CAMBRIDGE GREEK A

G000094943

GENERAL

P. E. EASTERLING
Regius Professor Emeritus of Greek, University of Cambridge

PHILIP HARDIE
Senior Research Fellow, Trinity College, and Honorary Professor of Latin, University of Cambridge

NEIL HOPKINSON
Fellow, Trinity College, University of Cambridge

RICHARD HUNTER
Regius Professor of Greek, University of Cambridge

E. J. KENNEY
Kennedy Professor Emeritus of Latin, University of Cambridge

S. P. OAKLEY
Kennedy Professor of Latin, University of Cambridge

GREEK LYRIC

A SELECTION

EDITED BY

FELIX BUDELMANN

Associate Professor of Classical Languages and Literature, University of Oxford

CAMBRIDGE
UNIVERSITY PRESS

CAMBRIDGE
UNIVERSITY PRESS

University Printing House, Cambridge CB2 8BS, United Kingdom

One Liberty Plaza, 20th Floor, New York, NY 10006, USA

477 Williamstown Road, Port Melbourne, VIC 3207, Australia

314–321, 3rd Floor, Plot 3, Splendor Forum, Jasola District Centre,
New Delhi – 110025, India

79 Anson Road, #06–04/06, Singapore 079906

Cambridge University Press is part of the University of Cambridge.

It furthers the University's mission by disseminating knowledge in the pursuit of
education, learning, and research at the highest international levels of excellence.

www.cambridge.org
Information on this title: www.cambridge.org/9780521633093
DOI: 10.1017/9781139049085

© Cambridge University Press 2018

First published 2018

Printed in the United Kingdom by Clays, St Ives plc

A catalogue record for this publication is available from the British Library.

ISBN 978-0-521-63309-3 Hardback
ISBN 978-0-521-63387-1 Paperback

CONTENTS

MAPS

PREFACE

It is always a good time to be reading Greek lyric. Even so, I would like to think, the case for a volume such as this is particularly evident now. The past two decades have been an unusually busy period, during which new approaches and a steady trickle of new finds have substantively changed the way we think about the corpus.

I have tried to write a commentary that different kinds of readers will wish to use. The emphasis is literary. However, I believe that even first-time readers of Greek lyric should have the opportunity to engage with more technical issues, such as supplementation, transmission, metre or dialect, which play a large role in this field.

In comparison with the standard volume of this kind in English, D. A. Campbell's *Greek Lyric Poetry* (1967, 1982²), the notes are full and the selection is narrow (not just because Campbell includes elegy and iambus). I hope that both designs have their use. Neither is there any attempt to compete with G. O. Hutchinson's *Greek Lyric Poetry* (2001), which covers some of the same texts but with somewhat different aims. The selection leans towards the well known, but makes space also for some less widely read texts, notably Timotheus and some *carmina popularia*. Excluded are Pindar and Bacchylides, who have their own volumes in this series (as will in due course elegy and iambus). There are several more texts I should have liked to treat if space had permitted, and readers will have their own wish lists. I nevertheless hope that the poems that *are* included will make an attractive and diverse, as well as manageable, selection.

Text and apparatus are my own. I rely on the standard critical editions for reporting the papyri and manuscripts, except that I have used photographs to check certain details. In the commentary section, the bulk of the space is given to the discussion of individual poems; introductions to authors are kept brief. Relatively full (though still in many cases highly selective) lists of secondary literature are provided for each text. Individual observations are not usually attributed to their author. My debt to earlier commentaries and discussions will nevertheless be obvious in every paragraph. For reasons of space the long reception history of the poems is not treated.

This book has taken an embarrassingly long time to write. In the process, I have accumulated many debts of gratitude, and it is a pleasure to acknowledge some of them here. Fellowships granted by the AHRC and Harvard's Center for Hellenic Studies gave me two years of relatively undisturbed research time. Friends and colleagues answered queries (frequently so, in many cases): Amin Benaissa, Ewen Bowie, Bruno Currie,

Giambattista D'Alessio, Katharine Earnshaw, Johannes Haubold, Simon Hornblower, Gregory Hutchinson, Adrian Kelly, Pauline LeVen, Polly Low, Al Moreno, Tim Power, Lucia Prauscello, Tobias Reinhardt, Peter Thonemann, Giuseppe Ucciardello, Hans van Wees, Tim Whitmarsh. Armand D'Angour and Beppe Pezzini gave unstinting advice on metrical issues, as did Andreas Willi, Philomen Probert and Stephen Colvin on questions of dialect, and Evert van Emde Boas on syntax. Henry Spelman and Peter Agócs commented in detail on substantial parts of the draft typescript, and made this a much better book. Oliver Taplin supplied the translations on pp. 1–2. Carolin Hahnemann and her students at Kenyon College test-drove sections of the commentary in class. Mirte Liebregts helped with checking references. Michael Sharp at CUP provided judicious guidance at all stages. Iveta Adams' astute and meticulous copyediting improved the typescript in a great many respects. Emma Collison efficiently oversaw production. The General Editors, Pat Easterling and Richard Hunter, joined in the latter stages by Neil Hopkinson, read at least two full sets of drafts. I am immensely grateful for their expert advice, wisdom, patience and encouragement throughout: I know how much time they spent on this. The final thank you, however, is to Henrietta, David and John, who would have every reason to take issue with my opening sentence.

Oxford
June 2017

CONVENTIONS AND ABBREVIATIONS

1. The following conventions are used in the Greek text:
   -]   left-hand limit of the papyrus
   - [right-hand limit of the papyrus
   - [α]   letter supplied by editor (gap in papyrus)
   - <α>   letter inserted by editor (no gap in papyrus or manuscript)
   - {α}   letter deleted by editor
   - ạ   letter cannot be identified with certainty
   - str.   strophe
   - ant.   antistrophe
   - ep.   epode

2. For the sake of concision, generally accepted minor emendations are adopted in the text without indication in the apparatus, and variant readings, even in superior manuscripts, are not reported if they are evidently erroneous. Where a general editorial position on a recurring question of dialect is set out in the commentary, individual interventions in line with that position are made 'silently'; an example is the systematic adoption of -σδ- rather than -ζ- in Alcaeus and Sappho (stated on p. 88), which is not indicated in the apparatus.

3. Sigla for the papyri and manuscripts cited in the apparatus of each lyric text are set out under 'Source' in the relevant section of the commentary.

4. Principles of indentation and metrical conventions are set out on pp. 23–4 of the Introduction. Greek phrases printed alongside the schemata indicate potentially problematic aspects of scansion. For example, '50 ἢ οὐχ', next to the first period in the schema for Alcm. 1 (p. 64), denotes an instance of synizesis in line 50, which is the first line of a stanza.

5. Under 'Discussions', asterisks indicate items judged particularly important or helpful.

6. The numeration used for the lyric texts is that of the following editions (details under 10 below): *PMG* and *SLG* for Alcman, Ibycus, Anacreon, Simonides, Timotheus, *carmina convivalia* and *carmina popularia* (*SLG* numbers start with S); Voigt for Sappho and Alcaeus (with indication of major deviations from LP); Finglass for Stesichorus; Maehler for Pindar and Bacchylides. For elegy and iambus *IEG*² is used, unless otherwise noted. With the exception of Stesichorus, therefore, the numeration of lyric, elegy and iambus is that of the most recent Loebs.

7. The word 'fragment' or 'fr.' is omitted where this creates no ambiguity. Thus: Anacr. 358 = Anacr. fr. 358 *PMG*.
8. The works of Homer are cited by title alone: *Il.* and *Od.*
9. Abbreviations of journals are those of *L'Année philologique*.
10. Editions, commentaries and works of reference are abbreviated as follows:

AB	C. Austin and G. Bastianini, *Posidippi Pellaei quae supersunt omnia*, Milan 2002
ARV²	J. D. Beazley, *Attic red-figure vase-painters*, 3 vols., 2nd edn, Oxford 1963
BAPD	*Beazley Archive Pottery Database*, www.beazley.ox.ac.uk
Barrett	W. S. Barrett, *Euripides: Hippolytos*, Oxford 1964
Bekker	I. Bekker, *Apollonii Sophistae Lexicon Homericum*, Berlin 1833
BNJ	*Brill's New Jacoby*
Bond	G. W. Bond, *Euripides: Heracles*, Oxford 1981
Braswell	B. K. Braswell, *A commentary on the fourth Pythian ode of Pindar*, Berlin 1988
CA	J. U. Powell, *Collectanea Alexandrina: reliquiae minores poetarum Graecorum aetatis Ptolemaicae 323–146 a. C.*, Oxford 1925
Cairns	D. L. Cairns, *Bacchylides: five epinician odes*, Cambridge 2010
Caizzi	F. D. Caizzi, *Antisthenis fragmenta*, Milan 1966
Calame	C. Calame, *Alcman*, Rome 1983
Campbell	D. A. Campbell, *Greek lyric*, Loeb, 5 vols., Cambridge, MA, 1982–93
Carey	C. Carey, *Lysiae orationes cum fragmentis*, Oxford 2007
CEG	P. A. Hansen, *Carmina epigraphica Graeca*, 2 vols., Berlin 1983–9
CGCG	E. van Emde Boas et al., *The Cambridge grammar of Classical Greek*, Cambridge 2018
CLGP	G. Bastiani et al. (eds.), *Commentaria et lexica Graeca in papyris reperta*, Munich 2004–
Consbruch	M. Consbruch, *Hephaestionis Enchiridion*, Leipzig 1906
Cousin	V. Cousin, *Procli philosophi Platonici opera inedita*, Paris 1864
Diehl	E. Diehl, *Anthologia lyrica Graeca*, 3rd edn, 3 vols., Leipzig 1949–52

DK	H. Diels and W. Kranz, *Die Fragmente der Vorsokratiker*, 6th edn, 3 vols., Berlin 1951–2
Drachmann	A. B. Drachmann, *Scholia vetera in Pindari carmina*, 3 vols., Leipzig 1903–27
Fabbro	E. Fabbro, *Carmina convivalia Attica*, Rome 1995
FGE	D. L. Page, *Further Greek epigrams*, revised by R. D. Dawe and J. Diggle, Cambridge 1981
FGrHist	F. Jacoby, *Die Fragmente der griechischen Historiker*, Berlin/Leiden 1923–
FHG	K. O. Müller, *Fragmenta historicorum Graecorum*, 5 vols., Paris 1848–73
Finglass	M. Davies and P. Finglass, *Stesichorus: the poems*, Cambridge 2014
Gerber	D. E. Gerber, *Greek elegiac poetry from the seventh to the fifth centuries BC*, Loeb, Cambridge, MA, 1999
Gostoli	A. Gostoli, *Terpander*, Rome 1990
GP	B. Gentili and C. Prato, *Poetarum elegiacorum testimonia et fragmenta*, 2nd edn, 2 vols., Leipzig 1988–2002
Greene	W. C. Greene, *Scholia Platonica*, Haverford, PA, 1938
GVI	W. Peek, *Griechische Vers-Inschriften*, vol. I: *Grab-Epigramme*, Berlin 1955
HE	A. S. F. Gow and D. L. Page, *The Greek Anthology: Hellenistic epigrams*, 2 vols., Cambridge 1965
Hense	O. Hense and C. Wachsmuth, *Ioannis Stobaei anthologium*, 5 vols., Berlin 1884–1912
Hordern	J. H. Hordern, *The fragments of Timotheus of Miletus*, Oxford 2002
Hutchinson	G. O. Hutchinson, *Greek lyric poetry: a commentary on selected larger pieces*, Oxford 2001
IEG²	M. L. West, *Iambi et elegi Graeci ante Alexandrum cantati*, 2 vols., second edn, Oxford 1989–92
IG	*Inscriptiones Graecae*, Berlin 1873–
Jan	K. v. Jan, *Musici scriptores Graeci*, Leipzig 1895
KG	R. Kühner, *Ausführliche Grammatik der griechischen Sprache*, part 2 (*Satzlehre*), 3rd edn, 2 vols., revised by B. Gerth, Hannover 1898–1904
Lentz	A. Lentz, *Herodiani Technici reliquiae*, 2 vols. (= vols. III.1 and III.2 of *Grammatici Graeci*), Leipzig 1867–70
Leutsch	E. v. Leutsch and F. W. Schneidewin, *Corpus paroemiographorum Graecorum*, 2 vols., Göttingen 1839–51

LfgrE	B. Snell *et al.* (eds.), *Lexikon des frühgriechischen Epos*, 4 vols., Göttingen 1955–2010
LGPN	P. M. Fraser and E. Matthews (eds.), *A lexicon of Greek personal names*, Oxford 1987–
LIMC	*Lexicon iconographicum mythologiae classicae*, 18 vols., Zurich 1981–97
LP	E. Lobel and D. L. Page, *Poetarum Lesbiorum fragmenta*, corr. edn, Oxford 1963
LSJ	H. G. Liddell and R. Scott, revised by H. S. Jones, *A Greek-English lexicon*, 9th edn with supplement, Oxford 1996
Matthews	V. J. Matthews, *Antimachus of Colophon: text and commentary*, Leiden 1996
Maehler	H. Maehler, *Bacchylides: carmina cum fragmentis*, 11th edn, Leipzig 2003; H. Maehler, *Pindari carmina cum fragmentis*, vol. II, Leipzig 1989
MW	R. Merkelbach and M. L. West, *Fragmenta Hesiodea*, Oxford 1967
Neri	C. Neri, *Erinna: testimonianze e frammenti*, Bologna 2003
Olson	S. D. Olson, *Athenaeus: The Learned Banqueters*, Loeb, 8 vols., Cambridge, MA, 2006–12
PCG	R. Kassel and C. Austin, *Poetae comici Graeci*, 8 vols., Berlin 1983–2010
Perry	B. E. Perry, *Aesopica*, Urbana, IL, 1952
Pfeiffer	R. Pfeiffer, *Callimachus*, 2 vols., Oxford 1949–53
P.GC	*Papyri of the Green Collection*
PGM	K. Preisendanz and A. Henrichs, *Papyri Graecae magicae*, 2nd edn, Stuttgart 1973–4
PMG	D. L. Page, *Poetae melici Graeci*, Oxford 1962
PMGF	M. Davies, *Poetarum melicorum Graecorum fragmenta*, Oxford 1991
Poltera	O. Poltera, *Simonides lyricus: Tesimonia und Fragmente*, Basel 2008
P.Oxy.	*Oxyrhynchus Papyri*
P.Ryl.	*Rylands Papyri* (Manchester)
PSI	*Papiri greci e latini* (Pubblicazioni della Società Italiana per la ricerca dei papiri greci e latini in Egitto), Florence 1912–
Rabe	H. Rabe, *Hermogenis opera*, Leipzig 1913
Rose	V. Rose, *Aristotelis qui ferebantur librorum fragmenta*, Leipzig 1886
Σ	scholion/scholia

Schwyzer	E. Schwyzer, *Griechische Grammatik*, 4 vols., 2nd edn, Munich 1950–71
SEG	*Supplementum epigraphicum Graecum*, Leiden 1923–
SH	H. Lloyd-Jones and P. Parsons, *Supplementum Hellenisticum*, Berlin 1983
SLG	D. L. Page, *Supplementum lyricis Graecis*, Oxford 1974
Syll.[3]	W. Dittenberger, *Sylloge inscriptionum Graecarum*, 3rd edn, 4 vols., Leipzig 1915–24
Tarditi	G. Tarditi, *Archilochus: fragmenta*, Rome 1968
TrGF	B. Snell *et al.*, *Tragicorum Graecorum fragmenta*, 5 vols., 1971–2004
Schneider–Uhlig	R. Schneider and G. Uhlig, *Apollonii Dyscoli quae supersunt*, 3 vols., 1878–1910
Voigt	E. M. Voigt, *Sappho et Alcaeus: fragmenta*, Amsterdam 1971
Walz	E. Walz, *Arsenii violetum, ex codd. MSS.*, Stuttgart 1832
Wehrli	F. Wehrli, *Die Schule des Aristoteles: Texte und Kommentar*, 2nd edn, 10 vols., Basel 1967–9
Wellmann	M. Wellmann, *Pedanii Dioscuridis Anazarbei De materia medica libri quinque*, 3 vols., Berlin 1906–14
West	M. L. West, *Greek epic fragments: from the seventh to the fifth centuries BC*, Loeb, Cambridge, MA, 2003; M. L. West, *Homeric Hymns, Homeric Apocrypha, Lives of Homer*, Loeb, Cambridge, MA, 2003

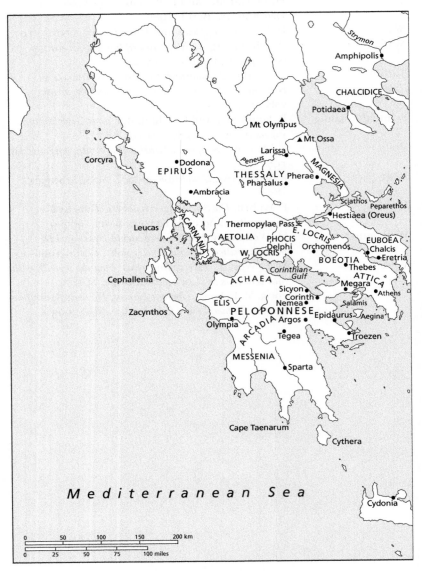

Map 1 The Aegean

Map 1 (cont.)

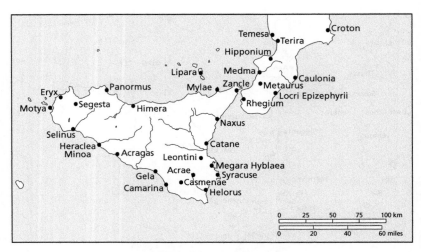

Map 2 Magna Graecia

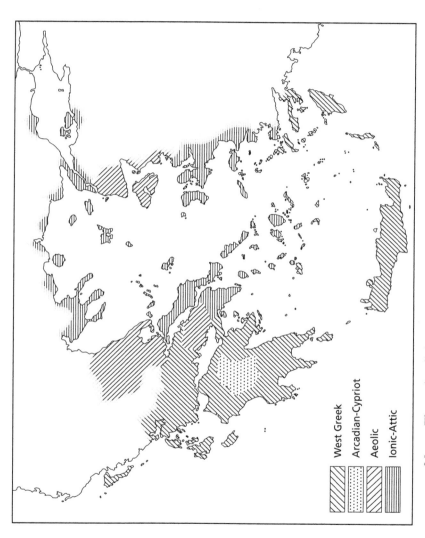

West Greek

Arcadian-Cypriot

Aeolic

Ionic-Attic

Map 3 The major dialect areas during the Archaic and Classical periods

INTRODUCTION

Thracian filly, why these scornful glances?
Why so cruelly run from me,
dismissing me as artless?

Trust me, I could slip the curb in deftly,
then with reins in hand could whirl
you round the turn-posts swiftly.

But instead you gambol in the pasture,
since you have no rider who's
a proper mounting-master.

Anacreon 417

Why can't you see what's obvious?
The racehorse is Enetian,
while cousin Hagesichora
has gleaming hair of purest gold,
and her complexion silvery –
what need to tell you this so plain?
Here's Hagesichora – her looks
come second after Agido –
she'll gallop, a Colaxian
against a swift Ibenian;
because the Pleiades are here
advancing through the deathless night,
which clash like Sirius with us
who bring a robe for Orthria.

extract from Alcman 1 (vv. 50–63)

io
Dynasty destroyed!
You galleons of the Greeks,
which singe like Sirius,
you massacred so many,
wiped out in their prime, my age.
Those boats shall not ship them back:
the force of black-smoke flame
shall burn them in its brutal body.
And there shall be groans and grief
through all the Persian provinces.

1

io
you weighty fall of fate
that dragged me here to Greece!
extract from Timotheus, *Persians*
(fr. 791.178–88): Xerxes at Salamis[1]

1 DEFINITIONS AND PERSPECTIVES

'Lyric' in contemporary literary criticism is a term as elusive as it is suggestive. It exists both as an adjective, expressing a poetic quality, and as a noun
denoting a poetic mode, and both are notoriously difficult to define. It is
this protean quality that has allowed 'lyric' to become a powerful creative
stimulus for both poets and theorists.

A foundational period for today's sense of 'lyric' was the end of the
eighteenth and beginning of the nineteenth century. Romantic thinkers,
especially in Germany, expanded earlier, looser ideas into a systematic
theory of three fundamental forms – lyric, epic and drama – each
characterised by distinctive qualities. Even though the triad of genres
never acquired the same prominence in Anglophone writing, the primary
quality accorded within this system to lyric certainly did: despite strong
counter-currents in twentieth-century criticism, 'subjectivity', a form of
poetic self-expression, often couched in the first person (the 'lyric "I"'),
still remains a chief feature of 'lyric' for many readers, maintaining
a special place on the long list of lyric qualities, alongside inwardness,
emotionality, concision, truth, poeticity and musicality.[2]

Each of these qualities has a critical history, which exerts influence
when applied to Greek lyric. Each therefore introduces forms of anachronism, and these can be detrimental when unintended or productive
when consciously exploited. This is perhaps especially obvious for subjectivity, but it applies equally to several of the others. The important
exception, at least to a point, is musicality, which poets and theorists across
the ages have traced back to early Greek lyric. Much modern lyric is read
rather than sung, and can be called 'musical' only metaphorically, because
it pays attention to the sound and flow of the verse (pop 'lyrics', lyric-
turned-*Lieder* and Italian '(opera) lirica' are among the exceptions that
prove the rule). Lyric in early Greece, by contrast, was literally 'lyric' in that

---

[1] The three translations are by Oliver Taplin.

[2] For a brief overview of the notion 'lyric' in the modern period, see Jackson
2012. For theorists of lyric since about 1920, see Jackson and Prins 2014. Culler
2015 sets out his own theory but also analyses Romantic and New Critical notions of
lyric. Johnson 1982 examines the idea of lyric by bringing together ancient and
Modernist poetry.

it was sung to the lyre (and other instruments) in various social settings. Unlike the notion of 'subjectivity' (etc.), music is there right at the beginning of our lyric record. This has various consequences for the nature of Greek lyric. Most immediately, it gives the Greek corpus the clear definition that modern lyric lacks: Greek lyric is poetry composed in what we think of as sung metres (see n. 3 for a different commonly used definition). It was not the only Greek poetry that could be sung; epic and elegy were both, at different times, sung in some way, but lyric was characterised by a greater variety of rhythmic and melodic expression. Metre thus provides Greek lyric with a defining criterion that is somewhat vague as an articulation of the realities of performance (not all poems can be classified categorically as either musical or not), but which is unambiguous in so far as we are concerned with written texts: we categorise a text as lyric on the basis of the pattern of long and short syllables. This sharp metrical criterion is taken over by Latin lyric (where it no longer reflects modalities of performance, as most Latin lyric was probably primarily for reading), but it is abandoned in modern lyric, which is not associated with any particular metre.

Despite this tidy definition, however, the corpus has only a loose coherence. Arguably, the contours appear sharpest when lyric is marked off against epic, a contrast that goes beyond the often radical difference in length. Unlike epic, much lyric is anchored in the present, or even altogether focused on the present and present-day concerns, and adopts a first-person voice, singular or plural. A good number of lyric poems, moreover, refer to their own performance ('I/we sing', etc.), and/or to the real or imagined circumstances of their performance, with an elaboration that is alien to early epic.

Individually and collectively, these features capture something important about Greek lyric. (They also, it is worth noting, capture something important about later lyric, which draws variously on Greek models). However, while they distinguish lyric from epic, they do not amount to a strict demarcation of the corpus in absolute terms. Brevity, present-tense and present-day perspectives, a prominent 'we' or 'I', and references to performance, were not unique to lyric. They were features also of elegy and iambus, genres that – specifics of metre apart – may be set off against epic in much the same way as lyric (hence the second, broader, definition of Greek lyric current today, though not adopted in this volume, which includes elegy and iambus, alongside lyric narrowly defined).[3] What is

---

[3] Narrow (as here): e.g. Campbell's *Greek Lyric* Loeb and Hutchinson's *Greek Lyric Poetry* commentary. Broad (incl. elegy and iambus): e.g. Campbell's *Greek Lyric Poetry* commentary, and the *Cambridge Companion to Greek Lyric*. The broad definition is entwined with the Romantic idea of lyric subjectivity and of lyric as one of only three broad literary kinds.

more, any sense of coherence gained from this set of shared characteristics
needs to be balanced against great variation in other respects (see section
2 below).

To understand why Greek lyric constitutes a rather loose group of texts
at the same time as boasting a clear definition, one needs to consider the
origins of the corpus. Greek lyric was created retrospectively. The term
'lyric' is first attested in the Hellenistic period, when poets such as Sappho,
Anacreon and Pindar were canonised as λυρικοί, and their poems gathered
and edited as a corpus (see sections 3 and 6 below). Originally, their
compositions were probably thought of simply as μέλη or ὕμνοι, 'songs'.[4]
The metrical criterion employed by the Alexandrian editors expresses
something crucial about these texts (they were sung), and produces
a collection of works that share further characteristics, at least loosely,
but what it does not do, and probably was never intended to do, is create
a tightly coherent or sharply demarcated poetic form. As a (loose) indication of musicality, lyric metre escapes the pronounced anachronism of
'subjectivity', but to a lesser degree it too bequeaths to us a retrospective
view, grouping together firmly, as it does, a set of texts that will not have
been grouped quite so firmly in the period in which the poems were
composed and first performed.

Greek lyric, then, is rich in tensions: precisely defined, yet enormously
varied; looking back to an original category (μέλος), yet a Hellenistic
invention; predating, and in certain respects standing apart from, the
subsequent tradition of lyric poetry and lyric theory, yet influencing it,
and in our perception coloured by it. These tensions have created
a vibrant and diverse field of study. By way of initial orientation, there
follow brief sketches of major scholarly perspectives on Greek lyric:
because of the thinness of the metrical criterion, 'lyric as ...' is
a necessary supplement to 'lyric is ...'

Greek lyric as literature. Since antiquity, the Greek lyric poets have been
considered literary classics. They are imitated, alluded to and named in
Hellenistic and Latin poetry, and their afterlives continue in early modern
and modern literature in many languages. The filly of Anacreon's poem
quoted at the beginning of the Introduction, for example, appears in odes
by Horace (*Carm.* 2.5) and Ronsard ('Pourquoy comme une jeune pou-
tre'). The popularity of individual poets has always fluctuated, but readers
of all periods have valued Greek lyric as a body of poems that repay close
engagement.

---

[4] The latter is the broader term; μέλος is for the most part restricted to what the
Alexandrians called 'lyric'. For the development of the terminology (μέλος, 'melic',
'lyric'), see Calame 1998.

In an obvious sense the same is not true for the immediate reception of
the poems: 'literature', never an easy concept, is an anachronistic term for
poetry that was originally sung and listened to more than it was read.[5] Yet it
is evident that these are poetically ambitious texts irrespective of medium.
The complex image-making of the Alcman passage quoted at the outset, or
the sustained erotic allegorising of Anacreon's filly poem, demonstrate the
kind of qualities that gave Greek lyric its place in the later canon.[6] Much of
the poetry that has come down to us, while operating within a tradition,
puts a premium on distinctive verbal artistry, an artistry that can be
appreciated as such both in performance and on the page. It is very
significant in this respect that the poems are firmly tied to individual,
named authors from early on.[7]

Greek lyric as performance. Greek lyric is a corpus of songs as well as poems
(and either term is used in this volume, depending on emphasis). Music-
making, and the performers' appearance, are thematised in a number of
texts, and lyric performers are a frequent motif in vase-painting. Timotheus
(author of the third quotation above) was a celebrity, his performances as
a kitharode sought after across the Greek world. Alcman's song was performed by well-rehearsed choruses of young Spartan women in eye-catching
outfits. Many scholars think that the description of the two leaders as
racehorses interacted with a choreography that drew attention to those
two dancers; certainly Alcman's text as a whole is predicated on performance, and on the interplay of vision and imagination. Other performances
were more impromptu. Relatively little rehearsal may be required to sing
Anacreon's short and simple filly song, but even in the most extempore
rendition the embodiment of the poetic voice in a singer added a musical
appeal, an individuality and an interpersonal dimension that are missing on
the page.[8]

Lyric as performance is compatible with lyric as literature. A performed
text can be judged literary, and a literary text can be performed. Moreover,
the history of lyric is rich in moments of imagined musicality. In their
different ways, poets of all periods use words of singing to make their
written lyric lyrical; Hellenistic readers, too, who created the label 'poets of
the lyre', imagined music where there was only text.

---

[5] On the anachronism of 'literature', see Williams 1983: 183–8, Goldhill 1999.
On Greek lyric as 'literature', see Maslov 2015, Budelmann and Phillips 2018a:
9–15.
[6] The three texts are discussed in further detail on pp. 58–83, 202–5, 232–52.
[7] With the exception of the anonymous *skolia* and *carmina popularia*, which thus
provide an instructive contrast; see pp. 252–5.
[8] The secondary literature on Greek lyric as performance is large; see esp. Stehle
1997, Power 2010, Peponi 2012 (on aesthetic response).

Greek lyric as performing a (cultural, social, political, religious) function. In the Archaic period, lyric was part of the fabric of everyday life. Lyric (as well as epic, elegy and iambus) expressed things that mattered to Greek communities. Much of it was occasional, composed to perform specific social, ritual and political functions at specific types of occasion. At the end of the Alcman extract, the young women describe themselves as involved in a ritual act, carrying a robe for a goddess called Aotis. The rest of the text suggests that the performance serves to flaunt their own, and their leaders', looks before the gathered community. Reflections of Spartan ideology can be detected throughout. Lyrics of unrequited desire, such as the Anacreon piece, were part of the glue that bonded groups of male symposiasts. Even Timotheus' extravagant star turns exploit ideological values; Xerxes' catastrophe, narrated complete with barbarian stereotypes, will have been heart-warming to Greeks of all periods, not least to Athenians coming to terms with loss, hardship and setbacks during the Peloponnesian War (the likely first audience). Greek lyric celebrates athletic victories, communicates with the divine, shapes ideologies, expresses identities, codifies social memory, enacts beliefs. The recognition that early Greece was a 'song culture', in which song was omnipresent and in countless formal and informal ways contributed to the lives of communities and individuals, transformed the study of lyric in the latter part of the twentieth century.[9]

Greek lyric as fiction and statement about self and the world. Greek lyric creates fictional settings and fictional personas. The Anacreon piece is not performed in a meadow, before a filly. A less pronounced form of fictionalising takes place in the Alcman extract, when (among other things) the chorus cast their leaders as exquisite horses. At the same time, however, Greek lyric is capable of meaningful self-expression and authoritative proclamation. Despite the imaginary meadow, the term fiction does not capture the whole effect of Anacreon's poem, which is also (*inter alia*) a statement about love, and in performance a form of self-presentation. It is at least possible that Alcman's girls are saying something about their feelings for their leaders as they sing the poem; if not, they nevertheless articulate values appropriate to themselves and important for their audience. This distinctive mode of speech, at one remove from reality yet capable of engaging with reality, is an important part of the appeal and efficacy of Greek lyric, as it is of elegy and iambus and of later lyric traditions.

Greek lyric as a philological challenge. The Greek lyric that survives is incomplete. We have only a fraction of the output of even the best-preserved

---

[9] See esp. Rösler 1980, Herington 1985 (introducing the notion of 'song culture'), Gentili 1988 [1984], Kurke 1991, Kowalzig 2007, Morgan 2015.

poets, and many of those poems we have are fragmentary. Notoriously, phraseology, dialect and metre are often complex. As a result, much Greek lyric scholarship is philological in emphasis, more so than most scholarship on epic and drama. Often interpretation and reconstruction are intertwined.

2 CHARTING THE CORPUS

The varied nature of the lyric corpus may be illustrated, and the corpus charted, under several headings.

Chronology. The earliest properly historical lyric poet, and the first in this volume, is Alcman in the late seventh century BC. He is preceded, probably earlier in the same century, by the shadowy figures Terpander and Eumelus and the first iambic poets, first among them Archilochus. The last poet presented here is Timotheus, who was active in the late fifth and early fourth centuries. The selection thus encompasses much of the Archaic period and extends well into the Classical age, two full centuries, during which Greek communities experienced substantial social, political, institutional, economic and military change.[10]

Geography. The surviving corpus is geographically diverse from the beginning. Alcman was active in Sparta, Sappho and Alcaeus on Lesbos, and Stesichorus came from Magna Graecia. From early on, some lyric poets moved around, and they did so at an increasing rate as trade and other forms of inter-*polis* connectivity increased during the Archaic period. Alcman's supposed origin in Lydia is probably a fiction, and Sappho's (involuntary?) exile in Sicily might be considered a special case, and may even be a later invention, but Ibycus certainly, and probably also Stesichorus, were active both in their native Magna Graecia and elsewhere in Greece. Anacreon, originating from Teos in Asia Minor, enjoyed successively the patronage of Polycrates on Samos and of the Pisistratids in Athens (and he is linked to other cities too). Simonides, Pindar and Bacchylides were genuinely panhellenic poets who took individual and civic commissions across the Greek world, and Timotheus was a touring star performer.[11]

Length. Most of the poems are relatively short, but many (including those by Alcman and Timotheus quoted above) ran to a hundred lines or more,

---

[10] The lyric production of the Hellenistic and Imperial periods is excluded, as it is in many treatments of Greek lyric, despite some continuities, and so is dramatic lyric.

[11] On individual poets, see the commentary. On the mobility of poets in general, see Hunter and Rutherford 2009, esp. the articles by Bowie and D'Alessio. See also pp. 18–19 below, on poems travelling without their poets.

and Stesichorean poems exceeded 1,000 lines (pp. 153, 154). Longer
poems usually contained a substantive past-tense mythological (or sometimes historical) narrative; some consisted more or less entirely of narrative.

Performers and instruments. Lyric was sung by men and women, adults and
children, choruses and individuals, impromptu or after extensive rehearsal. Much monodic (= solo) performance was by men. This is indicated
both by what we know of the *symposion* (see below), and by the usually male
speakers in Alcaeus, Anacreon, Ibycus and others. But Sappho shows (if
demonstration were needed) that women too sang monody, even though
her songs were subsequently performed also by men, and many anonymous 'popular songs' were clearly sung by women.[12] Solo performers of
lyric often accompanied themselves on the (typically seven-string) lyre.
Not least because of the level of instruction required, stringed instruments
were often primarily associated with the elite. The ideological concerns of
some of the surviving poetry also reflect an elite context. On the other
hand, 'popular song' and certain *skolia* show that there were forms of
solo-song that were performed by a wide range of social groups
(pp. 253–4, 266). Our evidence does not permit us to judge when, and to
what degree, familiarity with the poetry of elite monodic poets such as
Alcaeus, Sappho, Ibycus or Anacreon spread beyond elite circles.
Different again are the professional touring kitharodes of the high and
late Classical period (such as Timotheus), who performed their lengthy,
innovative and hugely popular solo pieces before mass audiences, accompanying themselves on larger instruments of up to twelve strings.[13]

Choral performances are fundamentally different from monody. Not
only are they the 'bigger' show – multiple singers, dance as well as song –
but they also come with a rich set of associations, of divine worship, of
order, of hierarchy, of communal action and communal values. Choral
performances could be accompanied by a lyre or by *auloi* (pipes, usually
played as a pair). Many choral texts are shaped to suit, or even advertise,
the identity of their intended performers. Alcman's song quoted above
was composed for a chorus of *parthenoi* (unmarried girls), for example,
and at the end of Bacchylides 17 the chorus identify themselves as male
Ceans. Other texts are non-specific, so that scholars disagree over whether
to assign them to choruses or soloists: this is the case for certain pieces by

---

[12] Female-voiced poems survive from male monodists, but it is unclear whether
they were intended for female performers; e.g. Alcaeus 10 Voigt (10B LP),
Anacr. 385.
[13] On performers, solo and choral, with a focus on gender, see Stehle 1997;
on stringed instruments, West 1992b: 48–80, Wilson 2004; on class ideology in
sympotic performance, Kurke 1992, Kurke 1997 ~ Kurke 1999: ch. 5, Hammer
2004.

Sappho (pp. 114, 148), all of Stesichorus (p. 153), some Ibycus (p. 174) and Simonides (p. 205), and the whole genre of the victory ode.[14] Chorally performed pieces need not emphasise their choral associations textually, and (vice versa) monody may adopt choral tropes for poetic purposes. Moreover, many originally choral texts subsequently received solo performances (see p. 19). While any single performance has to be either monodic or choral, the question whether a text is monodic or choral does not always have a simple answer, and poets certainly cannot be categorised as either choral or monodic.[15] This is not to say that the choral/solo distinction is artificial. It is notable that what appear to be originally choral texts are distinguished by their Doric dialect, and many share an AAB pattern of strophic response (see sections 7 and 8).

Occasion. The two most important types of occasion for the performance of lyric are the *symposion* and the festival. Both terms encompass a range of phenomena. The *symposion* is widely considered the default venue for many shorter lyric pieces (including the majority of songs in this volume), as well as much elegy and possibly iambus, and has been the subject of a large body of scholarship.[16] *Symposia* were closed, indoor events. Men sat or reclined on couches, jointly enjoying drink, conversation, banter, politicking, speechifying, games and musical and poetic performance. At some *symposia*, male youths would pour wine and be the object of flirtation (which may well have included lyric serenading). Most scholars think that any women present were normally not wives but *hetairai* and musical entertainers (who offered further targets for playful serenading).

Like the monodic texts, which vary greatly in tone, a *symposion* could be light-hearted or passionate and serious. Either way, institutionalised inebriation will have had its effect. Degrees of formality and intimacy, too, varied, as did the relationship between any one set of symposiasts and the *polis* at large. A *symposion* held by a tyrant like Polycrates, hosting Anacreon, will have differed in character from one of a political faction, such as Alcaeus' *hetaireia* (p. 87), that saw itself in opposition to the current regime; and the status and nature of song-making when a famous poet provided the chief attraction was not the same as when ordinary symposiasts took turns to perform. Most lyric performance at the *symposion* will have been solo, and for practical reasons alone elaborate choral dancing is

---

[14] Victory ode: the majority view (choral) is defended by Carey 1989. For an overview of the debate, see Morrison 2007: 43–4.
[15] On this last issue, see Davies 1988a.
[16] The foundational volume on the *symposion* is Murray 1990. On poetry at the *symposion*, see Stehle 1997: 213–61 and Cazzato *et al.* 2016. For the bibliography on the *symposion*, see Yatromanolakis 2016.

unlikely, but less elaborate forms of joint singing, for example of paeans and *skolia*, will have had their place.[17]

Greek *poleis* had a full festival calendar. Panhellenic sanctuaries, too, held regular festivals. These were diverse events, some stretching over several days and many attended by a broad mix of social groups and sometimes foreigners. They honoured the city's gods, offered a welcome holiday and an opportunity for social interaction, re-enacted mythical history, marked the seasons, celebrated the city's achievements. At many festivals, choruses played a role. Such choruses (and indeed the festival itself) combined what in today's Western societies would normally be thought of separately as the religious and the secular domain. Just as sacrifices constituted gifts for the gods and at the same time provided meat for the celebrants, so choral performances aimed to give pleasure to divine and human audiences alike. Festivals could accommodate the celebration of individuals and individual families, such as (probably) the named chorus-leaders in the Alcman passage above, and it is likely that some victory odes were performed in the context of established festivals. At certain festivals, such as the Spartan Karneia, the Delphian Pythia and the Athenian Panathenaia, musical and poetic performance took the form of major competitions (μουσικοὶ ἀγῶνες), which attracted high-profile performers from across the Greek world.[18]

Symposia and festivals are particularly well documented as occasions for lyric performance, but there were many others. Weddings, funerals, repetitive manual labour, military campaigns and ad hoc festivities of different sorts all provided opportunities for communal and individual song-making. Song was pervasive.

Scholarly reconstruction of the original occasion for which a particular song was composed almost invariably involves informed guesswork and needs to be mindful of the methodological challenges. There is considerable risk of circular reasoning when the poetic text is our only evidence, as is often the case. Moreover, since many lyric texts create some sense of a setting, the question arises how close the poetic setting is to the actual setting, and how the two interact.[19] Repeat performance in a different context (pp. 18–19) further complicates the picture.

---

[17] For paeans, see Rutherford 2001b: 51–2; more generally, Cingano 2003.
[18] On festivals in general, see Parker 2011: ch. 6. Choruses at festivals, and the work they do for their communities: Kowalzig 2007. Songs as gifts to gods: Depew 2000. Victory odes in the context of festivals: Krummen 2014 [1990], Currie 2011. μουσικοὶ ἀγῶνες: Shapiro 1992 (concise discussion of the Athenian Panathenaia), Power 2010: Part I (discursive treatment across geographies and periods).
[19] On such questions of pragmatics, see in the first instance D'Alessio 2009b: 115–20.

3 GENRE AND GENRES

The notion of genre looms large in the study of Greek lyric and will appear repeatedly in this book, but it raises difficult questions. Above all, what makes this a challenging subject is that much of the evidence, and most of the terminology, have been shaped by the aims and methods of the Hellenistic editors. For them, genre served as a classificatory tool: faced with the task of organising a polymorphous corpus, scholars allocated many of the texts to one or other of a manageable number of distinct types. To be sure, different poetic kinds existed already in the song culture of early Greece (as they do in all poetry), and the editors took into account what evidence they had about them, but in contrast to what was to become the case in Alexandria these poetic kinds were neither codified nor systematised, nor did they serve editorial purposes. This section therefore has two parts. The first is concerned with the terminology of genres that we have inherited from the Alexandrian editors (see also section 5 for an overview of Hellenistic scholarship on lyric), the second with the question as to what genre may have meant to the poets themselves and their audiences.[20]

The use of genre by the Hellenistic editors is illustrated by the organisation of the Alexandrian edition of Pindar: the poems were divided into separate books (one or more each) of hymns, paeans, dithyrambs, *prosodia* (procession-songs), *partheneia* (maiden-songs), *hyporchemata* (dance-songs), *enkomia* (see below), *threnoi* (dirges), *epinikia* (victory odes).[21] Such divisions by genre are of interest not only as a matter of history of scholarship. All these genre terms are still in use today, and for good reason. The Alexandrians had a much larger corpus at their disposal, which they studied carefully. We depend on their work for our own understanding of the poets and poems in question. It is because of this reliance on Hellenistic terminology and classifications that it is important to note their limitations. Three points in particular deserve remark.

First, the Alexandrian editors seem to have systematised and simplified what was originally a mass of partially overlapping, Greece-wide as well as local, terms. A fragment of a Pindaric *threnos* (fr. 128c), for example, lists, among other genres, three different types of lament (Linus-song, Hymenaeus-song and Ialemus-song), none of which seems to feature in the Alexandrian editions. It may be that the canonical poets happen not to have composed in those genres, but it is in any case clear that Alexandrian categories such as *threnos*, paean or dithyramb, while narrower than 'lyric', can be subdivided further.

---

[20] For an overview of genre and genres in Greek lyric, see Carey 2009.
[21] Some of the detail is uncertain because the surviving lists vary slightly.

Secondly, the Hellenistic scholars did not classify the whole lyric corpus by genre. While the editions of Simonides, Pindar and Bacchylides were categorised more or less entirely by genre, those of Sappho and probably Anacreon were organised predominantly by metre (see the introductions to individual poets in the commentary section). The reasons are debated, but it would be hasty to assume that genre is irrelevant to the poems of Sappho or Anacreon just because the Alexandrians did not classify them by genre.

Thirdly, and most important, many genre terms changed their meaning over time (and had locally divergent meanings). Alexandrian lyric terminology goes back a long way, but it acquired its eventual scholarly meaning only gradually. *Hymnos*, for example, which designates a specific genre in Alexandrian editions (including that of Pindar, above), meant 'song' in early epic and lyric, with only incipient associations of praise and celebration. *Enkomion*, which in Hellenistic classifications is the label for a small-scale sympotic piece, was in the fifth century used for the victory ode. That fifth-century usage in turn developed out of the characterisation of the victory ode as ἐγκώμια μέλη and ἐγκώμιοι ὕμνοι ('*komos*-songs'), which we find in Pindar.[22]

Entangled with these specific questions of definition and terminology, which require assessment genre by genre, is the much discussed general question as to how lyric genre functioned in the Archaic period, before the advent of scholarship. A good starting point is a frequently cited formulation by L. E. Rossi: genre conventions were not written down and yet adhered to in the Archaic period, written down as well as adhered to in the Classical period, and written down yet not adhered to in the Hellenistic period.[23]

Rossi's dichotomy written/not written draws attention to the role of wider cultural developments in shaping the working of genre. One obvious issue here is codification, and the lack of it. For the Archaic poets and their audiences, unlike for Hellenistic scholars, readers and poets, genre will typically have been a matter of explicit or implicit expectations formed by the experience of song in performance. At a very early stage, some poetic forms may not even have had names (which is, however, not to say that they would not have been recognised). Even more important is the issue of performance and text. In a period in which lyric was composed for performance, genre manifested itself not in textual

---

[22] On terminological changes over time, see Harvey 1955 (*enkomion* on pp. 163–4). A particularly incisive study of terminology, drawing out the implications for our understanding of genre, is D'Alessio 2013 on the dithyramb.

[23] Rossi 1971. Further important discussions of the nature of genre in lyric (taking different views): Käppel 1992, Rutherford 2001b: 3–17, Yatromanolakis 2004, Agócs 2012, Maslov 2015: esp. 62–77, 246–317.

properties alone, but in the interplay between text (subject matter, addressee, metre, other formal properties) and performance (occasion, performers, mode of performance). The genre *partheneion* is a good example. On the page, *partheneia* are characterised by a set of recurring features, notably extensive passages in which the first-person speakers talk about their identity, status, dress and performance. However, these textual characteristics are best seen as an expression of what for audiences will have been the essence of the genre: performance by choruses of *parthenoi*.[24]

Even when such differences between Archaic and later notions of genre are taken into account, however, the central thrust of Rossi's idea requires qualification. Archaic poets, he suggests, comply with genre conventions whereas their successors creatively break them. It is indeed easy to imagine that in many settings, not least at festivals, lyric performance gained efficacy from reinforcing generic expectations more than from deviating from them. One might compare modern religious liturgy, which encodes essential religious meaning in formulaic phrases that gain emotional charge from the familiarity created by their regular reuse. The genre-defining cry *ie paian* that makes a paean a paean, and the three-part prayer form that underlies many lyric prayers (address, narrative, request; see p. 115), but also the conventions of praise and celebration that recur in many epinicians, are resonant with significance because they are familiar to their audiences. They express, and in performance enact, something fundamental. It is because lyric song serves its occasion that it does not typically exploit genre to create outright clashes between occasion, performers and text, or elements of the text.

However, it would be wrong to conclude that for the lyric poets genre was a given, imposed by the requirements of the occasion. On the contrary, genre presented a constant spur to innovation. At the beginning of *Olympian* 9, for example, Pindar distinguishes his own, highly elaborate, epinician from the traditional celebratory victory song attributed to Archilochus. Bacchylides 17 was classified as a dithyramb by the ancient editors and is dominated by narrative in the way dithyrambs often are, but it ends with a reference to paeans and an invocation of Apollo, who normally receives paeans rather than dithyrambs. The interpretation of this mix of signals is disputed, but it is evident that Bacchylides does something striking in giving this unusual shape to the genre paean (or dithyramb). These are two particularly marked examples of a general phenomenon. While operating within traditional genres, lyric poets sought to put their own stamp on these genres and to create distinctive compositions.

Pindar and Bacchylides were active in the first half of the fifth century. The question whether genre was similarly manipulated in earlier periods,

[24] On *partheneia*, see the headnote to Alcman 1.

and by poets who were not classified by genre in the Alexandrian editions, is a difficult one. Sappho may serve as an illustration. The only genre the Alexandrian editors singled out in her work is the wedding song (see p. 114). Whether because of the nature of Sappho's poetry, or because we are limited to the genre categories we have inherited from the Alexandrians, we find it impossible ourselves to attribute most of the surviving poems to specific genres. What we can nevertheless see clearly is that genre is a concern in several of the texts. The narrative of the wedding of Hector and Andromache in fr. 44, itself not a wedding song, ends with a reference to wedding song, and the juxtaposition of heroic epic and wedding celebrations runs through the whole piece. Fr. 2 combines the tripartite prayer structure, a setting in a grove of Aphrodite, and the sympotic motif of shared conviviality. Different views may be taken on whether Sappho is mingling individually fluid forms or engaging in a self-conscious combinatory play with well-articulated generic elements.[25] Either way, it is evident that as early as 600 BC, in poems of uncertain genre, lyric authors could use generic associations for poetic effect. Both individual genres and notions of genre underwent constant development, throughout and after the Archaic period, and much of the detail is inaccessible to us, but there is no good reason to doubt that different kinds of lyric were recognised, and creatively manipulated, well before our record begins.

4 PERFORMERS, AUTHORS AND THE LYRIC VOICE

Many lyrics, ancient and modern, speak with a voice that can feel direct and personal, and yet is hard to categorise. We seem to be listening to another person, but we find it difficult to say who this person is. Is it the author, expressing his or her thoughts and feelings (the subjectivity of the Romantics)? Or a textually constructed persona (the response of New Criticism)? Or is this the wrong question to ask? Attempts to come to terms with the 'I', the 'subject', the 'voice', the 'speaker', have long been a major strand of lyric criticism (and the choice of terminology itself is part of the debate). What sets Greek lyric apart is again the interplay between text and performance, which adds a further dimension to the voice.[26]

For performers, Greek lyric texts are scripts. The voice the audience hears is most immediately that of the singers, but the singers perform a text

[25] The former view is developed by Yatromanolakis 2004.

[26] The bibliography on the lyric voice is large. For general accounts of the issues set out in this section (adopting different approaches), see Slings 1990, Morrison 2007: ch. 2, Kurke 2007, Budelmann 2018. There are important general points that arise from the debate about the Pindaric first person specifically; on this, see D'Alessio 1994 and Currie 2013. On authorship, see Bakker 2017.

and tune that are very often not theirs. Anacreon and Timotheus both performed their own compositions, but Alcman's *partheneia* were performed by choruses, and Anacreon's songs will have been sung countless times by symposiasts other than Anacreon. (In fact, even when authors perform their own songs, they present themselves in a manner very different from everyday interaction. They are not straightforwardly 'being themselves'.) Performers can inhabit the song in different ways. The song may feel personally meaningful to them, in its words or in its rhythm and tune. They may use it as a vehicle for all manner of self-presentation: as a cultured symposiast, as a modest girl, as an accomplished singer and dancer, etc. They may assume a detached distance, 'just' singing a song. Their own voice may mesh with that of the song or jar with it, may be inaudible behind it, or may drown it out.

In some poems, or indeed in some passages of some poems, the lyric voice has an impersonal, indefinite dimension. Choral lyric especially is capable of abrupt shifts between the individual and the anonymous; it rarely has a stable voice. Before Alcman's chorus sing about themselves and their leaders in the section quoted at the outset, they narrate Spartan myth and make gnomic pronouncements. These passages are not shaped as the personal views of the girls. They give voice to things that need to be said, without a strong sense of whose voice this is. In such contexts, the enunciation can be more important than the question who enunciates. Lyric performance is never *just* impersonal – the presence of the performer(s) makes sure of that – but neither is it always just personal, especially if it is perceived as discharging a societal function.

The role of the author has waxed and waned in scholarship on Greek lyric. Nobody any longer regards Greek lyric as unmediated authorial self-expression. Not just the influence of New Criticism, but also proper attention to performers and occasions, have severely circumscribed the role of the author, which once was at the centre of thinking about lyric. It is recognised that the 'I' of every poem is shaped by convention and by the purpose for which the poem is composed.

Nevertheless, authors matter. Several lyric poets name themselves (including already Alcman and Sappho); express the hope that their poetry will be remembered (including already Sappho); or dramatise their own lives in their poems (including already Alcaeus, who sings about his exile, and Sappho, who composes a set of songs centred on relationships between the members of her own family).[27] All the surviving

---

[27] The publication in 2014 of Sappho's 'Brothers Poem' demonstrated the extent of Sappho's use of her own family as characters in her poetry. No doubt their portrayal involves fictionalisation, but it seems unlikely that they are altogether invented; for a range of views, see Bierl and Lardinois 2016.

lyric poets have a distinctive ἦθος and poetic style (or a set of distinctive ἤθη and poetic styles) that are recognisable across their output.

Lyric autobiography involves fictionalisation. No poem provides unmediated access to the life of the poet (and the same goes for later biographical accounts, many of which were based primarily on the poems).[28] However, the notion of secure biographical knowledge puts the bar too high. It is more productive to point to the *interest* (informed or otherwise) that lyric poems generate in the person who created them. Such interest is well documented from the late sixth and early fifth centuries onwards, not just in textual references but also in the appearance of named poets in vase-painting.[29] We do not know for certain when authors first became objects of interest, but it stands to reason that the phenomenon goes back to the very period, early on, when lyric developed the kind of features listed in the previous paragraph, which create the sense of an authorial presence behind the poem.

There is no one lyric voice, then. Each poem and each performance has its individual shape. What they have in common is a layering that gives authors and performers considerable flexibility. The layered voice creates a poetry that is variously, and even simultaneously, capable of self-expression (on the part of both author and performer), make-believe, inwardness, authoritative pronouncements, provocation, argument and glittering performance acts.

5 RELATIONSHIP WITH EPIC

Lyric and epic coexisted long before either mode began to leave a textual record, and they continued to coexist during the period in which the poems of the lyric corpus were composed: epic too was composed and performed throughout the Archaic period.

Lyric's relationship with epic involved both borrowing and competing.[30] The language of lyric draws heavily on epic diction, adopting as well as modifying established phraseology. Instances, noted throughout the commentary, are particularly frequent in dactylic and related metres but by no means confined to them. However, there is always a difference. Even lyricists

---

[28] On biographical writing about the lyric poets, see Kivilo 2010, Lefkowitz 2012: 30–45.

[29] See esp. *BAPD* nos. 510, 4979, 204129 (Sappho, Sappho and Alcaeus), and 200207, 200522, 201684 (Anacreon), most of them discussed in Schefold 1997 and Yatromanolakis 2007: 51–164. See also below, p. 227.

[30] In keeping with the remit of this volume, the focus is on how lyric relates to epic. However, traffic was not all one way. Epic refers to lyric genres, such as *threnos* and paean, and it is likely that some phenomena that we think of as epic have an origin in pre-historical lyric, including perhaps the hexameter; see Nagy 1974: 49–102, Gentili and Giannini 1977.

closest linguistically to epic, such as Stesichorus, do not fully participate in the formulaic system of oral-derived hexameter poetry. Very little, if any, surviving lyric was composed in performance as epic originally was, and lyric phraseology reflects a much more pronounced pursuit of originality.[31] Similarly, myths were often shared with epic (as well as non-epic) traditions, but were given a distinctively lyric shape. Lyric narrative is typically less expansive, more allusive and more narrowly focused on discrete scenes and visual tableaux.

Such preferences should be seen in the context of the broader tendencies noted above (p. 3), which distinguish lyric from epic: (relative) brevity, a prominent first person, a focus on the present, metrical and musical variation, textually inscribed occasionality. Lyric shares certain linguistic and mythical building blocks with epic (and see below on dialect), but is a very different kind of poetry.[32] Often the differences are unmarked. Lyric poems can adjust material shared with epic to suit their purposes without thematising either similarities or differences. In other instances the relationship with epic becomes a poetic focus. Among the texts in this anthology, this is the case most obviously in Sappho 44 and Ibycus S151, poems that mark out their position vis-à-vis epic. Several others create poetic effects from their use of particular epic passages, e.g. Alcaeus 347 and Stesichorus' *Geryoneis*.

The interpretation of what may be epic echoes in any particular poem is complicated by two factors. First, the loss of almost all 'cyclic' epic skews interpretation towards Homer and Hesiod.[33] Secondly, uncertainty over the genesis of the Homeric and Hesiodic text raises a particular set of questions for the oldest lyric authors. There is wide agreement that by the late sixth century the text of Homer and Hesiod was broadly stable and widely known, but we do not have sufficient evidence to be certain what, if any, version of the *Iliad, Odyssey, Works and Days, Theogony* or older *Homeric Hymns* the audiences of Alcman, Sappho or Stesichorus knew.[34] A case in point is early Lesbos. The poetic dialect of Sappho and Alcaeus suggests that they drew on both epic and local Aeolic poetic traditions. This observation is supported by what we know of seventh-century Lesbos. Later accounts link several poetic figures, lyric as well as epic, to the island, notably the kitharodes Terpander and Perikleitos and the epic poet

---

[31] The distinction is less clear for elegy than for lyric; see Aloni and Iannucci 2007: 92–101, Garner 2011.

[32] For a succinct exploration of the differences between lyric and epic, see Graziosi and Haubold 2009.

[33] For 'cyclic' material in lyric, see, among the poems in this volume, p. 139 (on Sappho), p. 173 (on Ibycus).

[34] For an overview of the major theories, see Haslam 2011, who inclines towards early fixation in writing.

Lesches. It is disputed whether there was a specifically Aeolic epic tradition, distinct from those on the Ionian mainland (no such doubts about
specifically Aeolic *lyric* traditions), but in any case Sappho and Alcaeus
operated in a musical and poetic melting pot.[35] As a result, any phrase,
character or story in Sappho and Alcaeus that seems to be Homeric or
Hesiodic can in principle be interpreted in four different ways: (a) allusion
to a passage or story in Homer or Hesiod; (b) allusion to a passage or story
in a lost epic or lyric tradition of one kind or other; (c) generic epic
colouring; (d) use of an inherited poetic language without particular
epic resonance.

The choice between these options can sometimes be narrowed down by
considering the specificity and frequency of the apparent echoes. To take
three examples discussed in the commentary, the points of contact
between Alcaeus 347 and Hes. *WD* 582–96 are considerably closer and
more numerous than those between Aphrodite's chariot ride in Sappho 1
and Hera's and Athena's chariot ride in *Iliad* 5, and therefore more likely
to constitute an allusion. Linguistic features found in epic but not in
vernacular Lesbian are considerably more numerous in Sappho 44 than
in most poems by Sappho and Alcaeus, and therefore likely to evoke some
form of epic. Considerations such as these can clarify the role of epic
material, but the limits of our knowledge are such that different views can
often be justified, whether on individual phrases or on Sappho's and
Alcaeus' poetics more broadly.[36]

6 DISSEMINATION AND TRANSMISSION

During the Archaic period, Greek lyric was disseminated primarily in
performance. Songs were sung more than once, many again and again.
Symposiasts memorised the pieces they heard, and performed them themselves at the next *symposion*. Much repeat performance will have been
informal in this way, and centred on the *symposion*. Revivals of larger,
choral, pieces could take different forms. Some compositions created for
a particular festival will have been performed on the same occasion in
consecutive years, and/or revived at a later point, and victory odes may
sometimes have been restaged to celebrate an anniversary of the victory.

[35] For linguistic evidence for Aeolic literary traditions, see Hooker 1977: 56–83,
Bowie 1981, Sa. 44.16–20n. (Περάμοιο). For a summary of the related debate over
the origin of Aeolic elements in Homeric epic, see Willi 2011: 460–1. For kitharodic song in Lesbos, see Power 2010: 258–67 and 378–85. See also Sa. 106 and
Archil. 121, and in general on Lesbos as a musico-poetic centre, Liberman 1999:
xi–xiv.
[36] West 2002 provides a survey of the evidence. For the methodological issues,
see Fowler 1987: ch. 1 (who is sceptical).

We should also reckon with the possibility that famous choral songs were taken up by choruses elsewhere, divorced from their original occasion. A less resource-intensive and probably more frequent mode of giving originally choral pieces a new outing was by adapting them, in whole or in part, for solo rendition at *symposia*. Finally, at least from the early fifth century, and perhaps earlier, upper-class boys learned to sing famous pieces as part of their education.[37]

We do not have sufficient evidence to trace the performance history of any one song down to the Classical period (when performance of early lyric gradually diminished). We need to reckon with a wide range of trajectories, just as we should allow for a broad variety of reasons why an old piece would be sung again: its promotion by poet or patron, its status as a classic, its encoding of a relevant personal, communal or mythical past, its place in a recurring ritual, its ideology, and very much else, not least individual taste.[38]

Our oldest lyric papyrus is that of Timotheus' *Persians*, dating to the second half of the fourth century BC, and it is close to certain that the great majority of our surviving texts were written down no later than the Classical period.[39] However, there are good reasons to believe that written transmission of the texts played a role much earlier.[40] Even though lyric song must go back a long way, none survives from the period before writing became available in Greece in the eighth and seventh centuries. Whether or not writing was used in composition, it is easy to imagine that poets, communities or patrons and their families would sometimes want to preserve a written copy. As in the case of epic, the extent to which writing contributed to the early transmission of the poems is uncertain. Some form of co-presence of written and oral transmission seems likely from early on, with writing relatively more important for longer and more complex pieces, and more frequent at the end of the Archaic period than at the beginning. Writing eventually became the dominant modality,

[37] For poetry in schools, see Ford 2003: 24–30.

[38] On reperformance in general, see Herington 1985: 48–50, 207–10, and Hunter and Uhlig 2017. On specific authors/genres, see e.g. Currie 2004 (epinician), Yatromanolakis 2007 (Sappho), Carey 2011 (Alcman, reperformance and written transmission), Hubbard 2011 (non-epinician choral lyric, reperformance and writing).

[39] Even older are the very fragmentary wooden tablets and papyrus from the Attic 'tomb of the musician' (see Pöhlmann and West 2012) and the Derveni papyrus, which preserves an allegorical commentary on an Orphic theogonical poem.

[40] On the use of writing alongside performance, see Herington 1985: 45–7, 201–6, Pöhlmann 1990: 18–23, Tedeschi 2015, and (for Pindar) Irigoin 1952: 11–20. Levels of literacy in the Archaic period are difficult to gauge. Sixth-century graffiti by Attic shepherds suggest that writing may have been more widespread than was once thought; see Langdon 2015.

but performance may still have shaped some aspects of the texts in the late Classical era and beyond.[41]

Research into the poetry and music of the past began in the Classical period, with pioneering figures such as Hellanicus of Lesbos and Glaucus of Rhegium in the latter part of the fifth century,[42] and it became an established strand of Peripatetic scholarship at the end of the fourth century. However, it was the Hellenistic scholars, in particular Aristophanes of Byzantium (c. 265/257–190/180) and Aristarchus (c. 215–144), who first systematically collected, categorised, edited and annotated the lyric texts. The Alexandrians created editions of each of the nine canonical lyricists (Alcman, Alcaeus, Sappho, Stesichorus, Ibycus, Anacreon, Simonides, Bacchylides, Pindar), and the text and the colometry (= layout with line breaks determined by the metre) of these editions seem to have become the default point of reference later on.[43]

The canon was not the work of any one person or even any one period. It is best thought of as the result of a drawn-out process that began as early as the fifth century (eight of the nine poets are mentioned or cited already in Athenian Old Comedy), and to which the work of the Hellenistic scholars made a relatively late contribution.[44] Its subsequent influence was substantial. The nine poets dominate the reception of Greek lyric, in Greece, Rome and beyond. However, uncanonical texts were not eradicated. Timotheus, for example, was still performed in the Imperial period, and we have several papyri of Corinna from the second century AD.[45]

With the exception of Pindar's epinicians, the works of the lyric poets have not come down to us by way of their own medieval manuscript traditions. (The same is true for early elegy, with the exception of Theognis, and for iambus.) We therefore rely on two considerably more haphazard forms of transmission, papyri ('direct' transmission) and ancient quotations ('indirect' transmission). Knowledge of Greek lyric has been transformed by a steady stream of papyrus finds, starting in the mid to late nineteenth century. The most recent find presented here,

---

[41] For arguments for the continuous influence of a living performance tradition in the case of the dialect of Alcman, see Hinge 2006: 304–14 and Willi 2012: 273–8.

[42] Hellanicus wrote a treatise on the victors at the Spartan Karneia festival (*FGrHist* 4 F 85–6); Glaucus composed *On the Ancient Poets and Musicians* (fr. 2 *FHG* (vol. II, p. 23)). Hellanicus' pupil Damastes of Sigeum is credited with *On Poets and Sophists* (*FGrHist* 5 T1). See further Franklin 2010: 12–34, Barker 2014: 29–55; and below, pp. 193, 197 for the Peripatetic scholar Chamaeleon.

[43] For a concise summary of Alexandrian scholarly activity on lyric, see Barbantani 2009: 297–303. Wilamowitz-Moellendorff 1900 remains fundamental on the transmission and canonisation of the lyric poets.

[44] The list of nine is first attested in two epigrams of the third/second century, *AP* 9.184 and 571. On Old Comedy, see Carey 2011: 452, 457–60.

[45] Timotheus: Hordern 2002: 73–9. Corinna: e.g. *PMG* 654 and 655.

Cologne papyrus inv. 21351 + 21376, which gave us much of the text of Sappho 58b, was first published in 2004.[46] The single largest and most significant cache of papyri, lyric and otherwise, is derived from a rubbish heap in the Egyptian town of Oxyrhynchus, edited in the series *Oxyrhynchus Papyri* (*P.Oxy.*). Lyric papyri date from the late Classical period (Timotheus, see above) to Late Antiquity. Many of them derive from meticulous scholarly editions, with and without annotation (scholia), while at the other end we have what seems to be a pupil's school exercise, written on a sherd and riddled with errors (*PSI* XIII.1300 = Sappho 2). Most papyrus texts are damaged and have gaps, some of them large. The choices made in reconstructing what is lost often make a difference to the interpretation of the poem as a whole. In order not to influence readers unduly, this edition prints only supplements that are judged to have a high degree of likelihood, and relegates less certain restorations to the apparatus and notes.

The other source of lyric texts is quotations in later ancient authors. Athenaeus (late 2nd cent. AD) cites a large number of lyric texts in his fifteen-book *Scholars at Dinner*, a fictional conversation among twenty-nine learned diners. Metricians, above all Hephaestion (2nd cent. AD), cite lyric lines to illustrate metrical phenomena. Stobaeus (5th cent. AD) includes lyric in his wide-ranging *Anthology*. Lexicographers, such as Hesychius (*c.* 5th cent. AD), yield individual words. Such authors deserve proper consideration as part of the reception history of Greek lyric. Even when they are, as here, used as sources of lyric texts, it is still necessary to understand the context and purpose of each quotation in order to assess whether a text is quoted in its entirety (it very often is not) and what may have been left out.

All textual transmission introduces error. Where we can compare a papyrus and a quotation of the same text, the indirect transmission often turns out to be more error-prone. This is unsurprising, since more stages are involved and the scribes of the quoting authors do not always understand the metre, dialect and other aspects of the lyric texts. Changes made by performers, too, will sometimes have entered the textual tradition.[47]

Finally, the lengthy process of transmission affected not just individual texts but also the balance of the corpus that has come down to us. Biases operated at several stages. Throughout antiquity, poems of interest to broader constituencies had a higher chance of survival. It is likely that obscurely local poetry was altogether lost at an early stage. This edition tries to counterbalance the effect of canonisation by giving due space to

---

[46] It is not, however, the most recent important find: see above, n. 27.
[47] See p. 254 on the remodelling of Alcaeus 249 in the *skolion PMG* 891. Cf. n. 41 above, and p. 25 below.

Timotheus and the anonymous *skolia* and *carmina popularia*. In the indirect transmission, the particular interests of the source authors come into play. For example, we owe a large number of texts concerned with drinking to the convivial setting of Athenaeus; there is no equivalent for e.g. political texts. Accounts in later texts, as well as papyrus finds, can help to adjust the picture. Ancient lexica, for example, sometimes list the genres represented in the work of a particular lyricist (not always reliably so), and thanks to papyrus finds Bacchylides, whose work previously was known only in short quotations, now fills over a hundred pages of the modern editions.

7 METRE

Melody and rhythm were central to the appeal of lyric in performance. The melodies employed by voices and instruments are now lost, but rhythms were very strongly guided (if not always wholly determined) by the patterns of short and long syllables, and are therefore more or less accessible to us from the poetic texts.[48]

Unlike epic, which is invariably cast in dactylic hexameters, lyric employs a wide variety of metres. Some of these metres, and groups of metres, bear geographic labels and thus might appear to correspond to groups of poets. It is indeed the case that aeolic metres (many of which feature the verse-initial 'aeolic base' × ×, e.g. the glyconic × × – ∪ ∪ – ∪ –) are frequent in Sappho and Alcaeus from Lesbos (in Aeolia), and that ionics (∪ ∪ – –) are found repeatedly in the Ionian poet Anacreon. But if regional metrical traditions were ever properly discrete, they had started cross-fertilising before the late seventh century. All poets in this volume employ more than one type of metre.

With a small number of notable exceptions (in this anthology Timotheus' *Persians*), the rhythms of Greek lyric, like those of most Greek and Latin poetry, are based on manifest repetition. Rhythmical repetition gives shape to a poem and is an essential component of the listening and reading experience. The level at which repetition occurs varies, and it is useful to distinguish between 'stichic' and 'strophic' compositions. Stichic rhythms (< στίχος 'line') are made up of an ever-repeating single verse. Both the epic hexameter and the iambic trimeter of drama are stichic. A stichic text in this anthology is Alcaeus 347: the poem is composed entirely of greater asclepiads (– × – ∪ ∪ – – ∪ ∪ – – ∪ ∪ – ∪ –). Strophic lyric poems (the majority) are formed from repeating stanzas of

---

[48] The standard Anglophone handbook of Greek metre is West 1982a. For questions of music (instruments, tunes, developments), see West 1992b. For an overview of the metres of Greek lyric, see Battezzato 2009.

anything between two and over a dozen lines. There may be as few as two strophes (e.g. Anacreon 358) or a large number, and the pattern of each strophe may be fairly uniform or richly varied. Longer, more elaborate poems are often triadic, taking an AAB shape: the strophe is first repeated identically (as the 'antistrophe'), and then followed by a different stanza (the 'epode'). This triad of str.–ant.–ep. is then repeated several times. Triadic compositions are common in the choral songs of tragedy and are associated with choral performance already in lyric. It is likely that rhythmical repetition (and variation) was accompanied by some form of corresponding patterning in the melody and the choreography. Strophe-end is indicated by ⫼ in the schemata printed in the commentary section.

Strophes are composed of smaller metrical units. 'Cola' ('limbs') are regularly occurring rhythmical patterns such as the hemiepes (– ⏑ ⏑ – ⏑ ⏑ –) or the glyconic (above). They are the building blocks from which any longer sequence is composed. (The yet smaller units of 'feet' or 'metra', such as the dactyl (– ⏑ ⏑), are on the whole less significant in lyric.) 'Periods' are self-contained sequences within the strophe, like sentences in language, which are followed by a pause of indeterminate and no doubt varying length. A period may consist of one or, more often, several cola (or a run of successive feet) strung together without pauses.

In stichic metres (such as the greater asclepiads of Alcaeus 347 above) each period inhabits one line of the printed text, but in flowing strophic forms a period will often be too long to be presented in a single printed line (and/or will encompass more than one line of the ancient colometry, which is reproduced in many modern editions). Such continuation of a period beyond the line-end on the page is here represented by indentation. By contrast, period-end is conveyed by absence of indentation, and in the schemata marked by ‖. The strongest indicators of period-end are hiatus (a word ending, followed by one beginning, with a vowel, without elision or change to the quantity of either vowel) and *brevis in longo* (a short syllable where the metre requires a long one): both interrupt the flow of the rhythm. However, performers will have paused also in other places and, vice versa, may have glided over instances of hiatus or *brevis in longo* without pausing, so that a strophe could have been articulated in varying ways. This edition tentatively posits some period-ends where, although there is neither hiatus nor *brevis in longo*, other indications suggest the possibility of a pause (e.g. a marked change in the character of the metre, or a strong break in the rhetorical structure of the text); these period-ends are marked in the schemata by ?‖. The key point, however, to remember with any attempt to indicate the articulation of a particular rhythmical sequence is that the text alone, which is all we have, will never permit complete and confident reconstruction of performance practice.

As is conventional, labels are appended to most of the schemata, to indicate the cola or feet into which a particular period may be broken down, e.g. *gl* = glyconic, *da* = dactyl (the symbols and abbreviations are those set out in West 1982a: xi–xii). These help to convey the structure and nature of the rhythm. But many lines and strophes can legitimately be broken down into different combinations of cola or feet; what matters most, therefore, in trying to grasp the rhythm is not the labels but the development and flow as the strophe unfolds.

8 DIALECT

During the Archaic and Classical periods, the regions of Greece spoke different dialects (see Map 3), and it is unsurprising that the lyric corpus exhibits considerable linguistic variety. However, for dialect as for metre, no simple mapping is possible between poetry and geography. The dialects of lyric are artificial literary languages which combine forms from different vernacular dialect groups. All lyric dialects have some forms associated with traditional poetic (above all epic) language rather than with any particular vernacular dialect. The mix of dialects in any given poem is driven not only by the place of performance or the origin of the poet, but also, and often above all, the genre of the poem. This link between genre and dialect is a feature of most Greek literature.[49]

The most important distinction is between the dialects of monody and choral lyric. Of the two, monody is closer to the vernaculars, such as Aeolic in the case of Sappho and Alcaeus or Ionic in the case of Anacreon. Even monodists, however, not least the Lesbian poets, admit traditional epic forms, just as they draw on epic phraseology.

The dialects of choral lyric are more complex. They mix Doric forms and forms that belong to a traditional poetic language, chiefly epic but including some non-epic Aeolic elements. In the case of Alcman, there are prominent forms specific to the Doric of Sparta (Laconian, a form of 'severe' Doric). His language, therefore, like that of monody, has a strong local flavour. Doric remains a feature of choral lyric in Stesichorus, Ibycus, Simonides, Pindar and Bacchylides (and in tragedy), even though some of them were Ionic-speaking by origin (and the Boeotian Pindar presumably Aeolic-speaking), and all of them composed poems for performance

---

[49] For chapter-length introductions to the lyric dialects, see D'Alessio 2009b: 120–8 and Silk 2010 (who also covers issues of style). On literary dialects in general, including lyric, see Cassio 2008 and, more briefly, Tribulato 2010. Colvin 2007 and Miller 2013 provide dialect-focused commentaries on a selection of literary and non-literary texts, including lyric. Both have general introductions setting out the distinctive features of the various dialect groups. For treatments of the dialect of individual poets, see the relevant introductions in the commentary section below.

outside Doric-speaking areas. However, the Doric veneer becomes thinner over time. While Doric (though not of course Laconian) forms are still prominent in Stesichorus, despite his heavily epic diction, the dialect of Pindar and Bacchylides is far more epic than Doric.

A major caveat to any account of lyric language (and a major problem in establishing the text) is that dialect is particularly vulnerable to changes in the process of transmission. (i) The Archaic alphabets had only one letter for short and long *o*, and short and long *e*. It is therefore likely that the distinction between the metrically equal ου and ω and between η and ει, which can determine whether a form is (e.g.) Doric or Ionic, or 'mild' or 'severe' Doric, was not codified when some of the poems were first recorded. (ii) Reperformance in a different place or period will often have introduced changes, conscious or unconscious.[50] (iii) Hellenistic editors imposed their own notions of the poets' original dialects – some of these are hypercorrections that make the texts look *too* Lesbian or *too* Laconian ('hyper-Lesbian', 'hyper-Laconian').

In any case, many details of the poets' own linguistic choices are irrecoverable. The text presented here is therefore on the whole conservative. Problematic dialect forms are often discussed in the notes rather than emended. As in most of the recent editions of Greek lyric, little attempt is made to reconstruct the appearance of the text prior to the Hellenistic editions, even where it is evident that the text established by the Alexandrian editors cannot be the same as that of the poets (see for example p. 63 on the choice between σ and θ in Alcman).

---

[50] See nn. 41 and 47.

GREEK LYRIC

A SELECTION

ALCMAN 1 *PMG* (3 CALAME)

× – ⏑ ⏑] Π̣ωλυδεύκης.
οὐκ ἐγὼ]ν Λύκαισον ἐν καμοῦσιν ἀλέγω
– Ἐνα]ρσφόρον τε καὶ Σέβρον ποδώκη
– ⏑ –]ν τε τὸν βιατὰν
– ⏑ –] ̣ τε τὸν κορυστὰν
Εὐτείχ]η τε ϝάνακτά τ᾽ Ἀρήϊον
– ⏑]ά τ᾽ ἔξοχον ἡμισίων

– ⏑ –]ν τὸν ἀγρόταν
× –] μέγαν Εὔρυτόν τε
– ⏑ –]πώρω κλόνον
× –]ᾳ̣ τε τὼς ἀρίστως
– ⏑ –] παρήσομες.
× – ⏑ γ]ᾳ̣ρ Αἶσα παντῶν
καὶ Πόρος] γεραιτάτοι
× – ⏑ -π]έδιλος ἀλκά.
– ⏑ ἀν]θ̣ρώπων ἐς ὠρανὸν ποτήσθω
– ⏑ πη]ρήτω γαμὲν τὰν Ἀφροδίταν
– ⏑ – ϝ]ᾳ̣νᾳ̣σσαν ἤ τιν᾽
– ⏑ –] ἢ παίδα Π̣ό̣ρ̣κω
– ⏖ – Χά]ριτες δὲ Διὸς δό̣μον
– ⏖ –]σ̣ιν ἐρογλεφάροι

– ⏑ – × –]τάτοι
× – ⏑ ⏑ –]τ̣α δαίμων
– ⏑ – ×]ι φίλοις
× – ⏑ ⏑]ωκε δῶρα
– ⏑ – ×] ̣γαρεον
× – ⏑ ⏑]ώ̣λεσ̣᾽ ἥβα
– ⏑ – × –]ρ̣ονον
× – ⏑ ⏑ – μ]ᾳ̣ταίας

Alcm. 1 suppl. et corr. Blass exceptis quae infra memorantur 2 Blass ex Σ Pind. *Ol.* 3 Egger in init. οὔτ᾽ Snell, ἀλλ᾽ Bergk 6 Ahrens ex *Epim. Hom.* 8 ἀγρέταν Ahrens 12 οὐ] Ahrens 13 Ten Brink 15 Ahrens : ἀπ]έδιλος Blass 16 μήτις ἀν] Blass 17 μηδὲ πει] Blass 20 Egger

```
– ◡ – × – ]έβα. τῶν δ' ἄλλος ἰῶι                                    30
– ◡ – × – ◡ ] μαρμάρωι μυλάκρωι
– ◡ – × – ] ‧ εν Ἀιδας
   – ◡ – × – ◡ ]αυτοι
– ᷉ – ◡ ◡ – ]πον. ἄλαστα δὲ
```
ϝέργα πάσον κακὰ μησαμένοι.   35
ἔστι τις σιῶν τίσις‧
ὁ δ' ὄλβιος ὅστις εὔφρων
ἀμέραν [δι]απλέκει
ἄκλαυστος. ἐγὼν δ' ἀείδω
Ἀγιδῶς τὸ φῶς‧ ὁρῶ   40
ϝ' ὥτ' ἄλιον, ὄνπερ ἇμιν
Ἀγιδὼ μαρτύρεται
φαίνην. ἐμὲ δ' οὖτ' ἐπαινῆν
οὔτε μωμέσθαι νιν ἀ κλεννὰ χοραγός
οὐδ' ἀμῶς ἐῆι. δοκεῖ γὰρ ἤμεν αὐτά   45
ἐκπρεπὴς τὼς ὥπερ αἴ τις
   ἐν βοτοῖς στάσειεν ἵππον
παγὸν ἀεθλοφόρον καναχάποδα
   τῶν ὑποπετριδίων ὀνείρων.

ἦ οὐχ ὁρῆις; ὁ μὲν κέλης   50
Ἐνητικός‧ ἁ δὲ χαίτα
τᾶς ἐμᾶς ἀνεψιᾶς
Ἁγησιχόρας ἐπανθεῖ
χρυσὸς ὡς ἀκήρατος‧
τό τ' ἀργύριον πρόσωπον,   55
διαφάδαν τί τοι λέγω;
Ἁγησιχόρα μὲν αὔτα‧
ἁ δὲ δευτέρα πεδ' Ἀγιδὼ τὸ ϝεῖδος
ἵππος Ἰβηνῶι Κολαξαῖος δραμεῖται.
ταὶ Πελειάδες γὰρ ἇμιν   60
   Ὀρθρίαι φᾶρος φεροίσαις
νύκτα δι' ἀμβροσίαν ἅτε Σείριον
ἄστρον ἀϝειρομέναι μάχονται.

---

38 Bergk   39 ἄκλαυτος Sitzler   40–1 quidam ὁρῶ|σ', alii ὁρῶ | ἐ leg.   45 αὔτα
Fowler   61 Ὀρθρίαι : ὀρθρίαι (nom. pl.) quidam editores, ὀρθίαι ΣΑ, ϝορθείαι
Davison

οὔτε γάρ τι πορφύρας
τόσσος κόρος ὥστ' ἀμύναι,　　　　　　65
οὔτε ποικίλος δράκων
παγχρύσιος, οὐδὲ μίτρα
Λυδία, νεανίδων
ϝιανογ[λ]εφάρων ἄγαλμα,
οὐδὲ ταὶ Ναννῶς κόμαι,　　　　　　70
ἀλλ' οὐδ' Ἀρέτα σιειδής,
οὐδὲ Συλακίς τε καὶ Κλεησισήρα.
οὐδ' ἐς Αἰνησιμβρ[ό]τας ἐνθοῖσα φασεῖς,
"Ἀσταφίς τέ μοι γένοιτο,
καὶ ποτιγλέποι Φίλυλλα　　　　　　75
Δαμαρέτα τ' ἐρατά [τ]ε Ϝιανθεμίς"·
ἀλλ' Ἁγησιχόρα με τείρει.

οὐ γὰρ ἁ καλλίσφυρος
Ἁγησιχ[ό]ρ[α] πάρ' αὐτεῖ·
Ἁγιδοῖ . ε . . αρμένει　　　　　　80
θωστήριά [τ'] ἄμ' ἐπαινεῖ.
ἀλλὰ τᾶν . . . . . σιοί
δέξασθε· σιῶν γὰρ ἄνα
καὶ τέλος. [χο]ροστάτις,
ϝείποιμί κ', ἐγὼν μὲν αὐτά　　　　　　85
παρσένος μάταν ἀπὸ θράνω λέλακα
γλαύξ· ἐγὼν δὲ τᾶι μὲν Ἀώτι μάλιστα
ϝανδάνην ἐρῶ· πόνων γὰρ
ἆμιν ἰάτωρ ἔγεντο·
ἐξ Ἁγησιχόρας δὲ νεάνιδες　　　　　　90
ἰρ]ήνας ἐρατᾶς ἐπέβαν.

τῶ]ι τε γὰρ σηραφόρωι
. [ ]τῶς εδ . . . .
τῶι κυβερνάται δὲ χρή
κἠν νᾶϊ μα . . . .　　　　　　95
ἁ δὲ τᾶν Σηρηνίδων
ἀοιδοτέρα μὲν . . . .

77 Π, ΣB : τηρεῖ quidam editores　79 Ten Brink　91 Page　93 ᾳ[ὺ]τῶς
Blass　97 αὐδά Von der Mühll, οὐδέν Page

σιαὶ γάρ, ἀντὶ δ' ἔνδεκα
παίδων δεκ . . . . ει·
φθέγγεται δ . . . . ἐπὶ Ξάνθω ῥοαῖσι   100
κύκνος· ἁ δ' ἐπιμέρωι ξανθᾶι κομίσκαι

ALCMAN 89 *PMG* (159 CALAME)

εὕδουσι δ' ὀρέων κορυφαί τε καὶ φάραγγες
πρώονές τε καὶ χαράδραι
†φῦλά τε ἑρπετά θ'† ὅσα τρέφει μέλαινα γαῖα
θῆρές τ' ὀρεσκῷοι καὶ γένος μελισσῶν
καὶ κνώδαλ' ἐν βένθεσι πορφυρῆς ἁλός·   5
εὕδουσι δ' οἰωνῶν φῦλα τανυπτερύγων.

ALCAEUS 42 VOIGT

ὡς λόγος κάκων ἀ[‿ − ‿ − −
Περράμω<ι> καὶ παῖσ[ι ‿ − ‿ − −
ἐκ σέθεν πίκρον, π[‿ ‿ − ‿ − ×
Ἴλιον ἴραν.

οὐ τεαύταν Αἰακίδαι[ς ‿ − −   5
πάντας ἐς γάμον μάκ[αρας ‿ − −
ἄγετ' ἐκ Νή[ρ]ηος ἔλων [μελάθρων
πάρθενον ἄβραν

ἐς δόμον Χέρρωνος· ἔλ[υσε δ' − −
ζῶμα παρθένω· φιλο[− ‿ − −   10
Πήλεος καὶ Νηρεΐδων ἀρίστ[ας·
ἐς δ' ἐνίαυτον

παῖδα γέννατ' αἰμιθέων [‿ − −
ὄλβιον ξάνθαν ἐλάτη[ρα πώλων·
οἱ δ' ἀπώλοντ' ἀμφ' Ἐ[λέναι ‿ − ×   15
καὶ πόλις αὔτων.

99 αεκ Π, δεκὰς οῖ' (ᾶδ' Wilamowitz, ὡς Puelma) ἀεῖδει Blass   105 coronis
Alcm. 89   3 φῦλά θ' ἑρπετῶν ὅσα fere D'Ansse de Villoison, φῦλά τ' ἑρπέτ' ὅσα
Page, ἑρπετά θ' ὅσσα (del. φῦλά τε) West   5 βένθεσ<σ>ι Welcker, Bergk
Alc. 42   suppl. Hunt   6 in fin. [καλέσσαις Hunt   10 [τας δέ Hunt
13 [φέριστον Diehl   16 coronis

ALCAEUS 129 VOIGT

× – ‿] ‗ ρατα τόδε Λέσβιοι
× –] ‿ ς εὔδειλον τέμενος μέγα
ξῦνον κάτεσσαν· ἐν δὲ βώμοις
ἀθανάτων μακάρων ἔθηκαν,

κἀπωνύμασσαν ἀντίαον Δία,   5
σὲ δ' Αἰολήιαν κυδαλίμαν θέον
πάντων γενέθλαν, τὸν δὲ τέρτον
τόνδε κεμήλιον ὠνύμασσ̣[α]ν

Ζόννυσσον ὠμήσταν. ἄγ[ι]τ' εὔνοον
θῦμον σκέθοντες ἀμμετέρα[ς] ἄρας   10
ἀκούσατ', ἐκ δὲ τῶνδε μόχθων
ἀργαλέας τε φύγας ῥ[ύεσθε·

τὸν Ὕρραον δὲ παῖδα πεδελθέτω
κήνων Ἐρ[ίνν]υς, ὤς ποτ' ἀπώμνυμεν
τόμοντες ἄ φ[̣]ν ̣ν   15
μηδάμα μηδένα τὼν ἐταίρων,

ἀλλ' ἢ θάνοντες γᾶν ἐπιέμμενοι
κείσεσθ' ὑπ' ἄνδρων οἶ τότ' ἐπικ ̣ην,
ἤπειτα κακκτάνοντες αὔτοις
δᾶμον ὑπὲξ ἀχέων ῥύεσθαι.   20

κήνων ὀ φύσγων οὐ διελέξατο
πρὸς θῦμον, ἀλλὰ βραϊδίως πόσιν
ἔ]μβαις ἐπ' ὀρκίοισι δάπτει
τὰν πόλιν ἄμμι δέδ[ ] [ ] εἴπαις

οὐ κὰν νόμον [̣] ̣ε [   ] ̣[ ]   25
γλαύκας ἀ[– × – ‿ ‿ – ‿ –
γεγρα ̣[‿ – × – ‿ – ×
Μύρσιλ[ο – ‿ ‿ – ‿ – –

Alc. 129 suppl. Lobel   12 ρ[Π¹ : ϙ[Π¹ supra lineam   15 ἄμφ[εν- Lobel
26 Ἀ[θανάας Diehl

ALCAEUS 130B VOIGT

ἄγνο{ι}ς τοὶς βιότοις . ις ὀ τάλαις ἔγω
ζώω μοῖραν ἔχων ἀγροϊωτίκαν,
ἰμέρρων ἀγόρας ἄκουσαι
καρυ[ζ]ομένας ὦ Ἀγεσιλαΐδα

καὶ β[ό]λλας· τὰ πάτηρ καὶ πάτερος πάτηρ   5
καγγεγήρασ᾽ ἔχοντες πεδὰ τωνδέων
τὼν ἀλλαλοκάκων πολίταν·
ἔγω [δ᾽] ἀπὺ τούτων ἀπελήλαμαι

φεύγων ἐσχατίαισ·· ὠς δ᾽ Ὀνυμακλέης
Ὠθάναος ἐοίκησ᾽ ἀλυκαιχμίαις,   10
φεύγων τὸν πόλεμον· στάσιν γάρ
πρὸς κρ [. . .]ς †οὐκ ἄμεινον† ὀννέλην;

.] [. .]τ[.] μακάρων ἐς τέμ[ε]νος θέων
ἐοίκησ[α] μελαίνας ἐπίβαις χθόνος
.λι[× –]. συνόδοισι ταύταις   15
οἴκημι κάκων ἔκτος ἔχων πόδας,

ὄππαι Λε[σβί]αδες κριννόμεναι φύαν
πώλεντ᾽ ἐλκεσίπεπλοι, περὶ δὲ βρέμει
ἄχω θεσπεσία γυναίκων
ἴρα[ς ὀ]λολύγας ἐνιαυσίας   20

× × –]. ἀπὺ πόλλων πότα δὴ θέοι
              ] [᾽]σκ . . . ν . . . πιοι
                       ]. . . . . .
.να[   ] . . . μεν.
. . .

ALCAEUS 140 VOIGT

μαρμαίρει δὲ μέγας δόμος   1
χάλκωι. παῖσα δ᾽ Ἄρηι κεκόσμηται στέγα

Alc. 130b   suppl. Lobel   1 ἄγνο{ι}ς uel ἄγνοις Π   8 Gallavotti : ἔγω[γ᾽]
Page   10 -κησ᾽ ἀλυκ- diu. Porro, -κησα λυκ- multi   12 interrog. notam dub. add.
Ferrari (ὀννέλην· Π)   15 Πac : μ᾽ αὔταις Πpc, -σιν αὔταις dub. Page   22 in fin.
Ὀλύμπιοι Lobel   24 coronis
. . .

λάμπραισιν κυνίαισι, κὰτ
τᾶν λεῦκοι κατέπερθεν ἴππιοι λόφοι
νεύοισιν, κεφάλαισιν ἄν-
δρῶν ἀγάλματα· χάλκιαι δὲ πασσάλοις   5
κρύπτοισιν περικείμεναι
λάμπραι κνάμιδες, ἔρκος ἰσχύρω βέλεος,
θόρρακές τε νέω λίνω
κόϊλαί τε κὰτ ἄσπιδες βεβλήμεναι·   10
πὰρ δὲ Χαλκίδικαι σπάθαι,
πὰρ δὲ ζώματα πόλλα καὶ κυπάσσιδες.
τῶν οὐκ ἔστι λάθεσθ᾽ ἐπεὶ
δὴ πρώτιστ᾽ ὐπὰ ἔργον ἔσταμεν τόδε.

ALCAEUS 347 VOIGT

τέγγε πλεύμονα οἴνωι, τὸ γὰρ ἄστρον περιτέλλεται,
ἀ δ᾽ ὤρα χαλέπα, πάντα δὲ δίψαισ᾽ ὐπὰ καύματος,
ἄχει δ᾽ ἐκ πετάλων ἄδεα τέττιξ < ∪ ∪ – ∪ – >,
ἄνθει δὲ σκόλυμος, νῦν δὲ γύναικες μιαρώταται
λέπτοι δ᾽ ἄνδρες, ἐπεὶ < – > κεφάλαν καὶ γόνα Σείριος   5
ἄσδει.

SAPPHO 1 VOIGT

ποικιλόθρον᾽ ἀθανάτ᾽ Ἀφρόδιτα,
παῖ Δίος δολόπλοκε, λίσσομαί σε,
μή μ᾽ ἄσαισι μηδ᾽ ὀνίαισι δάμνα,
    πότνια, θῦμον·

ἀλλὰ τυίδ᾽ ἔλθ᾽, αἴ ποτα κἀτέρωτα   5
τὰς ἔμας αὔδας ἀΐοισα πήλοι
ἔκλυες, πάτρος δὲ δόμον λίποισα
    χρύσιον ἦλθες

ἄρμ᾽ ὐπασδεύξαισα. κάλοι δέ σ᾽ ἄγον
ὤκεες στροῦθοι περὶ γᾶς μελαίνας   10

Alc. 140   4 Π¹ et Π² (κατεπ[ ) : καθύπερθεν Athen.   14 -τιστ᾽ ὐπὰ τῶργον Lobel,
-ιστον ὐπ᾽ ἔργον Maas
Alc. 347   1 -μονα uel -μονας fontes   Ϝοίνωι Grotefend   5 <δὴ> Bergk
Sa. 1   1 Π ( ]ικιλόθρο[ ), PF, epit. codd. alii, Heph. : -φρον᾽ epit. codd. alii, Choreob.
in Heph. (p. 249–51 Consbruch)

πύκνα δίννηντες πτέρ' ἀπ' ὠράνω αἴθε-
ρος διὰ μέσσω·

αἶψα δ' ἐξίκοντο. σὺ δ', ὦ μάκαιρα,
μειδιαίσαισ' ἀθανάτωι προσώπωι,
ἤρε' ὄττι δηὖτε πέπονθα κὤττι 15
δηὖτε κάλημι

κὤττι μοι μάλιστα θέλω γένεσθαι
μαινόλαι θύμωι· "τίνα δηὖτε πείθω
]̣ †σαγην ἐς σὰν† φιλότατα; τίς σ', ὦ
Ψάπφ', ἀδικήει; 20

καὶ γὰρ αἰ φεύγει, ταχέως διώξει·
αἰ δὲ δῶρα μὴ δέκετ', ἀλλὰ δώσει·
αἰ δὲ μὴ φίλει, ταχέως φιλήσει
κωὐκ ἐθέλοισα."

ἔλθε μοι καὶ νῦν, χαλέπαν δὲ λῦσον 25
ἐκ μερίμναν, ὄσσα δέ μοι τέλεσσαι
θῦμος ἰμέρρει τέλεσον, σὺ δ' αὖτα
σύμμαχος ἔσσο.

SAPPHO 2 VOIGT

δεῦρύ μ' ἐ<κ> Κρήτας πρ[⏑ ⏑ –] ⏑ ναῦον 1
ἄγνον ὄππ[αι –] χάριεν μὲν ἄλσος
μαλί[αν], βῶμοι δ' ἔνι θυμιάμε-
νοι [λι]βανώτωι·

ἐν δ' ὕδωρ ψῦχρον κελάδει δι' ὔσδων 5
μαλίνων, βρόδοισι δὲ παῖς ὀ χῶρος
ἐσκίαστ', αἰθυσσομένων δὲ φύλλων
κῶμα †καταιριον†·

19]̣ σαγην[Π : βαισαγην Pᵖᶜ, καὶ σάγην F, epit.   ἄψ σ' ἄγην ἐς ϝὰν φιλότατα Lobel
(ϝὰν iam Edmonds)   20 ἀδικήει Et. Gen. AB cit. 90 Calame 1970, Herodian.
1.454.21 et 2.332.1 Lentz : -κη P, epit., -κης F
Sa. 2   1 Theander : δευρυμμεκρητας ostr.   Lobel : ναυγον ostr., ξναυλον
Pfeiffer   2 et 3 suppl. Lobel   2 τοι] Page   3 δ' ἔνι Pfeiffer, Vogliano : δεμι
ostr., δὲ τε- Norsa   4 Vogliano   6 Hermog. : μαλίαν ostr.   8 καταιριον ostr.,
καταρρεῖ Hermog. : κατέρρει Sitzler

ἐν δὲ λείμων ἱππόβοτος τέθαλε
†τωτ . . . ρ“ιννοισ† ἄνθεσιν, αἰ δ᾽ ἄηται   10
μέλλιχα πνέοισιν < ᵕ − ᵕ − ×
− ᵕ ᵕ − − >.

ἔνθα δὴ σὺ − ᵕ ἔλοισα Κύπρι
χρυσίαισιν ἐν κυλίκεσσιν ἄβρως
ὀμμεμείχμενον θαλίαισι νέκταρ   15
†ωνοχοαισα†

SAPPHO 16 VOIGT

ο]ἰ μὲν ἰππήων στρότον, οἰ δὲ πέσδων,
οἰ δὲ νάων φαῖσ᾽ ἐπὶ γᾶν μέλαι[ν]αν
ἔμμεναι κάλλιστον, ἔγω δὲ κῆν᾽ ὄτ-
τω τις ἔραται.

πά]γχυ δ᾽ εὔμαρες σύνετον πόησαι   5
π]άντι τ[ο]ῦτ᾽· ἀ γὰρ πόλυ περσκέθοισα
κάλλος [ἀνθ]ρώπων Ἐλένα [τὸ]ν ἄνδρα
τὸν [. . . ἀρ]ιστον

κ̣αλλ[ίποι]σ᾽ ἔβα ᾽ς Τροΐαν πλέοισα,
κωὐδ[ὲ πα]ῖδος οὐδὲ φίλων τοκήων   10
πά[μπαν] ἐμνάσθη, ἀλλὰ παράγαγ᾽ αὔταν
−᾽ ᵕ ᵕ −]σαν

− ᵕ −]αμπτον γὰρ [ᵕ −] ν̣όημμα
− ᵕ] . −̣ . κούφως τ[ᵕ ᵕ −] ν̣οήσηι·
−]μ̣ε νῦν Ἀνακτορία[ς] ὀνέμναι-   15
σ᾽ οὐ] παρεοίσας·

τᾶ]ς κε βολλοίμαν ἔρατόν τε βᾶμα
κ̣ἀμάρυχμα λάμπρον ἴδην προσώπω

10 ἠρίνοισιν Vogliano (τέθαλε<ν> supplens), ἐράννοισ᾽ Page   13 ἔνθα ostr. : ἔλθε
Norsa ex Athen.   15 Gallavotti, Lanata : ἀμμείχ- ostr., συνμεμιγ-
Athen.   16 ωνοχοαισα ostr. : οἰνοχοοῦσα Athen., οἰνοχόαισα Diehl, οἰνοχόαισον
Theiler
Sa. 16   suppl. Hunt exceptis quae infra memorantur   8 [πανάρ]ι̣στον Page, [μέγ᾽
ἄρ]ι̣στον Gallavotti   9 Lobel   11 Theander   13 Κύπρις᾽ ἄγν]αμπτον
Schubart   15 κ̣ἄ]με Lobel, τῶ̣]με Lidov, West   16 Agar

ἦ τὰ Λύδων ἄρματα κἀν ὄπλοισι
πεσδο]μάχεντας.   20

‒ ‿ ‒] μὲν οὐ δύνατον γένεσθαι
‒]ᾳν ἄνθρωπ[‒ · π]εδέχην δ᾽ ἄρασθαι
‒ ‿ ‒ × ‒ ‿ ‿ ‒] δ̣᾽ ἔμ᾽ αὔται
‒ ‿ ‿ ‒ ‒]

SAPPHO 31 VOIGT

φαίνεταί μοι κῆνος ἴσος θέοισιν
ἔμμεν᾽ ὤνηρ ὄττις ἐνάντιός τοι
ἰσδάνει καὶ πλάσιον ἆδυ φωναί-
σας ὐπακούει

καὶ γελαίσας ἰμέροεν· τό μ᾽ ἦ μάν   5
καρδίαν ἐν στήθεσιν ἐπτόασεν.
ὠς γὰρ <ἔς> σ᾽ ἴδω βρόχε᾽, ὤς με φώνασ᾽
οὐδὲν ἔτ᾽ εἴκει,

ἀλλὰ κὰμ μὲν γλῶσσα ἔαγε, λέπτον
δ᾽ αὔτικα χρῶι πῦρ ὐπαδεδρόμακεν,   10
ὀππάτεσσι δ᾽ οὐδὲν ὄρημμ᾽, ἐπιρρόμ-
βεισι δ᾽ ἄκουαι,

†έκαδε μ᾽ ἴδρως ψῦχρος κακχέεται†, τρόμος δέ
παῖσαν ἄγρει, χλωροτέρα δὲ ποίας
ἔμμι, τεθνάκην δ᾽ ὀλίγω 'πιδεύσην   15
φαίνομ᾽ ἔμ᾽ αὔται.

ἀλλὰ πὰν τόλματον ἐπεὶ †καὶ πένητα†

SAPPHO 44 VOIGT

<   >
<   >
<   >
Κυπρο̣ [   ]ας·   1
κᾶρυξ ἦλθε θ̣. [   ]ελε[. . . .] θεις

20 Rackham, Vogliano
Sa. 31   3 φωναί|σας Forssman : -φων· σαῖς P   7 <ἔς> fere Ahrens   Danielsson :
φωνάς P   9 <μ'> ἔαγε Sitzler, πέπαγε Cobet   10 P : χροῖ Blomfield   13 P : ἀδέμ᾽
ἴδρώς κακὸς χέεται *Epim. Hom.*, κὰδ δ᾽ ἴδρώς ψυχρὸς χέεται Muretus, κὰδ δέ μ᾽ ἴδρως
ψῦχρος ἔχει Page   15 P : 'πιδεύην Ahrens, 'πιδεύης Hermann
Sa. 44   suppl. Hunt exceptis quae infra memorantur   2 θέ[ων Jurenka

Ἴδαος τάδεκα... φ[ ] ις τάχυς ἄγγελος·

< "   >   3a

τάς τ' ἄλλας Ἀσίας [ ]δε αν κλέος ἄφθιτον·

Ἕκτωρ καὶ συνέταιρ[ο]ι ἄγοισ' ἐλικώπιδα   5

Θήβας ἐξ ἴερας Πλακίας τ' ἀπ' [ἀϊ]ννάω

ἄβραν Ἀνδρομάχαν ἐνὶ ναῦσιν ἐπ' ἄλμυρον

πόντον· πόλλα δ' [ἐλί]γματα χρύσια κἄμματα

πορφύρ[α] καταῦτ[με]να, ποίκιλ' ἀθύρματα,

ἀργύρα τ' ἀνάριθμα ποτήρια κἀλέφαις."   10

ὢς εἶπ'· ὀτραλέως δ' ἀνόρουσε πάτ[η]ρ φίλος.

φάμα δ' ἦλθε κατὰ πτόλιν εὐρύχορον φίλοις.

αὔτικ' Ἰλίαδαι σατίναι[ς] ὐπ' ἐϋτρόχοις

ἆγον αἰμιόνοις, ἐπ[έ]βαινε δὲ παῖς ὄχλος

γυναίκων τ' ἄμα παρθενίκα[ν] τ [ ] σφύρων,   15

χῶρις δ' αὖ Περάμοιο θυγ[α]τρεσ[∪ – ∪ –.

ἴππ[οις] δ' ἄνδρες ὔπαγον ὐπ' ἄρ[ματ ∪ – ∪ –

π[ᵜ]ες ἠίθεοι, μεγάλω[σ]τι δ[∪ – ∪ –

δ[ ] ἀνίοχοι φ[. . . . .] [

π[ ]ξα ο[20

desunt nonnulli uersus

ἴ]κελοι θέοι[ς   21

] ἄγνον ἀολ[λε –

ὄρμαται [∪ ∪ – ∪ ∪ –]νον ἐς Ἴλιο[ν.

αὖλος δ' ἀδυ[μ]έλης [∪ ∪ –] τ' ὀνεμίγνυ[το

καὶ ψ[ό]φο[ς κ]ροτάλ[ων, ∪ ∪]ως δ' ἄρα πάρ[θενοι   25

ἄειδον μέλος ἄγν[ον, ἴκα]νε δ' ἐς αἴθ[ερα

ἄχω θεσπεσία γελ[∪ – ∪ ∪ – ∪ –,

πάνται δ' ἦς κὰτ ὄδο[∪ ∪ – ∪ ∪ – ∪ –

κράτηρες φίαλαί τ' ὀ[ ]υεδε[ ] εακ[ ] [

μύρρα καὶ κασία λίβανός τ' ὀνεμείχνυτο.   30

γύναικες δ' ὀλόλυσδον ὄσαι προγενέστερα[ι,

3a lacunam indicauit scriba   8 Wilamowitz   9 Maas, Theander : κατ' αὖτ[με]να
Lobel   18 π[άντ]ες Hunt   20 ἔ]ξαγο[ν Hunt   22 ἀόλ[λεες Hunt   26 ἄγγ[ον
suppl. Hunt, reliqua Lobel   27 γέλ[ος Hunt   28 ὄδο[ις Hunt, ὄδο[ν Lobel et
Page   31 ἐ]λέλυσδ[ο]ν Π¹, ὀλόλυζο[ν Π²

πάντες δ᾽ ἄνδρες ἐπήρατον ἴαχον ὄρθιον
πάον᾽ ὀνκαλέοντες ἐκάβολον εὐλύραν,
ὔμνην δ᾽ Ἕκτορα κ᾽Ἀνδρομάχαν θεοεικέλο[ις.

SAPPHO 58B

× – ᴗ ᴗ – – ἰ]ο̣κ[ό]λ̣πων κάλα δῶρα, παῖδες,
× – ᴗ ᴗ – –]ν φιλάοιδον λιγύραν χ̣ε̣λύνναν.

× – ᴗ ᴗ – –] ποτ᾽ [ἔ]ο̣ντα χρόα γῆρας ἤδη
× – ᴗ ᴗ λεῦκαι δ᾽ ἐγ]ένοντο τρίχες ἐκ μελαίναν·

βάρυς δέ μ᾽ ὀ [θ]ῦμο̣ς πεπόηται, γόνα δ᾽ οὐ φέροισι,   5
τὰ δή ποτα λαίψηρ᾽ ἔον ὄρχησθ᾽ ἴσα νεβρίοισι.

†τατ† στεναχίζω θαμέως· ἀλλὰ τί κεν ποείην;
ἀγήραον ἄνθρωπον ἔοντ᾽ οὐ δύνατον γένεσθαι.

καὶ γάρ π[ο]τ̣α̣ Τίθωνον ἔφαντο βροδόπαχυν Αὔων
ἔρωι δε[ ]α̣ εἰσανβαμεν εἰς ἔσχατα γᾶς φέροισα[ν,   10

ἔοντα̣ [κ]ά̣λο̣ν καὶ νέον, ἀλλ᾽ αὖτον ὔμως ἔμαρψε
χρόνωι πόλιον γῆρας ἔχ̣[ο]ν̣τ̣᾽ ἀθανάταν ἄκοιτιν.

× – ᴗ ᴗ – – ᴗ ᴗ – –]ι̣μέναν νομίσδει
× – ᴗ ᴗ – – ᴗ ᴗ – – ᴗ ᴗ]αις ὀπάσδοι·

ἔγω δὲ φίλημμ᾽ ἀβροσύναν < – ᴗ ᴗ > τοῦτο καί μοι   15
τὸ λάμπρον †ἔρος ἀελίω† καὶ τὸ κάλον λέλογχε.

STESICHORUS 8A FINGLASS (S17 *SLG*, 185 *PMG*)

†Ἅλιος† δ᾽ Ὑπεριονίδα <ἰ>ς   str. *uel* ant.
δέπας †ἐσκατέβαινε χρύσεον†, ὄ-
φρα δι᾽ Ὠκεανοῖο περάσας

34 coronis Π¹ et Π²
Sa. 58b suppl. G–D (3, 5, 9, 11, 12), Stiebitz (1, 10), Hunt (4, sed δ᾽ pro τ᾽
Lobel)   6 West : -σιν Π¹ Π²   7 τὰ <μὲν> West   στεναχίζω Π¹ : στεναχίσδω
West   10 δ̣έ̣π̣α̣ς εἰσανβάμεν᾽ G–D   15 τοῦτο om. Athen.   16 ἔρως anon.   τώελίω
Sitzler
Stes. 8a   1 West : -ίδας Athen.   2 -βαιν᾽ ἐς Pardini

ἀφίκοιθ' ἱαρᾶς ποτὶ βένθεα νυκ-
τὸς ἐρεμνᾶς   5
ποτὶ ματέρα κουριδίαν τ' ἄλοχον
παῖδάς τε φίλους·
ὁ δ' ἐς ἄλσος ἔβα δάφναισι †κατάσ-
κιον† ποσὶ παῖς Διός – ◡ ◡ –

STESICHORUS 15 FINGLASS (S11 *SLG*)

χηρσὶν δ[◡ ◡ – ‿‿ – ◡ ‿‿ τὸν
δ' ἀπαμ[ειβόμενος
ποτέφα [◡ ◡ – Χρυσάορος ἀ-
θανάτοιο̯ [◡ – ‿‿ – ◡ ◡ – ·

῞μή μοι θά[νατον ‿‿ – ‿‿ –   5 ep.
τα δεδίσκ[ε(ο) – ◡ ◡ – –
μηδεμελ[– ‿‿ – ‿‿ – ◡ ◡.
αἰ μὲν γὰ[ρ ◡ ◡ ἀθάνατος ‿‿
μαι καὶ ἀγή[ραος – ‿‿ – ‿‿ –
ἐν Ὀλύμπ[ωι,   10
κρέσσον[(◡) – ‿‿ – ‿‿ – ◡ ἐ-
λεγχέα δ[– ◡ ◡ –

καὶ τ[– ◡ ◡ – ◡ ◡ – –   str.
κεραϊ[ζ ◡ ◡ – ‿‿ – ‿‿ ἀ-
μετέρω[ν ‿‿ – ◡ ◡ – – ·   15
αἰ δ' ὦ φί[λ(ε) – ‿‿ – ‿‿ γῆ-
ρας [ἱκ]έσ̯θαι,
ζώ[ει]ν τ' ἐν ἐ[– ‿‿ – ‿‿ –
θε θ[ε]ῶν μακάρω[ν,
νῦν μοι πολὺ̯ κά̯[λλιον – ‿‿ –   20
ὅ τι μόρσιμ[ον – ‿‿ – ◡ ◡ –

καὶ ὀνείδε[◡ – ◡ ◡ – –   ant.
καὶ παντὶ γέ[νει ‿‿ – ‿‿ ἐξ-
οπίσω Χρυσ[άο]ρο[ς υ]ἱόν.

4 ἀφίκοιθ' Blomfield : ἀφίκηθ' Athen.   9 -σκιόεν Barrett
Stes. 15   suppl. Lobel (2, 3 ἀ-, 5, 6, 11, 14 ἀ-, 15, 16 [λε, 20, 25 μ]ή, 26 γ]), Page (9),
West (23 [νει), Führer (23 ἐξ-), reliqua Barrett   8 in fin. πέλο- Page, ἔσο-
Barrett   18 ἐ[παμερίοις Barrett   20 in fin. ἐστι παθεῖν Page

μ]ὴ τοῦτο φ[ί]λον μακά[ρε]σσι θε[ο]ῖ-   25
σι γ]ένοιτο
. . . .].[.]. . κε[. .].[.] περὶ βουσὶν ἐμαῖς
. . . .]
          ]κ̣λεος̣.[

STESICHORUS 17 FINGLASS (S13 *SLG*)

          ]μ̣.[

◡◡ – ◡] ἐγὼν [◡ ◡]α καὶ ἀλασ-   ep.
◡ ◡ –]αἰ ἄλ[ασ]τ̣α π̣αθοῖσα
– ◡ σε, Γ]αρυόνα, γωνάζομα[ι,
– ◡ ἐμ]όν τιν μαζ[ὸν]◡̣[– ◡◡   5
– ◡ ◡ –]ωμον γ[◡ ◡ – ◡◡ –
◡ ◡ – –]
– ◡◡ – ◡] φίλαι γανυθ[ε ◡◡
– ◡◡ εὐφ]ροσύναις.

◡◡ – ◡◡ –]δεα πέπλ[ον   10 str.
          ].[.]κλυ. . . .[
◡◡ – ◡◡ – ◡ ◡]ρευγων·
◡◡ – ◡◡ – ◡◡ –]γονελ[–

STESICHORUS 18 FINGLASS (S14 *SLG*)

– ◡◡ – ◡◡ μ]ι̣μνε παραὶ Δία
παμ[βασιλῆα ◡ – .

◡ ◡ – γλαυκ]ῶπις Ἀθάνα   str.
◡◡ – ◡◡ –]ς ποτὶ ὂν κρατερό-
φρονα πάτρω᾽ ἱ]πποκέλευθον·   5
" ◡◡ – ◡◡ –]ς μεμναμένος α[
◡ ◡ – –]
◡◡ – ◡◡ Γαρυ]όναν θ[αν]άτου

Stes. 17   suppl. Barrett (5 ἐμ], 9), Page (10), reliqua Lobel   2–3 [μελέ]α καὶ ἀλασ|[τοτόκος κ]αὶ Barrett   5 αἴ ποκ᾽ ἐμ]όν Barrett   in fin. ἐ[πέσχεθον Page   8 παρὰ ματρί] Barrett
Stes. 18   2 et 5 (πάτρω᾽) suppl. Page, reliqua Lobel   4 in init. φάτ᾽ Page   8 in init. μὴ βούλεο Barrett

STESICHORUS 19 FINGLASS (S15 + ?S21 *SLG*)

```
        ]ν.[
 ‾‾ - ‾‾]ναντ[ ᴗ ᴗ - -
 ‾‾ - ᴗ ᴗ ]αν δρι̣ω̣.[ ᴗ ᴗ -
 ᴗ ᴗ - - ]
 ‾‾ - ‾‾ - ]τα νόωι διελε̣[              5
 ‾‾ - ‾‾ - ]ν·
 ‾‾ - ‾‾ - ] πολὺ κέρδιον εἶν
 ‾‾ - ‾‾ ]οντα λάθραι πολεμε[ῖν
```

```
 ‾‾ - ‾‾ - ᴗ ] κραταιῶι·                 ant.
 ‾‾ - ‾‾ - ] ξ κατεφράζετ[ό] οἱ          10
 ‾‾ - ‾‾ πι]κρὸν ὄλεθρον·
 ‾‾ - ‾‾ - ἔ]χε̣ν̣ ἀσπίδα πρόσ-
 θ ᴗ ᴗ - - ]
 ‾‾ - ‾‾ - ]ε̣το· τοῦ δ᾽ ἀπὸ κρα-
 τός (ᴗ) - ‾‾ -]                          15
 ‾‾ - ‾‾ ἱπ]πόκομος τρυφάλει᾽·
 ‾‾ - ‾‾ - ᴗ] ἐπὶ ζαπέδωι.
```

```
 ]ν με̣ν̣ [     ] ρ̣ο̣νες ὠκυπετα[         ep.
 ‾‾ - ‾‾ - ᴗ] ν ἐχοίσαι
 - ‾‾ - ]επ[ ]άξαν ἐπ[ὶ] χθόνα·          20
 - ‾‾ - ]α̣πε.η κεφαλὰ χαρ[ᴗ
 ]ωσωα.[.]ε̣...[
```

desunt octo uersus (ep. 6–8 + str. 1–5)

```
 ‾‾ - ‾‾ - ‾‾]ων στυγε[ρ]οῦ              31
 θανάτοι]ο .. [
 κ]εφ[αλ]ᾶι πέρι̣ [- ᴗ ] ἔχων, πεφορυ-
 γ]μένος αἵματ[ι - ‾‾ - ]ι̣ τε χολᾶι,
```

```
 ὀλεσάνορος αἰολοδε[ίρ]ου                35 ant.
 ὀδύναισιν Ὕδρας. σιγᾶι δ᾽ ὅ γ᾽ ἐπι-
 κλοπάδαν ἐνέρεισε μετώπωι·
```

Stes. 19 suppl. Page (12, 13, 38, 42, 44), reliqua Lobel 5–6 διελέ̣[ξ]ατο
West 7 ἐδοάσσατό οἱ] Diggle 10 εὐρ]ά̣ξ Barrett 18–22 huc dub. transponunt
Page, Barrett 31 φέρ]ων Barrett, Führer 32 τέ̣[λος Barrett, Führer 33
[πότμον] Barrett

διὰ δ' ἔσχισε σάρκα [καὶ] ὀ[στ]έα δαί-
μονος αἶσαι·
διὰ δ' ἀντικρὺ σχέθεν οἶ[σ]τὸς ἐπ' ἀ-   40
κροτάταν κορυφάν·
ἐμίαινε δ' ἄρ' αἵματι πορφ[υρέωι
θώρακά τε καὶ βροτόεντ[‿ ‿ – .

ἀπέκλινε δ' ἄρ' αὐχένα Γαρ[υόνας   ep.
ἐπικάρσιον, ὡς ὅκα μ[ά]κω[ν   45
ἅ τε καταισχύνοισ' ἁπαλὸν [⏑⏑
αἶψ' ἀπὸ φύλλα βαλοῖσα ν[‿ – ⏑⏑

IBYCUS S151 SLG (282A PMG)

–]αι Δαρδανίδα Πριάμοιο μέ-   ant.
γ' ἄσ]τυ περικλεὲς ὄλβιον ἠνάρον
–]οθεν ὀρνυμένοι
Ζη]νὸς μεγάλοιο βουλαῖς

ξα]νθᾶς Ἑλένας περὶ εἴδει   5 ep.
δῆ]ριν πολύυμνον ἔχ[ο]ντες
πό]λεμον κατὰ δακρ[υό]εντα.
Πέρ]γαμον δ' ἀνέ[β]α ταλαπείριο[ν ἄ]τα
χρυ]σοέθειραν δ[ι]ὰ Κύπριδα.

νῦ]ν δέ μοι οὔτε ξειναπάταν Π[άρι]ν   10 str.
–] ἐπιθύμιον οὔτε τανίσφυρ[ον
ὑμ]νῆν Κασσάνδραν
Πρι]άμοιό τε παίδας ἄλλου[ς

Τρο]ίας θ' ὑψιπύλοιο ἁλώσι[μο]ν   ant.
ἆμ]αρ ἀνώνυμον· οὐδεπ[(⏑) – ⏑ ⏑   15
ἡρ]ώων ἀρετὰν
ὑπ]ερέφανον οὕς τε κοίλα[ι

νᾶες] πολυγόμφοι ἐλεύσα[ν   ep.
Τροί]αι κακόν, ἥρωας ἐσθ[λούς.
τῶν] μὲν κρείων Ἀγαμέ[μνων   20

43 -εντ[α μέλεα Page   46 [δέμας Page
Ibyc. S151   suppl. Maas (14 ἁλώσι[μο]ν), Wilamowitz (15 ἆμ]αρ), Barron (22, 27,
30 ἐν δ]ὲ, 36, 37), reliqua Hunt   3 Ἄργ]οθεν Hunt   11 ἦν] Hunt

ἄ]ρχε Πλεισθε[νί]δας βασιλ[εὐ]ς ἀγὸς ἀνδρῶν
Ἀτρέος ἐσθ[λὸς] πάϊς ἔκγ[ο]νος.

καὶ τὰ μὲν ἄ[ν] Μοῖσαι σεσοφι[σ]μέναι   str.
εὖ Ἑλικωνίδε[ς] ἐμβαίεν λόγω[ι·
†θνατός† δ᾽ οὔ κ[ε]ν ἀνὴρ   25
διερ [   ] τὰ ἕκαστα εἴποι,

ναῶν ὅ[σσος ἀρι]θμὸς ἀπ᾽ Αὐλίδος   ant.
Αἰγαῖον διὰ [πό]ντον ἀπ᾽ Ἄργεος
ἠλύθο[ν ἐς Τροία]ν
ἱπποτρόφο[ν, ἐν δ]ὲ φώτες   30

χ]αλκάσπι[δες, υἷ]ες Ἀχα[ι]ῶν.   ep.
τ]ῶν μὲν πρ[οφ]ερέστατος α[ἰ]χμᾶι
⏖ –] πόδ[ας ὠ]κὺς Ἀχιλλεύς
καὶ μέ]γας Τ[ελαμ]ώνιος ἄλκιμ[ο]ς [Αἴας
. . . . .] . . [. . . .]λο[ ]πυρος.   35

– ⏖ – κάλλι]στος ἀπ᾽ Ἄργεος   str.
– ⏖ – Κυάνι]ππ[ο]ς ἐς Ἴλιον
          ]
          ] . . [.] . . σ

. . . .]α χρυσόστροφ[ος   40 ant.
Ὕλλις ἐγήνατο, τῶι δ᾽ [ἄ]ρα Τρωΐλον
ὡσεὶ χρυσὸν ὀρει-
χάλκωι τρὶς ἄπεφθο[ν] ἤδη

Τρῶες Δ[α]ναοί τ᾽ ἐρό[ε]σσαν   ep.
μορφὰν μάλ᾽ ἐΐσκον ὅμοιον.   45
τοῖς μὲν πέδα κάλλεος αἰέν
καὶ σύ, Πο⟨λ⟩ύκρατες, κλέος ἄφθιτον ἑξεῖς
ὡς κατ᾽ ἀοιδὰν καὶ ἐμὸν κλέος.

IBYCUS 286 PMG

ἦρι μὲν αἵ τε Κυδώνιαι
μηλίδες ἀρδόμεναι ῥοᾶν

ἐκ ποταμῶν, ἵνα παρθένων
κῆπος ἀκήρατος, αἵ τ᾽ οἰνανθίδες
αὐξόμεναι σκιεροῖσιν ὑφ᾽ ἔρνεσιν   5
οἰναρέοις θαλέθοισιν. ἐμοὶ δ᾽ ἔρος
οὐδεμίαν κατάκοιτος ὥραν·
†τε† ὑπὸ στεροπᾶς φλέγων
Θρηΐκιος Βορέας
ἀΐσσων παρὰ Κύπριδος ἀζαλέ-   10
αις μανίαισιν ἐρεμνὸς ἀθαμβὴς
ἐγκρατέως πεδόθεν †φυλάσσει†
ἡμετέρας φρένας.

IBYCUS 287 PMG

Ἔρος αὖτέ με κυανέοισιν ὑπὸ
   βλεφάροις τακέρ᾽ ὄμμασι δερκόμενος
κηλήμασι παντοδαποῖς ἐς ἀπεί-
   ρ<ον>α δίκτυα Κύπριδος <ἐσ>βάλλει.
ἦ μὰν τρομέω νιν ἐπερχόμενον,   5
ὥστε φερέζυγος ἵππος ἀεθλοφόρος ποτὶ γήραι
ἀέκων σὺν ὄχεσφι θοοῖς ἐς ἅμιλ-
   λαν ἔβα.

IBYCUS 288 PMG

Εὐρύαλε γλαυκέων Χαρίτων θάλος, <   >
   καλλικόμων μελέδημα, σὲ μὲν Κύπρις
ἅ τ᾽ ἀγανοβλέφαρος Πει-
   θὼ ῥοδέοισιν ἐν ἄνθεσι θρέψαν.

ANACREON 348 PMG

γουνοῦμαί σ᾽ ἐλαφηβόλε
   ξανθὴ παῖ Διὸς ἀγρίων
δέσποιν᾽ Ἄρτεμι θηρῶν·

Ibyc. 286   8 ἄθ᾽ ὑπὸ Hermann, ἀλλ᾽ ἄθ᾽ ὑπὸ Mehlhorn   12 πεδόθεν Naeke : παῖδ᾽
ὅθεν Athen.   φυλάσσει Athen. : τινάσσει Naeke
Ibyc. 287   3-4 Schneidewin : ἄπειρα codd.   4 Clemm (εἰσ-) : βάλλει codd.
Ibyc. 288   1 <Ὡρᾶν> Page

ἤ κου νῦν ἐπὶ Ληθαίου
δίνηισι θρασυκαρδίων
ἀνδρῶν ἐσκατορᾶις πόλιν   5
χαίρουσ', οὐ γὰρ ἀνημέρους
ποιμαίνεις πολιήτας.

ANACREON 358 PMG

σφαίρηι δηῦτέ με πορφυρέηι
βάλλων χρυσοκόμης Ἔρως
νήνι ποικιλοσαμβάλωι
συμπαίζειν προκαλεῖται.

ἡ δ', ἔστιν γὰρ ἀπ' εὐκτίτου   5
Λέσβου, τὴν μὲν ἐμὴν κόμην,
λευκὴ γάρ, καταμέμφεται,
πρὸς δ' ἄλλην τινὰ χάσκει.

ANACREON 388 PMG

πρὶν μὲν ἔχων βερβέριον, καλύμματ' ἐσφηκωμένα,
καὶ ξυλίνους ἀστραγάλους ἐν ὠσὶ καὶ ψιλὸν περί
πλευρῆισι < − × − > βοός,

νήπλυτον εἴλυμα κακῆς ἀσπίδος, ἀρτοπώλισιν
κἀθελοπόρνοισιν ὁμιλέων ὁ πονηρὸς Ἀρτέμων,   5
κίβδηλον εὑρίσκων βίον,

πολλὰ μὲν ἐν δουρὶ τιθεὶς αὐχένα, πολλὰ δ' ἐν τροχῶι,
πολλὰ δὲ νῶτον σκυτίνηι μάστιγι θωμιχθείς, κόμην
πώγωνά τ' ἐκτετιλμένος·

νῦν δ' ἐπιβαίνει σατινέων χρύσεα φορέων καθέρματα   10
†παῖς Κύκης† καὶ σκιαδίσκην ἐλεφαντίνην φορεῖ
γυναιξὶν αὔτως < − ◡ − >.

Anacr. 358   1 πορφυρέηι Barnes : πορφυρενι Athen.
Anacr. 388   3 <δέρριον> siue <δέρμ' ἔβη> siue <δέρμ' ἤιει> Bergk   4 Schömann :
νεόπλουτον, νεόπλυτον codd.

ANACREON 395 *PMG*

πολιοὶ μὲν ἡμὶν ἤδη
    κρόταφοι κάρη τε λευκόν,
χαρίεσσα δ' οὐκέτ' ἥβη
    πάρα, γηραλέοι δ' ὀδόντες,
γλυκεροῦ δ' οὐκέτι πολλὸς   5
    βιότου χρόνος λέλειπται.

διὰ ταῦτ' ἀνασταλύζω
    θαμὰ Τάρταρον δεδοικώς·
Ἀΐδεω γάρ ἐστι δεινὸς
    μυχός, ἀργαλέη δ' ἐς αὐτόν   10
κάτοδος· καὶ γὰρ ἑτοῖμον
    καταβάντι μὴ ἀναβῆναι.

ANACREON 417 *PMG*

πῶλε Θρηικίη, τί δή με λοξὸν ὄμμασι βλέπουσα
νηλεῶς φεύγεις, δοκέεις δέ μ' οὐδὲν εἰδέναι σοφόν;

ἴσθι τοι, καλῶς μὲν ἄν τοι τὸν χαλινὸν ἐμβάλοιμι,
ἡνίας δ' ἔχων στρέφοιμ<ί σ'> ἀμφὶ τέρματα δρόμου.

νῦν δὲ λειμῶνάς τε βόσκεαι κοῦφά τε σκιρτῶσα παίζεις·   5
δεξιὸν γὰρ ἱπποπείρην οὐκ ἔχεις ἐπεμβάτην.

SIMONIDES 511 *PMG* (7 POLTERA)

fr. 1a

            Κέλητι
    τοῖς Αἰατίου παισίν

    ]α Κρόνοιο παῖς ἐρικυδ[ής   1
    ] Αἰατίου γενεάν
    ]ται καὶ χρυσοφ[όρ]μ̣ι̣[γξ
Ἀπόλλων ἑκαταβόλο̣[ς

Anacr. 395 2 τε Bergk : δὲ codd.   3 Schneidewin : οὐκ ἔθ' codd.   10 ἀργαλέη S :
ἀργαλὴ A   11 κάτοδος S¹ : κάθοδος S²A
Anacr. 417 4 Bergk
Sim. 511 suppl. Lobel praeter fr. 1(b) uers. 6 (Gentili)

σαμαίνει λιπαρά τε Πυθ[ώ   5
  θ᾽ ἱπποδρ[ο]μ.
.]. σε . [.]υν[

desunt nonnulli uersus

fr. 1b

        ].[1
        ]
        ].κ.λ..[
        ]σπασ[.]αν
βασιλῆα [τ]ελεσφόρον   5
ἀμφικ[τιό]νων ἔχρησαν
Πυρ<ρ>ίδαν· ἅμα δεγεν.. ο σὺν ὄλβω[ι
Θεσσαλῶν καὶ παντὶ δάμωι

SIMONIDES 531 *PMG* (261 POLTERA)

τῶν ἐν Θερμοπύλαισι θανόντων
εὐκλεὴς μὲν ἁ τύχα, καλὸς δ᾽ ὁ πότμος,
βωμὸς δ᾽ ὁ τάφος, †προγόνων† δὲ μνᾶστις, ὁ δ᾽ οἶ<κ>τος ἔπαινος.
ἐντάφιον δὲ τοιοῦτον {οὔτ᾽} εὐρώς
οὔθ᾽ ὁ πανδαμάτωρ ἀμαυρώσει χρόνος.   5
ἀνδρῶν ἀγαθῶν ὅδε σακὸς οἰκέταν εὐδοξίαν
Ἑλλάδος εἵλετο. μαρτυρεῖ δὲ Λεωνίδας,
ὁ Σπάρτας βασιλεύς, ἀρετᾶς μέγαν λελοιπώς
κόσμον ἀέναόν τε κλέος.

SIMONIDES 542 *PMG* (260 POLTERA)

ἄνδρ᾽ ἀγαθὸν μὲν ἀλαθέως γενέσθαι χαλεπὸν   str. 1
χερσίν τε καὶ ποσὶ καὶ νόωι
τετράγωνον ἄνευ ψόγου τετυγμένον·   3
desunt septem (uel septemdecim) uersus

---

fr. 1 (a)   6 αἰ θ᾽ ἱπποδρ[ο]μι- Lobel
Sim. 531   1 del. West   -λαισι uel -λαις codd.   3 πρὸ γόων Eichstädt,
Ilgen   οἶ<κ>τος Jacobs   4 οὔτ᾽ del. Bergk : οὔ τις West   6 Reiske : ὁ δὲ
codd.   Schneidewin : σηκὸς codd.   7 <καὶ> post δὲ Arsen.   8 ὁ del. Bergk

οὐδέ μοι ἐμμελέως τὸ Πιττάκειον νέμεται,   str. 2 11
καίτοι σοφοῦ παρὰ φωτὸς εἰ-
ρημένον· χαλεπὸν φάτ' ἐσθλὸν ἔμμεναι.
θεὸς ἂν μόνος τοῦτ' ἔχοι γέρας· ἄνδρα δ' οὐκ   14
ἔστι μὴ οὐ κακὸν ἔμμεναι,
ὃν ἀμάχανος συμφορὰ καθέληι.
πράξας {μὲν} γὰρ εὖ πᾶς ἀνὴρ ἀγαθός,
κακὸς δ' εἰ κακῶς < –   18
– ᴗ – ᴗ ᴗ – –
– ᴗ – ᴗ – – >

τοὔνεκεν οὔ ποτ' ἐγὼ τὸ μὴ γενέσθαι δυνατὸν   str. 3 21
διζήμενος κενεὰν ἐς ἄ-
πρακτον ἐλπίδα μοῖραν αἰῶνος βαλέω,
πανάμωμον ἄνθρωπον, εὐρυεδέος ὅσοι   24
καρπὸν αἰνύμεθα χθονός·
ἐπὶ δ' ὔμμιν εὑρὼν ἀπαγγελέω.
πάντας δ' ἐπαίνημι καὶ φιλέω,   27
ἑκὼν ὅστις ἔρδηι
μηδὲν αἰσχρόν· ἀνάγκαι δ'
οὐδὲ θεοὶ μάχονται.   30

desunt tres uel tredecim uersus   str. 4
ᴗ ᴗ – ᴗ – > μηδ' ἄγαν ἀπάλαμνος εἰ-   34
δώς τ' ὀνησίπολιν δίκαν,
ὑγιὴς ἀνήρ· †οὐ μὴν† ἐγώ
μωμήσομαι· τῶν γὰρ ἀλιθίων   37
ἀπείρων γενέθλα.
πάντα τοι καλά, τοῖσί<ν>
τ' αἰσχρὰ μὴ μέμικται.   40

SIMONIDES 543 *PMG* (271 POLTERA)

    ... ὅτε λάρνακι
ἐν δαιδαλέαι
ἄνεμός τέ μιν πνέων

Sim. 542   16 ὃν Bergk : ὃν ἂν codd.   Boeckh : ἀμήχ- codd.   17 μὲν del.
Hermann : γὰρ del. Aars   26 Bergk : ἔπειθ' ὑμῖν codd.   35 τ' Hermann : γ'
codd.   37 Schneidewin : ἠλι- codd.   39 Page
Sim. 543   1 P : ὅτι M, del. Poltera   3 Schneidewin : μὴν PM

κινηθεῖσά τε λίμνα δείματι
ἔρειπεν· οὐδ᾽ ἀδιάντοισι παρειαῖς   5
ἀμφί τε Περσέϊ βάλλε φίλαν χέρα
εἶπέν τ᾽· "ὦ τέκος, οἷον ἔχω πόνον.

σὺ δ᾽ ἀωτεῖς, γαλαθηνῶι δ᾽ ἤτορι   ˙ ?ep.
κνοώσσεις ἐν ἀτερπεῖ
δούρατι χαλκεογόμφωι   10
†δενυκτιλαμπει†
κυανέωι τε δνόφωι †ταδεις†.
ἄχναν δ᾽ ὕπερθε τεᾶν κομᾶν
βαθεῖαν παριόντος
κύματος οὐκ ἀλέγεις, οὐδ᾽ ἀνέμου   15
φθόγγον, πορφυρέαι
κείμενος ἐν χλανίδι, πρόσωπον καλόν.
εἰ δέ τοι δεινὸν τό γε δεινὸν ἦν,
καί κεν ἐμῶν ῥημάτων
λεπτὸν ὑπεῖχες οὖας.   20

κέλομ᾽ εὖδε, βρέφος,   ?str.
εὑδέτω δὲ πόντος, εὑδέτω <δ᾽> ἄμετρον κακόν.
μεταβουλία δέ τις φανείη, Ζεῦ πάτερ, ἐκ σέο.   23–4
ὅτι δ᾽ ἢ θαρσαλέον ἔπος εὔχομαι   25
ἢ νόσφι δίκας,
σύγγνωθί μοι."

SIMONIDES 581 *PMG* (262 POLTERA)

τίς κεν αἰνήσειε νόωι πίσυνος Λίνδου ναέταν Κλεόβουλον,
ἀεναοῖς ποταμοῖς ἄνθεσί τ᾽ εἰαρινοῖς
ἀελίου τε φλογὶ χρυσέας τε σελάνας
καὶ θαλασσαίαισι δίναις ἀντι<τι>θέντα μένος στάλας;
ἅπαντα γάρ ἐστι θεῶν ἥσσω· λίθον δέ   5
καὶ βρότεοι παλάμαι
θραύοντι· μωροῦ φωτὸς ἅδε βουλά.

4 τε Brunck : δὲ PM   5 Brunck : οὔτ᾽ PM, οὐκ Thiersch   7 Athen. : τέκνον
PM   8 Casaubon : αὖτε εἶς Athen., αὐταῖς PM   ἤτορι Athen. : ειθει P, ει M, ἠθεΐ
Bergk   9 P : κνώσσεις Athen., om. M   13 ἄχναν Page : αὐλέαν P, αὐλαίαν M, ἄλμαν
Bergk   ὕπερθεν PM   14 βαθειᾶν Ahrens   17 πρὸς ωπον κ. πρόσωπον P :
πρόσωπον κ. + *uac.* M   20 λεπτὸν Stephanus : λεπτῶν PM   21 Schneidewin :
κέλομαι PM   22 Thiersch   25 Blass : ὅτι δὴ PM, ὅττι δὲ Mehlhorn
Sim. 581   4 Schneidewin, Mehlhorn   6 Hermann : βρότ(ε)ιοι codd.

TIMOTHEUS, *PERSIANS*

788 PMG

κλεινὸν ἐλευθερίας τεύχων μέγαν Ἑλλάδι κόσμον

791 PMG

ὅ]τε δὲ τᾶι λείποιεν αὖραι	‿‿‿—— —‿—— 2tr	60
τᾶι δ' ἐπεισέπιπτον, †ἄφρωισ	—‿—‿ —‿†—— 2tr?	
δε† ἀβακχίωτος ὄμβρος,	‿†‿—‿ —‿—‿ 2tr?	
εἰς δὲ τρόφιμον ἄγγος	—‿‿‿‿—— ith (= 2tr₍ₐₐ₎)	
ἐχεῖτ'. ἐπεὶ δ' ἀμβόλιμος ἅλμα	‿ —‿—— ‿‿‿—— ‿2tr	
στόματος ὑπερέθυιεν,	‿‿‿‿‿‿—— ith (= 2tr₍ₐₐ₎)	65
ὀξυπαραυδήτωι	—‿‿——— δ	
φωνᾶι παρακόπωι τε δόξαι φρενῶν	——‿‿‿— ‿——‿— 2δ	
κατακορὴς ἀπείλει	‿‿‿—‿—— δ— (= ith)	
†γόμφοις ἐμπρίων	†————— δ	
μιμούμενος λυμεώ-	——‿— —‿— ia ₍ₐia	70
νι σώματος θαλάσσας·†	‿—‿— ‿—— ia ia₍ₐ	
"ἤδη θρασεῖα καὶ πάρος	——‿— ‿—‿— 2ia	
λάβρον αὐχέν' ἔσχες ἐμ	—‿— ‿—‿— ₍ₐ2ia	
πέδαι καταζευχθεῖσα λινοδέτωι τεόν.	‿—‿— ——‿‿‿ ‿—‿— 3ia	
νῦν δέ σ' ἀναταράξει	—‿‿‿‿—— ith (= 2tr₍ₐₐ₎)	75
ἐμὸς ἄναξ ἐμὸς πεύ-	‿‿‿—‿—— ith (= 2tr₍ₐₐ₎)	
καισιν ὀριγόνοισιν, ἐγ-	—‿‿‿‿‿—‿— ₍ₐ2ia	
κλήισει δὲ πεδία πλόϊμα νομάσι ναύταις·	——‿‿‿ ‿‿‿‿‿ ‿—— 2ia ia₍ₐ	
οἰστρομανὲς παλαιομί-	—‿‿‿—‿— ¨gl (= cho ia)	
σημ' ἄπιστόν τ' ἀγκάλι-	—‿————‿— ₍ₐ2ia	80
σμα κλυσιδρομάδος αὔρας."	‿‿‿‿‿‿—— ith (=₍ₐia ia₍ₐ)	
φάτ' ἄσθματι στρευγόμενος, βλοσυρὰν	‿—‿— —‿‿—‿— ia D	
δ' ἐξέβαλλεν ἄχναν	—‿—‿‿— dod¨	
ἐπανερευγόμενος	‿‿‿—‿‿— dod¨	
στόματι βρύχιον ἅλμαν.	‿‿‿‿‿‿—— ith	85

. . . .

Tim. 791   suppl. et corr. Wilamowitz exceptis quae infra memorantur
61–2 ἄφρει δ' Danielsson, ἀφρῶι δ' ἔ<ζε'> Gargiulo   69 γόμφους
Sitzler   71 θαλασασ Π : θαλάσ<σ>αι Wilamowitz   78 Danielsson, Sitzler :
νομμασιναυγαις Π   79 Hordern : παλεο- Π

ὁ δὲ παλινπόρευτον ὡς ἐσ-	◡◡◡−◡ −◡−◡	2tr	173
εῖδε βασιλεὺς εἰς φυγὴν ὁρ-	−◡◡◡− −◡−−	2tr	
μῶντα παμμιγῆ στρατόν,	−◡−◡ −◡−	2tr‸	175
γονυπετὴς αἴκιζε σῶμα,	◡◡◡−− −◡−◡	2tr	
φάτο δὲ κυμαίνων τύχαισιν·	◡◡◡−− −◡−−	2tr	
ἰὼ κατασκαφαὶ δόμων	◡−◡− ◡−◡−	2ia	
σείριαί τε νᾶες Ἑλλανίδες, αἳ	−◡−◡ −◡− −◡◡−	2tr‸ cho	
κατὰ μὲν ἥλικ’ ὠλέσαθ’ ἥ-	◡◡◡−◡−◡◡−	gl¨ (= tr cho)	180
βαν νέων πολύανδρον·	−◡−◡◡−−	ph	
νᾶες δ’ †οὐκὶ ὀπισσοπόρευ-	?		
τον ἄξουσιμ†, πυρὸς	?		
δ’ αἰθαλόεμ μένος ἀγρίωι	−◡◡−◡◡−◡−	dod^d	
σώματι φλέξει, στονόεντα δ’ ἄλγη	−◡◡− −◡◡−◡−−	cho ar	185
ἔσται Περσίδι χώραι.	−−−◡◡−−	ph	
<ἰ>ὼ βαρεῖα συμφορά,	◡−◡− ◡−◡−	2ia	
ἅ μ’ ἐς Ἑλλάδ’ ἤγαγες.	−◡− ◡−◡− ‸2ia		
ἀλλ’ ἴτε, μηκέτι μέλλετε,	−◡◡−◡◡−◡−	dod^d (= gl)	
ζεύγνυτε μὲν τετράορον ἵπ-	−◡◡−−−◡◡−	gl¨	190
πων ὄχημ’, οἱ δ’ ἀνάριθμον ὄλ-	−◡−−◡◡−◡−	-gl	
βον φορεῖτ’ ἐπ’ ἀπήνας·	−◡−◡◡−−	ph	
πίμπρατε δὲ σκηνάς,	−◡◡−−−	dod	
μηδέ τις ἡμετέρου γένοιτ’	−◡◡−◡◡−◡−	dod^d (= gl)	
ὄνησις αὐτοῖσι πλούτου.”	◡−◡− −◡−−	ia tr	195
οἱ δὲ τροπαῖα στησάμενοι Διὸς	−◡◡−−−◡◡−◡◡	4da	
ἁγνότατον τέμενος, Παιᾶν’	−◡◡−◡◡−−	dod^d (= gl)	
ἐκελάδησαν ἰήϊον	◡◡◡−◡◡−◡−	gl	
ἄνακτα, σύμμετροι δ’ ἐπε-	◡−◡− ◡−◡−	2ia	
κτύπεον ποδῶν	◡−◡− ia		200
ὑψικρότοις χορείαις.	−◡◡−◡◡−−	ar	
ἀλλ’ ὦ χρυσεοκίθαριν ἀέ-	−−−◡◡◡◡−	gl	
ξων Μοῦσαν νεοτευχῆ,	−−−◡◡−−	ph	
ἐμοῖς ἔλθ’ ἐπίκουρος ὕμ-	◡−−◡◡−◡−	gl	
νοις ἰήϊε Παιάν.	−◡−◡◡−−	ph	205
ὁ γάρ μ’ εὐγενέτας μακραί-	◡−−◡◡−◡−	gl	
ων Σπάρτας μέγας ἁγεμὼν	−−−◡◡−−	gl	
βρύων ἄνθεσιν ἥβας	◡−−◡◡−−	ph	

δονεῖ λαὸς ἐπιφλέγων	‿ − − ‿ ‿ − ‿ −	*gl*
ἐλᾶι τ᾽ αἴθοπι μώμωι,	‿ − − ‿ ‿ − −	*ph*	21(
ὅτι παλαιοτέραν νέοις	‿ ‿ ‿ − ‿ ‿ − ‿ −	*gl*
ὕμνοις Μοῦσαν ἀτιμῶ.	− − − ‿ ‿ − −	*ph*
ἐγὼ δ᾽ οὔτε νέον τιν᾽ οὔ-	‿ − − ‿ ‿ − ‿ −	*gl*
τε γεραὸν οὔτ᾽ ἰσήβαν	‿ ‿ ‿ ‿ − ‿ − −	*ar*
εἴργω τῶνδ᾽ ἑκὰς ὕμνων·	− − − ‿ ‿ − −	*ph*	21
τοὺς δὲ μουσοπαλαιολύ-	− ‿ − ‿ ‿ − ‿ −	*gl*
μας, τούτους δ᾽ ἀπερύκω,	− − − ‿ ‿ − −	*ph*
λωβητῆρας ἀοιδᾶν,	− − − ‿ ‿ − −	*ph*
κηρύκων λιγυμακροφώ-	− − − ‿ ‿ − ‿ −	*gl*
νων τείνοντας ἰυγάς.	− − − ‿ ‿ − −	*ph*	22(
πρῶτος ποικιλόμουσος Ὀρ-	− − − ‿ ‿ − ‿ −	*gl*
φεὺς <χέλ>υν ἐτέκνωσεν	− ‿ − ‿ ‿ − −	*ph*
υἱὸς Καλλιόπα<ς ‿ −	− − − ‿ ‿ − ‿ −	*gl*
− × > Πιερίαθεν·	− × − ‿ ‿ − −	*ph*
Τέρπανδρος δ᾽ ἐπὶ τῶι δέκα	− − − ‿ ‿ − ‿ −	*gl*	22
τεῦξε Μοῦσαν ἐν ᾠδαῖς·	− ‿ − ‿ ‿ − −	*ph*
Λέσβος δ᾽ Αἰολία ν<ιν> Ἀν-	− − − ‿ ‿ − ‿ −	*gl*
τίσσα<ι> γείνατο κλεινόν·	− − − ‿ ‿ − −	*ph*
νῦν δὲ Τιμόθεος μέτροις	− ‿ − ‿ ‿ − ‿ −	*gl*
ῥυθμοῖς τ᾽ ἐνδεκακρουμάτοις	− − − ‿ ‿ − ‿ −	*gl*	23(
κίθαριν ἐξανατέλλει,	‿ ‿ ‿ − ‿ ‿ − −	*ph*
θησαυρὸν πολύυμνον οἴ-	− − − ‿ ‿ − ‿ −	*gl*
ξας Μουσᾶν θαλαμευτόν·	− − − ‿ ‿ − −	*ph*
Μίλητος δὲ πόλις νιν ἁ	− − − ‿ ‿ − ‿ −	*gl*
θρέψασ᾽ ἁ δυωδεκατειχέος	− − − ‿ ‿ ‿ − −	*hï*	23
λαοῦ πρωτέος ἐξ Ἀχαιῶν.	− − − ‿ ‿ − ‿ − −	*hi*
ἀλλ᾽ ἑκαταβόλε Πύθι᾽ ἁγνὰν	− ‿ ‿ − ‿ ‿ − ‿ − −	*hi*
ἔλθοις τάνδε πόλιν σὺν ὄλβωι,	− − − ‿ ‿ − ‿ − −	*hi*
πέμπων ἀπήμονι λαῶι	− − ‿ − ‿ ‿ − −	‿*hï* (= *ia iaₐ*)
τῶιδ᾽ εἰρήναν θάλλουσαν εὐνομίαι.	− − − − − − ‿ − ‿ ‿ −	‿*iaₐ* ‿*iaₐ tl̈*	24(

CARM. POP. 848 PMG

ἦλθ᾽ ἦλθε χελιδών,
καλὰς ὥρας ἄγουσα

221 -μουσον   Wilamowitz   221–2 οριυσυν   Π   223–4 lacunam   indicauit
Page   224 **Page** : πιερiασενι Π   226 ζεῦξε Wilamowitz   236 πρωτέος susp.
multi   240 εὐνομίαν Π

καὶ καλοὺς ἐνιαυτούς,
ἐπὶ γαστέρα λευκά
κἀπὶ νῶτα μέλαινα.
παλάθαν οὐ προκυκλεῖς   5
ἐκ πίονος οἴκου,
οἴνου τε δέπαστρον
τυροῦ τε κάνυστρον;
καὶ πύρνα χελιδών   10
καὶ λεκιθίταν οὐκ ἀπωθεῖται.
πότερ᾽ ἀπίωμες ἢ λαβώμεθα;
εἰ μέν τι δώσεις· εἰ δὲ μή, οὐκ ἐάσομεν·
ἢ τὰν θύραν φέρωμες ἢ τὸ ὑπέρθυρον,
ἢ τὰν γυναῖκα τὰν ἔσω καθημέναν;   15
μικρὰ μέν ἐστι, ῥαιδίως μιν οἴσομεν.
†ἂν δὴ φέρῃς τι, μέγα δή τι φέροις·†
ἄνοιγ᾽ ἄνοιγε τὰν θύραν χελιδόνι·
οὐ γὰρ γέροντές ἐσμεν, ἀλλὰ παιδία.

CARM. POP. 853 PMG

ὦ τί πάσχεις; μὴ προδῷς ἄμμ᾽, ἱκετεύω·
πρὶν καὶ μολεῖν κεῖνον ἀνίστω,
μὴ κακὸν <σε> μέγα ποιήσῃς
κἀμὲ τὴν δειλάκραν.
ἁμέρα καὶ δή· τὸ φῶς διὰ τᾶς θυρίδος οὐκ εἰσορῇς;   5

CARM. POP. 869 PMG

ἄλει, μύλα, ἄλει.
καὶ γὰρ Πιττακὸς ἄλει
μεγάλας Μυτιλήνας βασιλεύων.

carm. pop. 848   9 CE : τυρῶ A, τυρῶν B   10 πύρνα Bergk : πυρῶν ἁ codd., πυρῶνα Hermann   11–12 uersus corruptos esse nonnulli censuerunt   12 ἀπίωμες A : -μεν CE   14 φέρωμες A : -μεν CE   17 φέρῃς A : -ροις CE   iamb. trim. latere censuerunt Hermann, alii
carm. pop. 853   3 κακὸν μέγα ποιήσῃς Athen., κ. <σε> μ. ποιήσηι Bergk   5 δή Bergk : ἤδη Athen.   εἰσορῇς Meineke : ἐκορης Athen.
carm. pop. 869   1 μύλ᾽ ἄλ- Wilamowitz   2 Koester : ἀλεῖ codd.   3 Wilamowitz : Μιτυλάνας uel -λήνας codd. plerique

CARM. CONV. 892 PMG

ὁ δὲ καρκίνος ὧδ' ἔφη
χαλᾶι τὸν ὄφιν λαβών·
"εὐθὺν χρὴ τὸν ἑταῖρον ἔμμεν καὶ μὴ σκολιὰ φρονεῖν."

CARM. CONV. 893 PMG

ἐν μύρτου κλαδὶ τὸ ξίφος φορήσω
ὥσπερ Ἁρμόδιος καὶ Ἀριστογείτων
ὅτε τὸν τύραννον κτανέτην
ἰσονόμους τ' Ἀθήνας ἐποιησάτην.

CARM. CONV. 894 PMG

φίλταθ' Ἁρμόδι', οὔ τί που τέθνηκας·
νήσοις δ' ἐν μακάρων σέ φασιν εἶναι,
ἵνα περ ποδώκης Ἀχιλεὺς
Τυδεΐδην †τέ φασι τὸν ἐσθλόν† Διομήδεα.

CARM. CONV. 895 PMG

ἐν μύρτου κλαδὶ τὸ ξίφος φορήσω
ὥσπερ Ἁρμόδιος καὶ Ἀριστογείτων
ὅτ' Ἀθηναίης ἐν θυσίαις
ἄνδρα τύραννον Ἵππαρχον ἐκαινέτην.

CARM. CONV. 896 PMG

αἰεὶ σφῶιν κλέος ἔσσεται κατ' αἶαν,
φίλταθ' Ἁρμόδιε καὶ Ἀριστόγειτον,
ὅτι τὸν τύραννον κτανέτην
ἰσονόμους τ' Ἀθήνας ἐποιησάτην.

carm. conv. 892   1 ἔφα Bentley
carm. conv. 894   1 Ἁρμόδι' οὔ τί που Σ Aristoph. *Ach.* 980 : Ἁρμοδίου πω Athen.

COMMENTARY

ALCMAN

Alcman was active in Sparta. Ancient scholarship offers two *floruits*, second and fourth quarter of the seventh century (see testimonia 1, 10 Campbell). The earlier date is rendered very unlikely by Alcm. 5 fr. 2, which seems to have mentioned not just king Leotychidas I (usually dated to the second half of the seventh century) but also a daughter and possibly granddaughter old enough to have a role in the performance; see West 1992a. It is likely therefore that Alcman was a broad contemporary of Sappho and Alcaeus, perhaps slightly older.

Seventh-century Sparta was already a *polis* with considerable military power and organisation, which had annexed neighbouring Messenia in a protracted struggle, but it was not the militaristic society that we find in Classical sources, and it certainly was not culturally austere. Surviving art, including work in bronze and ivory, suggests wealth and sophistication; see the surveys of Fitzhardinge 1980 and Förtsch 2001. An impressive number of poet-musicians composed and performed in Sparta a generation or two before Alcman. Best preserved is the elegist Tyrtaeus. The Pseudo-Plutarchian *De musica* (ch. 9) connects several names with the establishment of Spartan musical institutions: Terpander of Lesbos, Thaletas of Gortyn, Xenodamos of Cythera, Xenokritos of Locri, Polymnestos of Colophon, Sacadas of Argos. Despite the dearth of reliable information for each of these figures, it is clear that seventh-century Sparta was a major musical and poetic centre, attracting talent from across Greece.

Much of Alcman's poetry seems to have been tied closely and explicitly to Sparta's religious and social structures. Several *polis* festivals, cults and deities are named in the texts, as are certain tribes and individual members of aristocratic and indeed royal families (cf. 1.53n.). We do not know whether Alcman was commissioned by the *polis* or by families, but he certainly composed for major public occasions. A significant portion of these compositions were maiden-songs, for which Alcman was known in antiquity (e.g. [Plut.] *De mus.* 17 = test. 15 Campbell), and which seem to have filled at least two of the six books of the Alexandrian edition; see Steph. Byz. ε137 (quoting Alcm. 16) and probably Alcm. 5 fr. 49 col. ii. They are represented here by the best-preserved example, the *Louvre Partheneion.* Alcman composed also for choruses of male youths: an ancient scholar calls him an 'instructor for traditional choruses of the daughters and ephebes (of the Spartans)' (fr. 10(a) *PMG* = test. 9 Campbell). Fr. 98 speaks of paeans at banquets; and several of the festivals with which Alcman is associated are known to have featured performances by males.

In many cases, including fr. 89 (presented here), we have too little to be sure of the genre, performers or occasion. Some of the fragments may be sympotic; e.g. 58, 59a. However, it is at least possible that testimonia according to which Alcman was famous for his love poetry (*Suda* α1289 = Campbell test. 1, Athen. 13.600f) rest on a mistaken interpretation of erotic elements in the *partheneia*.

The close ties with Spartan institutions give Alcman's poetry a local flavour: local names, local festivals and local dialect forms are all prominent. However, just as Sparta itself was not a parochial city, so Alcman's poetry, too, participates in panhellenic poetic traditions. (An altogether parochial poet would hardly have survived; cf. p. 21.) As far as we can tell, his myths focus as much on widely known names such as Helen, Paris and Ajax as on more obscurely Laconian figures. His language adds Laconian forms to what fundamentally is the artificial dialect mix characteristic of all choral poetry (pp. 62–3). He names himself in several texts, and apparently declared that his work was widely known (Aristid. *or.* 28.54 ~ Alcm. 148). In general on Alcman's status as both local and panhellenic, see Carey 2011.

Alcman's poetry, especially its local features, was the subject of considerable scholarly activity in antiquity. There was also a lively debate over whether Alcman (like for example Terpander) arrived in Sparta from abroad (Sardis, in his case); see frs. 13c and d. It is likely that he was Spartan, and that the notion of his Lydian origin is a misinterpretation of texts in which he mentions Sardis; see fr. 16.

The fullest commentary is Calame 1983. For scholarship on *partheneia* and their setting, see on Alcm. 1. For a concise overview of early Spartan history, see Kennell 2010: ch. 3. On Spartan religion, see (briefly) Parker 1989 and (in detail) Richer 2012.

Alcman 1 PMG (3 Calame)

This is by far our longest fragment of Alcman, composed for performance at a festival by a chorus of unmarried girls. It is referred to also as *Partheneion* 1 and (because of the location of the papyrus) *Louvre Partheneion*. The chorus narrate local myth, celebrate their two female leaders and, with due humility, show themselves off to the audience.

The surviving text falls into two very different parts, linked by a short gnomic passage (36–9).

Part I (1–35) consists of two stretches of narrative drawn from the same myth or possibly two different ones, bridged again by gnomic thought. Some or all of the mythical material is taken from early Spartan history. Deaths and violence abound.

Part II (39–101), by contrast, is rich in images of light and beauty. The chorus sing about the two female leader figures, Agido and Hagesichora, and their admiration for them. They also sing about themselves, casting themselves as inferior to and dependent upon their leaders. They explicitly enact their identity as *parthenoi*, unmarried girls (86, cf. 90), and express sentiments suitable to their role.

Despite the strong contrasts, the two parts share several themes and thus invite the audience to create links that are not made explicit in the text. All these themes have relevance to Spartan girls and Sparta at large (but not exclusively so):

Hierarchy. Hierarchical relationships run through the whole poem. The proper order, modelled by the chorus' humility and submission to Hagesichora and Agido, and reinforced through *gnomai* in all parts of the text (13–21, 36–9, 83–4, possibly 92–5), is one of knowing one's place and paying respect to one's leaders and the gods. The significance of order reaches beyond the text, to the girls' place in their *oikoi* and the *polis*, and to *polis* hierarchies more widely (a topic central also to another early Spartan poem, Tyrtaeus' elegiac *Eunomia*). Choral dance serves as a display of social order in much Greek thought.

Pairs. Both parts set off two outstanding individuals against their many, individually named, cousins: the two Dioscuri vis-à-vis the Hippokoöntidai (1–12); Agido and Hagesichora vis-à-vis the chorus (64–77), who describe Hagesichora as their cousin (52). The Spartans cast the Dioscuri as a divine model of their dual kings (Hdt. 5.75), and it is tempting to think that the dual kingship is in the background also of this text. Several pairs of abstract concepts add to the effect (13–14n.). On pairs in Spartan religion, see Richer 2012: 225–42.

Beauty and desire. At least some erotic colouring is present in Part I (17–21, see also 1–12n.). In Part II, the pervasive language of beauty shades into language of desire in more than one passage (74–7, 88, 91). It is above all Hagesichora and Agido who are singled out as desirable, but, with self-effacement and deference to their leaders, the whole chorus put themselves on display (64–77).

Cosmic imagery and language. Agido is compared to the sun (41), the Pleiades and Sirius appear in 60–3, and a goddess of dawn seems to be named in 87 and possibly 61. The various abstract powers, notably Aisa and Poros (13–14), also have a cosmic dimension. Alcman's text repeatedly opens up a cosmic vista, and thus draws on the connection between choruses and stars in the Greek imagination, encapsulated in the image of the chorus of the stars frequent in later texts (see Csapo 2008 and cf. 60–3n.).

Fighting. The youthful heroes' mortal battling in the mythical section is echoed by the striking metaphorical language of fighting and peace that the chorus use of their own situation (63, 65, 91). Without martial overtones, the notion of competition appears at 58–9.

Horses do not appear in Part I (though see 1n.), but are used repeatedly as images for Hagesichora and Agido as well as the chorus in Part II (46–9, 50–1, 58–9, 92–3). Associations with aristocracy, beauty, erotics and education make horses a resonant image in this text; for these associations, see Griffith 2006. There may also be a particular Spartan dimension. Aristophanes' 'by the Eurotas girls jump like πῶλοι' (*Lys.* 1307–9), in the context of an evocation of Spartan song and cult, shows that certainly in fifth-century Athens the comparison of groups of girls to young horses could be considered characteristically Spartan. The priestesses of the Leukippides, a pair of Spartan figures whose cult involved adolescent girls, were at some stage called πῶλοι; see Hesych. π4496, and in general on the Leukippides (itself a name that evokes horses) Calame 1997 [1977]: 185–91.

Ever since the discovery of the text, scholars have sought to reconstruct realities beyond the poem (see below for the extensive bibliography). Those realities are highly uncertain; what follows is a necessarily dogmatic view, as almost every detail is contentious.

Personnel. The chorus was formed of, probably eight, aristocratic *parthenoi*, plus Hagesichora and Agido (for the number, see 64–77, 96–101nn.). Hagesichora is a 'chorus-leader' (44 χοραγός); Agido too has a role of prominence. The text does not permit us to determine the relationship between the two.

Performance. The various references to dawn (see above) make performance at sunrise an attractive possibility. The A scholia (see 'Source' below) believe that for part of the song the choral group split into two half-choruses, which celebrated Agido and Hagesichora respectively; see the scholia on 36, 43, 48, and for discussion *CLGP ad locc.* (Römer) and Schironi 2016. Some modern scholars, notably Rosenmeyer 1966 and Péron 1987, take up this idea, but it is difficult to divide the lines satisfactorily between the two putative half-choruses, and the default assumption of a single chorus does not pose significant problems. Hagesichora and Agido performed too, or in any case were in attendance, but did not dance in the same formation as the chorus; this arrangement provides the backdrop to the shifting play of presence and absence in the text (see 78–81, 96–101nn.). Whether the names are the real names of the first performers is unclear, but it is certainly possible; see 53, 64–77nn.

A song for parthenoi. The fundamental studies of Calame 1977 and 1997 [1977] have established that the singers' identity and status as *parthenoi* is central to text, performance and occasion. A group of girls, more or less close to marriageable age, advertise their looks, express erotic desire (albeit not for men), and acknowledge their subordinate position in social and cosmic hierarchies; cf. the widespread topos that choruses provided a forum in which girls presented themselves to onlookers, in myths of abduction from the dance floor (e.g. *h.Dem.* 417–34), literary allusions to ritual (e.g. Eur. *IT* 1142–51) and later accounts of education (e.g. Plut. *Lyc.* 14.2–3, imagining early Sparta). More specific reconstructions will remain speculative on our evidence. Calame himself, for example, suggested that the Spartans had instituted female educational groupings in which close ties were created between the girls and their leaders (here Hagesichora), and that Agido (and Agido alone) will soon leave the group in marriage; but the evidence for such institutions is not robust and the text does not make it clear that either Agido or Hagesichora are older than the other girls. For a related model, see Goff 2004: 85–98, and on the education of Spartan girls, which prominently included choruses, Ducat 2006: ch. 7. On the importance of visual display in choruses of *parthenoi*, see Swift 2016.

A public song. Despite the focus on the performing *parthenoi*, this is clearly a public song. The myth and the *gnomai* have broad relevance, and men are an obvious audience for the girls' display. A public dimension is suggested even more clearly by Alcm. 3, a very similar poem in many ways, and therefore important for understanding the genre (see p. 62); there, the leading female figure passes 'through the crowd, the darling of the people' (73–4). See further Stehle 1997: 30–9, 73–88, who explores how the girls in Alcm. 1 speak both for and to the community, and Lonsdale 1993: 193–205.

The occasion. The performance took place in the context of a festival (81). The nature of the festival and the identity of the presiding deity or deities are uncertain. The chorus carry an offering for Orthria (or possibly Orthia, 61) and invoke Aotis (87). Both names suggest dawn, but both are otherwise unknown; further on the identity of the goddess(es), see *ad locc.* It is conceivable that the whole festival centred on the girls of the chorus, and that those select girls represented the girls of Sparta at large, as did for example the 'bears' (*arktoi*) or *arrhephoroi* at Athens. However, a more diverse festival, to which the girls contributed, is also possible, for example a seasonal festival, marking harvest time (cf. 60–3n.).

There are two separate reasons why the realities behind the poem have proved so elusive. One is the state of the evidence: the fragmentary survival of the text itself, together with the dearth of firm knowledge about Alcman's Sparta, hamper any inquiry. Another factor, however, of equal importance, is the poetics of Part II. Throughout that section, the song does not so much factually describe an external reality as textually reconfigure that reality and indeed create its own reality. References and appeals to realities before the audience's eyes are frequent (see esp. 40n. (τό), 50n.), but most such references are to the chorus itself as well as

Hagesichora and Agido rather than to the context in which they perform, and even those references to the performers are not straightforwardly descriptive. The chorus stage themselves and their own concern, and stage Hagesichora and Agido whom they cast, variously, as horses, astral bodies, possibly doves, whereas the ritual acts and the festival are mentioned only briefly and intermittently; they are not the central focus. Better knowledge of the context would clarify the text, but the relationship of the text with that context was complex already in the first performance. See further Peponi 2004 and Budelmann 2013b: 90–3.

We have no evidence for how the text was classified by the ancient editors, but most modern scholars refer to it as a *partheneion*, a genre that is well attested for Alcman in ancient scholarship; see p. 57, and on genre in general pp. 11–14. An emphasis on the singers' identity as girls, references to their outfits, and attention to their relationships with named leader figures, all recur in Pind. *Parth.* 2 (fr. 94b) and Alcm. 3, which moreover shares the eroticism of Alcm. 1, in an even more pronounced form. For discussion of the genre *partheneion* see Calame 1977: 147–76 and Swift 2010: 173–85.

Finally, the numerous points of contact with the better-preserved and therefore better-understood genre of epinician merit emphasis. The combination of civic and elite, the celebration of both humans and gods, the alternation of myth, *gnomai* and praise sections, the complex metaphorical language, the often difficult train of thought, the elusive relationship with the real-life setting: all these are elements that connect this text with the victory odes of Pindar or Bacchylides. For all the problems of interpretation, Alcm. 1 is considerably less idiosyncratic than it might appear (to us) at first sight; its use of recognisable conventions would no doubt be more obvious if we had more of Alcman's output and more *partheneia*.

Dialect: Like all choral lyric (pp. 24–5), Alcm. 1 combines Doric with Ionic and Aeolic forms familiar from epic or other lyric traditions. At least as transmitted, however, Alcman's language differs from that of Stesichorus, Pindar or Simonides in the particular choice of Doric: many of the forms are Laconian, the dialect of Sparta, which belongs to the family of 'severe' Doric dialects.

It is these Laconian features that give Alcman's texts their distinctive appearance. However, they are not used consistently, and as a result Alcman's dialect cannot be reconstructed with confidence. Unless editors are willing to intervene heavily despite this considerable uncertainty, their text is bound to reflect at least some of the inconsistency of the papyri, and this edition is no exception. The major editorial decisions taken here are set out in the next paragraph. For treatments of Alcman's dialect, see Hinge 2006 and Cassio 2007.

The papyrus of Alcm. 1 presents numerous instances of σ for θ (e.g. 86 παρσένος), which are preserved here. This orthography is found in later Laconian texts, but Alcman would have written θ. What is less clear is how he would have pronounced this consonant. Pronunciation of θ as /θ/ (like Engl. <th>) rather than /th/ (as in other Greek dialects) is virtually certain already for fifth-century Laconian, and may or may not go back further. The preservation of σ can therefore be justified in two ways: as a reflection of Hellenistic editorial practice, or as an approximation of early pronunciation. (Vice versa, instances of θ are not amended to σ, despite the inconsistency, e.g. 81 θωστήρια.) **Word-initial digamma** is shown by inscriptions to be a feature of vernacular Laconian, and is metrically required in several instances across Alcman's corpus. In Alcm. 1, it is probably transmitted twice (6 ϝάνακτα, 41 ϝ(ε)), and it is here restored in all etymologically clear cases, including some in which it makes no difference to the metre. In addition, 63 αὐειρομέναι is emended to ἀϝειρομέναι in order to avoid two different ways of rendering digamma (ϝ/υ). The papyrus is inconsistent also in the choice of η/ει and ω/ου; e.g. ἦμεν and ὠρανόν (severe Doric) but τείρει and καμοῦσιν (mild Doric and *koine*). We do not know how severe Alcman's literary Doric was. Nor do we know whether the scribe used severe Doric vowels to approximate Laconian, or to remind the non-Doric reader that this is not *koine*-Greek (the latter is argued by Willi 2012). This edition maintains the transmitted readings *faute de mieux*. The alternative would be to write η/ω throughout, on the assumption that Alcman's dialect was consistently Laconian. **Short-vowel infinitives** are metrically guaranteed occasionally in Stesichorus (93.17 Finglass) and Bacchylides (19.25). This is a literary practice of disputed origin (Doric or Aeolic). Several instances occur in Alcman, none of them in unambiguously short positions. One in fact requires emendation to preserve the metre, 43 φαίνεν > φαίνην (× – required), a change that then strongly suggests parallel emendation of ἐπαινέν at the end of the same line. The other two instances are left intact (17 γαμέν, 44 μωμέσθαι). As in some other lyric papyri, there are a number of 'Doric' accents (for the most part in line with the rules formulated by ancient grammarians). These are kept as transmitted, e.g. 13 παντῶν, 14 γεραιτάτοι, 59 δραμείται, 65 ἀμύναι. (Elsewhere in this volume, see e.g. Stes. 19.20 ἐπ[λ]άξαν (supplementation uncertain) and Ibyc. S151.2 ἠνάρον (with note); and for general discussion Nöthiger 1971: 83–6.)

Source: Louvre papyrus inv. E 3320 (Π), 1st cent. AD, ed. Egger 1865, with a reproduction in the accompanying volume of plates. Remains of three columns present the text of eight stanzas (variously complete). For descriptions of the papyrus, see Page 1951a: 1–3 and (with a photograph of one column) Turner 1987: 44–5. The text reproduces Hutchinson's transcription, except that it follows Ucciardello forthcoming on lines 41 (ϝ'), 80 (δὲ παρμένει doubtful), 84 ([χο]ροστάτις probaby possible).

A *coronis* (an elaborate marginal sign) shows that only four lines are missing at the end, but we do not know how much preceded the first surviving line; the common suggestion of a total length of ten stanzas = 140 lines (viz. loss of one column) assumes a neat division into two roughly similar halves. Attribution to Alcman is secure because of short quotations in later authors: see 2, 6, 19nn., and for a full list Calame 1983: 31–2 and 312.

Π also carries a set of scholia (ΣA), and a further set (ΣB) survives in *P. Oxy.* XXIV.2389, also 1st cent. AD. ΣA and ΣB are edited with commentary as *CLGP*, Alcman nos. 5 and 1a, ed. Römer. They are here cited only where they make a significant contribution to the text or the interpretation.

Metre:

¹ – ᴗ – x – ᴗ – ‖ 2 *tr*ᴧ   50 ἦ̣ οὐχ
² x – ᴗ ᴗ – ᴗ – – ‖ *hag*
³ – ᴗ – x – ᴗ – ‖ 2 *tr*ᴧ
⁴ x - ᴗ ᴗ – ᴗ – – ‖ *hag*
⁵ – ᴗ – x – ᴗ – ?‖ 2 *tr*ᴧ
⁶ x – ᴗ ᴗ – ᴗ – – ‖ *hag*   69 ϝι̣ανο
⁷ ᵜ ᴗ – x – ᴗ – ‖ 2 *tr*ᴧ   98 σι̣αί
⁸ x – ᴗ ᴗ – ᴗ – – ‖ *hag*
⁹ – ᴗ – x – ᴗ – x – ᴗ ᵜ – ‖ 3 *tr*
¹⁰ – ᴗ – x – ᴗ – x – ᴗ – – ‖ 3 *tr*   87 Ἀώτī
¹¹ – ᴗ – x – ᴗ – x   2 *tr*   32 Ἄιδας (two syllables, not three)
¹² – ᴗ – x – ᴗ – – ‖ 2 *tr*
¹³ – ᴖ – ᴗ ᴗ – ᴗ ᴗ – ᴗ ᴗ   4 *da*
¹⁴ – ᴖ – ᴗ ᴗ – ᴗ x – ‖‖ 4 *da*ᴧ or *ar*ᵈ

One of the longest stanzas in early lyric. The first part (1–8) consists of four mixed trochaic–aeolic pairs (2 *tr*ᴧ and *hag*). A properly trochaic section follows (9–12), before double shorts (which were present in the aeolic cola of 2, 4, 6, 8) return in the dactyls of the final two lines. There is some freedom of responsion throughout, most remarkably so in the variation between two versions of the last line of the stanza: a dactylic close in 7, 21, 35, 91, and a pendant ('aeolic') one in 49, 63, 77. Lines are divided by pauses in much of the stanza, but the last part is more flowing. Further on the metre, see Page 1951a: 23–5. (The schema supplied in the lacunae in the poetic text marks the first syllable of the trochaics as long, even though line 56 shows that resolution occurs occasionally.)

Discussions: Schironi 2016, Tsantsanoglou 2012, Bowie 2011, Ferrari 2008, Goff 2004: 86–9, *Peponi 2004, *Stehle 1997: 30–9 and 73–88, Too 1997, Lonsdale 1993: 193–205, Clay 1991, *Robbins 1991, Nagy 1990:

345–52, Hamilton 1989, Péron 1987, Segal 1983, Vetta 1982, Hooker 1979, *Calame 1977, *Calame 1997 [1977], *Puelma 1995 [1977], Griffiths 1972, Rosenmeyer 1966, West 1965: 194–202, *Page 1951a.
Commentaries: *Hutchinson 2001: 76–102, Pavese 1992a, *Calame 1983: 311–49, Garzya 1954: 9–76.

1–35 Part I falls into three sections: the myth of the Dioscuri and the Hippokoöntidai (1–?12), a set of *gnomai* (?13–21), continuation of the myth or a new myth (22–35). It is clear that the myth began before our line 1, but the content of any earlier section(s) is a matter of speculation. There may have been an invocation of the Muses as in Alcm. 3, and references to the chorus' situation or the festival need not have been reserved altogether for Part II. See also 'Source' above.

1–12 (or 1–15) *The myth of the Dioscuri and the Hippokoöntidai (continued).* Much of the passage is taken up with a catalogue of the slain sons of Hippokoön. Hippokoön and his brother Tyndareus were mythical kings of Sparta. Polydeuces (named in 1) and Castor (named probably before 1) were the sons of, variously, Tyndareus and Zeus (hence 'Dioscuri'). Surviving versions of the Hippokoön myth focus mostly on the generation of the fathers: Hippokoön drives Tyndareus out of Sparta but is then killed, along with his sons, by Heracles, and Tyndareus returns; see e.g. Diod. Sic. 4.33.5–6, [Apollod.] 3.10.5, *FGrHist* 40 F 1.18–21 = *IG* XIV.1293. 56–62. We do not know whether the version narrated here, in which the Dioscuri and Hippokoön's sons are the protagonists, is Alcman's invention; in any case it creates a counterpart to the youthful figures in Part II. Alcman lists eleven Hippokoöntid names (or ten, if Lykaithos was not one; see 2–12n.); Page 1951a: 26–30 discusses options for supplementation.

It is possible (no more) that Alcman gave the myth an erotic inflection. The Hellenistic poet Euphorion (*CA* fr. 29) apparently treated the Hippokoöntidai and the Dioscuri as 'rival suitors' – presumably for the two Leukippides, seized by the Dioscuri in other versions, but in rivalry with a different set of youths, the Apharetidai (see Theoc. 22 and other texts and visual representations discussed by Gantz 1993: 324–6). No evidence links Euphorion's version back to Alcman, but what makes the idea attractive is that a clash between Hippokoöntidai and Dioscuri over prospective brides would give point to the prominence of the sons rather than the fathers in what remains, would resonate with the erotic tone of the *gnomai* in 17–21, and would be relevant to the chorus qua *parthenoi*; see further Calame 1977: 55–9 and Robbins 1991: 12–14, and on the passage in general Davison 1938: 441–4 and Page 1951a: 30–3.

Whatever the precise version of the myth, the names in this ringing roll call will have been resonant in Sparta. Castor and Polydeuces were popular figures in Laconian myth and cult; see Alcm. 7, Pind. *Nem.* 10.55–60, and the discussion of Wide 1893: 304–25 and Parker 1989: 147. Several of the Hippokoöntidai acquired at some point cult monuments in central Sparta, as Paus. 3.14.6–7 and 15.1–2 reports (dates unknown); see further Caciagli 2009b: 19–32. The fight between Tyndareus and one of the Hippokoöntidai was depicted on the late sixth-century throne of Apollo at nearby Amyklai (Paus. 3.18.11). Sparta's Heraclid kings used the myth of the return of Tyndareus to legitimate their rule, certainly in the Classical period; see Malkin 1994: 22–6.

1 Πωλυδεύκης: the normal Πολυ- is metrically lengthened on the model of epic πουλύς etc.; cf. Ibyc. S151.47 Πουλύκρατες. The resulting (etymologically fictitious) connection with πῶλος ('young horse') may play with the Dioscuri's association with horsemanship (for which see e.g. Alcm. 2).

2–12 Two reconstructions are possible, the first perhaps more attractive. (i) A negative connective like οὔτ' in 3 and no negative in 12: 'I take no notice of Lykaithos nor (the others); we will pass them over.' The sequence is a *recusatio*, comparable to Ibyc. S151.10ff. The emphatic refusal to give the Hippokoöntidai attention (οὐκ . . . ἀλέγω, παρήσομες) prepares for the moralistic stance in 13–21 and ultimately for the chorus' announcement of what they *are* singing about, 39 ἐγὼν δ' ἀείδω. It does not deprive the Hippokoöntidai of the glory the list of names bestows on them, just as Ibycus does not deprive the fighters at Troy of glory. For οὐκ . . . οὔτε . . . τε . . . τε (etc.), cf. Ibycus' οὔτε . . . οὔτε . . . τε . . . τε. See further p. 173 and Bonanno 1991. Lykaithos is one of the Hippokoöntidai also in the list at [Apollod.] 3.10.5. (ii) Alternatively, line 3 opens with 'but' (ἀλλ') and 12 contains a negative: 'I take no notice of Lykaithos but of (the others); we will not pass them over.' Unlike in Pseudo-Apollodorus, Lykaithos is not a Hippokoöntid, and he is singled out as the only hero not to be given respect. One has to make the somewhat awkward assumption that either the audience's knowledge of the myth or the missing parts of the song would give point to the rhetoric of singling out Lykaithos. This approach receives some support from ΣA, which refers to Lykaithos as a son of Derites, who according to the lineage at Paus. 7.18.5 is a remote uncle of Hippokoön: this would place Lykaithos in Hippokoön's generation. (But disconcertingly, ΣA also says that Alcman names 'the other Deritids', . . . οὐ μόνον τὸν Λύκαιο(ν) (*sic*) ἀλλὰ καὶ τοὺς λοιποὺς Δηρητίδας οὓς ἐπ' ὀνόματος λέγει: does ΣA confuse Hippokoöntids and Deritids?)

On both reconstructions, the παρήσομες sentence may either be a one-line emphatic summary ('Those we will (not) pass over'), with punctuation at the end of 11, or start earlier, e.g. in 8 ('X, Y and Z, we will (not) pass over'); the difference for the overall meaning is small.

2 'I do not include Lykaithos among the dead. . .' The text is reconstructed from a quotation in Σ Pind. *Ol.* 11.15a. The implication is: 'I take no notice of him, unlike of the other dead': ἀλέγω will express respect

(LSJ s.v. II.2), or here disrespect, also when it is construed with ἐν (s.v. III).
The chorus appear to use the first person singular (2, 39, 40, 43, 52, 56,
77, 85, 86, 87, 88) and plural (12, 41, 60, 81, 89) without clear distinction.
3 Σέβρον: Paus. 3.15.1–2 calls him Sebros, [Apollod.] 3.10.5 Tebros.
4 τὸν βιατάν: the article turns the adjective into an honorary title,
'X the forceful'.
5 κορυστάν: cf. the Iliadic killing formula Τρώων ἕλεν ἄνδρα κορυστήν
(4.457, etc.).
6 Ἀρήϊον: Areios ('the warlike one') is not otherwise known as a son of
Hippokoön. ΣA reports that Pherecydes (5th cent. BC, *FGrHist* 3 F 6) knew
a Hippokoöntid called Areïtos, and conjectures that name here. The name
Euteiches at the beginning is reconstructed from *Epimerismi Homerici* ε154,
where the line is quoted.
7 ἔξοχον ἡμισίων (Attic ἡμιθέων) recalls epic phrases like ἔξοχον ἡρώων
(*Il.* 18.56, 437). The term ἡμίθεος looks back to a bygone age, and thus suits
a famous figure of the past or a hero of cult; see *Il.* 12.23, Hes. *WD* 160,
Sim. fr. eleg. 11.18 *IEG²*, and further Clay 2001 and Alc. 42.13n. below.
8 ἀγρόταν 'hunter'. Hunting played an important role in Spartan life
and ideology. Later texts know some of the Hippokoöntidai as participants
in the hunt for the Calydonian boar; Ov. *Met.* 8.314, Hyg. *fab.* 173. Many
editors nevertheless emend to ἀγρέταν 'leader'. See Fraenkel 1910–12: I.
57–8, who objects to ἀγρόταν because the word is derived from ἀγρός
('land') not ἄγρα ('hunt') and hence means 'rustic'; cf. LSJ Supplement
s.v. But (as Fraenkel notes) the related ἀγρότερα aquired the meaning
'hunter' irrespective of its proper etymology, e.g. Pind. *Ol.* 2.54, *Pyth.* 9.6,
carm. conv. 886.3; the same conflation should be possible for ἀγρότης.
10 is very difficult. An adj. πωρός or πῶρος is only attested in the lexicographers, glossed as 'blind' (*Suda* π2183) or 'suffering' (ταλαίπωρος,
Hesych. π4513). An established, longer adjective such as ταλαι]πώρω
might therefore be more likely, but no obvious text suggests itself, partly
because the noun κλόνος ('turmoil') is difficult to fit into a context that
demands an epithet or some other phrase that qualifies one or more heroes.
The frequently printed prepositional phrase Ἄρεος ἂν] πώρω κλόνον ('in the
turmoil of blind Ares', Bergk) would stand out in the otherwise syntactically
simple list.
11 ἀρίστως ~ Attic ἀρίστους.
12 παρήσομες ~ Attic παρήσομεν. For the use of the future, see Sim.
542.37n. Future forms with short -σο- are common in the literary Doric of
lyric; their relationship with vernacular Doric is uncertain. See Cassio
1999.
13–21 (or 16–21) *A gnomic sequence, alternating between divine and human,
and freedom and constraint. It moves from the power of fate (13–14) to
(probably) human powerlessness (15, reconstruction uncertain) and*

a warning to respect the limits of what is possible and right for humans (16–19), which is thrown into relief by a statement of what is possible for the Graces (20–1). These are traditional notions, generically phrased. They offer comment on the myth that precedes and follows, and are in keeping also with the chorus' stance in Part II.

13–14 Πόρος is supplemented on the basis of ΣA: 'because he has called the same figure Poros that Hesiod has called Chaos in his mythology'. The sentence is probably a gnomic statement (e.g. 'Ancient Aisa and Poros are . . .') rather than a summary conclusion to the myth (e.g. 'Ancient Aisa and Poros vanquished them all').

Elsewhere πόρος occurs both in a concrete sense ('passage', 'course') and an abstract one ('means', 'device'), the latter first attested in the fifth century. The precise meaning in this passage is irrecoverable, and in any case the point was probably not so much a specific cosmological proposition as an august expression of the order of things: fate and the course of life, fate taking its course, fixed fate and human freedom. For more specific reconstructions, see Tsitsibakou-Vasalos 1993: 130–9 and Ferrari 2008: 29–53. Alcman creates comparable pairs in lines 83–4 (ἄνα | καὶ τέλος), and in frs. 5(2) (ancient Πόρος and Τέκμωρ) and 102 (narrow path and ?pitiless necessity).

15 -π]έδιλος ἀλκά: the widely accepted ἀπ]έδιλος 'shoeless' has connotations of haste, e.g. [Aesch.] *PV* 135 with Griffith 1983 *ad loc.* Here it would have to suggest either an 'overly hasty' or 'unprotected' ἀλκά (in a statement about human short-coming), or a 'rapid' ἀλκά (in a statement about gods): see the survey of opinions in Tsitsibakou-Vasalos 1993: 139–51. But both images are odd: shoes are not emblematic fighting equipment in the way shields or swords are, and one expects the gods to be capable of putting on their shoes even when time is short. We may need another supplement. Punctuation is likely at the end of the line, as there seems to be a change of topic in 16.

16–20 Probably: 'Let (no) mortal fly to heaven, (nor) attempt to marry Aphrodite or queen . . . (or "marry . . . Queen Aphrodite") or some . . . or a daughter of Porkos.' See apparatus for supplements. Several myths come to mind: the celestial travels of Icarus, Bellerophon and Phaethon had dire consequences; Anchises and Adonis suffered after their affairs with Aphrodite, and see 19n. for Peleus and Thetis. But above all, both sentiments are generic injunctions against seeking something humans should not seek: the ability to fly, let alone fly all the way to heaven; and marriage to a goddess, let alone the most desirable of goddesses; cf. Sa. 27.12–13, Pind. *Pyth.* 4.87–92. The warning not to attempt inappropriate marriages takes on a particular inflection in the mouths of a chorus of young nubile women before a male audience. For the potential relevance to the Hippokoöntidai, see 1–12n.

17 γαμέν: infinitive; see p. 63.

19 Πόρκω: the reading rests on Hesychius' statement that Alcman used the name Porkos for the sea god Nereus (ν516). The Nereid Thetis, whose reluctant marriage with the mortal Peleus was short-lived and produced the ill-fated Achilles, had an ancient cult in Sparta, according to Paus. 3.14.4.

20–1 A 3rd pers. pl. verb (]σιν), meaning something like 'enter' or 'frequent', is lost. The progression of thought is by opposition, as often in gnomic sequences: as companions of Aphrodite (see Ibyc. 288.1n.) and divinities who live on Olympus (Hes. *Th.* 62–5), the Graces create a contrast with the improper human ambition of 16–19. As female deities of good cheer and as choral dancers (*Od.* 18.194, *h.Apol.* 194), they foreshadow Part II.

21 ἐρογλεφάροι ('love-eyed') is a *hapax* and ἐρο- an unusual prefix. Alcman seems to condense into an adjective Hes. *Th.* 910 τῶν καὶ ἀπὸ βλεφάρων ἔρος εἴβετο δερκομενάων (of the Graces). Cf. 69 ϝινογ[λ]εφάρων and 75 ποτιγλέποι.

22–35 *Further mythical narrative,* featuring violent deaths, capped by a moralising conclusion (34–5). The most persuasive attempts to identify the myth are as follows, in descending order. (i) Continuation of the earlier myth; see Robbins 1991: 14–15. Robbins further points to similarities with the Dioscuri's battle with the Apharetidai at Pind. *Nem.* 10.64–71 (esp. the hurling of a large stone), and suggests that Alcman conflated the myths. For possible points of contact with the Apharetidai myth, see also 1–12n.; for the likelihood that Pindar had this passage in mind, see 34–5n.; and for *gnomai* interrupting a mythical narrative, see Carey 1981 on Pind. *Pyth.* 2.34. (ii) The youths Otos and Ephialtes trying to ascend heaven and/or seeking an inappropriate marriage; see *Od.* 11.305–20, Callim. *Dian.* 264–5, and the discussion of Janni 1965: 68–71. (iii) The gigantomachy; see Page 1951a: 42–3.

31 μαρμάρωι μυλάκρωι 'glittering boulder'. μάρμαρος qualifies a stone already at *Il.* 16.734–5. Etymology and original meaning are disputed; see *LfgrE* s.v.

34–5 A comment on the myth and a lead-in for the *gnomai* that follow. The word order suggests construing ἄλαστα adjectivally with ϝέργα, and ϝέργα as object of πάσον (~ ἔπαθον). The phrasing is firmly grounded in epic language (cf. *Il.* 18.77, 24.105, *Od.* 24.199), but the most strikingly similar passage is Pind. *Nem.* 10.64–5 μέγα ἔργον ἐμήσαντ' ὠκέως | καὶ πάθον δεινόν, for which cf. 22–35n.

34 ἄλαστα 'terrible' (?). Precise meaning and etymology uncertain (not necessarily from λανθάνειν); see Barrett on Eur. *Hipp.* 877–80 and Chantraine 1968–80 s.v. Cf. Stes. 17.2–3(n.).

36–9 Gnomic section. A *gnome* about divine punishment continues the thought of the previous sentence in generalising form. It reflects on the related topic of the precariousness of the human condition; but with the kind of transition by opposition that is common in gnomic passages (cf. 20–1n.), it emphasises the positive (good fortune) rather than the negative (divine punishment), and so introduces the more cheerful tone of Part II.

36 This is the tone of wisdom poetry: for ἔστι τις ('there is such a thing as') in admonitory texts, see West 1978 on Hes. *WD* 11–46, and cf. Antimachus fr. 131 Matthews; and for divine τίσις in moralising statements, see *Od.* 1.32–43 and Sol. 13.25. Asyndeton, brevity and repeated sound patterns (s, t, i) add emphasis. σιῶν ~ θεῶν.

37 ὁ δ' ὄλβιος ὅστις: such rhetoric of defining what makes a man fortunate is traditional; e.g. Hes. *WD* 826–8 and Bacch. 5.50–5. The masculine is standard in such contexts, and in keeping with the chorus' authoritative voice throughout the gnomic and mythical sections. For the equally traditional notion that ὄλβος is unstable, see e.g. Sim. 521 and Pind. *Pyth.* 3.105–6.

εὔφρων 'cheerful' rather than 'sensible'.

38 ἁμέραν [δι]απλέκει 'weaves through a day'. Each day has to be got through without disaster. Cf. Semonides 7.99–100 οὐ γάρ κοτ' εὔφρων ἡμέρην διέρχεται | ἅπασαν (relative chronology uncertain). The metaphorical use of διαπλέκειν occurs elsewhere, usually with 'life' rather than 'day'; see Pind. *Nem.* 7.99 and LSJ s.v. II.

39–105 Part II comprises five stanzas. The first two celebrate first Agido, then Hagesichora, then (probably) both (39–59, perhaps 39–63). The third turns to the chorus' own looks, but again emphasises Hagesichora's superiority (64–77). It is followed by a stanza that combines deference to the gods with deference to Agido and Hagesichora (78–91). The final stanza opens with further expressions of subordination and then probably moves on to the chorus' only confident statement of the quality of their performance, perhaps because the chorus and their leaders now combine. The lost ending included a further statement about Hagesichora and/or Agido. This outline shows that the almost ceaseless celebration of Agido and Hagesichora has a simple overall structure, which is reinforced by the stanza-breaks; but it masks multiple shifts, as well as considerable uncertainty of interpretation throughout.

39–59 *Celebration of Agido and Hagesichora.* The chorus express admiration for the two leaders, first individually and, at the end of this section, in conjunction and comparison (probably). The language is visual, extolling their looks by means of various images, esp. horses. At several points it is difficult to determine whether the chorus sing about Agido or Hagesichora; see the schematic overview of different views in Calame

1977, after p. 176. The notes below set out a preferred interpretation: 39–51 Agido, 51–7 Hagesichora, 58–9 both, with Agido pre-eminent. But it is important to realise that (a) choreography, and perhaps audience knowledge, will have been crucial here; (b) the excellence and pre-eminence of both leaders is more important than the differences.

39–43 A further emphatic first person (cf. 2–12n.) announces Agido programmatically as the new theme. At the same time it marks a broader shift from the mythical past to the actors here and now. The statement connects to the preceding *gnome* by appealing to the speaker's experience; Agido on this day is a positive instantiation of the generalisation.

ἐγὼν δ' ἀείδω: ἀείδω + acc. declares the subject matter of a work; cf. *Little Iliad* fr. 1, *h.* 12.1, Pind. *Isthm.* 2.12. 'I sing' introduces the language of performance that was absent in the myth; contrast 2 ἀλέγω.

40 Ἀγιδῶς: see 53n.

τό: the frequency of definite articles in Part II creates a sense of concrete reality, irrespective of whether the people and things pointed to are real or imaginary; see 44, 50, 51, 52, 55, ?60, ?70; cf. pp. 61–2.

φῶς exploits several connotations: joy and salvation (e.g. formulaic φόως Δαναοῖσι γένηαι | γένωμαι, *Il.* 8.282, etc.), radiance and beauty (cf. Sa. 96.9, Praxilla 747 *PMG*), glorious reputation (Pind. *Ol.* 4.10). The combination of φῶς with a personal name in the genitive is unusual; Agido is strikingly exalted at first mention. In a dawn or nighttime performance there could be a literal dimension too, if the performers carry torches.

ὁρῶ: the chorus see Agido looking like the sun, and invite the audience to see her so, too. They do much the same again at 50–9(n.), starting with the same verb, now in the second person: ἦ οὐχ ὁρῆις.

41 ϝ' 'her': ϝε ~ ἑ, the 3rd pers. acc. pronoun. Π's reading is uncertain, with some editors transcribing σ (i.e. ὁρῶ|σ') or ε (possibly = ϝε). Uncertainty is compounded by the metre; as an enclitic, ϝ' metrically does not open the verse but closes the previous one, which should however end with a pause rather than an elision, and the same holds for ὁρῶ|σ'; see Pavese 1967: 36 n. 24 and Hutchinson on Sa. 31.9–10 for the closest parallels.

ὥτ' (~ ὥστε) **ἄλιον** introduces the cosmic imagery that will recur at 60–3, while maintaining the associations of φῶς.

41–3 ὅνπερ ... φαίνην: probably 'which indeed Agido calls upon to shine for us as witness'. ὅνπερ is the object of μαρτύρεται, and φαίνην (~ φαίνειν) is best described as an infinitive of purpose; see further Puelma 1995 [1977]: 66–9. The idea that the all-seeing sun is a witness of human action is common, e.g. *Il.* 3.276–80, Sim. fr. eleg. 16 *IEG*². Here Agido is said to invoke it, figuratively or ritually, for the sake of 'us' (ἄμιν, construable with both verbs): the sun is to witness the chorus'

performance, and perhaps the celebrating community at large. On the
'witnessing' of and by choruses as a motif, see Martin 2007: 42–8.

43–5 ἐμέ … ἐῆι: best taken as a version of the break-off formulae
familiar to us from Pindar. Probably, (i) the chorus purport suddenly
to recall or receive their leader's (= Hagesichora's) injunction not to
praise or blame Agido. It is not for them (emphatic ἐμέ) to pronounce
judgement on her, inferior as they are. For Agido stands out without the
chorus' doing (45 αὐτά, 'by herself'). The chorus, that is, continue to
celebrate Agido, while presenting themselves as too inferior to her to do
even that. For this reading, see e.g. Bowie 2011: 42–3 and, with a change
of αὐτά to αὗτα 'this woman' (accompanied by a gesture to Agido),
Fowler 1995. Alternatively, (ii) the leader does not let the chorus praise
Agido because she (the leader, Hagesichora) is herself (αὐτά) extraordinary. The chorus, that is, shift their attention to Hagesichora; see
further Calame 1977: 46–8. This reading avoids the conceit of
Hagesichora orchestrating the chorus' praise and makes αὐτά easier,
but the pronouns are problematic: emphatic ἐμέ and unemphatic νιν
put the focus on the chorus, while we would want it to be on Agido
('not *her* but Hagesichora'). Moreover, there would be an unwanted
hint of jealousy.

43–4 οὔτ' ἐπαινῆν | οὔτε μωμέσθαι: a polar statement amounting to
'not say anything at all about', cf. *Il.* 10.249. The previous sentence puts
the emphasis firmly on praise, but in a context of potential comparison
between the two girls blame is more than a meaningless balancing com-
plement. For the (uncertain) ε in μωμέσθαι, see p. 63.

44 κλεννά (~ κλεινή) **χοραγός:** this must be Hagesichora, in view of her
name (*pace* Puelma 1995 [1977]: 74–7 and Pavese 1992a: 51–2); cf. 53n.
The reference by title underlines the authority of the prohibition.
We know little about what was involved in the role; see Calame 1997
[1977]: 43–73 for the evidence. However, it is clear that the Spartan
χοραγός was more literally a chorus-leader than the χορηγός who financed
performances in Classical Athens. The masculine equivalent of κλεννά
χοραγός occurs at Alcm. 10b σιοφιλὲς χο[ρα]γὲ Ἀγησίδαμε κλεε[νν]ὲ
Δαμοτιμίδα; the expression may have had a formulaic ring. (The dialect
form κλεννά is problematic and should perhaps be emended; see Hinge
2006: 117.)

45 οὐδ' ἀμῶς = οὐδαμῶς. The rough breathing is in the papyrus.

45–9 δοκεῖ … ὀνείρων: Alcman may be reworking *Il.* 2.480–3, where
Zeus makes Agamemnon stand out among his fellow Greeks (ἐκπρεπής)
like a bull among a herd of cows. If he is, he has replaced the bull of the
epic simile with a horse and has marked the scene as imaginary ('just as if
somebody were to', 'dreams'), thus enhacing the contrast between chorus-
leader and chorus to the point of incongruity.

45 ἦμεν (Laconian) ~ εἶναι.

αὐτά: see 43–5n.

47 βοτοῖς: cattle or sheep rather than horses, e.g. *Il.* 18.521–4, Aesch. *Ag.* 1415–16.

47–8 ἵππον | παγὸν ἀεθλοφόρον is epic: *Il.* 9.123–4, 9.265–6 ἵππους | πηγοὺς ἀθλοφόρους. The meaning of πηγός was debated already in antiquity ('strong', 'white', 'black'); see Matthews on Antimachus fr. 185. Callimachus plays with this uncertainty at *Dian.* 90. A somewhat mysterious epic word would add grandeur to an already grand simile. ἀεθλοφόρον is the first of several references to competition in Part II; cf. pp. 59–60.

48 καναχάποδα: very rare, but perhaps also taken from hexameter poetry. It occurs, as here of horses in a race, in a hexameter couplet attributed to Homer at *Certamen* 8 and to Hesiod at Plut. *Mor.* 154a.

49 τῶν ὑποπετριδίων ὀνείρων: lit. '(a horse) of those under-the-rock dreams', viz. a dream-horse. ὑποπετρίδιος is obscure. As creatures of darkness, dreams naturally belong to dark places; cf. ΣA 'because they live in a sunless place'. But that is not enough to give point to the adjective (and indeed the scholiast goes on to produce more far-fetched explanations). Page 1951a: 87 and others follow Herodian 2.237–8 Lentz in taking ὑποπετριδίων as the equivalent of ὑποπτεριδίων, 'winged'. This produces a simpler expression since dreams commonly fly, but the evident derivation from πέτρος is difficult to sidestep.

50–9 The visual focus on Agido and Hagesichora intensifies. The dominant image continues to be extraordinary horses, but after the simile in 46–9 ('like a horse'), the audience is now prompted to configure the two leader figures as those horses ('the horse'); see further Peponi 2004: 299–303.

50 ἦ οὐχ ὁρῆις; 'Don't you see?' The chorus address in the first instance themselves (in the singular, just as they often use the first person singular), but the question is also a request to the audience to share their way of seeing. There may be a playful self-consciousness in presenting as obvious what is far from obvious (there is no racehorse here, just girls). Cf. 56 διαφάδαν for the same self-consciousness.

50–1 It is simplest to assume that the horse refers to the same woman as that in the simile. On the interpretation of 43–5 above, this would be Agido, and μέν … δέ would mark the transition from Agido to Hagesichora, the undisputed topic of 51–7. Alternatively, ἦ οὐχ ὁρῆις could make a new start, directing attention to Hagesichora, which would have the benefit of giving most of the stanza to Hagesichora, after most of the previous stanza belonged to Agido; μέν … δέ would have to mark the shift from Hagesichora as horse to Hagesichora as human, cf. 58–9n.

51 Ἐνητικός 'Enetic'; a reference probably not to Homer's Enetoi from the south coast of the Black Sea (*Il.* 2.852), but to the Enetoi who lived at the top of the Adriatic (Lat. *Veneti*) and who bred famous horses; see Eur. *Hipp.* 231 with Barrett and Σ *ad loc.*

51–4 ἁ δέ... ἀκήρατος: a new comparison (unadulterated gold) brings out the beauty of Hagesichora's hair. But since χαίτη is used for both human hair and horses' manes, the horse imagery is kept alive.

52 ἀνεψιᾶς 'cousin', either literally (which would be evidence for selection of the participants from a single family or φυλή) or metaphorically. Calame 1997 [1977]: 216–18 discusses (late) evidence for kinship terminology in Spartan educational grouping; see esp. Hesych. κ971 κάσιοι· οἱ ἐκ τῆς αὐτῆς ἀγέλης ἀδελφοί τε καὶ ἀνεψιοί. καὶ ἐπὶ θηλειῶν οὕτως ἔλεγον Λάκωνες.

53 Ἁγησιχόρας: like all names in the text, Hagesichora's is introduced without patronym, at least in what survives; the chorus are (purporting to be) talking to themselves or to an audience to whom these are all familiar figures. Whatever the identity of the performer on any given occasion, the name marks her role as a chorus-leader, and it is possible that it would in fact have been understood as a synonym of 44 χοραγός. The name Agido similarly suggests pre-eminence (ἀγ- ~ ἡγ-). These are names with a meaning. However, royal names like Agis and Agesilaos show that it is nevertheless possible that they were the names of the first performers. Evidently the Spartan elite (like other Greek elites) liked to express their leadership in their children's names. Cf. 64–77 and 73nn., and further significant names at Alcm. 3.73–4, 10b and 59b, at least some of which seem to be historical. For discussion, see Calame 1977: 140–2, Nagy 1990: 345–9, Hinge 2009.

54 ἀκήρατος: see Ibyc. S151.41–5n.

55–7 The chorus continue their exaltation of Hagesichora's appearance. Then, in a pseudo-spontaneous shift parallel to that in 43–5(n.), they interrupt themselves: 'Why am I telling you in an obvious way?' Hagesichora's beauty speaks for itself (as did Agido's in 43–5), 'This is Hagesichora here.'

55 ἀργύριον 'silvery' follows on from 'gold'. Light skin is a token of beauty in women from Homer on, e.g. *Od.* 18.196; for silvery skin, see *h.* 6.10 στηθέσιν ἀργυφέοισιν, of Aphrodite.

58–9 Probably, (i) 'And the second in beauty after Agido (viz. Hagesichora) will run as a Kolaxaian horse to an Ibenian.' Agido's beauty is extraordinary, but Hagesichora too is very beautiful indeed. For similar comparisons that praise both individuals, see Ibyc. S151.41–5(n.), *Il.* 2.673–4, *carm. conv.* 899 *PMG*; further Puelma 1995 [1977]: 79–82, 108. μέν... δέ presumably indicates the shift between two modes of demonstrating Hagesichora's beauty: from the actual evidence of her visible appearance to the putative scenario (see 59n. (δραμεῖται)) of how she would look racing against Agido. The alternative is (ii) to translate 'Whoever is second after Agido in beauty...', thus e.g. Hutchinson *ad loc.* and, differently, Page 1951a: 47–9. μέν... δέ would become more straightforward, but in this otherwise very concrete passage, with its focus on two particular women, an indefinite meaning of ἁ... δευτέρα ('whoever...') is arguably harder to understand.

58 πεδ' ~ μετ'.

59 Ἰβηνῶι Κολαξαῖος: both terms are obscure to us, and prompted discussion already in antiquity; see ΣA and ΣB. On the reading of the sentence advocated here, both must denote breeds that are excellent, albeit to different degrees. The Ibenians may have been a Lydian people; see ΣB, Steph. Byz. 118. 'Kolaxaian' may have amounted to 'Scythian', since Kolaxais was a mythical Scythian king (Hdt. 4.5, 4.7); Ivantchik 2002 and Zaikov 2004 speculate about more specific allusions to Scythian myth.

δραμείται: the future makes this a statement of assumption rather than fact, amounting to 'it will prove to be the case that...'; contrast the present tense at 39, 42, 45, 50, 53, 56 (but cf. 'if' + optative in 46–9). For the future expressing inference, see *CGCG* §33.45, Bakker 2002. The race is a metaphor for relative beauty, but has the potential to interact with the dancing moves of the chorus and (probably) their leaders. It also brings to mind the foot-races in which Spartan girls engaged; for the evidence, which goes back to the sixth century BC, see Calame 1997 [1977]: 186–7, Ducat 2006: 231–4. The unparalleled construction of τρέχειν with dative is best explained as by analogy with verbs of competition, which often take the dative; see KG 1.432–3 and Schwyzer 11.161β.

60–3 *The Πελειάδες fight the chorus: an expression of either the extreme superiority of Hagesichora and Agido (continued from 58–9) or of the precariousness of the moment.* 'For the Πελειάδες are rising up through the immortal night like Sirius and are fighting us as we are bringing a robe to Orthria.' This is the most difficult sentence in the text. Its poetic effect turns on the paradoxical notion of the Πελειάδες as fighters, and as comparable to Sirius, but it is unclear who or what the Πελειάδες are here, and hence what the sentence means. Two lines of approach suggest themselves, the first perhaps more persuasive.

Approach (i) assumes that Πελειάδες is an established title of Agido and Hagesichora, akin to the use of πελειάδες as the appellation of the priestesses of Zeus at Dodona (Hdt. 2.57.1). Such a title might be understood as either 'Pleiades' (women of myth, turned into stars) or 'Doves' (as at Dodona); see 60n. On this reading, the comparison with Sirius is yet another expression of the superiority of the two leaders, and μάχονται, hyperbolically, couches this superiority in the language of battle: the chorus' inferiority is a matter of life and death, they are in a battle against their radiant leaders. The conceit would continue with 65 ἀμύναι and 77 τείρει, and see also 87–91n. One benefit of this approach is that it makes sense of the γάρ: 'Two extraordinary horses race against one another, one even better than the other. I say that because (γάρ) I am up against the most baneful star.' The imagery changes from horses to stars, and the competition from one between the two leaders to one between leaders and chorus, but the emphasis on their exceptionality continues, with a climactic statement of their superiority. There is good continuity also with what follows (64–77n.). Yet the battle imagery is difficult, and one has to posit Agido and Hagesichora's institutional title Πελειάδες. Further on this approach, which goes back to ΣΑ and ΣΒ, see Puelma 1995 [1977]: 83–5 and Segal 1983.

   Approach (ii) interprets Πελειάδες as the star-cluster. The Greeks often used the Pleiades' heliacal rising (viz. the first day on which they are visible briefly before dawn) to mark the beginning of summer, e.g. Hes. WD 383–4, 571–81, and this passage might thus indicate the day on which the song was performed. More specifically, the rising Pleiades would 'fight' the chorus in the sense that they are signalling the imminent end of the ceremony at dawn (Burnett 1964); are delaying sunrise and thus impeding the ceremony (Hutchinson ad loc.); are marking the hottest time of the year (Stehle 1997: 79–85); or, as a chorus in the sky (for which see Eur. El. 467–8, Callim. fr. 693 Pfeiffer), are outdoing the performing chorus (Clay 1991: 58–63, Dale 2011b: 28–31). The comparison of the (notoriously dim) Pleiades to the (notoriously bright) Sirius emphasises the statement. This approach has the advantage that no title Πελειάδες needs to be posited, but the causal connection with the previous sentence (γάρ) is problematic, and there are difficulties also for what follows (64–77n.). As in (i), the metaphorical battle is difficult to understand.

   Other approaches appear to throw up yet more problems: Page 1951a: 52–7 and Rosenmeyer 1966: 343–5 interpret the Πελειάδες as a rival chorus, and Bowie 2011 as Sirens. Calame ad loc. unconvincingly takes ἆμιν as dative of advantage ('fight for us'). Caciagli 2009b: 32–41 argues for 'since they raise Sirius'. Priestley 2007 takes ἆτε Σείριον with φᾶρος, 'a cloak like Sirius'.

   60 Πελειάδες: the Pleiades, usually seven, are among the most important constellations in ancient thinking about stars; see Kidd 1997 on Aratus 254–67. In mythology, they were the daughters of Atlas, turned into stars when pursued by Orion: see Gantz 1993: 212–19. In this spelling with Πελ- rather than Πλ- (found also at e.g. [Hes.] frs. 288–90 MW, Pind. Nem. 2.11), the word is the same as πελειάδες 'doves'. Later authors refer to a story of metamorphosis into doves among various etymologies of the Pleiades; see Σ Aratus 254–5 and cf. Athen. 11.490e.

   61 Ὀθρίαι: the word order favours interpretation as a proper name in the dative ('to Orthria') rather than as a nom. pl. adjective ('at daybreak'). No goddess Orthria – a goddess of dawn? – is otherwise known. There is a case for amending to Ϝορθείαι ('to Orthia'), a reading already found in ΣA (ὀρθίαι). Orthia, later associated with Artemis, had a major sanctuary on the bank of the Eurotas; see Calame 1997 [1977]: 156–69, Pomeroy 2002: 106–11. An unknown Othria in a city with a major Orthia sanctuary would be a remarkable coincidence. The emendation receives some support also from Pind. *Ol.* 3.29–30, where the Pleiad Taygete consecrates a doe to Orthosia (~ Orthia). The reading Ὀθρίαι is kept here nevertheless, hesitantly, because of two considerations: (i) the strong possibility that Aotis in 87 is a dawn goddess (n.); (ii) Archaic Orthia inscriptions normally have Ϝορθεία and Ϝορθα(σ)ία rather than short Ὀρθία (for a possible exception see *SEG* 28.409); one would therefore have to assume correption Ϝορθείαι to produce the metrically required short vowel.

φᾶρος: an interlinear gloss and a marginal note, as well as Herodian 2. 941–2 Lentz, give the meaning as 'plough', which is otherwise attested only in the lexica and grammarians (see further Matthews on Antimachus fr. 154). But 'cloak' is the more obvious interpretation, both because it is the standard meaning and because garments are common gifts for deities.

φεροίσαις ~ φερούσαις. One of a handful of non-epic Aeolic forms in Alcman's language.

62 νύκτα δι' ἀμβροσίαν: an epic line-opening formula. It is uncertain what made night immortal in epic (see Heubeck *et al.* 1988 on *Od.* 4.429), but the phrase suits a sentence that refers to a ritual act.

Σείριον: the dog-star, known for brightness, heat, destruction and beauty; see *Il.* 22.25–32, Hes. *WD* 582–8, Archil. fr. 107; cf. Alc. 347.1n. As the dog of Orion, Sirius is sometimes involved in pursuing the Pleiades; e.g. Pind. fr. 74.

63 ἀϝειρομέναι: ἀείρειν regularly describes stars rising or moving across the sky; see LSJ Supplement s.v. i.1, Kidd 1997 on Aratus 326. It also suits dancers leaping up; e.g. Soph. *Trach.* 216, Aristoph. *Lys.* 539.

64–77 *The chorus-members' outfits and looks; Hagesichora's exceptionality (expressed in erotic language).* The rhetoric assumes the form of *praeteritio*: a catalogue of eight women (almost certainly chorus-members) culminates in a further statement of Hagesichora's exceptionality. The passage picks up the metaphor of the battle against the Πελειάδες, reframing it as a contest of attractiveness. If the Πελειάδες are Hagesichora and Agido, the thought runs: 'Here is proof that Agido and Hagesichora are superior fighters (γάρ). Despite their accoutrements and looks, these four chorus-members are not beautiful enough to ward off their two leaders; nor do those other four chorus-members have what it takes to make us fall in love with them. We are in love with Hagesichora; we cannot ward her off.' If the Πελειάδες are stars, the thought is more difficult, as the climactic sentence about Hagesichora consitutes a move in a new direction rather than linking back to the opening of the stanza (but see 77n.).

As may be the case also for the list of real fighters in 2–12(n.), to which this passage loosely corresponds, the expressions of insufficiency do not stand in the way of glorification: the girls are celebrated for their beauty and their glamorous outfits at the same time as they are subordinated to Hagesichora. The cultural connotations of the outfits and jewellery are discussed by Krummen 2013: 33–8, who highlights relations between Sparta and Ionia. There is no way of knowing how closely the descriptions matched the actual appearance of the original performers. The eight names may be the real names of the (first) performers. The evidence to the contrary is even less conclusive than for Hagesichora and Agido, for which see 53n.; contra Hinge 2006: 291–2. For the size of the chorus, see 96–101n.

64–5 Probably, 'For neither is an overabundance of purple at all enough to protect us . . .' ὥστ' is prepared for by τόσσος. Subsequently, (the equivalent of Attic) τοῖος/τοία is to be supplied with 66 δράκων, 67 μίτρα, etc.: '. . . nor is a ποικίλος δράκων <such that it can protect us>', etc.

64 πορφύρας: a marker of luxury and high status; cf. in this selection Sa. 44.9, Sim. 543.16–17.

66 ποικίλος: both the 'dappled' skin of the represented snake and the 'elaborate' workmanship; this double meaning is a trope, e.g. *Od.* 19.228 (ποικίλος fawn on brooch) and Pind. *Pyth.* 8.46 (ποικίλος snake on shield).

δράκων: a snake-shaped piece of jewellery such as a bracelet.

67–8 μίτρα | Λυδία 'Lydian headband'. This was obviously a prized luxury article. It appears also at Sa. 98a.10–11; see further Ulf 2014: 422–3.

69 ϝιανογ[λ]εφάρων ('dark-eyed', lit. 'violet-eyed') ∼ ἰοβλέφαρος/ ἰογλέφαρος, describing the Graces at Bacch. 19.5 and Aphrodite at Pind. fr. 307.

ἄγαλμα: (object of) 'pride', 'delight'.

71 ἀλλ' οὐδ' expresses progression: 'nor again'. In 77 ἀλλ' marks a contrast: 'no, . . .', 'rather'.

σιειδής ∼ θεοειδής. Even divine looks will not help.

73–6 The lesser attractiveness of the final four women (compared to Hagesichora) is conveyed vividly through a counterfactual mini-scene. No chorus-member (fem. ἐνθοῖσα ∼ ἐλθοῦσα) would go to their rehearsals (or whatever happens at Ainesimbrota's house) and there express desire for Astaphis, Philylla, Damareta or Vianthemis.

73 ἐς Αἰνησιμβρ[ό]τας 'to Ainesimbrota's house': we do not know who Ainesimbrota is, except that she evidently is not one of the chorus-members. Since she is named here she is presumably of significance to the performance or festival more widely, e.g. the chorus-trainer. See further Page 1951a: 65–6, Calame 1977: 95–7, Hubbard 2011: 357.

The very difficulty of establishing her role from the text alone suggests strongly that this is her real name.

75 ποτιγλέποι ~ προσβλέποι: for similar wishes, in different keys, see Anacr. 358.8 and Theoc. 3.39; and for the erotic gaze in general, lines 21 and 69 above, Alcm. 3.61–3, Ibyc. 287.1–2n.

76 Δαμαρέτα τ' ἐρατά [τ]ε Ϝιανθεμίς: the jingle underscores the final line of the mini-speech.

77 με τείρει 'wears me down'. The battle imagery is still felt, but in the context of 74–6 and 78–81 the primary meaning is erotic, and amounts to 'drives me mad (with desire)'. [Hes.] fr. 298 MW uses τείρειν of δεινός ... ἔρως and Telestes 805 of ὀξὺς ἔρως. If the Πελειάδες are not Agido and Hagesichora, the palaeographically minimal change τηρεῖ 'watches over' may be considered. It improves coherence with the opening of the stanza: 'we do not have what it takes to fight the Pleiads, but Hagesichora looks after us'. But it loses the neat connection with the immediately preceding lines ('I am in love not with those four, but with Hagesichora').

78–91 *Deference and ritual; the chorus vis-à-vis their human leaders and the goddess Aotis.* Ritual returns (cf. 61) in a stanza in which the chorus balance continued statements of dependence on their leaders, esp. Hagesichora, with paying respect to the gods, specifically Aotis. The train of thought is fundamentally one of alternation (see nn. for specific transitions): 78–81 *leaders*: Hagesichora is not with us, she is with Agido and commends our festival at a distance; 82–4 *gods*: gods, would that you accept their (?prayers); 84–7 *leaders (Hagesichora)*: chorus-mistress, by ourselves we cannot sing; 87–9 *gods (Aotis)*: we want to please Aotis, who healed our troubles; 90–1 *leaders (Hagesichora)*: Hagesichora led us to peace.

'Our festival', the invocation of the gods, the reference to Agido and Hagesichora's prayers, and the wish to please Aotis, create an impression of the wider festival and of the chorus' contribution to it, but the impression is hazy, and the ritual references are presented as incidental to the chorus' concerns; see p. 62.

78–81 Hagesichora's absence (οὐ ... πάρ' αὐτεῖ ~ οὐ πάρεστι αὐτοῦ) contrasts with her presence earlier (57), but there is no need to remove the contrast by punctuating the sentence as a – not very punchy – rhetorical question ('Is Hagesichora not here... ?'); contra Puelma 1995 [1977]: 91–2, Campbell in the Loeb. The chorus refer either to a piece of choreography that sets Agido and Hagesichora off from the rest of the dance formation, or to their prayers (82–3), imagined as performed simultaneously somewhere else. This interpretation is supported by the similar use of physical distance in Alcm. 3, where Astymeloisa excites the chorus' desire (61–3) but 'does not answer' (64) and is 'among the people' (73); see Peponi 2007 for discussion, and Hamilton 1989: 464–5 and Swift 2010: 195–6 for further comparative material.

80 .ϝ. ἀρμένει: the most popular restoration is Canini's δὲ παρμένει, which would produce 'she remains near Agido', but it is unclear that it fits the traces.

81 θωστήρια 'festival' (neut. pl.); ΣA's gloss ἑορτή is probably right. The etymological connection with θοίνη, θοινατήριον, θῶσθαι points to sacrifice and feasting, essential ingredients of Greek festivals. ΣA's gloss continues α[, possibly the beginning of the name of the presiding deity in the genitive: (festival of) Artemis (~ Orthia)?, Aotis?, Aphrodite? Cf. 87n. (Ἀώτι).

ἄμ' ~ ἡμέτερα. The metre shows that this is not ἅμα 'together'.

ἐπαινεῖ denotes ritual propriety and indicates Hagesichora's authority; contrast 43–5 and compare 87–8.

82–4 'Gods, may you accept their ?prayers. For fulfilment and completion rest with the gods.' From Agido and Hagesichora's approval of the θωστήρια, the chorus move on to prayers performed by them. This is the only address to the gods in what survives, and it is at one remove: a prayer that prayers be accepted. The *gnome* explains why the chorus turn to the gods, as well as reinforcing with variation the *gnomai* in 13–14 (another pair of overlapping abstracts) and 36–9.

82 ἀλλά often introduces prayers; see Denniston 1954: 15–16.

ϲιοί is reasonably certain in the context. For the space before, Hutchinson regards the usual supplement εὐχάς (Blass) irreconcilable with the traces and with misgivings contemplates λιτάς. The sense makes some such word very likely.

83 ἄνα: rare, but the form ἄνυσις is Homeric.

84–7 A statement of humility which explains why the chorus' request to the gods had to be a request at one remove. It balances due deference to the gods with due deference to the human leader; the address to the ϲιοί is succeeded by an address to the [χο]ροϲτάτιϲ. The screeching owl on the beam contrasts in the text with the melodious singing of the Sirens (96) and the swan (100–1), and in reality with the singing and dancing of the chorus; cf. Sa. 31.7–8.

84 [χο]ροϲτάτιϲ: lit. 'she who sets up the chorus', viz. Hagesichora. A respectful appellation: without her the chorus would not exist. The word is a *hapax* and may not be an institutional title (like the masc. χοροστάτης in later periods) but coined ad hoc on the basis of expressions such as χορὸν ἱστάναι; for such expressions, cf. Aristoph. *Birds* 219, *Clouds* 271 and the name Stesichorus (p. 153); and see further Calame 1997 [1977]: 43–8 and Henrichs 1994–5: 95 n. 36. Π's double accent on ρο and στα is peculiar; perhaps the scribe confused nominative χοροϲτάτιϲ (used as vocative) and vocative χορόϲτατι.

85 ϝείποιμί κ' 'so to speak'. κ(ε) ~ ἄν.

87 γλαύξ provides an emphatic climax to the statement. The nocturnal noise of owls is a nuisance at Aristoph. *Lys.* 760–1. The reading ἀπὸ θράνω ('from a rafter') is not fully secure, but an alternative is difficult to find.

87–91 A balanced expression of twofold indebtedness, τᾶι μὲν Ἀώτι ... ἐξ Ἁγησιχόρας δέ. The interpretation is very uncertain. The 'struggles' (πόνων) and 'peace' (ἰρ]ήνας) are probably metaphorical, and the statement as a whole perhaps best taken as marking 'peace' after the the earlier 'battling' (63) with the Πεληιάδες, in the sense that the performance, which is nearing its end, has been successful. If the Πεληιάδες are Hagesichora and Agido, their superiority no longer threatens the chorus. If they are stars, their challenge has been overcome. Either way, there has been a development from 77 Ἀγησιχόρα με τείρει to Hagesichora as the facilitator of 'lovely peace'. This development towards contentment will continue in 96–101 (n.). Metaphorical εἰρήνη is unusual (unlike e.g. English 'peace of mind'), but after daring metaphorical μάχονται (63) and ἀμύναι (65), the audience will be ready for a metaphorical 'peace'. Metaphorical πόνοι are common, e.g. Pind. fr. 70c.16 πόνοι χορῶν. For different interpretations of these lines, see Calame 1977: 116–19, Lonsdale 1993: 204–5, Puelma 1995 [1977]: 71–2 n. 50, Bowie 2011: 61–2.

87 ἐγὼν δέ after 85 ἐγὼν μέν emphasises the symmetry between the chorus' deference to Hagesichora and their eagerness to find favour with Aotis. ἐγὼν μέν/ἐγὼν δέ thus interlocks with τᾶι μέν/Ἁγησιχόρας δέ, as the chorus shift between human and divine.

Ἀώτι: unknown, but probably related to ἠώς ('dawn'), and hence compatible with Orthria in 61 (if that is the right reading). Various suggestions have been made about possible associations of Aotis with other deities, but the evidence is insufficient for more than speculation: Artemis, Helen, Aphrodite, Eileithyia, Hera and one or both of the Leukippides; see Bowie 2011: 60 n. 74 for doxography, and cf. 81n. (θωστήρια).

88 ϝανδάνην: through their contributions to the ritual, not least their performance, cf. similar language at Alcm. 45, 56; Pind. *Ol.* 3.1. But ἐρῶ is marked. The chorus now apply the kind of erotic language that they used already in 64–77 to the goddess they worship. In contrast to Part 1 (1–12, 16–20nn.), there is no question of transgression: the chorus desire to please.

90 νεάνιδες: the chorus – and possibly the girls of Sparta in general.

91 ἰρ]ήνας: the size of the gap suggests that Π had ιρηνας rather than the form of the word standardly transmitted for Pindar and other early poets, εἰρήν-. The earliest Laconian attestation is ℎιράναν at *SEG* 26.461.2 (5th/4th cent.). See further Hinge 2006: 9.

ἐπέβαν: lit. 'set foot on', viz. 'embarked upon'. The metaphor is often hardly felt (see LSJ s.v. A.1.4), but particularly appropriate for a χοροστάτις, who directs the chorus' steps. See Soph. *OC* 189 for a similar play of figurative and literal meaning.

92–5 *Two images of subordination to a leader.* The precise line of thought is irrecoverable, but it is clear that both trace-horse/yoke-horses and helmsman/crew are suitable images for Hagesichora's role of safely guiding the choral group, and thus follow on easily from 90–1.

92–3 Perhaps, '(Yoke horses follow/should follow) the tracehorse of their own accord (ἀ[ὐ]τῶς).'

92 σηραφόρωι: trace-horses ran unyoked on the side of four-horse teams, and had a particularly important role in negotiating turns. Their various associations are all relevant here: leadership (Eur. *HF* 446, Eur. *Or.* 1017, Hesych. σ339), dependability (Aesch. *Ag.* 842, and see Griffith 2006: 333–4), luxuriousness (Aesch. *Ag.* 1640–1, Aristoph. *Clouds* 1300–1).

95 cannot be reconstructed. Hutchinson and Ucciardello forthcoming rule out the often printed κἠν νᾶϊ μά[λιστ' ἀκούην ('and on a boat one pays the utmost obedience (to the helmsman)') as irreconcilable with the traces.

96–101 *Even though inferior to the Sirens, the chorus sing as beautifully as a swan.* Perhaps: 'The (?voice) of the Sirens is more tuneful (*sc.* than ours) – for they are goddesses – and (? this group of ten) children (sings) in place of eleven (Sirens). And yet it gives voice (?like) a swan on the waters of the Xanthos. But she (i.e. Hagesichora) with her lovely blond hair...' The supplement in 97 would be e.g. αὐδά 'voice' (μέν is highly likely on any interpretation); for the supplements in 98–100 see below. Thus e.g. West 1965: 200–2, Ferrari 2008: 97–100. The chorus maintain a certain humility, continuing on from the images of subordination in 92–5: their song does not match that of the Sirens, who are both divine and more numerous. However, in the comparison with the mellifluous swan the chorus evince an uncustomary self-confidence. For the first time they speak about themselves in an unreservedly positive tone. The reason, probably, is that the 'group of ten' includes Agido and Hagesichora; contrast the eight girls of 64–77(n.). As the song nears its end, the closural movement towards contentment that started with the end of the chorus' 'struggles' and their 'embarking on peace' under Hagesichora's leadership (88–91) continues. They cannot take on the Sirens, but together with Agido and Hagesichora they sing like a swan.

Other reconstructions are arguably less coherent, but the uncertainty is considerable and there are numerous options. Most fundamentally different are approaches according to which the entire passage refers to Hagesichora: 'This woman is (not) a better singer than the Sirens (supplementing e.g. οὐδέν in 97), for they are gods. But instead of eleven girls she sings like ten, and she gives voice like a swan...' Thus, broadly, Puelma

1995 [1977] 95–9, Peponi 2012: 85–6. The flow of the stanza is appealing, with the earlier images of leadership serving as a set of foils leading up to the praise of Hagesichora (a 'priamel'; cf. p. 127). 101 ἁ δ᾽ might bring back Agido. However, with Hagesichora as subject it is difficult to reconstruct the text of 98–9 in such a way that it both makes sense and is in keeping with ΣA (for which see below).

96 Σηρηνίδων: Sirens are exceptional singers as early as *Od.* 12. The chorus of Pind. *Parth.* 2.13–15 sing σειρῆνα δὲ κόμπον … μιμήσομ᾽ ἀοιδαῖς 'I shall enact in my songs the Siren vaunt.' The Sirens are also dangerous seductresses, which invests the comparison to the *parthenoi* of the chorus with a sense of frisson; cf. Swift 2010: 180–1, Power 2011: 98–101. The notion of eleven Sirens is obscure. West 1967a: 11–14 argues for the presence of Pythagorean musical theory; cf. Ferrari 2008: 92–100 with n. 78. Bowie 2011: 57–9 provides an iconographic parallel (as well as offering a more wide-ranging interpretation of the role of the Sirens in this text).

98–9 are reconstructed from ΣA: 'He [Alcman] said eleven (ἕνδεκα) … because the chorus was formed sometimes from eleven and sometimes from ten girls.' ἀντὶ δ᾽ ἕνδεκα is therefore highly likely in 98, and δεκάς … ἀείδει possible in 99; see further *CLGP ad loc.* Depending on the overall run of the sentence (96–101n.) one would then want either a demonstrative after δεκάς (ἅδ᾽, 'this group of ten') or a comparison (ὡς, 'like a group of ten').

100 Ξάνθω: known to Homer as a river in Lycia (*Il.* 12.312–13) and as an alternative name of the Scamander (*Il.* 20.74). Blass' δ᾽ ἄρ᾽ ὥτ᾽ would produce the comparison that seems to be needed.

101 κύκνος: the swan is noted for its song, not just at the point of death, e.g. *h.* 21.1, Eur. *IT* 1104–5, *Ion* 161–9, probably Alcm. S2 (= 12B Campbell). Contrasts suggest themselves with both the Sirens of 96 (who have bird-bodies in the iconography; see Hofstetter 1997) and the owl of 87.

ἐπιμέρωι ξανθᾶι κομίσκαι returns to the topics of beauty and allure. There seems to be a pun Ξάνθω/ξανθᾶι.

Four lines are lost; see 'Source'. Perhaps Agido made another appearance (if ἁ δ᾽ is Hagesichora); perhaps there was a divine address.

Alcman 89 PMG (159 Calame)

A short passage, describing the sleep of wild nature. The movement is from inanimate (1–2) to animate (3–6).

The paratactic list, with one or two elements per line, is appropriately simple and unhurried, while changing types of noun phrase ensure variation (noun, noun + relative clause, noun + epithet, noun + genitive).

The prominence of terms that would normally convey liveliness or movement, such as torrents, bees and wings (see *ad locc.*), increases the sense of the extraordinary. Even more arresting, for the opposite reason, is the opening: unlike the sea or winds, mountains do not sleep elsewhere in Greek literature, exactly because they do not move and hence do not cease to move. Alcman's scene is both suggestive and difficult to parallel because the sleep is so all-encompassing.

The text is almost certainly incomplete, since stand-alone descriptions of nature are unknown in early Greek literature, but we can only speculate about the context. Three possibilities deserve consideration. (i) The calm of the natural environs serves as a foil for the tortured sleepless speaker; cf. anxious characters in Homer who cannot find sleep while everybody else does (e.g. Zeus at *Il.* 2.1–2, Agamemnon at 10.1–4), and fuller instances of the topos in later texts, such as Eur. *IA* 9–13 and esp. Verg. *Aen.* 4.522–32; cf. Sim. 543 below. (ii) The lines set the scene for a night-time ritual in the mountains; cf. Alcm. 56. This might be a scene, moreover, that is pervaded by a sense of divine presence, since silence often attends epiphanies. Further on this view, see Calame 1983: 573–4. However, sleep is not the same as silence, and one might expect alertness in the face of the divine. (iii) As part of the myth section of a longer composition, Alcman is describing the dark world of the North, a land that is regularly cast as wrapped in darkness and as the place where the sun rests at night. Alcman treats the mythical North elsewhere. See esp. fr. 90, 'Rhipai, mountain flowering with forest, breast of black night', and further on this approach see Budelmann 2013a.

Uniquely among Alcman's more substantial fragments, the dialect of the transmitted text is epic-Ionic throughout, containing no characteristically Doric, let alone Laconian, forms. Unless one doubts attribution to Alcman, one has to assume either that Alcman drew more heavily than usual on epic forms in a text that is heavily epic in its vocabulary (a feature of other lyric descriptions of nature, as Harvey 1957: 215–17 points out), or that the text was changed in transmission and differs substantially from both Alcman's own and that of the Alexandrian edition. The truth may well be a combination of both explanations. In the absence of reliable criteria by which to make decisions on individual forms, the text is here printed as transmitted. The attractive metrical emendations 3 ὅσ<σ>α and 5 βένθεσ<σ>ι would both change one Homeric form for another. Further on the dialect, see Page 1951a: 158–62 and Morani 1990, and on Alcman's dialect in general pp. 62–3 above.

Source: Cited as Alcman's by Apollonius the Sophist (1st cent. AD), *Lex.* s.v. κνώδαλον (p. 101 Bekker), to illustrate the distinction between θῆρες/θηρία, ἑρπετά (which he takes to mean 'snakes' here, probably wrongly) and κνώδαλα (which he glosses 'sea-monsters', whales and such like'). We have only one manuscript.

Metre:

$- - \cup \cup - \cup \cup - \cup - \cup - -^?\|$ $- 2da\ ith\ (= - D\ pe)$ ὀρέων

$- \cup - \cup - \cup - -^?\|$ $- \cup\ ith\ (=2tr)$

$\dagger - \cup - \cup \cup \dagger \cup \times \cup - \cup - \cup - - \|$ ends with *ith* (preceded by 2*da* with West's

$- - \cup - - - - \cup - \cup - -^?\|$ $ia - - ith$ text)

$- - \cup - - \cup \cup - \cup - \cup - \|$ $3ia$ (with central *cho*, unless Heyne's βένθεσ<σ>ι is

$- - \cup - - - - \cup \cup - \cup \cup -^?\|$ $ia - - D$ adopted)

The rhythm combines iambo-trochaic and dactylic forms with considerable flexibility, but repeated patterns give structure to the stanza. The first four verses end with ithyphallics, the last three open with $- - \cup - -$. The dactylic blunt close of line 6 suggests strongly that the stanza continues. The pendant (– –) cadences otherwise, and the frequent changes of rhythm, make pause after each line likely, even though only those after 3 and 5 are guaranteed by *brevis in longo*; a steady regularity would also suit the subject matter. See further West 1982a: 52–3, who in particular discusses the unusual shape $- - \cup - - - -$ (4, 6).

Discussions: Magnelli 2015, Budelmann 2013a, Morani 1990, Alfageme 1978, Elliger 1975: 185–8, Cuartero 1972: 399–402, Pfeiffer 1959.

1 εὕδουσι: the metaphorical usage is common. See *Il.* 5.524–5 ὄφρ' εὕδησι μένος Βορέαο καὶ ἄλλων | ζαχρηῶν ἀνέμων, Sim. 543.22, Aesch. *Ag.* 565–6 (the sea sleeping at noon), and LSJ s.v. II. Alcman uses the conceit at unusual length, as well as in variation with real sleep.

ὀρέων κορυφαί: traditional phrasing; e.g. *Il.* 12.282 ὑψηλῶν ὀρέων κορυφὰς καὶ πρώονας ἄκρους. In Alcm. 56 a festival takes place ἐν κορυφαῖς ὀρέων.

φάραγγες: the only word in the text that is not otherwise attested before the fifth century.

2 χαράδραι are normally fast-flowing and loud; e.g. Aristoph. *Wasps* 1034.

3 †φῦλά τε ἑρπετά θ'†: ἑρπετά are animals that 'crawl', i.e. move on their legs; the word thus combines well with ὅσα τρέφει μέλαινα γαῖα. But φῦλα ('tribes') makes little sense by itself; contrast 6 οἰωνῶν φῦλα. The three most attractive corrections, all of them producing broadly the same meaning, are: the deletion of φῦλά τε as an intrusion from 6; φῦλά θ' ἑρπετῶν ('tribes of animals'); and φῦλά θ' ἑρπέτ' with (unusual) adjectival ἑρπετά ('creeping tribes'). Pfeiffer's frequently printed ὕλα θ' ἑρπετά θ' ('and the wood and animals') is less likely; 'forest' should come in the previous verse (from which it would be divided by hiatus), and one would expect a plural; for further objections, see Perotti 1988.

τρέφει ... **γαῖα:** ὅσα τρέφει εὐρεῖα χθών (*Il.* 11.741, etc.) and γαῖα μέλαινα (*Il.* 2.699, etc., cf. Sa. 16.2(n.)) are hexameter formulae. See also *Od.* 4. 417–18 ὅσσ' ἐπὶ γαῖαν | ἑρπετὰ γίγνονται, the only instance of ἑρπετόν in surviving early hexameter.

4 θῆρες ... **ὀρεσκῷοι** 'mountain-dwelling beasts'. Cf. *Il.* 1.268 φηρσὶν ὀρεσκῴοισι (the Centaurs).

γένος μελισσῶν: bees are probably chosen because they are emblems of activity, e.g. Hes. *Th.* 596–7. For the phrasing, cf. *Il.* 2.87 ἔθνεα ... μελισσάων, [Hes.] fr. 33a.16 MW μελισσέων ἀγλαὰ φῦλα.

5 κνώδαλ' 'creatures'. For the phrasing, cf. *Od.* 17.316–17 οὐ μὲν γάρ τι φύγεσκε βαθείης βένθεσιν ὕλης | κνώδαλον, the only instance of the word in the *Iliad* or *Odyssey*, and expressions such as *Il.* 1.358 ἐν βένθεσσιν ἁλός (of Thetis).

πορφυρῆς 'purple'. It is possible that the word evokes not just the darkness but also the motion of the sea; cf. πορφύρω 'heave' and see Stulz 1990: 176–8, *LfgrE* s.v. That motion would now be put to rest, along with the κνώδαλα.

6 εὕδουσι: the ring composition may be imaginary as neither the scene of sleep nor this sentence need have ended here.

οἰωνῶν ... **τανυπτερύγων** 'long-winged birds'. Cf. *Il.* 12.237 οἰωνοῖσι τανυπτερύγεσσι, and similar expressions. Those long wings are not now flapping.

ALCAEUS

Alcaeus of Lesbos is best known for what antiquity called 'poems of strife' (στασιωτικὰ ποιήματα, Strabo 13.2.3 = test. 1 Campbell), which, with their sometimes very specific detail, create autobiographical vignettes (accurate or otherwise) of a life of ambition, conflict and failure; but he also composed small-scale hymns (34, 45, 307, 308; for the genre, cf. Anacr. 348 below), drinking songs (represented here by 347), and poems of love and desire (mostly lost, but see Cic. *Tusc.* 4.71, Hor. *Odes* 1.32.9–12 = test. 26 Campbell, Quint. 10.1.63 = test. 21). Myth, too, was a frequent feature of his poetry (see on fr. 42 below). Poetically, the recurring political topics serve as material for variation on a theme (cf. variation on the theme of love in Latin elegy). Examples presented here are the contrasting pair fr. 129 and fr. 130b, and the altogether different fr. 140. Alcaeus can be aggressive and abusive as well as celebratory, he combines strongly individual first-person perspectives with extended narrative, allegory and ecphrasis, and overtly manipulates earlier poetic traditions, ranging from Hesiod (see 347 below), to epic (see 42 below) and Archilochus (esp. 401B Voigt = 428 LP).

Ancient chronology places Alcaeus' career *c.* 610 to 580 BC, and we are not in a position to offer an alternative estimate. Fr. 48.10–11 seems to refer to the fall of the Levantine city of Ashkelon, which can be dated to 604; on this fragment, see Fantalkin and Lytle 2016. For the apparently conflicting evidence of Hdt. 5.94–5, see Page 1955: 152–61 and Hornblower 2013 on 5.94.2. Further on Alcaeus' date, see Liberman 1999: xv–xvi and Hutchinson 2001: 187–8.

Two types of context are important for understanding Alcaeus, the first of them cultural. As set out in the Introduction, early Lesbos, like Alcman's Sparta, was a musical and poetic centre (pp. 17–18). This environment will have been instrumental in Alcaeus' own formation as a poet, and it is likely that he was familiar also with the poetry of the roughly contemporary Sappho.

The second relevant context is political. Alcaeus was active during a period of considerable unrest in his hometown of Mytilene. Several aristocratic clans were jostling for supremacy, fighting one another in closed political factions or *hetaireiai* (the term is only attested later, but Alcaeus himself speaks of his ἔταιροι, 'companions'). As is clear from the fragments themselves, and confirmed by ancient scholarship which drew on fuller knowledge of the corpus, Alcaeus was a prominent member of one such *hetaireia*, which, led perhaps by his brother, was in conflict with various rulers of the day. Success was at best intermittent, and Alcaeus was forced to spend repeated periods away from Mytilene. The most significant of the rival rulers is Pittacus (on whom see p. 94); other persistent names are Melanchrus and Myrsilus (see 129.28n. for the latter). All of them are referred to as 'tyrants' either by Alcaeus or in the later tradition, but it should not be assumed that their rule was necessarily either illegitimate or violent. For attempts to piece together a sequence of events, see Page 1955: 149–243, Liberman 1999: xiv–xxiii, and specifically for Alcaeus' periods of exile, p. 94 below. De Libero 1996, Anderson 2005 and Osborne 2009: 174–85 provide accounts of aristocratic rivalry and the nature of tyranny in this period.

It is likely that Alcaeus composed with two audiences in mind, his *hetaireia*, at whose *symposia* his songs (among other things) articulated group-internal attitudes, memories and ambitions, and a wider set of listeners, in Lesbos and beyond, for whom his songs (among other things) portrayed the vicissitudes of a political faction. For all their references to specific events and persons, these are portable poems that make sense also outside their original settings. Several of them create an elaborate (stable or shifting) *mise en scène* – a ship battered by waves, a lone exile at a sanctuary, a house full of weapons – which will have helped reperformance, both within the *hetaireia* and without.

The Alexandrian editors collected Alcaeus' poems in ten books; their criteria of classification are disputed, but in contrast to Sappho were not metrical; see Liberman 1999: xlviii–lx, Acosta-Hughes 2010: 134–40. Alcaeus was much read already in the Classical period. Herodotus, for example, uses him for his account of the conflict between Athens and Mytilene over the city of Sigeum in the Troad (see p. 87), Aristotle quotes him as a source for Pittacus (*Pol.* 3.14.1285ab = Alc. 348), and the Peripatetic scholar Dicaearchus wrote a treatise about him (frs. 94–9 Wehrli). Alcaeus continued to attract attention in Rome, and Horace selected him as his chief model for his lyric *Odes*.

The most useful edition, and closest to a commentary on the whole corpus, is Liberman 1999; Page 1955 is a fuller commentary on the larger fragments. The most important book-length study is Rösler 1980, which situates the poems in the context of performance for the *hetaireia*. See also Martin 1972 (an introductory monograph) and Burnett 1983: 107–205 (a literary study).

The dialect of Alcaeus and Sappho. Like all lyric language (pp. 24–5), the dialect of Alcaeus and Sappho blends inherited poetic, especially epic, forms and formulae with the local vernacular. The vernacular in question is Lesbian, a member of the Aeolic group of dialects. The vernacular colouring is more pronounced than in most other lyric poets, but the balance of the different elements varies (see p. 139 on the tilt towards epic in Sa. 44). Notable features include: psilosis (no rough breathings), recessive accentuation (accent as close to the beginning of the word as general Greek rules of accentuation permit), gemination (double consonants instead of lengthening of the preceding vowel, e.g. ἄμμι ~ ἡμῖν, ἰμέρρει ~ ἰμείρει), 'diphthongisation' (e.g. ὄδοις ~ ὀδούς, θέλοισα ~ θέλουσα, τάλαις ~ τάλας); αἰ 'if' and the modal particle κεν. For complete lists, see the handbooks in p. 24 n. 49. For book-length treatments of Aeolic and Lesbian, see Blümel 1982 and Hodot 1990. On the language of the Lesbian poets, see Hamm 1957, Hooker 1977 and Bowie 1981.

A further notable characteristic of the dialect as transmitted in the papyri is the use of σδ in place of word-internal ζ, e.g. πέσδων. This is not what the poets wrote: Lesbian inscriptions consistently have ζ. The spelling σδ was probably introduced to indicate that the Archaic pronunciation of ζ differed from that current in *koine* Greek ([z]). (Whether it was indeed [sd], as the editors evidently thought, or rather [ds], is disputed.) The papyri distinguish 'secondary' ζ (e.g. ζά ~ Attic διά), for which they maintain ζ. Modern editions usually replicate both conventions, emending if necessary (but see Sa. 58b 'Source').

Finally, the transmitted texts present a number of 'hyper-Lesbian' forms: these are Lesbian-looking forms introduced in the transmission even though they do not in fact exist in Lesbian. Examples in the texts presented here include μειδιαίσαισα (the second αι is genuine Lesbian 'diphthongisation', the first is not), δίννηντες and Ζόννυσσον (no gemination expected here). This edition reproduces transmitted hyper-dialectic forms, but since it is impossible to establish Hellenistic editorial practice with certainty, it does not introduce them by emendation. For example, ἐπτόασεν is not changed to ἐπτόαισεν, and by the same token -ημι in verbs like οἴκημι is not changed to (possibly hyper-dialectic) -ημμι.

Alcaeus 42 Voigt

Two mythical figures and their myths, set against one another. Helen is presented as the cause of the suffering of the Trojans, and then thrown into relief by Thetis, who in her marriage with Peleus exemplifies a female ideal.

The comparison hinges on the introduction of Thetis as οὐ τεαύταν, 'not such a woman' (as Helen), and is elaborated with ring composition: Helen and Troy at the beginning and the end (1–4, 15–16) frame Thetis, with ἀμφ' Ἐ[λέναι and πόλις αὔτων echoing ἐκ σέθεν and Ἴλιον ἴραν. Even though the song says little about Helen, it achieves a sense of total difference between her and Thetis. The proper marriage of Peleus and Thetis evokes the improper relationship of Paris and Helen. The smooth sequence of wedding, conjugal love and the birth of a child in the Thetis section contrasts in theme as well as narrative mode with the bald statements of death and destruction which characterise Helen. Helen is named (probably) twice but given (probably) no epithet, while Thetis is referred to by eulogistic periphrasis.

The neat polarity requires the omission of well-known aspects of the myths of Helen and especially Thetis. Thetis was not just a 'delicate girl' but also, and above all, a sea-goddess. In many versions, her marriage to Peleus was arranged by Zeus for ulterior motives, chief among them the hope to circumvent a prophecy that Thetis' son would be stronger than his father (first attestation Pind. *Isthm.* 8.31–41). Thetis was reluctant to marry Peleus (e.g. *Il.* 18.432–4), who in some accounts wins her only by wrestling with her (first *LIMC* s.v. 'Peleus' 78, mid-/late 7th cent.; in literature Pind. *Nem.* 3.35–6, 4.62–5). She soon left husband and son to live in the depths of the sea; this is where the *Iliad* situates her, without Peleus. In fact, her story and Helen's are intricately linked. It was at Thetis' wedding that Eris provoked the quarrel among the gods which led to the Judgement of Paris and, ultimately, to the Trojan War, and it was at the hands of Achilles, whose birth the poem narrates immediately before returning to Trojan deaths, that many of those Trojans died. Together, these omissions are striking. The sense that Alc. 42 demands to be interpreted against the mythological and poetic tradition is compounded by allusions in the phrasing (7, 13, 14nn.), by the opening ὡς λόγος, and by the poetic catchphrase ἀμφ' Ἐ[λέναι, which serves to encapsulate the Helen myth.

Helen provides obvious material for this type of mythological self-consciousness. Her morality is the subject of debate as early as Homer. She prompted metapoetic treatment in numerous later works, e.g. Stesichorus' *Palinode*, and foresees already in Homer that she and Paris 'will be things of song for people in the future' (*Il.* 6.358). She had currency in Lesbian poetry (Alc. 283, Sa. 16), as indeed did Thetis (Alc. 44, probably Sa. 141). The *Cypria* (often dated later than Alcaeus) narrates both the wedding of Thetis and Peleus and the birth of Helen and Judgement of Paris near the outset, presumably treating both episodes as causes of the Trojan War; see Proclus' summary and fr. 1, and the discussion of Currie 2015: 285–7.

Alcaeus drew on myth in a number of poems. In the case of some of them enough survives to indicate that the mythical narrative was not self-standing but illustrated sentiments or events in the here and now; see frs. 38a, 117b, 298. It is conceivable that in this poem, too, the (surviving) myth was preceded by a (lost) non-mythical section; see Rösler 1980: 221–38. However, the play with the mytho-poetic tradition gives the text sufficient point as it stands, and the elaborate ring composition makes the four stanzas a self-contained unit. There is therefore a good chance that it is indeed complete; see further 'Source' and 1n.

Source: *P.Oxy.* x.1233 fr. 2 col. ii.1–16 (2nd cent. AD), edited by Hunt, with *exempli gratia* supplements by Wilamowitz. A *coronis* shows that we have the end of the poem, but the papyrus does not help to decide whether we have the beginning: the text starts at the top of a column; the previous column-end is not preserved.

Metre: Four Sapphic strophes; see on Sa. 1.

Discussions: *Caprioli 2012, *Blondell 2010: 351–9, Pallantza 2005: 22–34, Race 1989, Davies 1986a, Maronitis 2004 [1984], Meyerhoff 1984: 91–113, *Burnett 1983: 190–8, Rösler 1980: 221–38, *Page 1955: 278–81. For poetic treatments of Helen, see esp. Blondell 2013 and Austin 1994; for Thetis, Gantz 1993: 228–31 and March 1987: 1–26.

1–4 *Helen and Troy.* The person addressed as the cause of the Trojans' bitter suffering (πίκρον + lost noun) must be Helen. She was probably named in line 1 or 2. Her specific role may have been left vague: it is possible that κάκων serves to pass moral judgement on her. Page's supplements (π[ύρι δ' was already suggested by Wilamowitz) convey an *exempli gratia* impression of the run of the stanza: ὡς λόγος κάκων ἄ[χος ἔννεκ' ἔργων] | Περράμωι καὶ παῖσ[ι ποτ', Ὤλεν', ἦλθεν] | ἐκ σέθεν πίκρον, π[ύρι δ' ὤλεσε Ζεῦς] | Ἴλιον ἴραν, 'As the story has it, because of wretched deeds bitter grief once came to Priam and his children, Helen, from you, and Zeus destroyed holy Troy with fire.' Pallantza 2005: 28–34 argues that the addressee is Paris, with Helen named in a lost first stanza. However, 5 τεαύταν is difficult if Helen has not been mentioned shortly before; and one expects the connection from 1–4 to 5–14 to be made through Peleus rather than Thetis, and Paris rather than Helen to reappear in 15–16.

1 ὡς λόγος: a common expression, which elsewhere rounds off or parenthetically interrupts rather than introduces a narrative; e.g. *Certamen* 11 ('Hesiod'), Aesch. *Suppl.* 230, *Eum.* 4. If this is the beginning of the poem, ὡς λόγος is a suitably striking means of situating the poem's treatment of myth in a tradition; cf. headnote. Notably, λόγος (but not ὡς λόγος) appears near the beginning of two other compositions about Helen, Stesichorus' palinode ('that λόγος is not true', fr. 91a, probably early in the work), and a piece of which we only have the first three words, Ἐ]λένην ποτε λόγος (Michigan papyrus inv. 3250c recto col. i.5, in a list of lyric and tragic incipits, see Borges and Sampson 2012: 27).

2 For the form Περράμωι, see Sa. 44.16n., for the phrasing cf. formulaic Πρίαμος/μον Πριάμοιό τε παῖδες/ας (4x in *Il.*).

3 ἐκ σέθεν can denote agency or first origin without attribution of agency. Apostrophe of mythical figures is rare in lyric. It here establishes Helen as the topic of the song.

4 Ἴλιον ἴραν: an epic formula, e.g. *Il.* 6.448. Troy perishes despite being sacred. On the sacredness of cities, see Scully 1990: 16–40, and on the interest Lesbians took in nearby Troy see pp. 139–40 below.

5–14 *Thetis, Peleus, Achilles.* The section is introduced as a comparison of Helen with Thetis, but soon develops into a self-standing, rapid account of the wedding and marriage of Peleus and Thetis, which flows across two stanza-breaks and culminates in the birth of Achilles. The detail highlights propriety; see the headnote for omissions that make this possible.

5 τεαύταν ~ τοιαύτην.

Αἰακίδαι[ς: the honorific patronymic refers to Peleus rather than Aiakos' grandson Achilles occasionally already in the *Iliad* (e.g. 18.433), and then does so frequently after Homer. At line-end perhaps ἄκοιτιν (Barkhuizen 1983), 'not such a bride'.

6 The gods' attendance is standard in the frequent representations of the wedding of Peleus and Thetis in song and image; e.g. *Il.* 24.62–3 and the François Vase (*LIMC* s.v. 'Peleus' 212). Here they come at Peleus' invitation. καλέσσαις would fit syntax and metre.

7 ἄγετ' ('led off', viz. 'married') is standard wedding language; see Sa. 44.5n. Peleus collects Thetis from her father's house, as though she were an ordinary bride. Only ἔλων suggests dissonance, hinting at the force he had to use; there may also be a pun on Helen's name (cf. the pun at Aesch. *Ag.* 689–90 ἑλέναυς ἕλανδρος ἑλέ|πτολις).

9 Χέρρωνος: Cheiron is Achilles' tutor; first at *Il.* 11.832, see Robbins 1993. In some versions he hosts Peleus' and Thetis' wedding; see [Apollod.] 3.13.5, cf. Pind. *Nem.* 3.56–7 and Eur. *IA* 700–10.

9–10 ἔλ[υσε δ᾽ − −] | ζῶμα παρθένω (gen.): cf. *Od.* 11.245 λῦσε δὲ παρθενίην ζώνην. As the sense is complete it is impossible to guess what is lost at line-end.

10 The punctuation after παρθένω is in the papyrus. The next sentence was probably concerned with the love or love-making of Peleus and Thetis. E.g. φιλό[τας δ᾽ ἔθαλε (Hunt, Page).

11 Νηρεΐδων ἀρίστ[ας: appropriately, the mother of the 'best of the Achaeans' is the 'best of the Nereids'.

12 ἐς δ᾽ ἐνίαυτον 'and within the year': normally 'for a year', and here too looking at the time that passed as she was pregnant.

13 αἰμιθέων depends on a lost superlative at line-end, e.g. φέριστον. As the son of Thetis and Peleus, Achilles is literally 'half-divine', but in the context the word evokes the destruction of the race of the ἡμίθεοι in the Theban and Trojan Wars (Hes. *WD* 156–73, cf. fr. 204.96–105 MW): Achilles is exceptional, but like the Trojans of 15–16 he died at Troy. Further on the term see Alcm. 1.7n.

14 ὄλβιον ('blessed') raises questions, since Achilles did not live to enjoy wealth or many other blessings.

ξάνθαν ἐλάτη[ρα πώλων: Achilles' horses, one of them called Xanthos, were a wedding gift to Peleus by the gods (*Il.* 16.380–1, etc.). In the *Iliad*, they reach their greatest prominence in the prophecy of his death (19. 404–24). πώλων is near-certain as the only metrically suitable word for 'horse'.

15–16 *Helen and Troy, resumed.*

15 οἰ δ᾽ must be the Trojans, because of πόλις αὔτων. As no supplement meaning 'Trojans' suggests itself, their identity is probably to be understood. Hunt's frequently printed Φρύγες τε is doubtful because the first author known to have conflated Phrygians and Trojans is Aeschylus (fr. 446), as Hall 1988 points out. In any case, the text opens out from its focus on individuals and ends with a bleak reference to the destruction of the Trojans and their city.

ἀμφ᾽ Ἐ[λέναι 'for the sake of Helen'. This and similar expressions are so frequent as to condense emblematically the ever-recurring question of Helen's role: see ἀμφ᾽ Ἑλένηι vel sim. at *Il.* 3.70, 3.91, *Od.* 22.227, Pind. *Pyth.* 11.33–4, *lyr. adesp.* 989 *PMG*; and related phrases at Alc. 283.14, *Il.* 3.157, Hes. *WD* 165, frs. 196.4, 200.11 MW and elsewhere. After the third-person account of Thetis and Peleus, the earlier second person (ἐκ σέθεν) is not resumed.

Alcaeus 129 Voigt

At a pan-Lesbian sanctuary of Hera, Zeus and Dionysus Alcaeus prays for relief from the hardship of exile and curses his rival Pittacus, the current

ruler of Mytilene. Interweaving past, present and future, the song combines
raw immediacy with elaborate self-presentation and self-dramatisation.
The text opens with an account of the establishment of the sanctuary in
the past (1–9). There follows an invocation of the three deities with
a request for delivery (9–12), which soon gives way to a curse on Pittacus
(13–14). The curse in turn prompts a solemn recall of the oath of mutual
loyalty sworn by the speaker, his companions and Pittacus (14–20).
The final section seems to be an account of Pittacus' (perceived) offences,
starting with his perjury (21–?). Asyndeta in 9 and 21 mark the two major
divisions. Our line 1 may well be the beginning of the poem (1–9n.), and
a *coronis* guarantees that 32, four lines below the last legible letters
(Μύρσιλ[), is the end.

Central to the poem's poetic and rhetorical strategy is a carefully constructed voice. The speaker is an exile but unlike in fr. 130b does not
represent himself as cut off. He speaks for the whole *hetaireia*, using plurals
in what is almost certainly a solo-song. What is more, the oath and the
condemnation of Pittacus' actions are expressed with a view to the well-
being of the whole δᾶμος and πόλις rather than in overtly partisan terms,
and the pan-Lesbian perspective of the opening stanzas would not be out
of place in a civic hymn. Throughout, the poem draws on ritual speech:
prayer, curse, oath (sealed with sacrifices).

While there is, therefore, a consistency to the speaker's voice and his
strategy of self-presentation, the linear experience of the text is nevertheless
one of abrupt changes of tone – a solemn opening followed by a curse and
abuse – and of information delayed and withheld. The speaker's presence is
felt from the beginning (the deictics 1 τόδε and 8 τόνδε, the second person 6
σέ), but is initially left undeveloped. He does not use the first person until 10
ἀμμετέρα[ς], and a fuller sense of who he is emerges only from 11–12 ἐκ ...
τῶνδε μόχθων | ἀργαλέας τε φύγας. The history of the *hetaireia*'s interactions
with Pittacus that is necessary for understanding the curse is held back until
the second half. And even at the end, when the scene has fully unfolded,
much is missing: we may never be given Hera's (1, 5–9, 6–7nn.) or Pittacus'
names, are never told quite enough about 14 and 21 κήνων, told rather little
about what went wrong with Pittacus, and even less about the exile
(who (else)? why?). The effect is partly one of tense immediacy, as the
song mimics the speaker's emotions and the turns and twists of his thought.
But there is also a sense that this is a song (that purports to be) directed at
a group of people who share experiences, knowledge and ways of speaking.
It situates itself within the world of Alcaeus' *hetaireia*, and for later audiences
and readers evokes that world.

This is one of several poems in which Alcaeus treats his exile in this
particular precinct: see 130b (where the remoteness of the location is
emphasised), as well as probably 130a and 131, all of them grouped with

129 in Π¹. These poems were evidently read together in later periods, and may well have constituted a recognisable group, and been performed as such, from early on. The same precinct is at the centre also of Sa. 17 (there traced back to the heroic age). Similarities with the 'Strasbourg epode', in which the narrator wishes a catalogue of ills upon a perjurious former comrade, raise the possibility of wider generic or even intertextual connections (Hippon. 115 *IEG*² = Archil. 193 Tarditi, cf. 22–3n.).

Both the precinct and the exile are real. The sanctuary was probably located at Messon near Pyrrha, to the west of the island; see Robert 1960 and Caciagli 2010, and for the less likely alternative of Cape Phokas on the south coast, Quinn 1961 and Picard 1962. Any reconstruction of Alcaeus' life is fraught with uncertainty, but there is no reason to doubt that he suffered one or more spells of exile; apart from the texts above, see esp. Σ on fr. 114 and fr. 306Ae Voigt (= test. 9c Campbell), and the attempts to reconstruct a sequence of events by Forsdyke 2005: 36–48 and Bowie 2007: 32–42. The processes that led to such periods of displacement may have been less formal and less institutionally enforced than the modern term 'exile' suggests. The word φυγή (12) in the first instance means 'flight'; cf. 130b.9n. The inter-*polis* sanctuary would have been a safe place for Alcaeus while he was unable to live in Mytilene.

The general picture of ever-shifting constellations in Mytilene that emerges from both Alcaeus' fragments and later testimonia suggests that the one-time alliance with Pittacus, as well as its eventual disintegration, may also be accepted as historical. By contrast, it is impossible to tell how far we can trust Alcaeus on the circumstances of its break-up and the rights and wrongs. His vilification of Pittacus here and elsewhere needs to be weighed against a later tradition in which Pittacus is a good ruler and a sage (e.g. Sim. 542, Pl. *Prt.* 343a, Aristot. *Pol.* 3.1285a33–40, Diod. Sic. 9. 11–12), and against his own declaration that Pittacus had, at least at one point, popular support (see 20n.). On Pittacus, see Hölkeskamp 1999: 219–26, Visconti 2004, as well as the general literature above, p. 87. See also *carm. pop.* 869 below.

It is possible that the song was performed at the precinct; sanctuaries often had sympotic spaces. However, the repeated use of deictic pronouns (1, 8, 11) and the whole opening section serve to conjure up the sanctuary setting wherever it was performed.

Metre:

```
x – ∪ – x – ∪ ∪ – ∪ –  ‖
x – ∪ – x – ∪ ∪ – ∪ –  ‖
x – ∪ – x – ∪ – x
– ∪ ∪ – ∪ ∪ – ∪ – –  ‖
```

Seven Alcaic strophes. The fourth line runs on from the third, forming a single period, as in the Sapphic strophe (p. 116).

Source: Mostly, *P.Oxy.* xviii.2165 fr. 1 col. i (= Π¹); the smaller *P.Oxy.* xviii.2166c no. 6 (= Π²) preserves a few letters of most lines down to 15, and fills in some minor gaps in Π¹. The text printed here does not record the individual contributions made by each papyrus, or any trivial discrepancies between the two. Both papyri date from the second century AD and were edited by Lobel.

Discussions: Gagné 2013: 218–20, Edmunds 2012, Caciagli 2010, Bachvarova 2007, Kurke 1994, Meyerhoff 1984: 211–18, *Burnett 1983: 158–63, *Rösler 1980: 191–204, Page 1955: 161–9.

1–9 *The precinct.* An account of the establishment, almost certainly in the distant past, of a pan-Lesbian sanctuary and cult of three deities. The speaker addresses Hera (6; cf. 1n.), but this is not (yet) a prayer; in fact the deictics τόδε and τόνδε are directed more at a human than a divine audience. The lines set the scene for the song, and are therefore likely to be the opening; the papyri offer no evidence either way.

1 The opening words cannot be recovered. Gallavotti suggests ὦ πότν]ι̣' Ἥρα, τᾶ<ι>. An address to Hera is conceivable, but not necessary as preparation for 6 σέ (see 5–9n.).

2 εὔδειλον 'well visible' (?); a unique variant of εὐδείελος, Homeric epithet of Ithaca and other islands. The meaning is uncertain: see Braswell on Pind. *Pyth.* 4.76 and García-Ramón 1998–9. The adjective probably goes with τέμενος, or possibly with a word lost at the beginning of the line.

3 ξῦνον 'common', in the first instance to all Lesbians, and therefore (it will turn out) also to the exiled speaker. The precinct is also common to the three deities, but those have not been mentioned yet.

κάτϵσσαν: aor. of what in Attic would be καθίζω. The τέμενος is 'established' first, then altars are set up.

ἐν 'therein', adverbial. βώμοις is acc. obj.

4 ἀθανάτων μακάρων: at 130b.13 the τέμενος similarly belongs to μακάρων ... θέων, but μάκαρ is too frequent in Alcaeus to permit the conclusion that the τέμενος was generally referred to by this term.

5–9 The Lesbians gave three deities their cult titles, viz. established their worship. A triad of Hera, Zeus and Dionysus appears in Sa. 17, which shows that the female deity in 6–7 is Hera. If Hera is not named in 1, the address by titles alone invokes the audience's familiarity with the sanctuary and situates the speaker right before her altar. His presence at the sanctuary is then reinforced by τόνδε.

Even though the triad can be placed within panhellenic religious patterns – Zeus is Hera's husband and Dionysus' father, and Dionysus and Hera occasionally receive joint cult, e.g. in Olympia – this particular triad is not attested elsewhere in Archaic or Classical Greece.

The numerous individual cult titles too combine the common and the uncommon (see below). Exiled from Mytilene, Alcaeus asserts his Lesbian identity by associating himself with this distinctly Lesbian sanctuary. For discussion of the triad, see Caciagli 2010: 228–38, with earlier references.

5 κἀπωνύμασσαν ~ καὶ ἐπωνόμασαν.

ἀντίαον 'of suppliants' (?), probably an equivalent of ἀνταῖος (< ἄντομαι 'beseech'). Π² carries a gloss ἱκέσιον. Sa. 17.9 Δί' ἀντ[ίαον] strongly suggests that this was indeed Zeus's cult epithet, but it assumes particular relevance in this prayer by a helpless exile.

6–7 σὲ ... γενέθλαν combines Anatolian and Greek elements, as suits a Lesbian deity. The title 'origin/mother of all (humans, gods, things)' associates this Hera with Cybele, the Eastern Magna Dea. Αἰολήιαν ('of Aeolus') makes her Greek. Aeolus was an ancestor of the Lesbians; see *h.Apol.* 37, Diod. Sic. 5.81.6. The second-person address to (initially) Hera alone is likely to reflect a pre-eminence within the triad that is appropriate to a Magna Dea figure and is suggested also by Sa. 17, even though Zeus, the patriarchal head of the Greek pantheon, is named first. Cf. also 'queen Hera' (βασίληαν Ἥραν) in Sappho's 'Brothers Poem', and see further Pirenne-Delforge and Pironti 2014, Boedeker 2016 and (more generally) Simon 1997.

6 κυδαλίμαν: in Homer reserved for warriors, but the related κυδρός is used of Hera and other deities close to Zeus; see *LfgrE* s.v. 2.

7 τέρτον ~ τρίτον.

8 κεμήλιον 'god of fawns'(?). The most promising explanation of this unknown epithet is the derivation from κεμάς 'young deer', an animal prominent in Dionysiac cult and myth; see originally Deubner 1982b [1943] 698–700, and for the subsequent discussion Catenacci 2007. The articulation τόνδε κεμήλιον, rather than τὸν δεκε-, is indicated by the accents in Π¹.

9 Ζόννυσσον 'Dionysus'; probably the local version of the name. For the different variants of the name in later Lesbian inscriptions, see Hodot 1990: 43–5; for 'secondary' ζ in the Lesbian papyri, see p. 88 above.

ὠμήσταν 'the raw-eater'. This title is best understood in connection with the eating of raw flesh in Dionysiac myth, and seems to have been ancient in the north-eastern Aegean. A Dionysus ὠμάδιος is attested for Chios, and ἀνθρωπορραίστης ('render of men') for Tenedos; see Euelpis fr. 1 *FHG* (vol. iv, p. 408) and Ael. *NA* 12.34, and for discussion and further references Graf 1985: 74–80 and Henrichs 1978: 144, 150–2. Column ii of *P.Oxy.* LIII.3711 fr. 1, a difficult fragment of an Alcaeus commentary, partially preserves ancient explanations of ὠμηστής, in terms of maenad myth and (possibly) Lesbian prehistory; see Haslam's *editio princeps* and Liberman 1999 on his fr. 306Ea. The bloodthirsty title

takes on extra resonance in a curse, especially a curse on a man who is
abused for inappropriate eating (21, 23–4).

9–12 *Prayer for release from the hardship of exile.* The mode shifts from
a loose apostrophe, addressing Hera, to a formal appeal to all three deities.
Both the request to listen and the hope that the gods will be well disposed
are common in prayers.

9 ἄγ[ι]τ': adverbial ἄγε and ἄγετε are only occasionally addressed to
deities (other than the Muse), e.g. *Od.* 13.386, *h.Dem.* 490, *h.Apol.* 165.
They probably convey urgency. Kretschmer 1917: 256 explains ἄγιτε/ἄγι
(8x in the Lesbian poets) as originating in a crasis of ἄγε and ἴτε.

10 σκέθοντες ~ σχόντες.
ἀμμετέρα[ς]: the Lesbians first called on you here; now *we* do. Who 'we'
are is left to be inferred. This is the first (emphatic) indication that this is
a joint request; several plurals will follow. By contrast, Pittacus is portrayed
as acting alone.

ἄρας: wishes both for help ('prayers'), benefiting the speaker and his
group (11–12), and for harm ('curses'), hurting Pittacus (13–14). On this
ambivalence in the meaning of ἀρά, see Aubriot-Sévin 1992: 293–401.

12 ἀργαλέας... φύγας specifies τῶνδε μόχθων.
ῥ[ύεσθε: the supplement is suggested by 20 ῥύεσθαι; cf. frs. 34.7 Voigt
(34a.7 LP), 350.4. Traces of what is probably a σ above the ρ may indicate
a correction. Lobel therefore considers ϲ[άωτε. Either way, the meaning
must be 'rescue'. Supplying the object 'us' is made easy by the presence of
ἀμμετέρα[ς].

13–14 *Curse on Pittacus.* The request for benevolence and help turns
into a curse on the enemy.

13 τὸν Ὕρραον ... παῖδα 'the son of Hyrrhas'. Ὕρραος is an adjective;
adjectives are common in expressions of parentage in Aeolic Greek; see
Hodot 1990: 211–29. With some variation in the form of the name,
Hyrrhas recurs as Pittacus' father at 298.47 and possibly 383, and is frequent
in the later tradition; see the passages collected as fr. 469 Voigt. Gagné 2013:
216–17 suggests speculatively that this is not a real name but a term of abuse.
πεδ- ~ μετ-.

14 κήνων is difficult. It is best understood as (i) neuter, 'for those
things'. The Erinys, traditional protector of oaths (*Il.* 19.258–62, Hes. *WD*
803–4), should persecute Pittacus for the suffering he has inflicted on
Alcaeus and his group; see Rösler 1980: 198–200, Hutchinson *ad loc.*
The alternative (ii) is to take κήνων as masculine, the Erinys 'of those
men'. The Erinys represents the curse of the victims (cf. *Od.* 11.280,
Aesch. *Sept.* 70), viz. *hetairoi* of Alcaeus (one is led to assume) who died
or suffered as a result of Pittacus' behaviour. (i) is easier than (ii) because
'those things' can loosely refer back to the μόχθοι and φύγα, whereas
Pittacus' victims have not been mentioned.

14–20 *The past oath of alliance.* Many ancient oaths amount to a self-curse that comes into effect if the oath is violated; see Sommerstein and Torrance 2014: chs. 1 (Sommerstein) and 2 (Konstantinidou). Therefore the implication here is that the preceding curse (13–14) is an inevitable consequence of the violation of the oath Pittacus had sworn. The lengthy paraphrase of the oath has two functions: it serves to parade the exemplary heroic value of Alcaeus and his *hetairoi*, and it is configured in such a way as to make Pittacus look maximally perjurious. He evidently is no longer allied with Alcaeus' *hetairoi* (violating the undertaking of 15–16), he (allegedly) harms the city (23–4, violating 20), and he may have made common cause with those he undertook to fight (25–8(n.), violating 17–19). Alcaeus probably spoke of Pittacus' oath in other poems too; see fr. 306g Voigt (306(9) LP) and perhaps frs. 67 and 167.

14 ὤς ποτ' 'since once'.

15 τόμοντες must refer to the slaughter and mutilation of animals that ritually reinforces the swearing of oaths; see LSJ s.v. τέμνω II.1 and 2, Faraone 1993: 65–72, Parker 2011: 156–8. The object may be ἄμφ[εν-'throat(s)' (~ αὐχέν-, attested at Theoc. 30.28). At the end of the line one wants an infinitive such as 'to betray', governed by ἀπώμνυμεν, as are 18 κείσεσθ' and 20 ῥύεσθαι.

17 γᾶν ἐπιέμμενοι: a solemn phrase. For the topos of earth as a garment of the dead, see e.g. Pind. *Nem.* 11.16, Aesch. *Ag.* 872, and further Wærn 1951: 19–26.

18 ὐπ' 'at the hands of', with θάνοντες.

ἐπικ´ην (two letters missing) has defied supplementation. A third person plural is needed. ἐπικρέτην (who 'were in power') does not appear to fit the space.

19 ἤπειτα ~ ἤ ἔπειτα 'or else'. Victory is more remote than death in this fierce oath.

20 δᾶμον ὐπὲξ ἀχέων ῥύεσθαι, reinforced by 23–4, implies that Alcaeus and his group fight on behalf of the community at large, and through the reminiscence of 11–12 ἐκ ... μόχθων ... ῥ[ύεσθε suggests that they share a predicament with the community at large. By contrast, in fr. 348 Alcaeus complains that the citizens installed Pittacus as ruler, 'all of them greatly praising him'. The chronology is uncertain, but it is clear that the attitude of the populace towards Pittacus is of substantial importance, rhetorically and actually. See also frs. 130b.6–7 and 70.12. On the uncertain question as to what parts of the population were included in the Archaic δῆμος, see Donlan 1970.

21–?32 *Pittacus' offences.*

21–2 κήνων ... θῦμον: another difficult κήνων, probably 'Pot-Belly (ὁ φύσγων) did not talk to his heart about those things', viz. did not take the things he swore to heart. The genitive depends on διελέξατο | πρὸς θῦμον, and is best explained as analogous to genitives with verbs expressing concern for something/somebody, e.g. φροντίζω, μέλει μοι. For people conversing with their θῦμος, see e.g. *Il.* 17.90 and Archil. 128, and for the phrasing cf. the formula ἀλλὰ τίη μοι ταῦτα φίλος διελέξατο θυμός (5x in *Il.*). Gallavotti 1942: 178 and Deubner 1982b [1943]: 700–1 suggest (roughly), 'Pot-Belly did not talk to the heart of those people', viz. did not take an interest in those who suffered because of his behaviour. The genitive is simpler, but the notion of talking to the θῦμος of somebody else, let alone somebody dead, is strange. For other constructions, see Gentili and Catenacci 2007: 183–4, who themselves advocate a (problematic) partitive genitive with φύσγων, 'Among those people, Pot-Belly did not...'

21 φύσγων: over-eating is a stock theme of abuse (e.g. Hippon. 118, 128). Here the invective language condenses the emotional charge of the accusations and characterises Pittacus' behaviour as self-debasing. The theme is developed by δάπτει | τὰν πόλιν; cf. 9n. (ὠμήσταν). An ancient list of abusive terms which Alcaeus directed at Pittacus includes the food-related γάστρων 'Belly' and ζοφοδορπίδας 'Diner-in-the-Dark' (Diog. Laert. 1.81 = Alc. 429). Across his output, Alcaeus seems to have turned Pittacus into a recognisable stock character, as Archilochus did with Lycambes and Aristophanes with Cleon. Further on Alcaeus' invective against Pittacus, see Davies 1985, Andrisano 1994, Kurke 1994. The term may have been in use as a nickname more widely; Edmunds 2012 points to its appearance on a dedicatory pot of the sixth century BC (*IG* IV.322), there apparently without opprobrious connotation. There is a case for amending to φύσκων, the spelling found in all other texts, including the list in Diog. Laert.

22 βραϊδίως 'recklessly', 'without a second thought' (~ ῥαιδίως); continuing from διελέξατο | πρὸς θῦμον.

22–3 πόσιν | [ἔ]μβαις ἐπ' ὀρκίοισι: for the metaphor of trampling oaths underfoot, see *Il.* 4.157 ὥς σ' ἔβαλον Τρῶες, κατὰ δ' ὅρκια πιστὰ πάτησαν (of Pandarus' wounding of Menelaus during the truce) and ?Hippon. 115.15 λ[ὰ]ξ δ' ἐπ' ὀρκίοις ἔβη; and further Masson 1951: 434–8. Despite the use of a less aggressive verb here, those parallels support the standard interpretation against the alternative suggestion that Alcaeus is referring to a (well-attested) type of oath-swearing ceremony in which the oath was reinforced by the act of stepping on the bloodied victims, a ritual Pittacus is accused of undertaking without serious intent (βραϊδίως); thus Faraone 1993: 70, similarly Caciagli 2009c. Plural ὅρκια, rather than ὅρκος, is used in particular for reciprocal agreements; see Cohen 1980.

23–4 δάπτει | τὰν πόλιν 'mauls the city'. The same expression occurs at 70.7 δαπτέτω πόλιν ὡς καὶ πεδὰ Μυρσί[λ]ῳ, again of Pittacus. It likens Pittacus to predators who tear apart and devour their prey (e.g. *Il.*

11.481, 16.159). He is wild and self-seeking. πόλιν picks up 20 δᾶμον, and δάπτει develops 21 φύσγων. Further on the motif, which goes back to Achilles' stigmatising of Agamemnon as δημοβόρος (Il. 1.231), see Fileni 1983. See also PMG 869 below.

24 ἄμμι ~ ἡμῖν. The second half of the line is very difficult to reconstruct.

25–8 Only guesswork is possible. οὐ κὰν (~ κατὰ) νόμον may accuse Pittacus of offending against what is right. γλαύκας (and the traces that follow) would suit Athena, but she is hardly expected here.

28 Μύρσιλ[ο will be Myrsilus, apparently one-time ruler of Mytilene and another hate figure of Alcaeus'. His pairing with Pittacus at fr. 70.7 (quoted 23–4n.) raises the possibility that the reference here accuses Pittacus of defecting to the enemy camp; cf. 14–20n. The matter is complicated by 18 τότ', which indicates that the enemy then is not the enemy now; see Hutchinson on 21. Perhaps Myrsilus is indeed dead now (as he is in fr. 332), but nevertheless mentioned as the then enemy in whose favour Pittacus had left the sworn alliance. Further on the shadowy figure Myrsilus, see Liberman 1999: xviii–xix and Dale 2011a.

Nothing recognisable survives of 29–32, other than the *coronis* below 32.

Alcaeus 130b Voigt

Expelled from the *polis*, Alcaeus lives at or near a countryside precinct. The way this life is presented changes considerably as the poem unfolds. We have (parts of) all lines; see 1, 21–4nn.

The shrine, and Alcaeus' exile at it, are evidently those of Alc. 129: both precincts are called τέμενος (130b.13, 129.2); both are dedicated to multiple gods (130b.13 μακάρων . . . θέων, 129.4 ἀθανάτων μακάρων); both belong to the Lesbians together (130b.17 Λε[σβί]αδες, 129.1 Λέσβιοι). On the shrine and the historical situation, see p. 94 and 129.5–9n. However, while both poems are born from the same circumstances, the poetic treatment is different and they invite reading side by side; see further pp. 93–4.

The poem has a complex temporal structure, articulated by the persistent use of verbs of living. The speaker starts by lamenting in the present tense a wretched existence away from civilisation, 1–2 ἔγω | ζώω. When he returns to the present with 16 οἴκημι, he lives at a pan-Lesbian sanctuary: the same life and same location, but viewed very differently. In between, he uses (inceptive) aorists to narrate his arrival in this place. The likeliest reconstruction of the fragmentary text in that middle section is perhaps that the arrival too is presented in two stages: 10 ἐοίκησα(α) in a sentence about settling down for (possibly) an unwarlike life away from the city is taken up by 14 ἐοίκησ[α] in a sentence about settling at the sanctuary.

The transition from what was forced upon him to what (within limits) he chose is helped by a further doublet; 9 φεύγων is taken up by 11 φεύγων, the first in a statement of expulsion, the second probably performing a shift towards a proclamation of the speaker's chosen stance: he avoids war and *stasis*.

The resulting sequence may be expressed as an ABB'A'C structure.

A (1–9) I lead a miserable life, driven away from the political institutions in which my ancestors participated.

B (9–12) I settled in the outmost regions, avoiding war.

B' (13–?14) I settled in a sanctuary.

A' (?15–20) There I live, keeping out of trouble. An annual pan-Lesbian festival takes place at the sanctuary (possibly now).

C (21–4) I hope the gods will release me some day (reconstruction very uncertain).

The misery of exile and displacement is a frequent theme in early Greek poetry; see Tyrt. 10.3–12, Sol. 36.10–12, Thgn. 332a–4, 1211–16; and in general Bowie 2007. Alcaeus' poem stands out for the varied and evocative description of the speaker's life away from the *polis*. Pervasive bitterness mingles with an emphasis on innocence and indeed propriety. The tone is set by the opening word, ἄγνος (probably). Bitterness and a sense of propriety combine suggestively in the festival witnessed by the speaker. On the one hand, the festival is a desperately inadequate substitute for participation in political life, all the more so as the rituals described in 17–20 are female; on the other, it serves as an emblem of the speaker's 'pure' existence. The prayer for divine help that may have occupied the final stanza would be well prepared. Further on the sacred setting, see Nagy 1993. Alcaeus seems to have exploited a similar contrast between his exile and a Lesbian festival in fr. 296b; see Spelman 2014.

Like 129 (p. 94), this song may or may not have been performed at the sanctuary. Even though Alcaeus' *hetairoi* are the likely first audience, the theme of displacement as well as the pan-Lesbian shrine give it broader appeal.

Source: *P.Oxy.* XVIII.2165 fr. 1 col. ii.9–32 + fr. 2 col. ii.1 (= Π); 2nd cent. AD, ed. Lobel. The same papyrus preserves fr. 129. Lines 9–11 (ὡς ... πόλεμον) are also preserved by *P.Oxy.* LIII.3711 fr. 1 col. ii.31–3; see *ad loc.*

Metre:

× × – ⏑ ⏑ – – ⏑ ⏑ – ⏑ – ?‖ gl^c
× × – ⏑ ⏑ – – ⏑ ⏑ – ⏑ – ‖ gl^c
× × – ⏑ ⏑ – ⏑ – – ?‖ *hipp*
× – ⏑ ⏑ – – ⏑ ⏑ – ⏑ – ‖‖ tl^c (= $_\wedge gl^c$)   ὦ_Ἀγε-

Two glyconics with choriambic expansion ('asclepiads') set the basic rhythm. They are followed by a hipponactean (same opening, different ending) and then a telesillean with choriambic expansion (same ending, different opening).

Discussions: *Ferrari 2016, Edmunds 2012, De Cristofaro 2005, Cavallini 2003, Andrisano 2001, *Burzacchini 1994, Kurke 1994, Nagy 1993, Burzacchini 1985, *Rösler 1980: 272–85, Burzacchini 1976, *Page 1955: 197–209.

1–9 *A miserable life, away from the city.*

1 Although preceded by several lines of text in the papyrus, which are not marked off with a *coronis*, this must be the beginning of the poem since the metre of what precedes (= Alc. 130a) is different.
The text is very uncertain. (i) If the horizontal stroke through the iota in ἄγνοις is a cancellation, intended to yield ἄγνος, Alcaeus describes himself as 'pure as regards my modes of life', an arresting phrase in the context of wretched exile, and at first almost mysterious. Interpretation becomes possible gradually: pure as he stays clear of the activities in the malfunctioning *polis* (7), of war and of strife (9–12), lives at a shrine (13–14), witnesses a festival (15–20). The reading is supported by Hor. *Odes* 1.22.1 *integer uitae scelerisque purus*, which would be an allusion. It is difficult to complete . . ις satisfactorily, and a separate stroke, sloping leftwards from the bottom of the iota, is left unexplained, but this is nevertheless the least unsatisfactory option; see Burzacchini 1985. (ii) If ἄγνοις (acc. pl.) is kept, it is a predicative qualification of βιότοις, '(I live?) my life as a pure one.' Horace's putative appropriation becomes looser, and both strokes are left unexplained. Completion of . .ις remains a challenge. (3) Ferrari 2016: 473–5 proposes ἀγνώστοις βιότοις τλαίς (τλαίς Hutchinson), 'enduring unknown modes of life. . .' He interprets the stroke stretching from the bottom of the ι in ἄγνοις towards the bottom of the ο as a correction which joins the two letters to turn them into ω. However, the instance of οι corrected to ω that he compares looks different.

βιότοις: the plural for one individual's life is unusual.

ὁ τάλαις ἔγω 'this wretched man that is me'. This idiom is less common and more marked in lyric than in tragedy, but cf. already *Il.* 22.59 πρὸς δ᾽ ἐμὲ τὸν δύστηνον. The song starts with a strong focus on the lone speaker, while the location is left vague until 13 τέμ[ε]νος. This is in contrast to fr. 129 (τόδε . . . τέμενος).

2 Life as a rustic has befallen the speaker as his μοῖρα; it is not his own doing. This is a despised sort of life; cf. the scorn for the lack of sophistication of a country-girl in Sa. 57.

3–7 The speaker imagines first a better place (the *polis* and political life) and then a better time (that of his father and grandfather, who participated in that life). The contrast characterises the here and now.

3–5 ἀγόρας ... καὶ β[ό]λλας (~ βουλῆς) 'assembly and council'. Those were probably more confined to the elite and less formalised than in fifth-century Athens; see Stein-Hölkeskamp 1989: 100–3. Presumably the meetings were held in Mytilene rather than at the sanctuary; Alcaeus does not even hear the heralds.

4 καρυ[ζο]μένας ~ κηρυσσομένης.

ὦ Ἀγεσιλαΐδα: Agesilaidas is unknown to us. There is a tension between the presence of an addressee (whether real or fictional) and the loneliness expressed in the poem. A further contrast is created by the etymology of the name (ἡγεῖσθαι, λαός).

5 τά: probably a loose reference ('these things') to the assemblies and councils, viz. to political participation. On this reading the sentence is complete after 7 πολίταν; and 8 τούτων is another reference back to 'those things'. The alternative view is to take τά as antecedent of τούτων, 'what my father..., from those things...' Punctuation at the end of 7 would be light, and the main clause in 8 would start with ἔγω[γ']. That reconstruction would account for the lack of punctuation after πολίταν in the papyrus and create a tighter construction. However, such pronounced subordination would be unusual for Alcaeus.

πάτηρ καὶ πάτερος πάτηρ: the repetition expresses the long tradition, now deplorably interrupted. The forefathers loom large in Alcaeus' songs; see 6.13–18, 72.13, 339, 371, 394.

6 καγγεγήρασ': the text may not be correct. The perfect stem γέγηρα is unparalleled (Homer only has aor. ἐγήρα, later one finds γεγήρακα), and the papyrus reading itself is uncertain. See Hamm 1957: §232.

τωνδέων (~ τῶνδε)... **πολίταν:** the deictic 'these' either expresses the vividness with which the hateful citizens appear before the speaker's mental eye, or refers to the citizens' presence at the sanctuary because the annual festival is currently taking place (13–20n.); for the latter suggestion, see D'Alessio 2018: 44, and cf. 15 ταύταις (text uncertain). For the unique form τωνδέων, cf. Homeric τοίσδεσ(σ)ι.

7 ἀλλαλοκάκων 'inflicting harm on one another', a *hapax*. The implication is that the speaker is not involved in this civil strife; cf. 11 στάσιν. The rhetoric of fr. 129 is different; see esp. lines 17–20.

8 ἔγω: the emphatic first person continues.

ἀπελήλαμαι: ἀπελαύνειν is used to refer to exclusion from political life also in later texts; e.g. Lys. 18.5, Isocr. 9.66.

9 φεύγων ἐσχατίαισ' 'as an exile in the outmost region'. We do not know how formal this banishment was; cf. p. 94. Similar terminology occurs at 129.12, 131.2. For the dative of place, cf. Soph. *Phil.* 144. The alternative is to read accusative ἐσχατίαις, and translate 'keeping clear of the frontiers (viz. of the *polis* territory)'. But Alc. 328 ἐπ' ἐσχατίαισιν οἴκεις suggests that the ἐσχατιαί are where the speaker lives rather than what he must avoid.

9–12 *Settling in the wilderness, avoiding war and strife.*

9–11 ὡς δ' ... πόλεμον: perhaps 'Like Onomakles the Athenian, I settled (here) as a spear-shunner, avoiding the war.' The speaker describes the change from his customary life of warfare to his current passive existence. The marked *hapax* ἀλυκαιχμίαις (< ἀλύσκω + αἰχμή; nom. sg.), and the provocative comparison with an enemy, probably serve to underline the extraordinary nature of this change. However, both text and interpretation are very uncertain. Hesych. λι369 has the word λυκαιμίας, and many modern editors divide -κησα λυκαιχμίαις ('wolf-fighter'?). The attraction of putative ἀλυκαιχμίαις is that φεύγων τὸν πόλεμον becomes a gloss of the difficult coinage that precedes. ἐοίκησα without an object raises questions; some editors therefore understand (ἀ)λυκαιχμίαις as acc. pl. Arguably, though, ἐσχατίαισ' makes it easy enough to supply 'there'/ 'here'; cf. Soph. *OC* 92. For the establishment of the text, with the help of a quotation in the scholarly text *P.Oxy.* LIII.3711 = *CLGP* Alcaeus no. 16, see Haslam 1986: 123–4. For the particular word-division and interpretation adopted here, see Porro 1989 and 1994: 176–81. For different proposals, see Burzacchini 1994: 32–4, Rodríguez Somolinos 1994, Bowie 2007: 36–40, Caciagli 2009a, Ferrari 2016: 477–8.

9–10 Ὀνυμακλέης | Ὠθάναος: unknown, and therefore probably contemporary rather than mythological; perhaps a well-known recluse. Athens features elsewhere in Alcaeus' work in so far as he portrays his participation in the conflict between Mytilene and Athens over Sigeum in the Troad; see Alc. 401ab Voigt = 428ab LP (where, tantalisingly, he seems to have described himself as escaping battle).

11 φεύγων τὸν πόλεμον will at first suggest cowardliness (e.g. *Od.* 14.213 φυγοπτόλεμος), before the next sentence explains (γάρ) this behaviour as in fact prudent. φεύγων repeats the opening of 9, but the object changes the meaning: rather than lamenting exclusion from what he wants, the speaker now says that he is avoiding what he does not want. This sets the tone for what follows, esp. 16.

11–12 στάσιν ... ὀννέλην; 'for is it not better to do away with strife against ... ?' As in 7, the speaker distances himself from civil discord. The question mark is adopted tentatively; it changes Π's punctuation of the sentence as a statement, which would require either emending to ὀννέχην (~ ἀνέχειν, 'sustain', Vogliano) or, irregularly, giving ὀννέλην (= ἀνελεῖν) the meaning 'take up'; contrast Pind. fr. 109.3 στάσιν ... ἀνελών 'removing strife' (from the mind). Again the text is very uncertain: the metre indicates corruption (which could be addressed e.g. with Page's οὐ κάλλιον), and no obvious supplement has been found for the beginning of the line; πρὸς κρέ[σσονα]ς would have to assume an unusually formed ε.

13–20 *Arrival and life at the sanctuary; annual festival.* It turns out that the speaker has made his home at a shrine frequented by the women of Lesbos. The section probably starts with his arrival at the shrine in the past (13–?14); see pp. 100–1. It ends with the description of an annual festival at the shrine (17–20). The textual difficulties in 15 make it impossible for us to tell whether the festival is said to be taking place at the moment. In any case, however, the passage evokes an image of the speaker at (or near) the festival.

14 μελαίνας ἐπίβαις χθόνος 'stepping onto the black earth' suggests making landfall. The speaker seems to have made the journey from Mytilene by boat. At Sa. 17.6–7 the Atridae arrive at the same sanctuary by sea, coming from Troy. For 'black earth', see Sa. 16.2n.

15 συνόδοισι 'gatherings', a suitable word both for a festival (see Thuc. 3.104.3, LSJ s.v. 1.2) and for a *hetaireia* (see Sol. 4.22, LSJ s.v. 1.1). It probably refers to the annual event described in 17–20, but Alcaeus adopts language that brings out the contrast with his former political life.

ταύταις: the text is very uncertain. This is the original reading in Π. It would create the strong sense that the festival is taking place now ('those gatherings'); cf. 6n. The first τ was subsequently changed by a different hand to μ. Many editors therefore print μ' αὔταις; this is possible but the position late in the sentence of the enclitic με (unusual, though not unparalleled), together with uncertainty over what αὔταις would mean here, raises questions; see Ferrari 2000b: 237. Ferrari 2016: 482–3 argues for χλίδ[αις δ' ἐ]ν συνόδοισιν αὔταις 'luxuriating in the very midst of the festive gatherings' (suppl. Kamerbeek, Koster).

16 κάκων ἔκτος ἔχων πόδας is an idiom; cf. [Aesch.] *PV* 263–4 πημάτων ἔξω πόδα | ἔχει and Braswell on Pind. *Pyth.* 4.289.

17–20 The festival contrasts with the assembly and council the speaker longed for at the beginning of the poem. The actors are female rather than male, the sound is that of ὀλολυγαί rather than heralds. The beauty contest is referred to in later sources; see Voigt's apparatus here, and Caciagli 2016: 428–9, 433–4. The ὄ]χλος | παρθέ[νων … γ]υναίκων at Sa. 17. 13–14, with reference to the same shrine, may or may not evoke the same festival.

18 πώλεντ' may refer to a procession.

ἐλκεσίπεπλοι: Sa. 57.3 'not knowing how to draw up (ἔλκην) her rags over the ankle' suggests the interpretation 'drawing up the robe' rather than 'trailing the robe', which is also more in keeping with the dances that are likely to be part of the festival programme; see *LfgrE* s.v.

19 ἄχω θεσπεσία 'wondrous reverberating sound': a variation on the Homeric formula ἠχῆι θεσπεσίηι. The expression appears also at Sa. 44.27, of *parthenoi* singing in a wedding procession, and at [Hes.] *Scut.* 279, of wedding music. It may activate the often dormant derivation of θεσπέσιος from θεός and ἐνέπειν ('divinely sounding').

20 ἴρα[ς ὀ]λολύγας depends on ἄχω, and has in turn γυναίκων depend on it. The ὀλολυγή is an emotional and often joyful female shout, typically in ritual settings; see e.g. Sa. 44.31, Aesch. *Sept.* 268 (ὀλολυγμὸν ἱερόν), and the discussion in Deubner 1982a [1941], Collins 1995, Karanika 2009.

21–4 There is little to go on. The speaker may be returning to his predicament, but now, after two stanzas about the sanctuary and the festival, expressing the wish that one day (πότα) the gods (reading 22 Ὀλύμπιοι) will release him from it. A *coronis* in Π indicates that this is the end of the poem.

Alcaeus 140 Voigt

The surviving text has two parts, and depends for its effect on the discrepancy between them: an expansive and intensely visual catalogue of arms displayed inside a building, and a brief first-person plural statement about 'this (unspecified) task'. We probably have the end but may not have the beginning (1, 13–14nn.).

Epic arming scenes regularly describe panoplies, and indeed the language of the fragment is more than usually epic; see Hooker 1977: 42–3. Moreover, the weapons are described in terms that are compatible not just with the hoplite panoply of Alcaeus' day but also with Homeric weaponry; see Del Freo 1993, and in general on the relationship between Homeric and historical hoplite weaponry, Snodgrass 1964, van Wees 1994, Schwartz 2009: ch. 2. However, these similarities with epic throw into relief a difference, which makes this catalogue unusual and arresting. Whereas arming scenes portray arms at the point of use, here they are offered for contemplation, ready to use but not in use. The effect is enhanced if 2 Ἄρηι κεκόσμηται alludes to dedication of arms in a shrine; cf. *ad loc.*, and see the discussions of Bonanno 1990: 125–46 and Cirio 1995 (who, however, go too far when they suggest an actually sacred setting), and for dedications of arms in temples, Aesch. *Ag.* 578–9, *Sept.* 478–9, Eur. *Hcld.* 695–9, each sharing phrasing with fr. 140.

The tone changes sharply in the final stanza. The users of the arms – 'we', Alcaeus and his *hetaireia* – enter (or re-enter) the poem. Ecphrasis and display give way to a determined focus on the task in hand, and the catalogue is retrospectively recast as one of objects that must and will be used. There is not, however, an immediate call to arms.

In sympotic performance, the 'great house' of the song will interact with the dining room that is the venue, and the warlike ethos of the song will interact with the peaceful ideology that characterises the *symposion*. In this respect the text may be contrasted with more conventional pieces such as

Xenophanes 1. Arms could have a place in banqueting halls, as in Odysseus' palace (*Od.* 16.284–90, 19.4–34) and the Lydian 'men's halls' at Hdt. 1.34.3, but here they become the only thing one sees, overwhelming in their abundance (παῖσα, κρύπτοισιν (with 6–7n.), πόλλα). **Source:** Athen. 14.627a–b. The text is quoted in the course of a discussion of the relationship between bravery and music. Even though μουσικώτατος, Athenaeus' character says, Alcaeus was unduly πολεμικός. This poem, with its catalogue of arms, is presented as a case in point in so far as 'it might in fact have been more appropriate for his house to be full of musical instruments'.

Our text of Athenaeus for this poem is derived from MS A. The epitome quotes only the first few words, as does Eustathius (*Il.* p. 1320.1–2). For Athenaeus' MSS, see p. 257. Two slim papyrus snippets, *P.Oxy.* XXI.2295 fr. 1 (Π¹, 1st cent. AD) and *P.Oxy.* XXI.2296 fr. 4 (Π², 1st/2nd cent. AD), preserve a few letters from a handful of lines and help correct minor errors in Athenaeus' text.

Metre:

− × − ∪ ∪ − ∪ −   *gl*

× × − ∪ ∪ − ∪ − × − ∪ − ||| *gl ia*   8 βέλεος, 10 κόϊλαι

Seven mini-stanzas, each consisting of a glyconic followed by another glyconic and an iamb. The layout of the two papyri shows that the Alexandrian edition broke the stanza after nine rather than eight syllables, i.e. *hi*, followed by *tl ia*. The modern analysis brings out better the regularity of the metre and takes better account of the word-divisions, but either way there is no marked break within the stanza.

Discussions: Fearn 2018: 102–6, Clay 2016: 204–7, *Spelman 2015, *Caciagli 2014, Clay 2013, Marzullo 2009, Cirio 1995 (similarly Cirio 2001), Colesanti 1995, Del Freo 1993, *Bonanno 1990: 125–46 (similarly Bonanno 1976), Latacz 1990: 247–54, Rösler 1980: 148–58, Maurach 1968, *Page 1955: 209–23.

1 Π¹ has illegible remnants of a further line immediately above line 1. Since both margins are missing, we cannot tell if there was a *coronis* (marking the end of a poem). The connecting particle δέ makes it more likely than not that the preceding text was part of the same poem, but we cannot be certain since δέ occasionally appears at the beginning of poems; see *carm. conv.* 892.1n.

μαρμαίρει: in Homer, weapons commonly gleam as warriors advance on the battlefield. Alcaeus translates the image and its connotations of fighting-strength to the stationary and artificially lit interior of the 'great house'. It will remain active throughout the whole song, reinforced by adjectives (λάμπραισιν, λεῦκοι, χάλκιαι, λάμπραι).

μέγας δόμος ('great house') is non-specific, unless the lost opening or the performance context provided further information. The phrase resembles the epic formula μέγα δῶμα, usually a royal palace, occasionally the residence of a god, i.e. a temple. Cf. 'Source'.

2 χάλκωι: bronze is the weapon material *par excellence* in Homer, and χαλκός can by itself signify various weapons; see LSJ s.v. II.1. In the Archaic period, when iron was used for offensive weapons such as spears and swords, bronze continued to be the metal of choice for helmets, the outer shell of (otherwise wooden) shields and much of the body armour including greaves. But bronze items are not weapons as a matter of course, especially within a house; e.g. Critias 2.8 'bronze, which decorates the house (κοσμεῖ δόμον) for any use'. Alcaeus is playing with expectations.

Ἄρηι κεκόσμηται 'has been decorated for Ares'. The phrase expresses both reverence for the god and, metonymically, readiness for war. Ἄρηι is an epicism. The Lesbian form is the metrically unsuitable Ἄρευι (Alc. 400.2 and probably Sa. 111.5).

στέγα: probably 'roof, ceiling' rather than 'room', thus producing a movement from the ceiling (2–6) via the walls (6–8) to the floor (9–12).

3–6 *Crested helmets.* The horse-hair crest is standard in Homer, codified in the formula δεινὸν δὲ λόφος καθύπερθεν ἔνευεν. However, the sharp distinction between Homer's 'plumes' and Archaic fixed crests that Page 1955: 212–13 makes is unwarranted: 'nodding from above' also suits some historical crests documented in the iconographic record, especially those of a forward-curving type; cf. the shaking of a λόφος at Alc. 388 and Tyrt. 11.26.

3 λάμπραισιν κυνίαισι: cf. *Il.* 17.269 λαμπρῇσιν κορύθεσσι, and for the whole sequence *Il.* 13.132–3 = 16.216–17 (of a tight battle-line) ψαῦον δ' ἱππόκομοι κόρυθες λαμπροῖσι φάλοισι | νευόντων, ὡς πυκνοὶ ἐφέστασαν ἀλλήλοισιν.

3–4 κὰτ | τᾶν ~ καθ' ὧν.

4 λεῦκοι: 'shining' as much as 'white'.

κατέπερθεν as equivalent of the standard καθύπερθε(ν) has not been satisfactorily explained, but is the reading of both papyri and is confirmed by fr. 208.15 ἔπερθα.

5–6 κεφάλαισιν ... ἀγάλματα continues the emphasis on splendour and serves as a reminder that all this equipment is there for wearing.

6–8 *Greaves* were worn by Homeric as well as historical fighters. They were important because the hoplite shield left the legs unprotected.

χάλκιαι ... κνάμιδες: cf. *Il.* 7.41 χαλκοκνήμιδες.

6–7 πασσάλοις (acc.) | **κρύπτοισιν περικείμεναι:** the greaves are so large, or so many, that one cannot see the nails on which they are arranged.

8 ἔρκος ... βέλεος 'defence against ... missiles', another apposition that points to the use of the equipment. The *Iliad* applies ἔρκος ... βέλεων

(5.316) and ἕρκος ἀκόντων (4.137, 15.646) variously to a bunched up robe, a belt (?), and a shield.

9 *Linen cuirasses.* Iconographic evidence suggests that they were used in Greece from at least the early sixth century as an alternative to the standard bronze cuirass, and in the guise of the epithet λινοθώρηξ they appear in two disputed Iliadic passages (2.529, 2.830). See Aldrete *et al.* 2013.

10 *Shields.* Cf. Tyrt. 19.7 and Mimn. 13a.2 κοίλης ἀσπίσι. 'Hollow' is appropriate for the concave round hoplite shield. Homeric shields are not called 'hollow', but neither are they flat. The catalogue comes to an end without ever mentioning the spear, a prominent weapon of both the Homeric and the Archaic warrior. Spears may not be visually imposing enough, as well as too normal: until 600 BC, they are often included in representations of civilian dress; see van Wees 1998b: 352–8.

κὰτ . . . **βεβλήμεναι** indicates a shift from walls to floor, even though syntactically ἄσπιδες is a further subject of 6–7 πασσάλοις | κρύπτοισιν. The image seems to be one of careless plenty ('tossed down'); contra LSJ s.v. II.3.

11 *Swords from Chalcis.* Euboea seems to have been known for its swords. See Aesch. fr. 356 *TrGF* and (perhaps) Archil. 3, and for Chalcis as an early centre of steel metallurgy, Bakhuizen 1977. The audience will have understood these swords as made of iron (cf. 2n.), but at the same time Χαλκι-keeps alive the bronze theme.

πάρ ~ πάρεισι 'there are', 'are ready'.

σπάθαι 'blades': *pars pro toto* referring to entire swords.

12 *Belts (?) and chitons.*

ζώματα: probably belts (for tying either the linen cuirasses or the κυπάσσιδες?); cf. 42.10. But the term, which occurs also in Homer, is rare and its meaning uncertain. See Page 1955: 220–1, Jarva 1995: 41, Marzullo 2009: 126–7.

κυπάσσιδες: a form of chiton, presumably worn underneath the corselet. See Gow 1955. It is not found in Homer.

13–14 Lit. 'These things cannot be forgotten, as a result of that moment when we originally took on this task.' ἐπεί-clauses that follow their main clause are normally causal, and some causal force is likely to be felt despite the temporal πρώτιστα; cf. *Il.* 19.9. In general on the effect of these lines, see the headnote. The focus on a shared task would make this a good conclusion to the song. The lack of detail about the nature of the (evidently military) task would create a (genuine or imagined) sense of knowledge shared among a closed group. There is also a metapoetic dimension: this song itself ensures that the arms are not forgotten.

14 ὑπὰ ἔργον: the hiatus is often amended, perhaps rightly. It is best defended as a further epic-looking feature: in Homer the digamma in (ϝ)έργον is metrically present in the majority of cases, e.g. formulaic μέγα ἔργον. See further Sa. 31.9n.

ἔσταμεν: either aorist ἔστᾱμεν (~ ἔστημεν) or perfect ἔστᾱμεν (~ ἐστήκαμεν); see Hamm 1957: §232. The perfect would emphasise that the undertaking is still in place. ὐπά . . . ἔσταμεν is an instance of 'tmesis'. The term ('cutting') is historically inaccurate. Preverb (here ὐπά) and verb were originally separate, before they merged into compounds; see Horrocks 1981. However, this process predates the surviving lyric poets, for whom tmesis therefore was a feature of traditional poetic style rather than ordinary language.

Alcaeus 347 Voigt

The beginning of a drinking song that recasts for effect Hesiod's instructions for the midsummer heat (*WD* 582–96), as well as (probably) interacting with other traditions.

The *Works and Days* passage is set out below. The indexed numbers indicate the lines of Alc. 347 that correspond to the underlined phrases.

Ἦμος δὲ ⁴σκόλυμός τ' ἀνθεῖ καὶ ³ἠχέτα τέττιξ
δενδρέωι ἐφεζόμενος λιγυρὴν καταχεύετ' ἀοιδήν
πυκνὸν ὑπὸ πτερύγων, θέρεος καματώδεος ²ὥρηι,
τῆμος πιόταταί τ' αἶγες, καὶ οἶνος ἄριστος,   585
⁴⁻⁵μαχλόταται δὲ γυναῖκες, ἀφαυρότατοι δέ τοι ἄνδρες
εἰσίν, ἐπεὶ ⁵⁻⁶κεφαλὴν καὶ γούνατα Σείριος ἄζει,
²αὐαλέος δέ τε χρὼς ὑπὸ καύματος· ἀλλὰ τότ' ἤδη
⁽¹⁾εἴη πετραίη τε σκιὴ καὶ βίβλινος οἶνος
μάζα τ' ἀμολγαίη γάλα τ' αἰγῶν σβεννυμενάων   590
καὶ βοὸς ὑλοφάγοιο κρέας μή πω τετοκυίης
πρωτογόνων τ' ἐρίφων· ⁽¹⁾ἐπὶ δ' αἴθοπα πινέμεν οἶνον,
ἐν σκιῆι ἑζόμενον, κεκορημένον ἦτορ ἐδωδῆς,
ἀντίον ἀκραέος Ζεφύρου τρέψαντα πρόσωπα·
κρήνης δ' ἀενάου καὶ ἀπορρύτου ἥ τ' ἀθόλωτος   595
τρὶς ὕδατος προχέειν, ⁽¹⁾τὸ δὲ τέτρατον ἱέμεν οἴνου.

Alcaeus' echoes are sufficiently clear and frequent to evoke the Hesiodic passage. The connection is developed gradually, delaying the moment of recognition on first hearing. Neither the command to drink in 1 nor 2 ὥρα are by themselves recognisable as an allusion, 2 ὐπά καύματος may be, 3 ἄχει . . . τέττιξ certainly is, and 4 σκόλυμος (which appears in the first line of the Hesiodic passage and is rare in poetry) is emphatic in its reference to Hesiod.

Alcaeus starts where Hesiod ends, with an exhortation to drink, and so turns the rest of the passage into reasons for drinking and the simple outdoor scene into a *symposion*. The entry in a farmer's calendar becomes a self-standing drinking song. In the resolute focus on drink, Hesiod's references to food disappear, as indeed does the moderate mixing of wine with water. Sex stays. The relationship with Hesiod is one of playful reappropriation rather than simple imitation. (For the *Works and Days* as a text that invites reuse, see Hunter 2014 and Canevaro 2015; for Alcaeus as an intertextual poet, cf. in this vol. fr. 42, and see in general Martin 1972: 87–111.)

Alcaeus' poem (or the beginning of it) was long-lived. When citing the first line, Plutarch labels it 'universally familiar' (πρόχειρον ἅπασιν, *Mor.* 697f). The considerable textual variation in the transmission of that line (the apparatus is very selective), and the further variation demonstrated by the evidently related fr. 352 (πώνωμεν, τὸ γὰρ ἄστρον περιτέλλεται), may result from creative reuse in performance as much as misquotation. Poetic adaptations of the line appear in Philodemus (*AP* 11.34.7) and in an anonymous fragment cited in the *Suda* (τ212). Evidently Alcaeus shaped a tradition, but there is a strong chance that a tradition also preceded him, and that Hesiod is a privileged intertext in what is in fact a rich web of high and low song-making traditions, both lyric and hexametric. Such traditionality is suggested by the recurrence of the themes and language of the Hesiodic passage not just in this song but also in Sa. 101A (cf. 3n.) and the Hesiodic *Scutum* (393–401), and by the nature of the themes themselves: the cicada as a harbinger of summer, the dog-star as a token of heat and suffering, and women as seasonally lascivious are all common and probably very old motifs; see Petropoulos 1994. One attraction of the song may therefore have been tonal richness. The case for traditionality is made by Hooker 1977: 79–81, who however presents allusion to Hesiod and use of other traditions as mutually exclusive. More broadly on Alcaeus' use of popular traditions, see Lelli 2006: 23–70 (on proverbs).

We almost certainly have the beginning since all quotations start from line 1. What and how much is lost at the end is impossible to tell, but see 5–6n.

Source: The fragment has interested different writers for different reasons. Only Proclus' commentary on the *Works and Days* quotes all of it, on 582–7 (fr. 215 in Marzillo 2010). Numerous authors quote part of the opening (from three words up to two lines); see the apparatus of Voigt and Liberman. The ancient tradition of the fragment is discussed by Ponzio 2001.

Metre:

$$- \times - \cup \cup - - \cup \cup - - \cup \cup - \cup - \; \| \; gl^{2c}$$

A run of greater asclepiads, viz. glyconics expanded with two choriambs, a metre used repeatedly by both Alcaeus and Sappho.

Discussions: Cazzato 2016: 200–2, *Hunter 2014: 123–6, Petropoulos 1994: esp. 16–17 and 81–2, Burnett 1983: 132–4, Rösler 1980: 256–64, Page 1955: 303–6.

1 τέγγε πλεύμονα: an exhortation to drink opens also Alc. 38A, 332, 346. The singular τέγγε may have been taken up by an address to a named individual in the lacuna. The notion that drink is taken in through the lungs is persistent in the poetic and medical tradition; see Eur. fr. 983 *TrGF*, Eupolis, *PCG* fr. 158, Pl. *Tim.* 70c, 91a. It is probably connected to the idea that the lungs are the seat of emotions, which themselves are often conceptualised as liquids; see Onians 1951: 35–8 and Clarke 1999: 90–2. Singular πλεύμονα is (hesitantly) adopted as the *lectio difficilior*: unlike πλεύμονας, it requires οἴνωι to behave metrically like ϝοίνωι; see further Sa. 31.9n.

τό ... ἄστρον: viz. Sirius, the dog-star, as is made explicit in 5. The heliacal rising of Sirius marked the period of the greatest heat (Hes. *WD* 414–19; Kidd 1997 on Aratus 332). Drink as a response to the heat of the dog-star was a topos; e.g. Thgn. 1039–40 and Eupolis, *PCG* fr. 158. Further on Sirius, see Alcm. 1.62n.

περιτέλλεται 'is revolving', viz. has become visible and is moving slowly from east to west, day by day; cf. Arat. 693, 709.

2 ἀ δ' ὤρα χαλέπα ('the season is arduous') explains the significance of τὸ γὰρ ἄστρον περιτέλλεται, and will in turn be explained by what follows.

δίψαισ' keeps alive the drinking theme. By contrast, in Hesiod it is the skin that is parched ὑπὸ καύματος. The form is either indic. sg. with hyper-Aeolic -αι-, or indic. pl.

3 ἄχει ... τέττιξ: the cicada suits the context of conviviality and music-making during debilitating heat because of its ability to make a sound while unable or unwilling to do much else: see *Il.* 3.151 (the elders, unable to fight, still talk like cicadas), the fable of the ant and the cicada (no. 373 Perry), Pl. *Phdr.* 258e–259d and Sa. 58b.9–12n.

The words shown by the metre to be missing at line-end probably continued the same clause; e.g. Seidler's πτερύγων ὔπα, based on Hes. *WD* 584. Some scholars postulate a lacuna of several lines, into which they fit Sa. 101A Voigt = Alc. 347B LP, an anonymous quotation about the song of the cicada which resembles Hes. *WD* 582–4. But the extra lines would break Alcaeus' fast-moving sequence of short clauses on individual seasonal characteristics; moreover, they need extensive emendation to suit the metre; see Stark 1956: 175–8 and Liberman 1992. They are therefore likely belong to the broader tradition but not to (this version of) this song.

4 σκόλυμος 'golden thistle' (*scolymus hispanicus*).

νῦν δέ contrasts with Hesiod's ἦμος ... τῆμος and τότ(ε): an exhortation here and now, rather than an entry in a calendar.

4–5 γύναικες ... ἄνδρες: Alcaeus foregrounds disgust as he changes Hesiod's μαχλόταται ('at their most lascivious') vs ἀφαυρόταται ('at their weakest'), to μιαρώταται ('at their most repulsive, tainted') vs λέπτοι ('feeble'). Hesiod's reference to sex still echoes in Alcaeus' phrasing, helped by the common notion that sex and especially female sexuality are dirty and carry pollution, on which see Parker 1983: 74–103 and Carson 1990. The binary opposition suits Hesiod's thinking about the sexes; at many *symposia*, it will (playfully) jar with a discourse of men pursuing women.

5–6 ἐπεί . . . ἄσδει continues the train of thought (ἐπεί), but also returns to 1 ἄστρον. Possibly the ring composition marked the end of the mid-summer heat section.

5 κεφάλαν καὶ γόνα (neut. pl.): like the head, the knees can stand for a person's vital powers. Cf. the Homeric formula γούνατ' ἔλυσεν and Thgn. 977–8 'as long my knees are nimble, and I carry my head without trembling'. For speculative discussion of the origin of this notion, see Onians 1951: 174–86.

Σείριος: Sirius scorches also at e.g. [Hes.] *Scut.* 153 and 397 and Archil. 107.1.

SAPPHO

Antiquity regarded Sappho as a contemporary of Alcaeus. Such synchronisation is common in ancient chronologies, and needs to be treated with caution, but we have no grounds on which to challenge it in this case, which is why the ordering of the two poets adopted here is alphabetical. What is beyond doubt is that Sappho and Alcaeus belong to a common tradition, sharing the same poetic language (p. 88) and many of the same metres. Sappho's mention of the exile of members of the clan of Kleanax (98b, Myrsilus was a Kleanactid), her attack on somebody who 'chose the friendship of women from the house of Penthilus' (71, Pittacus married into the Penthelid clan), as well as the tradition of her own exile (test. 5 Campbell, reliability uncertain), suggest that the political fault lines portrayed by Alcaeus affected her also. The sanctuary and worship of Hera, Zeus and Dionysus also feature in both poets (p. 94).

However, the world Sappho portrays in her poetry is very different from that of Alcaeus. It is a world of friendship, love and desire among women, of family life and relationships, of weddings, of poetry and music and of communion with the divine, above all Aphrodite. Sappho is best known for her first-person poetry of passionate love for other women, some of it set in the context of a hazily evoked all-female grouping. The selection here includes several of the most famous pieces, individually different in tone, focus and situation. The publication of the 'Brothers Poem' in 2014 (which is not included here) drew attention to a different strand in Sappho's work, familial and even domestic poetry (Obbink 2014, Bierl and Lardinois 2016). It is one of a sequence of poems in which the speaker is concerned with her brothers, and we also have fragments in which she addresses her mother and her daughter. Different again are the epicising narrative poetry that is preserved in fr. 44 (presented here), her wedding songs (frs. 103–117b), and formal cult song (esp. fr. 140, mourning Adonis). Several poems are mocking or invective (e.g. 55, 57).

Since antiquity, the realities behind Sappho's poetry have been the subject of fascination and debate. Leaving aside the wedding songs, only guesswork is possible. The once popular notion that Sappho led an educational institution has now long been considered anachronistic, and scholars have looked for better-documented paradigms of female sociality in the ancient world. The model of Alcman's *partheneia* with their expressions of female–female desire (pp. 60–1) has suggested to some a scenario in which Sappho's 'circle' is a more or less institutional grouping of adolescent girls who are together until they marry. Comparison with Alcman has given rise also to the theory that Sappho was a *chorodidaskalos* figure, composing her songs for public performance by a female chorus. (Choral performance is likely for wedding songs and for fr. 140; putative choral features of other fragments are controversial; see frs. 17, 27, 30, 43, and p. 148 on 58b.) For versions of these proposals, see Calame 1997 [1977]: 210–14, Lardinois 1996, Nagy 2007. Other scholars look instead to the *symposion*, and argue that Sappho performed her songs in female or male convivial settings; for different versions of this approach, see Parker 1993, Schlesier 2013, Bowie 2016; and cf. below, p. 123. We have to accept that the 'Sapphic question' cannot be settled. Sappho's poetry is striking for its suggestive poetic settings, which combine to form a distinctive world, yet it is equally striking for the dearth of tight connections between these settings and known performance contexts. See D'Alessio 2018 for a critique of some of the positions set out above, and for a discussion of Sappho's tendency to situate her poems on the margins of, rather than squarely within, formal ritual occasions.

Sappho had an unusually rich reception history from early on, in which admiration and imitation of her poetry mingled with curiosity about her life. See p. 195 on Anacr. 358, and in general on the early reception Yatromanolakis 2007. The Alexandrian editors arranged the poems in eight or nine books, the first of which ran to 1,320 lines. Much of the edition was organised by metre; the final book probably comprised wedding songs. See further Yatromanolakis 1999, Ferrari 2010 [2007]: 117–19, and esp. Liberman 2007.

The bibliography on Sappho is extensive. Yatromanolakis 2012 provides a guide. The standard edition is that of Voigt; regarding the most important subsequent finds, see below for 58b and additions to 16 ('Source'), and above for the 'Brothers Poem'. Page 1955 is a full commentary on the major fragments then known; Aloni 1997 offers brief annotations to most fragments. There are several book-length introductory treatments; see esp. Williamson 1995. Greene 1996 contains a number of influential essays. See also Stehle 1997: 262–318 and Ferrari 2010 [2007].

Sappho 1 Voigt

A distressed Sappho (named in line 20) prays to Aphrodite, recalling previous appeals and encounters with her. She does not specify the nature of her woes, but Aphrodite has understood them as a matter of betrayed or unrequited affection in the past, and we are invited to make the same inference now. The text is clearly complete (cf. 25–8n.).

The song manipulates the common three-part structure of hymns and prayers: (i) invocation, (ii) praise, reminder of past interactions, and/or narrative, (iii) request. It begins with an address and an appeal, and ends, in ring composition, by developing that appeal (1–5, 25–8). The long central section corresponds to the central part of the hymn structure but, with its description of a divine chariot ride and an encounter between goddess and mortal, it is reminiscent of epic narrative more than of cult song; see further 5–24, 7–13nn. On the tripartite structure, see Furley and Bremer 2001: 1.50–64, and on Sappho's manipulation of this form in several of her poems Burzacchini 2005. On the anachronism of the term 'hymn', see p. 12 above.

The allusion to epic may be an allusion to typical scenes and narrative sequences more than an allusion to particular Iliadic passages. Candidates for specific allusion would be Achilles' prayer to Thetis in book 1 (thus Krischer 1968: 12–14), the wounded Aphrodite's retreat to Olympus and complaint to her mother in book 5, and Hera's and Athena's chariot-ride from Olympus to earth in the same book (both suggested by Di Benedetto 1973, the latter by Svenbro 1975). Arguably, points of contact with all these scenes are generic rather than unique and specific, but this is a matter of judgement; see Fowler 1987: 38–9 and pp. 17–18 above.

The text is firmly anchored in the here and now (5 τυίδ' ἔλθ', 25 ἔλθε μοι καὶ νῦν), but the emphasis on repetition in the central section (5 κἀτέρωτα, 15, 16 and 18 δηὖτε) makes today's appeal to Aphrodite just one of several such occasions. Sappho's anguish is real, but even as she suffers she also knows that she is prone to such suffering. Some gentle humour adds to the effect (see esp. 13–24n.). The poem thus models both the despondency of unhappy love and a self-aware reflectiveness which, perhaps, tempers this despondency. The object of Sappho's love receives little attention in this, despite Aphrodite's questions in 18–20, as does the nature of Sappho's relationship with her: as in many of Sappho's poems, the focus is on her own involved state of mind.

The poem probably opened the Alexandrian edition (see 'Source'), and can indeed be read programmatically. Sappho names herself, and she portrays herself as somebody who regularly sings of unfulfilled desire for other women. She is intimate with Aphrodite, whom she can always call on, freely converse with and quote. Aphrodite in this poem, as elsewhere, is not just the all-powerful goddess of love, but also Sappho's long-standing audience, Muse and ally. Aphrodite is invoked in several other fragments: 2, 15, 33, 86, 101. Aphrodite and Sappho converse also in frs. 134, 159 and possibly 60.

Source: Dion. Hal. *Comp.* 23. The literary theorist and historian Dionysius (1st cent. BC) quotes the text as an example of the 'polished' style, and discusses it for its smooth sound patterns. The two main MSS are the Parisinus gr. 1741 (P, 10th cent.) and the Laurentianus LIX 15 (F, 10th/11th cent.); the text is also included in an epitome ('epit.' in the apparatus). For another lyric text cited in *Comp.*, see Sim. 543; cf. 'Source' there.

P. Oxy. XXI.2288 (= Π), a slim strip of papyrus of the first or second century AD, edited by Lobel, preserves a few letters from the left-hand side of each line down to 21, and helps correct minor errors in Dionysius' text. A number of ancient authors quote individual lines or words. One of them, Hephaestion 14.1 p. 43 Consbruch ('Heph.'), uses the opening to illustrate the Sapphic strophe. Since ancient metricians tend to quote opening lines, and since poems in the Sapphic strophe were collected in book 1 of the Alexandrian edition of Sappho (see test. 29 Campbell), it is likely that this poem was placed first in the edition. The choice would be notable, since the rest of the book seems to have been arranged alphabetically, whereas this poem starts with Ποικιλό-; see 16.1–4n.

Metre:

$- \cup - \times - \cup \cup - \cup - - \parallel$
$- \cup - \times - \cup \cup - \cup - - \parallel$
$- \cup - \times - \cup \cup - \cup - \times$ 11 ὠράνω‿αῖθε–
$- \cup \cup - - \parallel\!\parallel\!\parallel$ 24 κὦὐκ

Seven Sapphic strophes. The Sapphic strophe consists of three identical eleven-syllable lines, closed off by a shorter pattern, which repeats the $- \cup \cup -$ element that characterises the whole stanza (and which is common in many aeolic metres). The occurrence of hiatus at the end of lines 1 and 2 of the stanza (in this poem: 6, 14, ?18, 21, 22) indicates pause at those points; while the occasional bridging of lines 3 and 4 by single words (in this poem: 11–12) entails synapheia (i.e. unbroken continuity of the metrical pattern), with the option of either a short or long syllable in the final position of line 3.

Discussions: Purves 2014: 176–90, Schmitz 2013, Schlesier 2011a, Ferrari 2010 [2007]: 161–70, *Walker 2000: 242–8, Stehle 1997: 296–9, Lasserre 1989: 201–14, *Burnett 1983: 243–59, Winkler 1990 [1981]: 166–76, Carson 1996 [1980], Svenbro 1975, Di Benedetto 1973, West 1970a: 308–10, Krischer 1968, Privitera 1967, Page 1955: 3–18.

1–5 *An address with epithets, followed by the initial request.* As the goddess of love, Aphrodite is a source both of suffering (3 μή . . . δάμνα) and of help (5 ἔλθ’).

1 ποικιλόθρον’: a *hapax*, probably 'ornate-throned'. Aphrodite is imagined as majestically enthroned. The alternative is to derive -θρονος from the rare θρόνα (neut. pl., 'flowers'), and to translate 'with/of manifold flowers'; cf. the θρόνα ποικίλ(α) that Andromache weaves in a piece of cloth at *Il.* 22.441, and see Sa 2.6n. on Aphrodite's association with flowers. There is, however, no instance of a -θρονος compound that is evidently derived from θρόνα, whereas formation from θρόνος is manifest in several cases, e.g. ὁμόθρονος and δίθρονος. The less well-attested variant ποικιλόφρον’ ('of subtle mind') is probably a corruption that occurred under the influence of δολόπλοκε. See further Jouanna 1999: 101–16.

ἀθανάτ’ invokes Aphrodite's superior power and imperviousness to suffering, but also highlights the unusualness of the speaker's easy interaction with her in the subsequent stanzas. The word recurs at 14, and cf. 13 μάκαιρα.

2 δολόπλοκε 'weaver of plots'. Aphrodite's power to seduce and to overcome resistance is often expressed as a form of deceit; see *h.Aphr.* 7, 33, *Il.* 3.405. She is δολοπλόκος in several later texts, possibly under the influence of this poem; see Sim. 541.9, Thgn. 1386, and cf. already incert. Lesb. 42.7 Voigt. A guilefully weaving Aphrodite also suits this guilefully woven poem and its composer.

3 μή . . . δάμνα: the force of the present is probably 'stop overpowering me'.

ἄσαισι μηδ’ ὀνίαισι (~ ἀνίαις) 'discomfort and distress'. Similar sound patterns, and overlap in meaning, lend emphasis to the coupling.

4 θῦμον: the word recurs in Aphrodite's speech (18) and the final stanza (27). The speaker's θῦμος is a central focus of the poem.

5 τυίδ’ ἔλθ’: with more or less literal force, requests for deities to come are common in prayers, and particularly common in Sappho: see frs. 2 and 86 (Aphrodite); 53, 127 and 128 (Muses and/or Graces); and in general Pulleyn 1997: 136–44.

5–24 *Sappho's previous encounters with Aphrodite.* It is common for prayers to remind deities of their close rapport with the worshipper by recalling favours granted on earlier occasions; see *Il.* 5.116, Pind. *Isthm.* 6.42, Soph. *OT* 165 (all with εἴ ποτε). Sappho greatly elaborates this motif. She first describes the journey Aphrodite made when called upon by Sappho previously (7–13), and then recalls the earlier encounters and especially Aphrodite's words to her (13–24).

5 κἀτέρωτα: καὶ ἑτέρωτα, 'also on another occasion'.

6 τὰς ἔμας αὔδας: gen. sg., with Lesbian accentuation. 'My voice' amounts to 'my call for help', and at a different level to 'my singing'; Aphrodite is an audience.

πήλοι 'from afar'. When other singers perform the piece, the notion of listening to Sappho's voice from afar becomes an image for the dissemination of her work.

7 ἔκλυες 'you lent your ear', i.e. granted my wish.

7–13 The lengthy description of Aphrodite's journey retains the pictorial quality of 1–4. Prayers often speculate about the deity's possible whereabouts; e.g. *Il.* 1.37–8 and, in this anthology, Sa. 2.1 and Anacr. 348.4–7. But the house of Zeus, as well as the chariot, are reminiscent of epic rather than real-life prayer. The sparrows further complicate the tone.

8 χρύσιον: the stanza-break suggests joining the adjective with δόμον, as does already Π, which punctuates before ἦλθες. See further Slings 1991. Of course, singers can articulate the sentence differently.

ἦλθες picks up 5 ἔλθ'.

10 στροῦθοι: later sources attest erotic associations of the (randy) sparrow; see Athen. 9.391e–f and the discussion of Page 1955: 7–8. Sappho's flock of whirling sparrows is not inappropriate for Aphrodite; but it is novel, playful and memorable.

περί ~ ὑπέρ, 'over'. The usage is characteristic of Aeolic; cf. Alc. 365 and see Hodot 1990: 149–50.

γᾶς μελαίνας: see Sa. 16.2n.

11 πύκνα δίννηντες πτέρ': probably 'rapidly whirling their wings' rather than 'whirling their close-feathered wings'. Cf. *Od.* 2.151 ἐπιδινηθέντε τιναξάσθην πτερὰ πυκνά '(the two eagles) wheeled about, shaking their close-feathered wings'; Sappho is reworking traditional language. There is a case for emending δίννηντες to δίννεντες (cf. Sa. 16.20 πέσδο]μάχεντας from -μάχημι), but the inscriptional evidence is ambiguous (Blümel 1982: 218–19), and cf. Sa. 44.34 ὕμνην.

11–12 ἀπ'... μέσσω 'from the sky through the mid-air': the αἴθηρ is the level between earth and sky; see e.g. *Il.* 17.425, 19.351.

13–24 Sappho's recollection of Aphrodite's previous epiphanies is carefully structured and works towards a climax:

13 address;

14 Aphrodite's facial expression as she appeared before Sappho;

15–18 her open-ended enquiries about what woes it is this time that prompt Sappho to call on her, reported in indirect speech;

18–20 her specific enquiries about who it is this time that Sappho pines for, presented in direct speech;

21–4 her reassurances that the situation will change, still in direct speech.

Evidently, Sappho did not specify the nature of her concerns on previous occasions any more than she does now, but Aphrodite knew her well enough to interpret the matter as one of love. The passage operates at several interlocking levels. (i) Sappho is comforted in her helplessness by Aphrodite's words and presence. (ii) Aphrodite gently mocks Sappho for falling in love, and calling on her, again and again. (iii) Sappho metapoetically characterises herself as a composer with a repertoire of love poetry addressed to Aphrodite; cf. 15n. (δηὖτε). (iv) The passage exploits the close connection between memory and imagination. It reports past encounters, but since both indirect and direct speech are couched in the present, memories past gradually merge with imagination now. As Sappho remembers, Aphrodite seems to become present.

13 μάκαιρα expresses carefree serenity, and thus mirrors 1 ἀθανάτ'. For its use in addressing gods, see e.g. *h.Apol.* 14 (Leto), *h.* 8.16 (Ares).

14 μειδιαίσαισ' evokes Aphrodite's formulaic epithet φιλομειδής. Her laughter was variously elaborated. It often belonged to her erotic province (e.g. Hes. *Th.* 205, *h.* 10.2–3), but it could also be gleefully superior (*h. Aphr.* 49). Here the combination with μάκαιρα and ἀθανάτωι creates a sense of effortless divine superiority. But neither Sappho in the text nor the listener can be sure of her attitude: affectionate, mocking, or simply inscrutable.

15 ἦρε' 'you asked', aor. of *ἔρομαι.

δηὖτε 'again': characteristic of erotic poetry ('again I am in love'); see Anacr. 358.1n. Sappho manipulates that usage by giving δηὖτε to Aphrodite instead of saying δηὖτε herself, as well as repeating the word twice in the next three lines.

17–18 κὤττι (~ καὶ ὅττι)... **θύμωι** 'and what in my maddened heart I wanted above all to happen to me'. Much of the phrasing is broadly traditional; cf. e.g. *Od.* 18.113 (may Zeus give you) ὅττι μάλιστ' ἐθέλεις καί τοι φίλον ἔπλετο θυμῶι. What is not traditional in this context is μαινόλαι. Sappho's mind is out of control; cf. 3 ἄσαισι μηδ' ὀνίαισι. It is left open whether this is Aphrodite's accusation or Sappho's self-assessment.

18 The change from ὅττι in 15–17 (3x) to τίνα/τίς here, underscored by asyndeton, marks the shift from indirect to direct speech. Sappho's relationship with Aphrodite is such that she is able to impersonate her voice. For the switch from indirect to direct speech, cf. Pind. *Isthm.* 8. 31–45 and Bacch. 11.98–105.

πείθω: for erotic 'persuasion', see Ibyc. 288.3n.

19 Π probably had ἄψ σ' ἄγην (~ ἄγειν); see Lobel's *editio princeps* and Maehler *apud* Burzacchini 2007a: 85. That text cannot be right: 'once again whom shall I persuade to bring you back to your love?' The most promising emendation is ϝάν for σάν ('... to bring you back to her love'). Compare perhaps the use of ἄγειν in wedding contexts (Sa. 44.5n.), and cf. 21 for Sappho's strikingly passive role in this phrase. But the corruption may well be more extensive. For overviews of other proposals, see Saake 1971: 54–9, Caciagli 2011: 78–82.

φιλότατα 'love', taken up by 23 φίλει/φιλήσει.

19–20 ὦ | Ψάπφ': the address portrays Sappho as intimate with Aphrodite. It also memorialises her name. The closest early parallel is Hesiod's encounter with the Muses at *Th.* 22–35. Scott 1905: 32 argues that ὦ + voc. in lyric (and epic) 'denotes impatience, familiarity, or lack of reserve'. This would suit the context, but the evidence is complicated; see Dickey 1996: 199–206. Sappho names herself more often than our other lyric poets (as far as we can tell): 65.5, 94.5, 133.2. In all those instances the spelling is Ψάπ- (though never metrically guaranteed).

20 ἀδικήει portrays failure to reciprocate Sappho's love as an injustice; for the topos, cf. Thgn. 1283 μή μ' ἀδίκει, and see further Gentili 1972 and Bonanno 1973. Aphrodite may be characterising Sappho's viewpoint rather than expressing her own. The normal Lesbian form would be *ἀδίκει, but the metre requires four syllables; see Forssman 1975: 22–3, Colvin 2007: 219–20.

21–4 The change of fortunes is expressed in standard erotic vocabulary but striking syntax. The strict parallelism in all sentences heightens the sense of inevitability. It may even loosely recall repetition in magical incantations; cf. e.g. *PGM* iv.1510–20, and see the discussions of Cameron 1939, Petropoulos 1993, Faraone 1999: 133–46.

We learn that the object of Sappho's love was (and presumably is) female (ἐθέλοισα). Less clear, because of the lack of dative and accusative personal pronouns, is who it is that Aphrodite said the unnamed girl or woman would come to pursue, give presents to, and love. The most obvious supplement is 'you': Aphrodite promises that she will return to Sappho. But the unspecific phrasing introduces a generic note and places the emphasis not on the relationship with Sappho but on the imminent suffering of the girl or woman; see further Carson 1996 [1980], who compares Thgn. 1327–34 (though that passage treats the – eventual – transformation of pursued into pursuer as the consequence of ageing, while here it is the 'swift' result of divine intervention). In so far as 'you' is understood, the reciprocal exchange of roles between lover and beloved contrasts with the standard pattern of sympotic iconography and male erotic poetry in which the roles of pursuer (adult) and pursued (youth) appear irreversible; see further Williamson 1995: 163–5.

21 καὶ γὰρ αἰ '<don't fret>, for even if'. φεύγειν and διώκειν regularly appear as a pair in erotic contexts: e.g. *Cypria* fr. 10.7 West, Thgn. 1299.

22 ἀλλά emphasises the contrast between now and then; see Denniston 1954: 11–12.

24 κωὔκ (~ καὶ οὐκ) **ἐθέλοισα:** reluctance overcome is a trope of erotic poetry and an expression of Aphrodite's power; cf. Helen in *Il.* 3, Thgn. 1341–2, Sim. 541.8, *PGM* iv.2934–5; and cf. 2n. and 16.11n.

25–8 *The request is resumed and developed.* Tight ring composition establishes correspondence, 25 ἔλθε ~ 5 ἔλθ', 25 λῦσον ~ 2 δολόπλοκε, 26 μερίμναν ~ 3 ἄσαισι and ὀνίαισι, 27 θῦμος ~ 4 θῦμον. Sappho is still in dire straits; but in the course of recollecting Aphrodite's assistance in the past, the negative μή ... δάμνα (3) has turned into a set of equally unspecific but increasingly positive requests: that Aphrodite release her from her woes, that she fulfil her desires, and (perhaps with programmatic relevance beyond this poem) that she become her ally. The swift change of tone suggests Aphrodite's swift action (13 αἶψα; 21 and 23 ταχέως). See also 31.17n.

25 χαλέπαν ~ χαλεπῶν (gen. pl. fem.).

26–7 pick up Aphrodite's phrasing in 17–18. This occasion resembles previous ones very closely. Cf. also Sa. 5.3–4 and the epic formula τελέσαι δέ με θυμὸς ἄνωγεν, | εἰ δύναμαι τελέσαι γε καὶ εἰ τετελεσμένον ἐστίν (3x, once spoken by Aphrodite: *Il.* 14.195–6).

27–8 σύ ... ἔσσο (~ ἴσθι): gods are evoked as σύμμαχοι elsewhere (e.g. Archil. 108, Aesch. *Cho.* 2, 19). Nevertheless, the military language stands out in a request for support in a matter of love, addressed to a goddess who often is distinctly unwarlike (e.g. *Il.* 5.428; cf. above, p. 115). War (and epic) provides a contrast to love (and lyric) in several lyric poets and poems; in this selection, see esp. Sa. 16 and Ibyc. S151.

Sappho 2 Voigt

The poem takes the form of (what would later be called) a cletic hymn to evoke the setting of a grove and countryside shrine of Aphrodite, and Aphrodite's presence in it. We probably have the beginning, and quite possibly the end; see 'Source' and the paragraph below 15n.

A brief appeal to 'come here from Crete' (1) is followed by an extended, sensuous description of the setting, a shady, well-watered and sheltered grove and meadow, which (probably) belong to a temple (1–12). The final surviving stanza delivers the speaker's request, as Aphrodite is asked to pour nectar into cups (13–16). For the tripartite prayer form, and Sappho's adaptations of it, see the headnote to Sa. 1. The structure is simple and neat. Each stanza is a grammatical unit and opens with a marker of place: δεῦρυ – ἐν δ(έ) – ἐν δέ – ἔνθα.

Much is left to the listeners' inference and imagination. Until 13 Κύπρι, the goddess' identity is to be inferred from the particulars of the scene, which are redolent of Aphrodite and what she stands for (see notes). 1 μ' apart, humans are present at first only by implication, as the altars are scented with sacrifices and sleep descends from the quivering foliage. The setting of the first three stanzas shares several elements with other *loci amoeni*, without however specifying what precisely it is a setting for; cf. *Od.* 17.208–11 (sanctuary of the nymphs), *Il.* 14.346–60 (scene of Hera's seduction of Zeus), *Od.* 7.112–31 (Alcinous' seasonless garden), Pind. fr. 129 (paradisiacal afterlife of the blessed). The result is a scene that mingles eroticism and purity, human and divine, and despite all the visual detail is drawn suggestively rather than with precision.

The grove is populated explicitly in the fourth stanza. The image of a deity pouring nectar into golden cups recalls the divine conviviality of epic; e.g. *Il.* 4.2–4 μετὰ δέ σφισι πότνια Ἥβη | νέκταρ ἐωινοχόει. τοὶ δὲ χρυσέοις δεπάεσσι | δειδέχατ᾽ ἀλλήλους. Yet the setting is not Olympus but the grove, and Aphrodite is asked to make herself manifest among, and even to serve, what one assumes are human feasters (of unspecified gender, at least in what survives). Sappho leaves it open whether one is to imagine a festival in Aphrodite's precinct, attended by the goddess herself, or a (female?) outdoor banquet in a ritualised setting, or whether Aphrodite and her grove adumbrate metaphorically what are more informal, erotically charged interactions between the speaker and her unspecified companions. On any interpretation, though, the song transports listeners into the eroticised atmosphere of a place where extraordinary things are possible, as it creates a scene of carefree celebration and easy interaction with the goddess of love.

Aphrodite's hoped-for arrival resembles her journey to Cyprus at *h.Aphr.* 58–63 (cf. *Od.* 8.362–6): ἐς Κύπρον δ᾽ ἐλθοῦσα θυώδεα νηὸν ἔδυνεν | ἐς Πάφον· ἔνθα δέ οἱ τέμενος βωμός τε θυώδης· | ἔνθ(α)... Sappho and her audience may have known the *Hymn*, or the tradition behind it; see Sa. 58b.9–12n. If they did, the poem pointedly redirects Aphrodite from Cyprus to where she and her audience are. She is still called Kypris but is now Sappho's or Lesbos' Aphrodite.

The original performance context is irrecoverable; see D'Alessio 2018: 36–8 and, in general, p. 114 above. A cultic occasion at a countryside shrine of Aphrodite is no more likely than a more intimate convivial occasion (presumably all-female), or something different altogether. We cannot assume that the (vague) poetic setting maps onto the performance context. For cultic interpretations of the poem, see Ferrari 2010 [2007]: 153–4 and Caciagli 2011: 145–8. For our sparse, difficult and mostly later evidence for women's commensality, ritual and otherwise, see Burton 1998 and James and Dillon 2012: 144–7, 161–3. For the use of an outdoor setting in (male) sympotic poetry, see esp. Ibyc. 286, which seems to draw on Sa. 2.

Source: *PSI* XIII.1300, a sherd of probably the late third century BC, represented in the apparatus by 'ostr.' (= ostrakon). The scribe, perhaps a school pupil, struggled with the dialect and introduced numerous errors, some harmless, others defying correction. Moreover, the hand is difficult to read and the writing in places poorly preserved, which makes the transcription more than usually uncertain. The first edition is Norsa 1937, the fullest discussion of what the scribe wrote Lanata 1960. For more recent attempts to improve on the transcription and on the restoration of the text, see Malnati 1993, Ferrari 2000a, Tsantsanoglou 2008, Ferrari 2011 and (with digitally enhanced reproductions of details) Caciagli 2015. The sparse apparatus presented here is unable to give a properly representative picture of the assessment of the ostrakon.

Indirect traditions provide support in two places. Hermogenes, *Types of Style* 2.4 p. 331 Rabe (2nd/3rd cent. AD) cites parts of the second stanza, and Athenaeus 11.463e much of the fourth.

Before what is printed here as the first line, the ostrakon has οὐρανόθεν κατιοῦ[σα 'descending from the sky' (transcription Pintaudi 2000: 47). Four considerations suggest that the phrase does not belong to the poem, despite the thematic connection and even though it is not clear why the scribe wrote it. (i) Dialect and metre do not fit: substantial emendation would be needed. (ii) Before the ostrakon lost its top right corner, there probably was a gap after κατιοῦ[σα, which seems to be the only such gap in the text. (iii) Elsewhere Sappho seems to place δεῦρυ and δεῦτε in the opening verse: see frs. 53, 127, 128. (iv) 'From the sky' and (if correct) 'from Crete' are difficult to combine in one sentence, especially in this order. The different positions are rehearsed by Burnett 1983: 261–2 n. 86.

Metre: Sapphic strophes. See on Sa. 1.

Discussions: Caciagli 2011: 137–48, Ferrari 2011, Ferrari 2010 [2007]: 151–5, Burzacchini 2005: 18–25, *Yatromanolakis 2004: 63–7, Furley and Bremer 2001: I.163–5 and II.113–15, *Burnett 1983: 259–76, Jenkyns 1982: 22–38, McEvilley 1972, West 1970a: 315–18, Lanata 1996 [1966]: 15–17, *Page 1955: 34–44. See also 'Source' above, for discussions primarily focused on transcription and reconstruction (particularly important for this text).

1–4 *Request to come; initial description of the setting.* More so than in the later stanzas, a place of worship is suggested: temple (text uncertain), sacred grove, altars. The speaker is trying to persuade Aphrodite.

1 δεῦρύ μ' ἐ<κ> Κρήτας appears to be the only viable way of interpreting the traces, even if it requires two (minor) corrections; see Ferrari 2000a: 37–8, and for other reconstructions Tzamali 1996: 95–6. Aphrodite was prominent in Crete: see Diod. Sic. 5.77.7, Pirenne-Delforge 2001 and Pugliese Carratelli 1990: 73–5, who suggests that the Panormos that is listed as one of Aphrodite's haunts in Sa. 35 is in Crete.

μ': i.e. μοι. The speaker appears fleetingly, and then disappears again.

πρ[‿ ‿ –] ‿ : a verb meaning 'come (to)!' is most likely, e.g. Turyn's πρ[οσίκοι]ọ.

ναῦον 'temple', an emendation of the nonsensical ναυγον, supported by the occurence of ναός ἀγνός at Alcm. 14b and in the cletic cult song *carm. pop.* 871, and by νηόν at *h.Aphr.* 58 (see headnote). The alternative emendation ἔναυλον 'haunt' is just as easy (the previous word would lose one syllable), but 'haunt' clashes with 'altars', and while the nymphs have χαρίεντας ἐναύλους at Hes. *Th.* 129, it is not a suitable term for Aphrodite or her celebrants. For the palaeographical considerations involved, see Lanata 1960: 81 and Caciagli 2011: 139–40.

2 ἄγνον 'sacred', in the sense not of demarcation (ἱερός) but of the majesty of the divine which requires human reverence. See Parker 1983: 147–51.

ὄππ[αι –]: Page's supplement τοι (~ σοι) may well be right. The grove is Aphrodite's.

ἄλσος: ἄλση were sites both of encounters with divinity and of recreational activity; see Bonnechere 2007. They were often joined to a temple; see Bacch. 3.19, Hdt. 2.138.3, and the formulaic νηόν τε καὶ ἄλσεα δενδρήεντα (3x in *h.Apol.*).

3 μαλί[αν] 'of apple trees' (~ μηλεῶν). The typical μῆλον is the apple, but the term covers other round fruit like quinces and pomegranates. All of them are erotic symbols, in myth as well as ritual. See Littlewood 1968 and Burnett 1983: 267–8, who points out that the association can be both with virginity and its loss.

ἔνι 'in (it)', viz. 'in the grove'. The ostrakon has the nonsensical εμι. An alternative emendation is the perfect τεθυμιάμε|νοι (preceded by δέ), which requires slightly more substantial intervention.

3–4 θυμιάμε|νοι 'fuming', lit. 'being filled with smoke/scent'. The altars are being scented with burning frankincense, as in the hexameter formula τέμενος βωμός τε θυήεις/θυώδης (e.g. *Il.* 8.48, *h.Aphr.* 59).

4 [λι]βανώτωι: incense and other perfumes were regular sacrifical offerings, not least to Aphrodite (cf. *h.Aphr.* 61–3, Pind. fr. 122.3–4, Emped. DK 31 B128), and a staple at weddings, both as offerings and for their sensual appeal; see Sa. 44.30, Xen. *Symp.* 2.3, Men. *Sam.* 673–4, and further Detienne 1994 [1972] and Mehl 2008.

5–8 *Flowing water, roses, sleep.* It turns out to be the natural scene that is being described further, not the human-built temple or altars. The notion of sleep ?descending from the foliage introduces an unmistakably figurative turn of phrase for the first time.

5 ἐν δ' picks up 3 ἔνι (if ἔνι is correct).

5–6 ὔσδων (~ ὄζων) | μαλίνων: the apple trees are kept at the heart of the scene. The adj. μαλίνων (viz. 'apple-branches') is marginally preferable to the noun μαλίαν because it avoids the double genitive, lit. 'of the branches of the apple-trees', and 3 μαλί[αν] explains the error.

6 βρόδοισι: roses are associated with Aphrodite; see *Il.* 23.186, *Cypria* fr. 5.4 West (among other spring flowers), Bacch. 17.114–16, Irwin 1984: 161–8.

παῖς (Lesb.) ~ πᾶς.

7 αἰθυσσομένων ... φύλλων 'flickering leaves'. The verb expresses both motion and the play of light; see Stanford 1939: 132–6. The genitive is probably governed by κατ- ('down from'), or else absolute, depending on the reading in the next line.

8 κῶμα 'sleep', often pleasant, often preternatural. In both Homeric instances of this word, it is induced by deities in an erotic context; see *Il.* 14.359 (Zeus put to sleep after making love to Hera on a bed of flowers on Ida), *Od.* 18.201. Here it is either the hypnotic natural surroundings or Aphrodite that cause the sleep. See further Wiesmann 1972.

†καταιριον† ostr., καταρρεῖ Hermogenes (see 'Source'). A verb is likely, with κῶμα as subject, but a suitable word is not easy to find. (i) κατέρρει 'moves down' is not otherwise attested, except in the similar but often emended Erinna fr. 3 Neri (*SH* 402) τὸ δὲ σκότος ὄσσε κατέρρει. The simple verb ἔρρειν usually means 'to leave', but can also be a synonym of εἶμι; see *LfgrE* s.v. B.2. (ii) κατάρρει 'flows down' would require no emendation (of Hermogenes' reading) and would provide good sense, but the non-Aeolic form (Aeol. καρρέει) would stand out in this poem (in contrast to e.g. Sa. 44). For κατά rather than Aeolic κάτ, see Sa. 44.12, 105b.2 Voigt (105c.2 LP); for the ending -ει < -εει, see Sa. 43.5, Alc. 5.11. (iii) κατάγρει 'seizes, overpowers' (~ καθαιρεῖ), argued for most fully by Risch 1962, is very difficult without an object.

9–12 *Flowery meadow, breezes.* Meadows are sites of erotic encounters, see Anacr. 417.5n.

9 ἱππόβοτος subtly adds to the eroticism; see p. 60, and cf. Anacr. 346(1).6–9.

10 †τωτ ... ριννοισ† has proved incurable, probably because of scribal error. An adjective qualifying ἄνθεσιν is likely, such as ἠρίνοισιν (– ⌣ – ⌣, 'spring-') or ἐράννοισ' (⌣ – –, 'lovely'). But some of the letters at the beginning of the line must have been written in error since only four syllables (– ⌣ – ×) are required before ἄνθεσιν.

ἄηται: gentle breezes are a staple of pleasant natural settings, e.g. *Od.* 4. 567–8 (Elysian fields). Aphrodite blows sweet breezes at Eur. *Med.* 836–40.

11–12 If the structure is the same as in the previous stanzas, the omitted words continued and completed the sentence.

13–16 *Address to Aphrodite, and request to pour nectar.* See headnote for the interpretation of this image. Sappho uses related images at 96.26–9 and 141.3. Evidently an imperative is required. There is much to be said for (i) conjecturing it at the end (in view of 16 ϝωνοχοαισα, hyper-dialectic οἰνοχόαισον seems more likely than οἰνοχόησον): 'take the..., and pour the nectar!' The main alternative is (ii) to replace the ostrakon's ἔνθα with ἔλθε and print a participle at the end. ἔλθε would pick up 1 δεῦρυ. This approach is based on Athenaeus (see 'Source'), who cites the sequence from Κύπρι to the end, prefaced by ἔλθέ, and with the last word as οἰνοχοοῦσα. However, arguably 'come... pouring' is awkward; Aphrodite would be pouring as she approaches; see Nicosia 1977: 100–4 for further objections. (iii) For an altogether different approach, see Ferrari 2000a: 41–4: Aphrodite is asked for nectar that the speaker herself will pour. But see the criticism of Di Benedetto 2006: 14–15 n. 14.

13 . ‒ .⌣. ἔλοισα: if ἔλοισα is correct we have lost the accusative object to go with it, but a noun that fits the traces has proved elusive; emendation may be be required.

14 κυλίκεσσιν: a sympotic rather than cultic type of cup. The gold makes the cups divine or extravagantly luxurious or both.

ἄβρως can be construed with both ὀμμεμείχμενον and †ϝωνοχοαισα†. All activity here is sensuous and delicate.

15 ὀμμεμείχμενον (~ ἀνα-) **θαλίαισι νέκταρ** 'nectar mingled with festivity' (or 'with the festivities'). The metaphor exploits the notion of sympotic mixing of wine and water as a token of communal good cheer. Cf. Xenophanes 1.4 κρητὴρ δ' ἕστηκεν μεστὸς ἐϋφροσύνης, Pind. *Pyth.* 9.71–2.

νέκταρ is the drink of the gods, as wine is that of humans. Depending on how literally one conceives the goddess' presence, nectar may be read as a divine drink unusually served to humans or as a metaphorical expression for 'wine'. Poured by Aphrodite, moreover, the nectar also invites interpretation as the sweet desire that is her gift, even though the fixed erotic connotations of nectar are a later development (e.g. *AP* 5.305, Hor. *Odes* 1.13.15–16). Alc. 296b.4 has youths 'scented with ambrosia', in the context of festivities presided over by Aphrodite.

It is more likely than not that this is the end of the poem. Both Athenaeus and the ostrakon stop quoting in the same place, and there is still space on the ostrakon. If the poem did continue, the continuation may have included a reference to the companions sharing in the festivities, as Athenaeus continues the sentence in prose with τούτοις τοῖς ἑταίροις ἐμοῖς τε καὶ σοῖς, 'pouring wine for these companions of yours and mine'. Some scholars think he is adapting a phrase that originally had the feminine ἑταίραις (cf. Sa. 160). See further Nicosia 1977: 93–99 and de Kreij 2016: 65–6 (verse 16 is the end), and Di Benedetto 2006: 13–16 (poem continues).

Sappho 16 Voigt

The poem falls into three parts, connected by transitional sentences: a priamel culminating in the claim that the best thing is 'whatever somebody loves' (1–4); an account of Helen's desertion of her husband and family under the influence of (almost certainly) Aphrodite (6–13); the speaker's wish to see the absent Anactoria (15–20). If 21–4 belong to the same poem (which is unlikely), there would be a fourth section, a gnomic reflection; see 'Source'.

The third (and probably final) section makes the poem an expression of love and yearning for Anactoria, who is moreover celebrated through approximation to Helen. The earlier sections are not, however, mere preparation; this is a text with a broad intellectual and emotional range. As a whole it meditates on the value, the subjectivity, the transience and the pain of love, and the voice modulates from the provocative and argumentative to the personal and intimate. The poem makes good sense on a linear reading, but some of its meaning becomes apparent only at the end.

The priamel is 'a focusing or selecting device in which one or more terms serve as foil for the point of particular interest' (Bundy 1986 [1962]: 5; for general discussion, see Race 1982). This particular priamel introduces beauty and above all love as themes of the poem. It also puts forward an arresting claim, the ramifications of which are worked out as the poem continues. This claim can be read in two ways. Above all, the speaker argues that judgement is subjective and varies from person to person: κάλλιστον is '*whatever* someone loves'. It is this idea that the Helen myth picks up in the first instance. In this sense, the final term does not just present a superior alternative to the earlier terms, as it does in many priamels, but altogether subsumes them by shifting to a higher level. Secondly, in particular with hindsight, the choice of the marked ἔραται also creates the notion that the κάλλιστον thing is 'whatever someone *loves*'. In this sense, the priamel makes the case for love as something worthwhile, no less so than the cavalries, infantries and navies. This idea, too, is relevant to Helen, and it comes to the fore especially in the last stanza when the speaker reshapes the claim of the first stanza as a personal preference for Anactoria over chariots and infantries.

The Helen myth illustrates the claim that judgement is subjective. Helen abandoned everybody who should be dear to her and went to Troy – her husband, outstanding man though he was, as well as her parents and child. In so far as she acted out of love the myth also develops the idea that love matters and drives all judgement. Helen, then, corresponds to the speaker in the opening and closing stanzas, and the rejected Menelaus and the deserted family correspond to the military splendours that the speaker does not value. Yet nothing is made of Paris, the object of Helen's love, and it is Helen herself who is of surpassing beauty and not, as one would expect on this interpretation of the exemplum, Paris. With hindsight, a different match of myth to present suggests itself. Helen corresponds to Anactoria (the only other mortal to be named), and with gentle plaintiveness the poem hints at the loss of those left behind: Helen's husband and family who have been abandoned by Helen, and the speaker herself who wishes to see Anactoria again.

Helen is an ambivalent character already in epic, where she is both criticised and defended and is the cause of much suffering as well as a sympathetic victim of Aphrodite, plagued by remorse. Sappho uses this complex figure to create her own complex Helen. At the same time, there are significant differences. In keeping with the rejection of military matters in the priamel, the Trojan War and Helen's role in it are notably absent. The poem clearly takes the story of the war for granted but hardly refers to it. This omission is even more obvious in comparison with Alcaeus' two surviving Helen fragments. Both in fr. 283, which probably stands in an intertextual relation with Sa. 16 (direction uncertain), and in fr. 42, Alcaeus dwells less on love and beauty than Sappho, and more on death and destruction, with Helen as the cause. See further Race 1989, Segal 1998, Calame 2015: 205–7.

Source: *P.Oxy.* 1231 fr. 1 col. 1 (= Π¹), 2nd cent. AD, edited by Hunt in vol. x, with some additions by Lobel in vol. xxi, p. 122. Green Collection papyrus inv. 105 fr. 2 col. 1, early 3rd cent. AD (= Π²), edited by Burris *et al.* 2014 and then again by Obbink 2016a, is a thin strip which preserves the endings of many of the lines. It adds a few words (13 νόημμα, 14 νοήσηι, 23 δ' ἔμ' αὔται) as well as some letters where Π¹ has gaps; see also West 2014: 2–3. Both papyri are copies of book 1 of Sappho. Lines 3–4 are quoted by Apollon. Dysc. *Synt.* 2.419 Schneider–Uhlig.

Π² also helps assess where the poem ends. It shows that there are at least five stanzas after line 20 and before the beginning of poem 17. Since a length of ten stanzas would be very unusual for what we know of the poems in book 1, we must be dealing with two poems, frs. 16 and 16a, and the question is where to divide them. There is a very strong case for ending Sa. 16 at line 20. It rests on the ring composition of 1–4 ~ 17–20 (n.), the overall sense that the poem is complete, and the likelihood that 21–4 start a new thought (n.). The extra stanza is nevertheless printed here, in smaller type, because too little survives to be certain.

Metre: Sapphic strophes (11 ἐμνάσθη ἀλλά). See on Sa. 1.

Discussions: *Blondell 2010: 377–86, *Pallantza 2005: 61–79, Bierl 2003, Greene 2002: 97–102, Pfeijffer 2000b, *Foley 1998: 58–62, Segal 1998, Rosenmeyer 1997, Williamson 1995: 166–71, Pelliccia 1992, Race

1989, Calame 2005 [1987], Burnett 1983: 277–90, *Most 1981, Liebermann 1980, des Bouvrie Thorsen 1978, Koniaris 1967. See also 'Source' above.

1–4 *Priamel about what is κάλλιστον.* See the headnote for discussion; and des Bouvrie Thorsen 1978, Liebermann 1980 and Zellner 2007 for entry points into the extensive scholarship. The overtly abstract argument attracted intellectuals in later periods, esp. Gorgias in his *Helen*; see Race 1989 and Pelliccia 1992, and for Plato, Foley 1998: 58–62.

This is clearly the beginning of a poem, just as the lines that precede in Π¹ clearly are the end of one (fr. 15). Corroboration comes from the fact that the first word starts with o (ο]ἰ): the poems of book 1 were probably arranged alphabetically by first word (see Obbink 2016b: 41–5), and poem 17 starts with π (πλάσιον); for the intervening poem 16a (first word ὄλβιον?), see 21–4n.

1–2 ἰππήων ... νάων: cavalries, infantries and fleets are a pointedly narrow ideal of beauty. Sappho creates a rhetorical foil for her own broad claim, as well as perhaps mocking male and/or epic preoccupations. The tripartite division occurs first here; later see Pind. *Nem.* 9.34, Aesch. *Pers.* 18–19. Homer pairs only ἰππῆες and πεζοί, e.g. *Il.* 4.297–8, 23.133. The evidence for the beginnings of Greek naval warfare is very thin; see Wallinga 1993.

2 μέλαι[ν]αν: acc. sg. with γᾶν, rather than gen. pl. (μελαίναν) with νάων, because of the word order. 'Black earth' has a formulaic ring; in Sappho's corpus see frs. 1.10, 20.6.

3 κάλλιστον: at first probably understood as 'best'; the aesthetic meaning ('most beautiful') gains prominence as the poem continues. Various things are called κάλλιστον in early Greek poetry, e.g. *Od.* 9.11, Tyrt. 12.14 = Thgn. 1004; and καλόν appears in remarkably abstract statements elsewhere, e.g. Sa. 50, 58b.15–16, Thgn. 255–6. Sappho's statement thus is of a recognisable kind.

3–4 κῆν' ὄτ|τω ~ ἐκεῖνο ὄτου.

4 ἔραται: the metre indicates that this is subjunctive ἔρᾱται rather than indicative ἔρᾱται. The subjunctive expresses a temporal dimension: any time somebody loves something, that thing is the most beautiful at that moment; see Probert 2015: 90–2 and cf. Sa. 31.1–5n. The sense that love may be time-bound will be developed much more explicitly with Helen's change of heart in the myth section.

5–6 πά]γχυ ... τ[ο]ῦτ' 'It is utterly straightforward to make this understood by everyone.' Both the claim itself (lines 1–4 stake out a non-standard position) and the tone of public demonstration jar with what precedes. There may be a hint of humour.

6–13 *Helen.* After the brisk argumentative style of 1–6, the myth is couched in one long, flowing sentence. Despite the claim that this is a straightforward demonstration, the connection with what precedes it requires interpretation; see headnote.

6–7 περσκέθοισα (~ περισχοῦσα) | **κάλλος [ἀνθ]ρώπων** 'far surpassing humans in beauty': the genitive (rather than accusative) after περιέχειν may be accounted for by analogy with the genitive common after verbs of comparison (including e.g. περιεῖναι), or possibly by explaining περ- as Aeolic for ὑπερ-; see Sa. 1.10n.

8 τὸν [. . . ἀρ]ιστον: perhaps [μέγ᾽ ἄρ]ιστον. In Homer Menelaus is only ἄγαθος. The most beautiful woman was married to the best of men – but it was not to last. The passage as a whole expresses the power of love by means of a kind of rhetoric that elsewhere expresses Helen's eventual regret. See esp. *Od.* 4.261–4, 'I regretted the derangement that Aphrodite inflicted on me, when she led me there from my dear fatherland, and I deserted my daughter, my bedchamber, and my husband, who was wanting in no respect, neither mind nor appearance'; cf. *Il.* 3.173–5, 3. 428–9. Whether Sappho is making an allusion rather than just drawing on traditional phrasing is unclear. For the repeated article, rare in the Lesbian poets, cf. Alc. 141.3.

9 καλλ[ίποι]σ̣᾽ ~ καταλιποῦσ(α).

10–11 κωὐδ[ὲ] . . . ἐμνάσθη 'and did not even think about'. Sappho often entwines memory and love, e.g. 94.7–11, 96.15–17, 129a, and in this poem see 15–16 ὀνέμναι|σ᾽. Here she uses this nexus to express the dark side of single-minded passion.

10 πα]ῖδος: Hermione, mentioned also in Sa. 23. Like Menelaus (7 [τὸ]ν ἄνδρα) and like the parents she remains unnamed.

τοκήων: usually Zeus and Leda, but Leda's husband Tyndareus is sometimes mentioned in connection with Helen ([Hes.] frs. 199, 204.60–2 MW, Eur. *Hel.* 17).

11 παράγαγ᾽: the sense suggests that the lost subject is something like Κύπρις. Aphrodite led Helen (αὔταν) astray. The statement would characterise Helen's act as improper and at the same time probably provide a degree of exculpation. If the stroke visible in Π¹ above the second letter of 12 is correctly identified as a grave accent, Κύπρις is impossible in that line and has to be placed at the opening of 13, emphatically, as the final word in the sentence. Line 12, then, seems to have been occupied by a qualification of Helen's state of mind, e.g. Obbink's κωὐκ (~ καὶ οὐκ) ἐθέλοι]σαν 'even though she did not want to'; cf. Sa. 1.24n. The grave accent (which in ancient convention often denotes the absence of a 'real' – viz. acute or circumflex – accent) would serve to remind the reader that κωὐκ should be pronounced without accent (also in Lesbian); see Hamm 1957: §91b1 for other examples.

13–14 Probably a generalising statement, providing the transition from Helen (6–13) to the speaker's longing for Anactoria (15–20), rather than a continuation of the myth. Lidov 2016: 89–92 suggests (incorporating earlier proposals): ἄγν]αμπτον γὰρ [ἔχει] νόημμα | [καὶ τέ]λει κούφως τ[ό κέ ποι] νοήσηι 'For she (viz. Kypris, at the beginning of the line) has an unbendable mind and easily accomplishes whatever she intends.' See the apparatus of Obbink 2016a for this and other proposals.

15–20 *Anactoria.* As in line 6, the connection with what precedes – the myth section – requires interpretation; see headnote.

15–16 Perhaps: 'That (supplying τώ]με ~ τό ἐμέ) now made me think of Anactoria who is not here'; cf. Sa. 31.5.

15 νῦν marks the shift from myth to the here and now, as repeatedly in epinician.

Ἀνακτορία[ς]: she probably appeared in further Sappho poems. [Ovid] *Her.* 15.17 and Maximus of Tyre 18.9 (= testt. 19 and 20 Campbell) include her in selective lists of women loved by Sappho. Cavallini 2006 uses further late sources to speculate that Anactoria came from Miletus, to where she may or may not now have returned (which would give special point to the comparison with Λύδων ἄρματα).

ὀνέμναι[σ' continues the mental language of 13–14, and contrasts with 10–11 κωΰδ[έ] ... ἐμνάσθη (n.): love lets Helen forget and Sappho remember.

16 οὐ] **παρεοίσας:** Anactoria's absence is explained no more than that of the women who are no longer with the speaker in Sa. 94 and 96.

17–20 By ring composition, the specific statement about Anactoria exemplifies the general pronouncement in 1–4. The speaker prefers Anactoria to chariots (cf. 1 ἰππήων) and to soldiers fighting in armour (cf. 1 πέσδων). 17 ἔρατον picks up 4 ἔραται, and 18 ἴδην the aesthetic dimension of 3 κάλλιστον.

17–19 κε βολλοίμαν ... ἤ 'I would rather... than' (LSJ s.v. βούλομαι IV). Opt. + κε because the scenario is hypothetical.

17 βᾶμα ('step') makes Anactoria comparable to the soldiers of 19–20.

18 κἀμάρυχμα 'and sparkle'. Evidently a token of attraction; cf. Χαρίτων ἀμαρύγματ' ἔχουσα(ν), a formula in the Hesiodic *Catalogue of Women*. See further Brown 1989.

19 τὰ Λύδων ἄρματα: chariots had largely fallen out of use in Greek military practice in Sappho's day; they may have remained a reality in Lydia; see Aesch. *Pers.* 45–8. Certainly in later periods, Lydian chariots were proverbially excellent; see e.g. Diogenianus 3.13 (vol. II.38 Leutsch); and cf. already Pind. fr. 206.

19–20 κἀν ... [πεσδο]μάχεντας 'armed foot-soldiers'.

21–4 See 'Source' on the status of this stanza. This is probably the beginning of a new poem. Sa. 31.17ff. provides an example of a shift towards a more reflective mode at the end of what would have appeared to be a complete poem without the continuation, but it is difficult to connect 21–4 to what precedes; the unfulfilled wish of 17–20 is not a prayer (22 ἄρασθαι). For the opposite view see Lidov 2016: 92–3. Milne's ὄλβιον at the beginning of 21 would suit the alphabetical sequence of opening lines (see 1–4n.). Adopting ὄλβιον, West 2014: 3 suggests supplements that amount to: 'No one can be completely fortunate, but one may pray to enjoy a share of joy/happiness. I am conscious of this.'

Sappho 31 Voigt

A poem about the unbearable pain of love. Its remarkably mobile train of thought has prompted numerous interpretations and poetic treatments, most famously Catullus' close adaptation in poem 51. Sappho starts with the scene of a man who sits next to and converses with the female addressee; any such man, the (female) speaker says, seems to her equal to the gods (1–5). The focus then shifts to the speaker's response. She describes in detail the debilitating symptoms that afflict her whenever she looks at the addressee (7–16). Only one, corrupt, line remains of the rest (17), but the outlook seems to have become more reflective and less despairing.

The surviving stanzas take the form of a priamel; see Race 1983 and Furley 2000 (and above, p. 127 on priamels in general). The god-like man makes for an attention-grabbing opening and serves as a contrast which throws the speaker's condition into relief, but then recedes from view. He is god-like in so far as he is capable of conversing with the addressee, whereas the speaker falls apart when she merely looks at her. The contrast is highlighted by ring composition, 1 φαίνεταί μοι ... 16 φαίνομ' ἔμ' αὔται.

However, Sappho uses the priamel structure very lightly, and does not articulate the contrast sharply. The foil is not introduced as such: the opening sentence raises the false expectation of a poem about the man, or about the man and the addressee. In addition, 1 ἴσος θέοισιν is purposefully vague (appearance? status? ability?); the strength to withstand the addressee's presence suggests itself as the most obvious interpretation only when the speaker's own weakness becomes the focus of the poem, and even then ἴσος θέοισιν retains a somewhat open-ended quality. Pind. fr. 123. 2–9 both illustrates the type of contrast Sappho creates, and shows that she places the emphasis differently: 'He who sees the rays flashing from Theoxenus' eyes and is not tossed on the waves of desire has a black heart forged from adamant or iron with cold flame ... But I melt ...'

Because of Sappho's more fluid train of thought, the man always remains a lingering presence. One wants to know what he does in this otherwise female poem, where and why he is pictured sitting opposite the addressee, and whether his position vis-à-vis the addressee contributes to the speaker's suffering. All the poem allows one to say is that the two are engaged in easy and intimate conversation. The more specific reading, according to which the man and the addressee are imagined as a bridal or married couple (present or future), goes beyond the text; for different versions of this reading, see Snell 1931, Latacz 1985: 74–93 and Rösler 1990.

As in other poems (esp. fr. 1), Sappho combines vividness – the addressee's laughter and sweet voice, the speaker's crippling physical symptoms – with reflective distance. The speaker does not just stand back from her predicament in the (lost) final stanzas; the opening scene is (probably) couched in generic language too (1–5n.), but then followed by a (probably) non-generic statement about the effect on the speaker (6n.). Similarly, the symptoms are framed by a generalising clause ('whenever I look at you', 7), but then listed in such detail and with such vividness that they impress themselves as acutely present (7–16).

These shifts between generalising reflection and emotional immediacy locate the here and now of the poem in the speaker's mind. The sense of witnessing a mental world is enhanced by the absence of any indication of an internal or external setting. The address to the beloved (2, 7) is evidently imaginary in so far as she is pictured in conversation with somebody else and in so far as the speaker proclaims herself incapable of existing in her presence.

Source: The text is quoted by 'Longinus' at *On the Sublime* 10.2 for its skilful selection and combination of the symptoms of 'the madness of love' (ταῖς ἐρωτικαῖς μανίαις). All surviving MSS ultimately depend on the Parisinus gr. 2036 (= P). A second/third-century AD papyrus, *PSI* xv.1470 col. ii, partially preserves a commentary on part of the poem (= Sa. 213B Voigt, not in LP), which quotes lines 14–16. See Voigt's and Hutchinson's editions, and 13n. below, for shorter quotations in various ancient authors.

Metre: Sapphic strophes (1 ἴσος); see on Sa. 1.

Discussions: D'Alessio 2018: 57–61, Wiater 2010, Ferrari 2010 [2007]: 171–92, Radke 2005, Aloni 2001, *Furley 2000, Prins 1999: 28–40, *Stehle 1997: 288–96, *Rösler 1990, Svenbro 1993 [1988]: 150–6, Carson 1986: 12–17, Latacz 1985: 74–94, Race 1983, *Winkler 1996 (1981) 98–101 ~ Winkler 1990 [1981]: 178–90, Robbins 1980, *Privitera 1969, Page 1955: 19–33, Snell 1931, Wilamowitz-Moellendorff 1913: 56–61.

1–5 'That man to me seems equal to the gods, whoever sits opposite you (τοι ~ σοι), and listens to you close by as you speak sweetly and laugh delightfully.' The definite antecedent κῆνος … ὤνηρ (~ ὁ ἀνήρ), combined with the indefinite ὄττις-clause, probably picks out one man from a set of such men and focuses on him: any man who sits opposite you, that man seems to me. Further on this construction, as well as other interpretations of the disputed syntax, see Probert 2015: 111–18, who compares *Od.* 8. 209–11. The detailed description makes the scene concrete, despite the generalising construction. See headnote for what we can and cannot say about the man and his relationship with the addressee.

1 φαίνεταί μοι: the speaker's perspective is prominent straightaway. Sa. 165 φαίνεταί ϝοι κῆνος ('that man seems to himself'), quoted as Aeolic by Apollon. Dysc. *Pron.* 1.82 Schneider–Uhlig, may be from a different poem or an altered version of Sappho's opening; see Aloni 2001: 35–6.

ἶσος θέοισιν: see headnote. Such terminology can be used of grooms and brides (see Sa. 44.21n.) but is by no means exclusive to them. In epic, ἰσόθεος, δαίμονι ἶσος, θεὸς ὥς and similar epithets point to various kinds of extraordinary qualities and behaviour.

2–3 ἐνάντιός . . . ἰσδάνει: in Homer men and women sit opposite one another only if they are familiar with one another, so Odysseus and Penelope (*Od.* 23.89, 23.165), Odysseus and Calypso (5.198), Penelope and Telemachus (17.96); see Neuberger-Donath 1977.

3–5 ἆδυ φωναί|σας . . . καὶ γελαίσας ἰμέροεν: the 'sweet' voice and 'lovely' laughter describe an intimate scene, as well as hinting at the woman's effect on the speaker. φωναί|σας and γελαίσας are fem. ptcpls. gen. sg. The forms φωναί|σας and 7 φώνασ(αι) adopted here assume formation from *a*-stem φώναμι (rather than φώνημι); see Forssman 1966: 79–81.

5–6 τό . . . ἐπτόασεν: the speaker forcefully shifts the focus to her own reaction. The imprecise τό ('that'; cf. Sa. 16.15–16n.) leaves it open whether she is affected by the whole scene or just by the woman's laughter and voice, which immediately precedes the sentence. When the next sentence narrows attention to the speaker and the addressee, dropping the man, it is likely that this sentence too will be understood narrowly.

5 ἦ μάν marks an emphatic assertion, common e.g. in oaths, effectively 'believe me!' The speaker wants to express her plight with the greatest insistence even though (or because) she does not have the addressee's attention.

6 ἐπτόασεν 'has struck, excited', a strong word. In erotic contexts, see Alc. 283.3–4 ἐν στήθ[ε]σιν [ἐ]πτ[όαισε] | θῦμον, Anacr. 346(1).12, Thgn. 1018 (cf. 7–16n.). The aorist probably refers to the very immediate past: the speaker has just now been (and still is) affected. The shift away from the indefinite phrasing that precedes ('whoever'), as well as the assertive ἦ μάν, convey the speaker's process of visualisation: the scene presents itself vividly to her mind; see further p. 133. Alternatively, one might treat the aorist as 'gnomic' and translate as a present. However, the personal and emphatic tone would be untypical of the gnomic aorist.

7 'For whenever I as much as glance at you, immediately...'
The sentence explains (γάρ) the one that precedes by presenting the effect on the speaker's heart as a particular instance of a recurring type of response (if ἐπτόασεν = 'has struck'), or by elaborating the effect with more and stronger detail (if ἐπτόασεν = 'strikes'). For the lack of modal particle (κε, ἄν) in a temporal clause in the subjunctive, cf. Sa. 98.3, and for epic examples see Chantraine 1942–53: II.256. ὡς... ὡς is common in epic, three times with forms of εἶδον, *Il.* 14.294, 19.16, 20.424.

<ἔς> σ᾽ ἴδω: this restoration of the metre is accepted by most editors. Most 1995: 29–31 revives Hermann's <εἰ>σίδω, which would leave it open what or who precisely the speaker looks at; but εἰσοράω normally requires an object.

βρόχε᾽ ~ βραχέα, neut. pl., used adverbially. Even the briefest of glances has a violent effect.

7–16 A sequence of symptoms describes graphically how the speaker is affected. She has lost control of her body, above all her speech and her senses, and is shut off from the world. Individually, several of the afflictions occur in epic descriptions of heroes who strain and suffer on the battle-field, but Sappho amasses and lists them in the manner known to us from much later medical writers, and uses some untraditional, often hyperbolic, language. This is an arresting passage, and even more arresting as a description of suffering arising from love. See further Burnett 1983: 239–41, and cf. Sa. 58b for a shorter description of physical afflictions (caused by old age). The passage seems to be echoed in Thgn. 1017–22 (as well as later texts); alternatively, if Thgn. 1017–22 is taken wholesale from Mimnermus (see fr. 5 in *IEG²*), then Sappho may be influenced by earlier poetry.

7–9 *Loss of speech.*
7–8 φώνασ᾽ (aor. infin.) **οὐδέν** contrasts with 3–4 φωναί|σας.
8 ἔτ᾽ marks the sudden change; cf. 10 αὔτικα. The passage describes the onset of the symptoms.

εἴκει is dubious. If correct, it must be the equivalent of impersonal παρείκει 'it is possible'. No obvious emendation suggests itself, whether with the infinitive φώνασ᾽ or the genitive φώνας.

9 κἀμ... γλῶσσα ἔαγε 'my tongue is broken'. The language may evoke Homer's hypothetical 'ten tongues' and 'unbreakable voice' (*Il.* 2. 489–90), an allusion that would strengthen the paradox of the singer who says she cannot sing. See Bonanno 1993 for the motif in later texts. The hiatus before ἔαγε could easily be emended, with <μ᾽> ἔαγε or πέπαγε ('is fixed'), but it is probably satisfactorily explained as a poetic phrase that survived the loss of digamma in original *ϝέϝαγε; cf. Hes. *WD* 534 νῶτα ἔαγε, and Alc. 140.14 and 347.1nn., and see Bowie 1981: 84–6. The Lesbian of Sappho's time no longer had digamma. For

a compatible, alternative explanation (enactment of broken speech), see
Nagy 1974: 45 and Ford and Kopff 1976. For the so-called 'tmesis' (κἀμ ...
ἔαγε), see Alc. 140.14n. (ἔσταμεν).

9–10 *Heat.* πῦρ refers in the first instance to a sensation of heat spreading through the body; cf. the meaning 'fever', attested later (LSJ s.v. 1.7).
It also evokes the metaphor of desire that burns (e.g. Sa. 48, Pind. *Pyth.*
4.219), parches (e.g. Archil. 193) or warms one (e.g. Alcm. 59a).

9 λέπτον: the kind of 'thin' fire that can steal beneath the skin.

11 *Loss of vision.*
ὀππάτεσσι ... ὄρημμ' ~ ὄμμασι ... ὁράω.

11–12 *Loss of hearing.* 'My ears ?roar'; a contrast with 4 ὐπακούει.
The verb ἐπιρρόμ|βεισι is probably a suggestive ad hoc formation, evoking
the vibrating roar produced when the ῥόμβος ('bullroarer') is whirled.
The only other attestation is in Σ Pind. *Isthm.* 4.77c. For a full discussion,
see Prauscello 2007, who considers possible medical implications.

13 *Sweating.* The overall sense is clear: the speaker sweats. But there are
two (related) problems with the text. (i) The line is too long: by three
syllables as preserved in 'Longinus' (reproduced in the main text), by one
syllable as quoted in the *Epimerismi Homerici* 114 (reproduced in the apparatus). (ii) The beginning of the line is corrupt: ἔκαδε ('Longinus') clearly
so; ἀ δέ (*Epim.*) almost certainly so, since the article would emphasise ἴδρως
at the expense of the other afflictions, and since ἴδρως is masculine
(according to the *Epim.* it is fem. in Aeolic Greek, but that claim may
well be based on just this text). The simplest approach is to lose one of the
first two syllables in 'Longinus'' text, e.g. amending to κἀδ δέ, and then to
delete two further syllables later in the line. But ψῦχρος (absent from
Epim.) is common as a qualification of sweat, and was almost certainly in
'Longinus'' source, as is shown by ψύχεται in his paraphrase (10.3);
καταχεῖσθαι too is singularly appropriate for sweat: several times thus
used in the Hippocratic corpus, and cf. *Il.* 11.811 and 16.109–10. Both
words could be kept by adopting κἀδ δ' ἴδρως ψῦχρος χέεται, but one expects
a first-person pronoun, and ἴδρ- would be unusual in Sappho, though not
impossible; for a defence, see Neri and Citti 2005 and Privitera 2013. Less
difficult would be Page's κἀδ δέ μ' ἴδρως ψῦχρος ἔχει.

ἴδρως: sweat flows in battle and athletic exertion in epic (*LfgrE* s.v.).

13–14 *Trembling.* τρόμος ... ἄγρει resembles a range of epic expressions
with τρόμος, usually expressing fear; e.g. *Il.* 3.34 (combined with paleness),
5.862, 22.136.

14 παῖσαν ~ πᾶσαν, the first indication that the speaker is female.

14–15 *Loss of colour.* Greenness attends various medical conditions in
the Hippocratic corpus; e.g. *Prog.* 2.2, *Morb.* 2.39.1, *Loc. Hom.* 28.2.
In Homer, it is associated with fear; e.g. *Il.* 7.479, 15.4. The hyperbolic
comparison 'greener than (the quintessentially green) grass' is

characteristic of Sappho; cf. frs. 98a.6–7 ('yellower than a torch'), 156 ('more golden than gold'), 167 ('whiter than an egg'), and see the discussion of Zellner 2006. Since freshness is central to many uses of χλωρός (LSJ s.v. III) the translation 'paler', viz. parched, is unlikely.

15–16 τεθνάκην . . . αὔται: lit. 'it appears to me that I shall not want much in order to be dead' (West 1970a: 312). (Near-)death caps the list of the speaker's sufferings.

15 ὀλίγω ~ ὀλίγου (neut. gen.). **'πιδεύσην** is often emended to present 'πιδεύην or adjectival 'πιδεύης, but may well be correct. Even though active ἐπιδεύω is only found late, both Homer and Alcaeus use δεύω, and ἐπιδέω occurs from Herodotus onwards. Future infinitive after φαίνεσθαι is rare but attested, e.g. Hdt. 7.48. See further Tzamali 1996: 187–8.

16 φαίνομ' ἔμ' αὔται picks up 1 φαίνεταί μοι κῆνος. The speaker considers a man who sits opposite the girl equal to the (immortal) gods, and considers herself close to death.

17 The poem continues with what seems to be a general statement: 'But all may be endured (or "dared") since. . .' As elsewhere in Sappho, notably in fr. 1, the tone becomes less despairing as the poem approaches the end, and the perspective broadens; cf. 16.21–4n. and pp. 147–8. One can only speculate about what is lost, as do (e.g.) West 1970a: 312–15, Di Benedetto 2010, D'Angour 2013, Livrea 2016. Catullus 51 has one stanza after the list of afflictions, but is not a reliable guide since that stanza does not seem to resemble Sappho's line 17.

†καὶ πένηταt is unmetrical. In addition, there is probably a lacuna in the 'Longinus' MSS since the quotation is left dangling without a verb.

Sappho 44 Voigt

The most substantial text in Sappho's surviving corpus, an account of Hector's arrival at Troy with his bride Andromache. We have the end; two or three lines are missing at the beginning. The lost opening aside (on which see 1n.), the poem falls into four parts: (i) the herald Idaeus announces to Priam that Hector and his companions have brought Andromache and many gifts in their boats (2–11); (ii) the news spreads and the Trojans immediately rush off to meet the couple and their entourage (12–20, possibly continuing into the lacuna); (iii) (probably) the two groups meet and set off towards Troy (lacuna and 21–3); (iv) the celebrants, and presumably the couple, process back (24–34).

Sa. 44 is almost certainly a stand-alone mythological narrative rather than a wedding song celebrating a non-mythical couple, as sometimes used to be thought: too little is lost at the beginning to allow one to posit a major non-mythical section; see 'Source', 1n. Performance (probably

solo) may nevertheless have taken place in the context of weddings, but
poetic competitions are equally possible, as are *symposia* or the kind of all-
female context often assumed for the performance of Sappho's love songs
(on Sappho's context, see p. 114).

Sappho 44 stands in a tradition of representing weddings in texts and
images: see *Il.* 18.491–6, [Hes.] *Scut.* 272–80, Eur. *IA* 1036–79, Theoc. 18,
Catull. 61–2 and 64, X.Eph. 1.8–9; and for the iconography Lissarrague
1996. Like many texts in this tradition, some of them looking back to this
poem, Sa. 44 exploits an inherent tension between heroic epic and the
wedding. This is clear above all in respect of narrative technique and tone,
but also in the choice of metre and language. (More generally on Sappho's
relationship with epic, and the methodological questions involved, see
above, pp. 17–18.)

Narrative. As a piece of sequential mythological narrative, unusual in
Sappho's extant corpus (but see fr. 44a), Sa. 44 clearly looks to epic.
Characteristically epic elements enhance the effect: a messenger speech
(3a–10), a catalogue (8–10), a departure scene (13–20). The account of
wedding celebrations in the final part (24–34), with its public focus and its
detailed depiction of the celebrating community at large, has much in
common with the two fullest representations of weddings in early hexameter, those on Achilles' shield in the *Iliad* and in the Hesiodic *Shield*
(references above). On the other hand, Sa. 44 is distinctly unepic in its
(relative) brevity. Moreover, despite a sense of urgency in the lead-up to
the climactic procession (3 τάχυς, 11 ὀτραλέως, 13 αὖτικ'), the narrative is
characterised not so much by a drive towards a final outcome in the
manner of Homeric epic as by visual tableaux (the gifts, the Trojans
leaving, the procession) and by a proliferation of speech acts (Idaeus'
report, the news spreading through the town (12n.), the songs sung by the
celebrants, including the wedding song that Sappho does not quite sing
herself (33, 34nn.). Fundamentally, weddings offer scope for visual scenes
and for meta-representation more than for teleological or sequential
narrative impetus. Already in the *Iliad*, the fullest wedding scene (on the
shield of Achilles) is an ecphrastic set piece that sits outside the plot.

Tone. Heroic epic and the wedding diverge also in mood, one a genre
replete with death and suffering, the other an occasion of harmony and
joy. Along with the rest of Achilles' shield, the wedding scene in *Il.* 18
stands in contrast to the main narrative; see Taplin 1980. Sappho's choice
of Hector and Andromache adds a further dimension. In the *Iliad* their
marriage is doomed. Their wedding is referred to only once, in the
emblematic vignette of Andromache's faint after Hector's death: as she
sinks down she throws off 'the headscarf that golden Aphrodite had given
her on the day on which Hector of the gleaming helmet brought her from
the house of Eëtion, after bestowing countless gifts' (22.470–2).

Andromache's home city of Thebe, named by Sappho in line 6, is in the *Iliad* a city sacked and plundered, presaging the fate of Troy itself; see esp. Andromache's own account at 6.414–28, with Zarker 1965 and Easterling 1995, and on Thebe in the lost epic tradition more widely, *Cypria* fr. 24 West with Burgess 2002: 151–2. Behind Sappho's story of joyful celebration lies a story of doom. (For uncertain attempts to go further, and detect verbal references to the *Iliad*, see Rissman 1983: 119–48 and Schrenk 1994.)

Two opposed interpretations of this dark backdrop suggest themselves, and may have suggested themselves already in antiquity. (i) Sappho is pointedly turning darkness into light. She extracts what is happy in the marriage of Hector and Andromache and implicitly declares her power to select and tell her own story. We are to think of the darkness only to let the text dispel it. Or (ii) Sappho exploits the contrast between marriage and death, which appears already in the *Il.* 22 passage, and indeed in the story of the most famous epic couple, Helen and Paris, and which tragedy later develops extensively. Wistfully, she sings of Hector's and Andromache's pre-Iliadic youth, conscious that their happiness will not last and is the more precious for it. For celebratory readings, see Rösler 1975 and Pallantza 2005: 79–88 (unnecessarily tying this interpretation to performance at a wedding procession), for ominous readings, Kakridis 1966 and Schrenk 1994. (Alc. 42 raises related questions regarding the marriage of Peleus and Thetis: pp. 89–90.)

The engagement with epic extends to *metre* and *language*. For metre see below. The dialect of Sa. 44 is the same artificial composite as elsewhere in the Lesbian poets (see p. 88), but with a different balance. Along with a small handful of other fragments, Sa. 44 contains a larger than usual proportion of elements that we associate with epic and which are non-standard in Lesbian Greek, many of them guaranteed by the metre, e.g. the ending -οιο instead of Lesbian -ω in 16, and κατὰ πτόλιν in 12 rather than standard κάτ and πολ-. Page 1955: 66–70 gives a full, annotated list. Hooker 1977 and Bowie 1981 have challenged several of his instances, but a degree of difference from most of Sappho's other surviving texts is certain. The epicising effect is greatly strengthened, moreover, by the large number of epithets and adaptations of epic formulae (see commentary, and again pp. 17–18 for questions of methodology).

In imagining the significance of Sappho's narrative to her Lesbian audiences, geography needs to be borne in mind. Lesbos exerted considerable influence in the Troad in this period (Hdt. 5.94–5, Strabo 13.1.38). The Iliadic geography of the Troad is vague, but later texts situate Andromache's Thebe near the Gulf of Adramyttium, right across the straits from Lesbos (Hdt. 7.42.1, Strabo 13.1.61–3, *Barrington Atlas* 56E2). It has been suggested that Sa. 44 reinforced claims of descent from the Trojan royal house by Lesbian aristocratic families with interests in the Troad; see Aloni 1986, Coppola 2005. This is merely speculation, but even without such a hypothesis it is obvious that for Sappho's audiences this story of the distant past was also a story close to home. For another poem of Sappho's that uses epic myth with local relevance, see fr. 17.

Source: The text is derived from two partly overlapping paypri, the third-century AD *P.Oxy.* x.1232 (= Π^1) and the first- or second-century AD *P.Oxy.* xvii.2076 (= Π^2), both first edited by Hunt (Π^1 with some supplements by Wilamowitz). Π^1 preserves at least part of most surviving lines: 1–26 in col. ii and 29–34 in col. iii. Π^2 gives us the left-hand side of 23–34, filling in gaps in Π^1. The combination of two observations suggests that only three lines are lost at the beginning; see Sampson 2016: 54–6: (a) col. i. of Π^1 carries a different text (fr. 43), followed by blank space; fr. 44 therefore starts in col. ii; (b) the continuous text of 23–34 in Π^2 shows that only two lines (27–8) are lost at the top of col. iii of Π^1; it follows that a similar amount is lost at the top of col. ii.

The poem was the last in book 2 of the Alexandrian edition of Sappho, as is indicated by the *subscriptio* Σαπφ[οῦς μέλων] β in Π^2. It is attributed to Sappho's book 2 also by Athen. 11.460d, who cites most of line 10. Book 2 gathered poems in gl^{2d} (Hephaestion 7.7, p. 23 Consbruch); the surviving fragments (43–52) are varied in content.

Metre:

x x – ∪ ∪ – ∪ ∪ – ∪ ∪ – ∪ – ‖ gl^{2d} 9 πορφύρᾱ, 10 ἀργύρᾱ

A period consisting of glyconics expanded with two dactyls is repeated identically. The dactylic central section of each verse resembles the body of an epic hexameter verse; but unlike the hexameter, and in common with other aeolic metres, Sappho's line opens with the two-syllable aeolic base (≍ ≍) and never contracts dactyls into spondees (it always has fourteen syllables). Despite these differences, Sappho's expression in this metre is clearly affected by epic as it accepts instances of epic (and distinctly un-Lesbian) prosody, esp. 'epic' correption (5 -ρ[ο]ῖ ἄγ-) and short vowels before plosive and liquid/nasal (8 -ατᾰ χρύ-, 14 ὄχλος); see again the list of Page 1955: 66–7. For discussion of the metre, including the phraseology in relation to the metre, see Nagy 1974: 118–39, Hooker 1977: 56, 76–7, Ferrari 1986. Prauscello 2006: 188–202 argues that, musically, the poem was articulated in two-verse mini-strophes (cf. Sa. 58b below).

Discussions: Spelman 2017, Sampson 2016, Bowie 2010: 70–4, Power 2010: 258–67, Ferrari 2010 [2007]: 128–33, Coppola 2005, *Pallantza 2005: 79–88, Pernigotti 2001, Schrenk 1994, Meyerhoff 1984: 118–39, Burnett 1983: 219–23, Rissman 1983: 119–48, *Rösler 1975, *Kakridis 1966, *Page 1955: 63–74. See also 'Metre' above. On wedding songs, see Swift 2010: ch. 6 and Contiades-Tsitsoni 1990.

1 We can only speculate about the content of this and the preceding three lines (for the extent of the loss, see 'Source'). They may have formed a mini-prologue; cf. epic proems and Stes. 100. Alternatively, the poem may have settled straight into the narrative; cf. Alc. 42 (perhaps), Bacch. 17, Theoc. 18. Either way, punctuation at the end of 1 (which is in Π¹) and the asyndeton at the beginning of 2 mark at least a small break. What is very unlikely in this brief space is an enunciative frame that relates the narrative to a wedding here and now.

Κυπρο.: 'Cyprus' or a compound adjective 'Cyprus- . . .', almost certainly a reference to Cyprian Aphrodite, who is prominent in weddings. Cf. *Il.* 22.470–2, quoted on p. 138.

2–11 *The herald reports the arrival by boat of Hector and his bride Andromache.*

2–3 Idaeus is the principal herald of Priam and Troy in the *Iliad*. Epic phrasing is evident, even though much of the text is irrecoverable: cf. *Il.* 3.248 etc. κῆρυξ Ἰδαῖος, 18.2 πόδας ταχὺς ἄγγελος ἦλθε, 11.715 etc. ἄγγελος ἦλθε θέουσ'. This last phrase suggests the supplement θέ[ων in 2: 'The herald came running.' At line-end perhaps ἔλε[γε στ]άθεις (Jurenka), and in 3 τάδ' ἔκαστα (Diehl).

3a A diagonal line to the left and the word ἄνω ('above') to the right of this line would seem to indicate that some text was accidentally omitted and subsequently added at the top of the page. If just one line is missing it will be the opening of Idaeus' speech, since 4 begins mid-sentence. (We also lack a phrase introducing the speech, but this may have been placed within 2–3.)

4 Perhaps: 'The unperishing glory ?extends across (or ?"reaches") ?Troy and the rest of Asia.' But reconstruction is difficult. According to Lobel the most likely letter before αν is γ, i.e. accusative γᾶν, which would govern the genitive Ἀσίας. But no suitable verb that fits   [ ]δε has been proposed. Alternatively, if restoration starts with Hunt's plausible-looking τ[ό]δε, it becomes hard to restore . αν, even if letters other than γ are considered. Punctuation at line-end is in Π¹.

Ἀσίας: not a precise term in this period, but the western stretches of the Anatolian peninsula (and thus both Troy and Thebe) were certainly considered part of Asia; see *Il.* 2.461, [Hes.] frs. 165.11, 180.3 MW, Mimn. 9.2, and for the intricate debate, Dryer 1965 and Allen 1993: 80–1.

κλέος: evidently the glory of Andromache and/or her marriage with Hector. Sappho's usage notably contrasts with that of the *Iliad*, which ties κλέος, above all the κλέος ἄφθιτον of Achilles (9.413), to fighting and death. For such pointedly un-Iliadic κλέος, cf. *Od.* 24.196 (the κλέος of the faithful Penelope) and Ibyc. S151.46–8. There is also a self-conscious dimension, since Sappho's poem contributes to this κλέος.

5 ἄγοισ' ~ ἄγουσι: wedding language. The middle ἄγεσθαι is standard for the groom leading the bride to his home. The active is rarer, but see *Il.* 18.493, *Od.* 11.324, Hes. *Th.* 998.

ἐλικώπιδα: meaning uncertain, perhaps 'flashing-eyed'; used in early hexameter of maidens in the context of marriage or sex, e.g. Hes. *Th.* 998, fr. 43a.19 MW. The hyperbaton throws emphasis on Andromache.

6 ἰέρας: on cities as sacred, see Alc. 42.4n. Thebe is ἰερή at *Il.* 1.366.

Πλακίας τ' ἀπ' [ἀϊ]ννάω: in the *Iliad* Thebe is situated below the mountain Plakos, ὑπὸ Πλάκωι (6.396, etc.). By contrast, Sappho has 'ever-flowing Plakia', evidently a spring or river (which does not dry up in summer). This suits the indication of origin: the *Iliad* uses the combination of ἐκ + a city and ἀπό + a river to express the faraway place from which somebody or something is brought, e.g. 2.659; see Voigt 1961.

7–8 ἐνὶ ... πόντον: the journey from Thebe to Troy is made by boat also at *Il.* 23.829 (by Achilles), but the notion that it takes a sea voyage to travel from Thebe to the present location gains particular meaning in performance on (the nearby island of) Lesbos. ἐν νήεσσι is formulaic in early hexameter; ἐπ' ἄλμυρον | πόντον combines the epic line-end formulae ἐπὶ οἴνοπα πόντον and ἁλμυρὸν ὕδωρ; for the positioning across line-end, see Ferrari 1986: 445.

8–10 A long and artfully varied list of gifts demonstrates the value of the marriage to Hector and the Trojans, as well as the wealth of Thebe and its royal house. The list is in the nominative, as its last member κἀλέφαις shows, and requires supplementing 'there are'. For the switch from accusative (Ἀνδρομάχαν) to nominative in some lists, see KG 1.45–6 and Friis Johansen and Whittle 1980 on Aesch. *Suppl.* 714–15.

The practice of dowries – the flow of wealth from the family of the bride to the groom – was standard in Athens from at least the sixth century. In Homer it is often, vice versa, the suitor who brings the gifts, notably Hector at *Il.* 22.472. But Homer also has some notion of gifts accompanying the bride, and Andromache's epithet πολύδωρος (at 6.394 and 22.88) is suitably vague. Sappho thus differs subtly rather than radically from Homer, conceivably in line with contemporary Lesbian practice. Further on wedding-related gifts in Homer, see Snodgrass 1974: 115–18, Morris 1986: 104–10, Ormand 2014: 237–41; and on the changes during the Archaic period, Vernant 1980 [1973].

8 [ἐλί]γματα: twisted or curved jewellery, such as bracelets (~ epic ἕλιξ). **κάμματα:** ἔμμα ~ εἷμα.

9 πορφύρ[α]: for the unexpected neut. pl. ending -ρᾶ here and in 10 ἀργύρα, see Page 1955: 69 and Hooker 1977: 87–8.

καταΰτ[με]να: unresolved, despite the tantalisingly similar πορφύραι †καταυταμενα† at Sa. 101.3. If the word exists as printed here, it must mean 'perfumed'; cf. ἀϋτμή = 'scent' (LSJ s.v. 2) and see Treu 1954:

198–9. The more obvious articulation is κατ' ἀΰτ[με]να, which might just possibly mean '(clothes) that float with the breezes' (West 1993: 39), but the prepositional phrase does not suit the flow of the sentence. **ἀθύρματα** 'playthings', 'treasures'; of women's objects also at *Od.* 15.416. The phrase is in apposition to 8 [ἐλί]γματα . . . κἄμματα. **10 κἀλέφαις ~** καὶ ἐλέφας. A bald singular caps the list. Homer has a range of luxury objects wholly or partially made from ivory: reins, weapons, furniture, a mirror.

11 πάτ[η]ρ φίλος: Priam responds to the good news in his role as Hector's beloved and loving father, as he does to his death and defilement at *Il.* 22.408, ὤιμωξεν δ' ἐλεεινὰ πατὴρ φίλος.

12–20 *The Trojans set out to meet the couple.* The Trojans are classified by sex and marital status: females on mule-drawn carriages (13–16) vs males on horse-drawn chariots (17–18), the females subdivided into (married) women and unmarried girls (with Priam's daughters as a separate subgroup), and the males described specifically as unmarried youths. This taxonomy will be repeated in 24–34(n.) and befits the wedding as a ritual that formally orchestrates transition into adulthood and the coming together of the sexes. Cf. *Il.* 18.494–6 and [Hes.] *Scut.* 278–84.

12 The herald reported to Priam, now the news spreads anonymously; ἦλθε picks up 2 ἦλθε. The unperishing and thus translocal κλέος of line 4 is at this point manifest in the form of Trojan φάμα. Weddings give rise to rumour also in Homer: *Od.* 6.27–30, 23.148–51. For the phrasing cf. *Od.* 23.362, *Little Iliad* fr. dub. 32 West.

φίλοις (dat.) is inclusive here; family, friends, and *polis* are not sharply distinguished in this happy event. The reading has been called into question because of the repetition after 11 φίλος; see esp. Massimi 1959: 26–9. However, φιλία is central to weddings, and the repetition contributes to the sense that news is disseminating.

13 Ἰλίαδαι 'descendants of Ilus'. The Trojans share a common ancestor; cf. 12 φίλοις. The term comprises both sexes.

σατίναι[ς]: see Anacr. 388.10n. for the associations of gender and elegance. More practical and comfortable than horse-drawn chariots, wagons (typically mule-drawn) were standard in wedding processions, e.g. [Hes.] *Scut.* 273. By contrast, chariots, the ἄρ[ματ(α) of line 17, were reserved for depictions of heroic and divine weddings. See further Oakley and Sinos 1993: 29–30 and Griffith 2006: 233–41. Sappho blends myth and contemporary practice.

14 αἰμιόνοις ~ ἡμιόνους.

παῖς (~ πᾶς) **ὄχλος** is contrasted with the daughters of Priam in 16, but not in a derogatory way; cf. Sa. 17.13–14 ὄ]χλος | παρθέ[νων . . . γ]υναίκων. The scene is crowded as everybody takes an interest.

15 [ ] σφύρων: attested epic -σφυρος compounds do not seem to fit the space and traces. Perhaps Lavagni's τ' ἀτ[αλ]ροσφύρων, which would involve a transfer of the tenderness from the girls to their ankles.

16–20 Perhaps: 'Separately, next, ?went the daughters of Priam. ?All the unmarried young men yoked horses to ... chariots. Greatly ... the charioteers ... ?conveyed them out [of the city].'

16 αὖ reinforces χῶρις by marking the shift to a different group; on this particle, see Bonifazi 2012: ch. 4. Everybody joins, but royalty and/or family are treated distinctly.

Περάμοιο is a hybrid form, combining a Lesbian version of the name (cf. Alc. 42.2 Περράμ-) with an epic genitive ending (Lesbian -ω); its significance for the history of the poetic traditions of Lesbos is discussed by West 2002: 218.

θυγ[α]τρεσ[: probably nom. θύγ[α]τρες, governing a verb lost at line-end, rather than dat. θυγ[ά]τρεσ[ι. They are of course Hector's sisters and half-sisters, but the focus remains on Priam, whose lead they follow and from whose palace they depart.

18 π[ ]ες: quite possibly π[άντ]ες, cf. 14 and 32.

ἠΐθεοι '(unmarried) youths', the male equivalent of *parthenoi*. The term appears to qualify ἄνδρες; it is difficult to restore the sentence in such a way that those are two separate classes, like the women and *parthenoi* in 15. In 32, too, there is only one class of ἄνδρες.

20]ξα ο[: the likeliest restoration is ἔ]ξαγο[ν. This would produce a neat contrast with 5 ἄγοισ'. One group approaches, the other exits, the city.

Lacuna to 23 (*Probably:*) *The two groups meet and jointly set off for the city.*

Lacuna A smallish number of lines is lost between 20 and 21, since the fragments of Π¹ which, respectively, carry 1–20 and 21–6 are from the same column. Sampson 2016: 57–9 estimates six to seven, but the margin of error is large.

21 ἴ]κελοι θέοι[ς: no doubt Hector and Andromache, probably in the narrator's voice; cf. 34n. Hyperbolic comparisons are a topos of wedding song; see e.g. Sa. 105a (like an apple), 111 (like Ares), Eur. fr. 781.27 *TrGF* ('greater than a king in happiness', text uncertain). See also Sa. 31.1n.

22–3 Something like: 'all together (the people) set out for Troy'. The reference of ἄγνον is irrecoverable.

23 ὄρμαται raises questions because the historic present is not properly attested for this early period. If Sappho does indeed use it here, it probably serves to punctuate the narrative and indicate the beginning of a new section; for this usage in Classical texts, see Rijksbaron 2002: §7.3 and Willi 2017: 237–41.

24–34 *Procession and celebration.* Sounds are prominent in a multi-sensory sequence of instrumental music, singing, laughter, drink, perfumes, cries and more singing. The movements in space are hazy: what starts as a procession into the city turns imperceptibly into city-wide festivities (esp. 28). A pervasive sense of communal festivity and serene worship is more important than structure and order, but as in 12–20(n.) the crowd is organised into *parthenoi* (25–?), older women (31) and men (32–4).

24–5 αὖλος ... [κ]ροτάλ[ων: a wind and a percussion instrument. Presumably a string instrument is lost in the gap, e.g. κίθαρις (Lobel and Page). Exuberantly mixed instrumentation is frequent in literary wedding scenes; see *Il.* 18.495, [Hes.] *Scut.* 278–80, Eur. *IA* 1036–9. It probably symbolises boundless celebration as well as reflecting some form of reality. On music-making at weddings, see Kauffmann-Samaras 1996.

24 ἀδυ[μ]έλης: unremarkable as an epithet of string instruments (e.g. Sa. 156), but striking for the *aulos*, known for its piercing sound. ὀνεμίγνυ[το ~ ἀνεμίγνυτο (impf.).

25 ⌣ ⌣]ως: probably an adverb qualifying ἄειδον, e.g. λιγέ]ως (Lobel). ἄρα probably marks what follows (*parthenoi* singing) as an elaboration of what preceded (general music-making). See *LfgrE* s.v. 11.3 for this usage.

26 ἄγν[ον: 'pure' (since sung by *parthenoi* in an appropriate manner) as well as 'inviolable, sacred' (since belonging to the gods).

26–7 ἴκα]νε ... θεσπεσίᾳ: a variation on epic phrasing, e.g. *Il.* 13.837 ἠχὴ δ'... ἴκετ' αἰθέρα. For ἄχω θεσπεσία, see Alc. 130b.19n.

27 γελ[: probably a reference to laughter. Laughter suits the convivial language of the next lines, and more generally the joyous and sometimes ribald atmosphere of weddings; see Sa. 110, Theoc. 18.9–15, Halliwell 2008: 198.

28 Probably: 'Everywhere in the streets there was ...' ὀδο[ις (acc. pl.) is more likely than ὀδο[ν, which would yield 'along their route'. ἦς (Lesb.) ~ ἦν. See Bacch. fr. 4.79 for a similar evocation of all-inclusive sympotic street celebration, and Bond on Eur. *HF* 783.

29 κράτηρες are mixing bowls; the shallower φίαλαι are used both for drinking and for offering libations, of wine or perfume.

30 For incense and its place at weddings, see Sa. 2.4n. Exotic spices like myrrh and cassia, associated in later writers especially with Arabia, are absent from Homer and will not all have been everyday goods in Sappho's world; see further Hdt. 3.107.1 with Asheri *et al.* 2007 *ad loc.*, and Amigues 2005: 372–5.

31–3 Either (i) 'All the elder women performed the *ololyge*; all men cried out the lovely soaring paean, calling upon the far-shooter with the fair lyre'; or (ii) '... cried out a lovely soaring tune, calling upon Paian the far-shooter...' The sentence may be playing with the ambivalence of *paian* as both a name of Apollo and a song addressed to Apollo; see Ford 2006: 291–2. For the enjambment in interpretation (i) (ὄρθιον | πάον'), cf. 5–7,

7–8(n.). Interpretation (ii) requires the usage ὁ ὄρθιος = ὄρθιος νόμος (for which see Aristoph. *Ach.* 16, with Olson 2002 *ad loc.*) to go back to Sappho's period. Later texts attribute this famous nome (roughly = 'tune') to the early Lesbian kitharode Terpander; see Power 2010: 261–2. Female *ololyge* and male paean are combined also at Bacch. 17. 124–9 (again near the end of the poem, and leading on to a final self-referential statement) and Xen. *An.* 4.3.19. The joyful emotionality of both *ololyge* and paean, as well as the suggestion of a joint performance, create a sense of climax.

31 ὀλόλυσδον: augmentless impf. On the ὀλολυγή, see Alc. 130b.20n.

32 ὄρθιον 'clarion', 'soaring'; both loud and high-pitched. The term often describes 'shrill' cries of lament or fear, but suits also the full-throated paean cry; cf. Soph. *Trach.* 210–11 παιᾶνα παι|ᾶν' ἀνάγετ' ('raise the paean').

33 πάον': for celebratory paeans at weddings, see Aesch. fr. 350.4 *TrGF*, Aristoph. *Thesm.* 1034–5, and further Rutherford 2001b: 56–7. Audiences familiar with the *Iliad* may think of the rather different paean that the Greeks sing as they take Hector's body back to the ships at *Il.* 22. 391–2; see Nagy 1974: 135–8 and Rutherford 2001b: 123–6. With ἴαχον Sappho points to the cry ἰὴ παιάν that constitutes the essence of the paean, while ἐπήρατον suggests beautiful song; for this combination of cry and song, cf. Thgn. 779 παιάνων τε χοροῖς ἰαχῆισί τε. On the form πάον', see Page 1955: 67.

34 The description of the procession ends climactically with the celebration of the couple. The (presumably solo) song ends with a representation of choral performance, the medium appropriate to wedding song. See also the headnote. The emphatic final θεοεικέλο[ις picks up 21 ἴ]κελοι θέοι[ς (n.). Voices merge: both the speaker and the ἄνδρες praise the couple as 'godlike'.

ὔμνην: 3rd pers. pl. impf. For -ην (here metrically guaranteed) rather than -εν, as expected in Aeolic, see Sa. 1.11n.

Sappho 58b

The speaker puts her own old age at the centre of a song performed before a (real or imaginary) group of παῖδες.

The constitution of the text is unusually intriguing. It rests on two papyri, the early third-century BC Π¹, published in 2004, and the late second-century AD Π², known since 1922 (see 'Source' for details). Π¹ preserves (part of) lines 1–12 of the sixteen lines printed here, with what are evidently different, though thematically linked, texts preceding and following: it treats 1–12 as a complete poem. Π² was probably a copy of

Sappho's book 4 (see 'Metre'). It preserves (part of) all sixteen lines printed here, within a longer run of lines. Since the left-hand margin is missing we cannot tell where Π² indicated divisions between poems. (This is why the text appears in pre-2004 editions, including Voigt, as fr. 58.11ff.)

There are therefore two possibilities. The first is that Π², like Π¹, presented lines 1–12 as a complete text, with a new poem, also by Sappho, starting at 13, and running beyond 16. The sixteen-line version would then be a phantom created by the loss of the left-hand margin in Π². This is the much simpler, and therefore likelier, scenario; see Luppe 2004, West 2005, Bernsdorff 2005. Alternatively, Sappho may have composed a poem of sixteen lines, which was shortened at a later point, whether or not by the compiler of Π¹, to create an alternative version. This and similar scenarios are argued for by Livrea 2007, Yatromanolakis 2008, Boedeker 2009, Lardinois 2009. External support for the existence of the sixteen-line poem has been sought in possible allusions, arguably none of them overwhelmingly close, at Eur. Alc. 994–5, Posidippus epigr. 52 AB (see Puelma and Angiò 2005), Cercidas, CA fr. 7. For fuller overviews of the constitution of the text, see Hammerstaedt 2009 and Obbink 2009. This edition provides lemmatised notes only for 1–12, but presents the text also of 13–16.

The *twelve-line version* is one of Sappho's darker texts. It is dominated by a catalogue of the symptoms of the speaker's old age in 3–6, and ends sharply and suggestively after an account of the myth of Eos and the ageing Tithonus in 9–12; see Bernsdorff 2005. But it is not simply an unrelieved lament of old age. The poem opens with the speaker singing in the company of παῖδες. After describing her symptoms, she attempts in 7–8 to console herself by placing her suffering in a universal perspective; and the Tithonus narrative is sufficiently allusive to invite readings beyond the demonstration that old age is inevitable.

The poem is organised with tight symmetry. Lines 3–6, 7–8 and 9–12 are all construed around contrasts. 1 κάλα is picked up by 11 [κ]άλον, 1 παῖδες by 11 νέον, 5 φέροισι by 10 φέροισα[ν, 'white' in 4 by 'grey' in 12, ποτα in 3 and 6 by another ποτα in 9, and γῆρας in 3 by γῆρας in 12, probably both half-personified as the subjects of their respective sentences.

The (very possibly non-existent) *sixteen-line version* would be considerably lighter in tone, extending in its last two lines the incipient move towards contentment and bringing undeveloped aspects of the myth into view in retrospect. Lines 15–16 appear to associate the speaker with the very beauty that could not coexist with old age in 3–6 and 11–12, and they dwell on love rather than age. As in frs. 1 and 31, the speaker's mood and focus gradually develop as she contemplates her condition, with a particularly sharp inflection near the end. Again, there are symmetries. The overall structure is the more standard ABA, with an emphatic return to the first person (15 ἔγω). 16 κάλον looks back to the previous two instances of καλ-, 16 ἔρος to 10 ἔρωι, and the sun in 16 to Eos ('dawn') in the myth.

In both versions, the poem combines themes that are well established individually but not usually joined: youth/old age, song, love. It also combines a range of different modes: personal outcry, address to παῖδες, universal truth, myth. Looked at as a statement about old age, the most striking thing about the text is the integration of old age into a greater whole. Sappho treats old age and all the suffering it brings as integral to human existence, rather than wishing it away or longing for death.

For old age in early Greek literature, see pp. 200, 201. For points of contact with Mimnermus, who probably predates Sappho, see Johnson 2009. Sappho treats the theme also in frs. 24a and 121, possibly in 63, and above all in 21, which exhibits some notable similarities with 58b; see further Ferrari 2010 [2007]: 201–4.

The poem has been used as evidence for the hypothesis that Sappho is a choral poet (for which see p. 114). On this reading, the παῖδες are a young chorus led by Sappho, and she sings while they dance. This is possible, but two points need to be noted. First, choral performance is only implicit in what survives. The word 'chorus' does not appear (but is sometimes reconstructed in 1–2, and see 5–6n.), and the only mention of dance concerns Sappho's youth (6). The tortoise-lyre (2) is a versatile instrument, used for both solo and choral song; see Maas and Snyder 1989: 34–9. Secondly, even if the παῖδες are a chorus, the text is best seen as straddling individual self-expression (the speaker's meditation on her old age) and chorality (the internal audience of παῖδες); on Sappho's blending of 'private' and 'public' elsewhere, see Winkler 1990 [1981] and Snyder 1991, and on the marginal position vis-à-vis communal festivity adopted by many of her texts, D'Alessio 2018 (fr. 58b on pp. 52–3).

Source: Π¹ (Cologne papyrus inv. 21351 + 21376; two fragments of the same papyrus) was first edited in Gronewald and Daniel 2004a and 2004b ('G–D'), and subsequently included as no. 429 in *Kölner Papyri* vol. XI. It predates the Alexandrian edition, which may explain the form στεναχίζω (rather than -ίσδω; cf. p. 88). Π² (*P.Oxy.* xv.1787 fr. 1) was edited by Hunt. Much of lines 15–16 is preserved by the Peripatetic philosopher Clearchus (fr. 41 Wehrli), as quoted by Athenaeus (15.687a–b). Clearchus is discussing the connection between luxury and virtue.

Metre:

× – ◡ ◡ – – ◡ ◡ – – ◡ ◡ – ◡ – – ‖   *hag²ᶜ = ᴧhipp²ᶜ*

Hagesichoreans (= acephalous hipponacteans) with double choriambic expansion. The metre repeats line by line. In both Π¹ and Π² the text is marked off into two-line stanzas by means of *paragraphoi*, and there is indeed a tendency for pairs of verses to form syntactic units.
Poems in *hag²ᶜ* were probably collected in book 4 of the Alexandrian edition; see Liberman 2007: 48–52, Prauscello 2016. For discussion of Sappho's handling of *hag²ᶜ* in this poem, see Lidov 2009.
Discussions (in addition to first editions, for which see 'Source'): Bierl 2016, Boehringer 2013, Calame 2013, Brown 2011, Schlesier 2011b: 11–17, the articles in *Greene and Skinner 2009 and in Aloni 2008, Yatromanolakis 2008, Austin 2007, Burzacchini 2007a, Ferrari 2010 [2007]: 193–200, Livrea 2007, Di Benedetto 2006, *Rawles 2006, *Bernsdorff 2005, Geißler 2005, Hardie 2005, *West 2005, Luppe 2004.

1–2 Both the music-making, in which the speaker participates, and the παῖδες whom she addresses form a contrast with her old age in what follows. One possible train of thought would be as follows. Request that the παῖδες dance while I play the lyre (1–2). I too was once young but now I am old (3–4), and no longer dance myself (5–6). The text could be supplemented, *exempli gratia*, αἰ στέργετε Μοίσαν ἰ]ο̣κ[ό]λπων κάλα δῶρα, παῖδες, | [χορεύσατε κὰτ τὰ]ν̣... χ̣ε̣λύνναν (Ferrari 2010 [2007]: 194–5, χορεύσατε Di Benedetto). For the contrast between singer and dancing παῖδες, cf. Anacr. 374, Pind. *Isthm.* 8.1–5 (νέοι). However, it is also possible that the παῖδες are just an audience; e.g. φέρω τάδε Μοίσαν ἰ]ο̣κ[ό]λπων κάλα δῶρα, παῖδες, | [λάβοισα πάλιν τὰ]ν̣... χ̣ε̣λύνναν (G–D).
1 ἰ]ο̣κ[ό]λπων 'violet-bosomed', an adjective unique to Sappho, suggesting fragrance.
δῶρα: the gen. pl. Μοίσαν is almost certain earlier in the line. The 'gifts of the Muses' are a well-established expression for poetry, song and dance, e.g. Archil. 1 and Alcm. 59b. Sappho presents herself as a singer and devotee of the Muses elsewhere, esp. frs. 55, 150, and the new text in Π¹; see Hardie 2005 and Burzacchini 2007b.
παῖδες: gender-neutral, but since the author is Sappho one assumes 'girls'. Inc. Lesb. fr. 18c]σα φύγοιμι, παῖδες, ἄβα may be similar; a probably female speaker addresses παῖδες in a statement involving 'youth'.
2 χ̣ελύνναν: Sappho plays and addresses her personified 'divine χέλυς' in fr. 118. Here the two adjectives give the lyre special status; the article τὰ]ν̣ that features in several proposed reconstructions would contribute to the effect.
3–6 *The symptoms of the speaker's old age.* Such catalogues appear elsewhere, see esp. *Od.* 13.430–3, Archil. 188, Mimn. 1, later Anacr. 395.

3–4 The subject of the sentence, and the emphatic agent of the change, is probably γῆρας. E.g. ἐμοὶ δ' ἄπαλον πρίν] ποτ' [ἔ]ọντα χρόα γῆρας ἤδη | [κάρφει μάλα, λεῦκαι δ' ἐγ]ένοντο τρίχες ἐκ μελαίναν 'age now completely withers my skin which once was supple, and my black hair has turned white' (suppl. Di Benedetto, Austin). The sequence χρόα γῆρας ἤδη appears also in the very fragmentary description of old age in Sa. 21; further on ἤδη, see Anacr. 395.1n.

4 [λεῦκαι] ... **τρίχες:** Bacch. fr. 20A.12 may be drawing on this passage; see Danielewicz 2006. However, 'white hair' itself is frequent; see Anacr. 395.1–2n.

5 βάρυς ... **πεπόηται:** βαρύθυμος is found from the fifth century onwards, meaning 'sullen', but here 'my spirit has grown heavy' probably still has a strongly metaphorical quality; see further Bernsdorff 2004. Sappho inserts herself into a discourse about the effect of old age on the θυμός. See Il. 4.313–14 and Alc. 442 for the idea that the θυμός is more resilient in old age than the body, and Mimn. 1.7 (cf. 2.15) for the opposite notion of old age causing psychological strain.

5–6 γόνα ... **νεβρίοισι** 'My knees don't carry me, which once were nimble in the dance (lit. "for dancing") like little fawns.' The final symptom, climactically, is described most expansively. Alcm. 26.1–2 similarly complains that 'my limbs can no longer carry me', apparently contrasting himself with a chorus of girls. For comparison of young female dancers to fawns, see Bacch. 13.87–90 with Cairns ad loc., and Eur. El. 860–1.

6 ἔον (Lesbian) ~ ἦσαν; for documentation, see Bettarini 2005: 34–6.

7–8 The speaker shifts to a more reflective and self-conscious position. She notes that she laments 'frequently'; cf. δηὖτε in Sa. 1 (1.15n.). The strong verb στεναχίζω contributes to the sense of self-consciousness. The rhetorical question ἀλλὰ τί κεν ποείην; then dismisses the lament as fruitless, and introduces the gnomic statement of human limitation in the next line: 'It is impossible for a human being to be ageless.' Line 7 is imitated at Anacr. 395.7(n.).

7 †τα†: we need either < × >τα or τα < – > to restore the metre. τὰ <μέν> is attractive. Other options are discussed by Lundon 2007.

8 ἄνθρωπον: a gender-neutral term. The male example that follows applies also to women.

9–12 *The myth of Eos and the ageing Tithonus.* The only substantive early narrative of the myth to survive is h.Aphr. 218–38. Eos falls in love with the youthful Tithonus, abducts him and then lives with him. She asks Zeus to make him immortal but forgets also to ask for eternal youth. As he grows old she no longer sleeps with him and eventually shuts him away. Only his voice continues incessantly. This last detail is developed more fully in later versions, in which Tithonus is turned into a cicada; see Hellanicus, FGrHist 4 F 140 (the first attestation, 5th cent.) and Callim. fr. 1.29–38 Pfeiffer

(with reference to poetry). The youthful Tithonus, pursued by Eos, sometimes holds a lyre in fifth-century iconography; see *LIMC* s.v. 'Eos' III.A.b.
A number of similarities suggest that Sappho may have known *h.Aphr.* or
the tradition behind it (the relative dating of Sappho and our *h.Aphr.* is
uncertain); see notes below and compare the symptoms in 3–6 with those
at *h.Aphr.* 228–9 and 233–4. In general on Sappho and *h.Aphr.*, see
Faulkner 2008: 45–7 and cf. above, p. 122. These correspondences highlight the sparseness of Sappho's treatment. Her Tithonus too grows old,
but what happens to him is left open, and Eos' viewpoint is never developed. As a result, we are presented with one clear primary, and several
uncertain secondary, linkages between myth and frame.

   Primarily, the myth serves as a paradigm for the ineluctability of old age,
presented in terms of the same contrast as in 3–6: youth is long lost (ποτα
for the third time), old age has grasped its victim. The aged, deathless
Tithonus continues to linger as the myth (and quite possibly the song)
ends with the present participle phrase ἔχ[ο]ντ᾽ ἀθανάταν ἄκοιτιν.

   It is left to the audience to make further connections, two in particular.
(i) The persistence of Tithonus' voice in old age (present in *h.Aphr.* but
not here) may bring to mind not just Sappho the frequent lamenter (7–8),
but also Sappho the aged singer (cf. 1–2n.), especially so if the cicada myth
was already known: youth goes but song remains. There may even be a hint
at the eternal survival of Sappho's song, a motif probably in frs. 55, 65, 147,
and in the text that precedes in Π¹. (ii) Gender and status make Eos
a better match for Sappho than is Tithonus. Eos the female and divine
lover of the young and beautiful Tithonus may thus point to the speaker's
relationship with the παῖδες, and perhaps more generally to Sappho's
relationship with the women addressed in her love poems. For Sappho's
treatment elsewhere of myths of goddesses who love mortal men, and the
fragility of those constellations, see Stehle 1996 [1990]. Further on the
Eos and Tithonus myth here, see Geißler 2005 and Rawles 2006. Eos
appears also at Sa. 103.10, 123, 157, 175, but we do not have the contexts.

   9 ἔφαντο is difficult. The past tense is very unusual for introducing
a mythic paradigm; see Edmunds 2006. Perhaps 'there was a story'; she
heard it before and recalls it as relevant now. For attribution of received
stories to anonymous speakers, see *carm. conv.* 894.2n.

   βροδόπαχυν 'rosy-armed', like ῥοδοδάκτυλος 'rosy-fingered', can suggest
both the colour of the morning sky and the beautiful arms of the personified goddess. In many (later) vase images Eos pursues Tithonus and other
youths with outstretched arms; see *LIMC* s.v. 'Eos' III.A. On the ancient
orthographic convention of using βρ- to indicate original ϝρ- in the text of
the Lesbian poets, see Hooker 1973.

   10 δε[ ]α εισανβαμεν: a very difficult crux. The transcription printed
here, essentially that of Hammerstaedt 2009: 26 who adjusted the join of

the two papyrus fragments, rules out most proposals to date, and leaves as the least unlikely the first editors' ἔρωι δέπας εἰσάνβαμεν' '(they said that Eos) went up into the bowl out of desire'. The bowl would be that of Helios, for which see on Stes. 8a. Eos ('dawn') and Tithonus live tradition- ally in the far east, and Sappho would be casting their journey there in terms of the sun's nightly return east after setting in the west. See further Watkins 2007. However, (i) since Dawn and Tithonus do not elsewhere travel in Helios' bowl, the reference is difficult to understand; (ii) Austin 2007: 117 declares π impossible papyrologically; (iii) the emendation εἰσόμβαμεν' would probably be needed to adjust the dialect. Equally pro- blematic are attempts to make -εισαν the ending of a participle in agree- ment with Αὔων; no satisfactory verb suggests itself; see West 2005: 5. For discussion of the aorist infinitive form βάμεν(αι), certain on any reconstruc- tion, see Bettarini 2005: 36–9.

εἰς ἔσχατα γᾶς: it is natural for Eos to live on the edges of the earth, where the sun rises; so also at *h.Aphr.* 227.

11 [κ]ά̣λ̣ο̣ν καὶ νέον: Tithonus was the epitome of good looks; see Tyrt. 12.5.

ὔμως ~ ὅμως 'all the same', viz. despite the love of a goddess.

ἔμαρψε: similar expressions occur at *Od.* 24.390 and [Hes.] *Scut.* 245. At an earlier stage of the story it is often Eos who 'seizes' Tithonus; e.g. *h.Aphr.* 218 ἥρπασεν Ἠώς.

13–16 For the status of these lines, see the headnote. Too little is left of 13–14 to attempt supplementation. One possibility is a poem-opening priamel, capped with ἔγω δὲ φίλημμ' ἀβροσύναν, as an expression of the speaker's preference, couched in strong, personal language; see West 2005: 7.

καὶ ... λέλογχε (15–16) would continue the thought in more general form; perhaps: 'and love obtains/has obtained for me the radiance and beauty of the sun.' Others construe (in line with a paraphrase in Clearchus/Athenaeus), 'and love of the sun has obtained/obtains for me radiance and beauty'. Both word order and phrasing are problematic.

Very scrappy remnants of three lines follow in Π². The partially pre- served marginal sign after 16 may have been either a *paragraphos* (a horizontal line marking off pairs of lines; see 'Metre') or a *coronis* (a more elaborate sign, indicating end of poem); see Hammerstaedt 2009: 24.

STESICHORUS

Stesichorus (first half of the sixth century; see below) composed a type of narrative lyric that is not otherwise attested in the surviving corpus. It resembles epic in its mythical subject matter and unobtrusive narrator, and draws extensively on epic vocabulary and formulae. Some fragments allude in detail to epic passages. The metres have a dactylic component (dactylo-anapaestic or dactylo-epitrite), but are clearly lyric, and the dialect is a version of the mix that characterises choral lyric: Doric with epic and other elements (pp. 24–5).

According to the *Suda* (σ1095 = test. 1 Campbell), the Alexandrian edition contained twenty-six books, which makes Stes. the most prolific lyric poet known to us, despite the strong possibility that not all works are correctly attributed to him. Individual poems were very extensive, and (unusually for lyric) were given individual titles. The *Oresteia* took up two books (or more), see frs. 175a, 176a and b (the numeration used here is that of Finglass); cf. p. 154 for the *Geryoneis*. The range of myths treated is wide.

The likeliest primary performance context for such large-scale compositions is festivals (subsequent sympotic performance, presumably of extracts, is attested for Classical Athens: Eupolis, *PCG* fr. 395). The proem of the *Oresteia* speaks of Χαρίτων δαμώματα 'public songs of the Graces' (fr. 173). Performance may or may not have been competitive. Most scholars now think that the original performers were choruses rather than soloists. Stes.'s name ('he who sets up the chorus'), even though it does not appear in the poems themselves, points to choruses. The triadic str.–ant.–ep. structure of his metres, though found in monody later on (e.g. Pind. fr. 123), is characteristic above all of choral song, where it permits choreographic repetition and variation (cf. p. 23). The word μολπή ('dance and song') appears in three fragments (90.9, 271, 278). The only argument against choral performance is the physical challenge of simultaneous singing and dancing for what must often have been more than an hour. One can imagine intervals, less vigorous forms of dance, or perhaps even variation between choral and monodic song. On Stesichorean performance, see Cingano 2003: 25–34 and Ercoles 2013: 494–503.

It is evident that Stes. drew extensively on epic, but we know less than we would like about the way his poetry relates to other lyric traditions. Those arguing for monodic performance compare him to the kitharodes, who performed solo-songs, often on epic themes, often in public settings, often in dactylic metres; thus West 1971. On the choral hypothesis, this widespread and long-standing performance tradition, which we can properly grasp only in the much later nomes of Timotheus (pp. 230–52), is still relevant poetic context: Stes.'s poetry may well have recalled that performed by kitharodes. Even less is known about putative early narrative poetry for choruses. Further on Stes.'s interaction with other poetic traditions, see Burkert 1987, Power 2010: 234–43, Carey 2015.

Stes. is the earliest surviving poet of the Greek west. The testimonia link him to a variety of cities in Magna Graecia, above all Himera on the northern coast of Sicily and Metaurus in modern-day Calabria. Some of the myths he treats, and indeed his treatment of them, probably had particular resonance in the west; see Burnett 1988: 147–53, Willi 2008: 82–9, and below, pp. 156–7 on the *Geryoneis*. However, on the whole Stes. is remarkably devoid of local reference. This is a further point of contact with epic, and possibly evidence for early performances or even premieres outside Magna Graecia; see further Davies and Finglass 2014: 23–9 and Carey 2015: 51–5. It is also the reason why Stes. is even harder to date than some other lyric poets. Ancient accounts vary substantially. The modern consensus centres on the first half of the sixth century: Stes. may already have known the Hesiodic *Shield* (fr. 168), which would prevent a date before the very late seventh century, and he is a famous poet of the past for Simonides (Sim. 564), which suggests he did not live to the end of the sixth century. Stes. had an extensive influence on later literature, not least Attic tragedy.

The standard commentary is Davies and Finglass 2014. The testimonia are edited, with extensive notes, by Ercoles 2013. Finglass and Kelly 2015 is a collection of essays, Segal 1985 a general literary account; Willi 2008: 51–118 assesses Stes. through the lens of language.

The *Geryoneis*

Heracles' abduction of the cattle of the three-bodied Geryon was eventually canonised as his tenth labour. The outline of the story first survives at Hes. *Th.* 287–94, and the myth was popular during the Archaic period, before and after Stes. A number of pots and textual references survive; see Pisander fr. 5 West, Ibyc. S176, Hecataeus, *FGrHist* 1 F 26, Pind. *Isthm.* 1.12–13, frs. 81 and 169a.4–8, and for discussion Gantz 1993: 402–8 and (with a focus on iconography) Brize 1980 and 1990, Schefold 1992: 121–9 and Muth 2008: 65–92

Stes.'s *Geryoneis* was a long work. One of the papyrus fragments (25) indicates the line number 1300 in the margin. It is in principle possible that the papyrus contained more than one poem, but none of the fragments of *P.Oxy.* xxxII.2617 looks out of place in the context of a Geryon narrative. We have no way of telling how far the song went beyond those 1,300 lines, except that we never hear of separate books for the *Geryoneis*.

Attempts to establish the order of the fragments and thus reconstruct the narrative are guided by two types of evidence. One is the summary of the myth in Pseudo-Apollodorus (2.5.10), which provides useful pointers even though it is never certain that his source for any particular detail is Stes. The other is metrical and papyrological. The length of each triad of strophe, antistrophe and epode is twenty-six lines, while the column length of the papyrus is probably thirty lines. It follows that it takes 13 columns = 15 triads = 390 lines for the same verse of a triad (e.g. the first line of a strophe or the second line of an epode) to reappear in the same line of a column. This observation helps with estimating the minimum distance between certain fragments, and with placing fragments from the top or bottom of columns. See Page 1973: 146–8 in general, and 17 headnote, 18 headnote and 19.18–22n. for examples.

The narrative presented a series of substantial episodes: Heracles' sea journey in Helios' golden vessel to the island of Erytheia, home of Geryon; two separate dialogues in which Geryon rejects warnings and pleas from those who care for him, one of them male, the other his mother Callirhoe; a divine assembly scene, apparently concerned with Geryon's impending death; and Heracles' defeat of Geryon. The longer fragments carrying parts of these episodes are included in this edition. Shorter fragments show that Stes. also mentioned (*inter alia*) the birth of Geryon's herdsman Eurytion (9), a journey to the land of the Hesperides (10) and Heracles' drink from the cup of the Centaur Pholus (22a). For a schematic overview, see Davies and Finglass 2014: 247.

Even from our fragmentary remains we can tell that the narrative was richly varied. Full accounts of some episodes were mixed with rapid treatment of others, foreshadowing the narrative technique of later poets such as Pindar. Third-person narrative was interspersed with speeches; the focus shifted between Heracles and Geryon; the cast of speakers was varied (men, women, gods and semi-human figures, major and minor characters). Geographic coordinates, mostly but not exclusively in the west, seem to have been frequent: Erytheia (fr. 9), which Stes. locates opposite Tartessus on the coast of modern-day Spain, the Hesperides (10), the island of Sarpedonia out west (6), Pallantium in Arcadia (21).

At several points the text alludes to Homeric epic, recalling not just broad story patterns but specific passages. Some of these echoes add further layers of meaning and emotive charge to the characters' actions, thoughts and suffering. See pp. 161–2 and 164 on allusions to Sarpedon and Hector in the presentation of Geryon, and see in general Kelly 2015.

It is likely that Stes. elicited admiration and sympathy for both Heracles and Geryon. He explores both protagonists' viewpoints, even in our scanty fragments, presenting both in the process of decision-making, and he avoids a straightforward admirable-hero-kills-abject-monster narrative. Geryon is on the one hand a monster with wings and three bodies (fr. 5), but on the other he is a sympathetic figure who speaks, acts and suffers in accordance with heroic values, and who engages in recognisably human social relations. The death of one of his heads is described in emotive language (fr. 19); and the allusions to Sarpedon and Hector further add to the sense that Geryon is a monster only in appearance. Heracles, the greatest of Greek heroes, is in later literature also the most problematic, portrayed variously as inappropriately violent, outlandish and a buffoon; and questions of ethics are prominent in several Classical references to the Geryon myth; see esp. Pind. frs. 81 and 169a, Pl. *Gorg.* 484b–c. Some such questions may be present already in Stes. Without doubt, Heracles commits a heroic feat, travelling to the end of the world and overcoming a dangerous opponent. On the other hand, the methods he uses are unconventional (see on fr. 19). It may also be relevant that Stes. (along with other poets) was subsequently credited with the invention of Heracles' iconic bandit outfit of club, lion-skin and bow (fr. 281 = Athen. 12.512f). Further on the treatment of Geryon and Heracles, see Willi 2008: 92–9, Franzen 2009: 62–5, Noussia Fantuzzi 2013: 246–52.

Connected to the weakening of the dichotomy of hero and monster is an interest in another boundary, that between mortality and immortality. Geryon eventually dies, probably one head at a time; yet sprung from part-divine ancestry, he appears to be uncertain whether he is mortal or immortal, and seems to be pondering this question before the fatal battle (fr. 15). His mortality is a theme probably also in the dialogue with his mother (fr. 17) and the divine council (fr. 18). For a discussion of the *Geryoneis* within the context of the 'immortals are mortal, mortals immortal' theme in Greek literature and poetry at large, see Vermeule 1979: 136–44.

It is tempting to locate the first performance of the *Geryoneis* in Stes.'s native Magna Graecia. Heracles was an important figure in the west, a hero who charted unknown territory, who was claimed as ancestor by several settlements and rulers in Sicily and southern Italy, and who was worshipped in several localities; see Jourdain-Annequin 1989 and Malkin 1994: 203–18. Most of the evidence is later, but origins in the early days of the colonisation of Magna Graecia are likely. The setting of the *Geryoneis* is mostly in the west even from a Sicilian perspective, and the west, despite increasing trade, will have suggested foreignness, adventure and danger. The westernmost area of Sicily itself was free of Greek settlements, partly controlled by the Phoenicians, and Tartessus (fr. 9) was a famed city far away, familiar probably only to a very few. In so far as the Greeks of Magna Graecia saw themselves as adventurers on the western limits of the Greek world, distant from their ancestral homes on the Greek mainland, the poem would have had an obvious appeal. At the same time, it is easy to imagine that the portrayal of Geryon, the sympathetic victim of the raider, would have resonated in what was a region rich in hybrid ethnicities and cultures, populated by both colonisers and colonised. For 'colonial' readings, see Franzen 2009 and Noussia Fantuzzi 2013, and for the historical and conceptual questions involved in speaking of 'colonisation' in Sicily,

Hall 2012. For the (very uncertain) evidence for a hero-cult of Geryon in Sicily, see Diod. Sic. 4.24.3, and Curtis 2011: 40–1.

Despite certain connections with Magna Graecia, the *Geryoneis* had a broader reach. Possible echoes in Aeschylus, Pindar and Euripides (albeit none of them beyond doubt) suggest that the poem was widely known by the fifth century; see 8a.2–7, 15.20–4 and 17.2–3nn. Dissemination may well have been much faster than that. Nothing in what survives of the text is obscurely local; cf. p. 154.

Source: Some fragments are quotations, one of them included here (8a), but most of the text is preserved in over sixty fragments of different sizes of *P.Oxy.* XXXII.2617 (Π), copied in the first century BC or AD. For questions of reconstruction, see above, pp. 154–5, and on individual fragments below.

Metre: Dactylo-anapaestic runs (= 'lyric dactyls'), a rhythm Stes. uses also in *Boar-hunters* and *Games for Pelias*. The strophe is anapaestic (base unit ∪ ∪ –), the epode starts with anapaests before changing to dactyls (base unit – ∪ ∪) after the first period.

str./ant.
¹ ⏗ – ⏗ – ∪ ∪ – – ‖
² ⏗ – ∪ ∪ – ⏗ – ∪ ∪ –
³ ∪ ∪ – ⏗ – ∪ ∪ – – ?‖
⁴ ⏗ – ∪ ∪ – ⏗ – ∪ ∪ –
⁵ ∪ ∪ – – ‖
⁶ ⏗ – ⏗ – ∪ ∪ – ∪ ∪ –
⁷ ⏗ – ∪ ∪ –
⁸ ⏗ – ∪ ∪ – ⏗ – ⏗ –
⁹ ⏗ – ∪ ∪ – ∪ ∪ – ∪ ∪ – ‖‖

ep.
¹ ⏗ – ∪ ∪ – ∪ ∪ – ∪ ∪ –
² ∪ ∪ – ∪ ∪ – ∪ ∪ – – ‖
³ – ∪ ∪ – ⏗ – ⏗ – ∪ ∪
⁴ – ⏗ – ⏗ – ∪ ∪ – ∪ ∪
⁵ – ∪ ∪ – ⏗ – ∪ ∪ – ⏗ –
⁶ ∪ ∪ – – ?‖
⁷ – ∪ ∪ – ∪ ∪ – ∪ ∪ – ∪ ∪
⁸ – ∪ ∪ – ∪ ∪ – ‖‖

The fundamental alternation of – and ∪ ∪ is shared with the epic hexameter, but Stes. has an un-epic freedom to use both rising (anapaestic) and falling (dactylic) openings, and to vary period-length. Periods end with pendant close (– –) inside stanzas and (a perhaps more dramatic) blunt close (∪ –) at the end of stanzas.

The rhythm balances regularity and flexibility. The double shorts ∪ ∪ can be contracted to –. When they are, word-end is avoided after the contracted

syllable and the neighbouring ⌣ ⌣ remain uncontracted. Moreover, in what
survives, contraction occurs only in certain positions (indicated above),
though we do not have enough text to be confident that contraction is
not permitted in further positions. (Hence in the text presented, the metre
of syllables lost in the lacunae is indicated without this restriction.)
    Further on the metre see Führer 1968, *Haslam 1974.
    Discussions (see also p. 154 for discussions of Stes. in general, and below
on individual fragments): Noussia Fantuzzi 2013, *Franzen 2009,
Rozokoki 2009, Lazzeri 2008, Prest 1989, Davies 1988b, Carmignani 1981:
27–44, Brize 1980, Gentili 1977, *Page 1973, *Barrett 2007a [1968].
    Commentaries: *Davies and Finglass 2014: 230–98, Curtis 2011.

Fr. 8a Finglass (S17 SLG, 185 PMG)

Helios embarks in his bowl and sails home; Heracles (who has just dis-
embarked) enters a grove.
    The bowl in which Helios sails the ocean every night while resting, and
which Heracles uses to travel to Geryon's island of Erytheia (ἐρυθρός 'red',
evoking the setting sun), was a popular motif in poetry, pre- and post-Stes.
(see 'Source'), and it appears also in late Archaic iconography (see Brize
1980: 51–2). Stes. may have sought to put his own stamp on the myth; see
2–7n.
    The fragment places Heracles in a primordial landscape populated by
major cosmic powers: Ocean is a son and Helios a grandson of Gaia and
Ouranos (Hes. *Th.* 132–6); Night is a daughter of Chaos (*Th.* 123–4).
Geryon himself is a grandson of Ocean (*Th.* 287–8). On the extreme west
in Stes. and the early Greek imagination, see Ballabriga 1986: ch. 2 and
Debiasi 2004: 94–104.
    The pace of the narrative is noteworthy and contrasts with the expan-
siveness of other episodes. Heracles traverses cosmic space within a small
number of lines.
    In Pseudo-Apollodorus (2.5.10) Heracles uses Helios' vessel twice, on
the way out from the mainland to Erytheia, and then again crossing back
after killing Geryon. If Stes. described only one of these journeys in detail it
is likely to have been the first, and indeed his treatment of the outbound
crossing is confirmed by Athenaeus, who states that 'Stesichorus claims
that Helios used to sail across the ocean in a drinking cup, and that
Heracles as well used it to get to the other side when he set off after the
cattle of Geryon' (11.781d = Stes. 8b, trans. Olson). This fragment is
therefore best placed before those describing Heracles' fight with
Geryon. For counter-arguments, see Page 1973: 149, and for the question
how Heracles acquired the bowl (threatening Helios? from Nereus?),
Davies and Finglass 2014 on fr. 7.

Source: Athen. 11.469e, in a treatment of texts that narrate Helios' or Heracles' journeys in a drinking vessel. Apart from Stes., Athenaeus quotes the earlier Mimn. 12, and the later Aesch. fr. 69 *TrGF* (*Heliades*) and Antimachus fr. 86 Matthews. Also referred to are *Titanomachy* fr. 10 West, Pisander fr. 5 West (both perhaps 7th/6th cent.) and some later texts.

Discussions (in addition to those listed on p. 158): Bowie 2014.

1 †Ἅλιος†: the metre requires ∪∪ -. If ἅλιος entered the text as a gloss of 'son of Hyperion', it is impossible to guess what word was ousted. This is at least as likely as an original τᾶμος (Barrett), with ΑΜΟΣ corrupted to ΑΛΙΟΣ.

Ὑπεριονίδα <ἶ>ς 'force of Hyperionides', a periphrastic expression amounting to 'forceful child of Hyperion', viz. Helios. This is an economical emendation of Ὑπεριονίδας, which is a syllable short. Digamma is operative in a number of passages in Stes. (e.g. 97.224, 170.1), and would explain the hiatus here (-ίδα ϝίς).

2 δέπας '(mixing) bowl'. The word is frequent in epic; as the term for Helios' vessel, it is first attested here and in Pisander (fr. 5) but is standard subsequently. Gold is a suitable material; the sun gleams even in the dark night.

†ἐσκατέβαινε χρύσεον† is unmetrical. The easiest emendation is ἐσκατέβαιν' ἐς. For the repetition ἐσ- ... ἐς, more common in prose, see *Od.* 4.802, Eur. *Andr.* 657. The verb expresses Helios' descent from heaven (κατ-) as well as his entering into the vessel (ἐσ-); cf. Sa. 58b.10n.

2–7 ὄ|φρα ... φίλους: Helios' travel 'crossing through the ocean' and 'to the depths of holy, dark night' is unconventional. Elsewhere he journeys along the ocean and from west to east, where he rises the next morning; see esp. Mimn. 12. Here he is going (further) west: darkness is associated with the west, and ζόφος 'west' often forms a pair with ἠώς 'dawn, east' (LSJ s.v. ζόφος II); cf. Athenaeus' ἐπὶ τὴν δύσιν 'to his setting', when introducing the quotation. As suits a text about the far west, Stes.'s interest is in Helios' rest in darkness after setting rather than his preparation for rising in the east. The location of Helios' home is usually in the east, but the tradition is not fixed; see esp. Eur. *Alc.* 592–3, 'the dark stable of the sun', in a passage invoking the west, and further *RE* VIII.1 90–2 (s.v. 'Helios') and Ballabriga 1986: 77–81, 103–7. Aesch. fr. 69 *TrGF* may be 'correcting' Stes.: Helios escapes (rather than steers towards) the 'gloom of holy night'.

4–5 adapt and recombine traditional language: the depths of the sea (e.g. *Il.* 1.358 ἐν βένθεσσιν ἁλός; see further Silk 1974: 24), deep mist (e.g. *Od.* 9.144 ἀήρ ... βαθεῖ(α), in the context of a night-time sea journey), divine night (e.g. *Od.* 4.429 ἀμβροσίη νύξ), dark night (e.g. Hes. *Th.* 744

Νυκτὸς ἐρεμνῆς οἰκία) and the sunset formula δύηι τ' ἠέλιος καὶ ἐπὶ κνέφας ἱερὸν ἔλθηι (e.g. *Il.* 11.194).

6–7 Helios' peaceful, routine return to his family contrasts with Heracles' travel further away from home, to risk his life in battle and commit a unique feat.

8–9 As Helios embarks and Heracles disembarks, there are echoes and contrasts in the phrasing: 1 Ὑπεριονίδα vs 9 παῖς Διός, 2 δέπας †ἐσκατέβαινε† vs 8–9 ἔβα... ποσί, 4 ἱαρᾶς vs 8 ἄλσος, 4–5 νυκ|τὸς ἐρεμνᾶς vs 8–9 †κατάσ|κιον†.

8 ἄλσος '(sacred) grove'; see Sa. 2.2n. An ἄλσος could be an appropriate setting for an encounter with a monster, see [Hes.] *Scut.* 70, Eur. *IT* 1246; but the battle is still many lines off and Stes. may have aimed for a more generally numinous atmosphere.

8–9 †κατάσ|κιον† scans ∪ − | ∪ − while we need ∪ − | ∞ −. The simplest of several possible emendations is κατα|σκιό<ε>ν. This would be a *hapax*, but κατάσκιος is well attested, as is σκιόεις (e.g. *h.Aphr.* 20 ἄλσεά τε σκιόεντα).

9 ποσί: presumably in contrast to his, and now Helios', journey in the bowl.

Fr. 15 Finglass (S11 SLG)

Geryon affirms his decision to face Heracles.

This fragment probably sits several hundred lines after 8a. Geryon starts speaking in line 5 and his speech continues beyond the end. In it he explains his decision, in reply to a speech by a male interlocutor (16 φίλε). If the very small fr. 13 (not printed here), in which somebody requests that Geryon consider his parents Callirhoe and Chrysaor, belongs to that preceding speech by Geryon's interlocutor, the narrator pointedly recalls the interlocutor's appeal by referring to Callirhoe and Chrysaor again in 15.3–4 whereas Geryon himself does not acknowledge it. Back-to-back speeches such as these are rare in extant early lyric.

The best guess at the interlocutor's identity is Menoites, herdsman of Hades, who according to [Apollod.] 2.5.10 brought Geryon the news that Heracles had come and killed his herdsman Eurytion and the dog Orthos. Chrysaor is unlikely because of the way he is (probably) named at 15.3, as is Heracles himself, who attacks Geryon stealthily in fr. 19 and is not a φίλος. Eurytion, who would be an obvious person to care about Geryon, is a possibility; this would mean, however, that Pseudo-Apollodorus follows a different version.

Geryon's decision to fight Heracles is a recurring theme in the *Geryoneis*. His mother appeals to him in fr. 17, and he silently ponders the question one more time just before the fight in fr. 19. On the ordering of the two appeals, see 17 headnote. Stes. uses speeches to focus attention on fateful decisions also in other works, see frs. 97 and 103.

In drawing the listener into Geryon's mind and giving him character-istically heroic concerns, the speech is part of the *Geryoneis'* programme of treating the monster as a human figure who elicits sympathy and pathos. An allusion to the sympathetic Iliadic character Sarpedon (8–24n.) inten-sifies this effect.

Source: Three pieces of *P.Oxy.* xxxii.2617, joined by Barrett: the sub-stantial fr. 13a and the small frs. 14 and 15. Davies and Finglass add a fourth scrap, 13b, which is not included here because it is separated by almost fifty lines from 29]κλεος.

Discussions (in addition to those listed on p. 158): Rozokoki 2008, Willi 2008: 93–7, Tsitsibakou-Vasalos 1991–2, *Barrett 2007b [1978], Bornmann 1978.

1 χηρσίν: possibly Heracles', in a warning or prediction delivered to Geryon by his interlocutor; cf. the Homeric χερσὶ δαμέντ', etc. (e.g. *Il.* 16.854). For the severe Doric χηρ- (rather than χερ-) in the mostly mild Doric text of Stes., cf. 17.4 γωνάζομα[ι, and see Willi 2008: 58–60. These are almost certainly editorial interventions.

1–4 τὸν] . . . **[ἀ]|θανάτοιο** probably describes Callirhoe, who has a stron-ger claim to immortality than Chrysaor; see 8–24n. Therefore, for 3–4 we may want something like ποτέφα [κρατεροῦ Χρυσάορος ἀ]|θανάτοιό [τε Καλλιρόας γενέθλα (Prest 1989: 69–70). The whole passage would translate: 'In reply to him, the offspring of mighty Chrysaor and immortal Callirhoe addressed him.'

3 ποτέφα (Dor.) ~ προσέφη.

5–7 Barrett supplements μή μοι θά[νατον θροέων κρυόεν]|τα δεδίσκ[ε' ἀγάνορα θυμόν ('Do not try to frighten my proud heart by speaking of chill death'). A further imperative follows in 7, such as Page's μηδέ με λ[ίσσεο.

6 δεδίσκ[ε(ο) ~ Homeric δειδίσσεο (*Il.* 4.184). Whether the o is elided depends on the word that follows.

8–24 Geryon considers two scenarios: if I am to be immortal I will not fight (8–15), if I am mortal I will (16–24). The detail of the first scenario is debated, but the overall structure (if immortal/if mortal) is virtually certain because of the combination of 9 ἀγη[, 10 ἐν Ὀλύμπ[and 16–17 γῆ]ρας. The passage manipulates a traditional line of reasoning, and alludes in particular to Sarpedon's words to Glaucus at *Il.* 12.322–8: if we were to be ageless and immortal after surviving this war I would not suggest we fight, but as we are doomed to die let us do battle. Cf. Callinus 1.12–17, Pind. *Ol.* 1.82–3.

Like Sarpedon, Geryon goes with the second scenario (mortality), and fights. His choice is obvious not just from 25–6(n.) and subsequent fragments, but indicated already by the rhetoric of this passage; see 16 ὦ φί[λε and 20 νῦν (nn.). Unlike Sarpedon, Callinus and Pindar, however, he considers immortality a possibility: 'if I am/shall be' (9 -μαι), not 'if I were' immortal. For the rhetoric of entertaining two first-person scenarios as possible, both expressed with εἰ + ind., but picking the second, see e.g. Xen. *Ap.* 27.

Geryon's willingness, at least temporarily, to entertain the possibility that he is immortal may perhaps be explained by his mixed ancestry. His mother was Callirhoe, daughter of Ocean and Tethys (Hes. *Th.* 287–8). His father Chrysaor was a son of Poseidon and (the mortal) Medusa (*Th.* 278–81). It nevertheless remains puzzling that he first considers this possibility and then dismisses it.

8–15 *Scenario 1: Geryon immortal.* The train of thought is difficult to reconstruct. Perhaps broadly: If after escaping from Heracles I am to be immortal and ageless, and to live on Olympus, it is better to accept reproach and look on as Heracles plunders the cattle. Thus Barrett 2007 (1978) supplements 8–10 αἰ μὲν γά[ρ πέπον ἀθάνατός τ' ἔσο]|μαι καὶ ἀγή[ραος ἀνέρα τόνδε φυγών] | ἐν Ὀλύμπ[ωι, and 14–15 κεραϊ[ζομένας ἐπιδεῖν βόας ἁ]|ιμετέρω[ν ἀπονόσφιν ἐπαύλων (ἐπιδεῖν is improved on by Davies-Finglass' ποτιδεῖν). This supplementation assumes a detailed remodelling of Sarpedon's speech. In particular, Stes. would be picking up Homer's πόλεμον περὶ τόνδε φυγόντε (*Il.* 12.322) with ἀνέρα τόνδε φυγών. For Sarpedon this phrase emphasises that immortality is impossible and serves as a rhetorical foil: if escape from this one war were all it takes for us to live forever...; Geryon, by contrast, is contemplating taking steps to preserve the chance of an immortal life on Olympus. With immortality within the realm of possibility but well short of certain (8–24n.), avoiding as dangerous an opponent as Heracles might seem a reasonable course of action. Barrett himself interprets his supplements differently and introduces an (unattested and overelaborate) notion that Geryon has received a prophecy of immortality contingent upon avoiding death at the hands of Heracles. This seems unnecessary. For other approaches to these lines, see Davies and Finglass 2014: 272–4, who themselves also favour Barrett's supplementation (as well as his suggestion of contingent immortality).

8 γά[ρ introduces the whole of 8–24. On either scenario, he will not be intimidated, either he hopes for immortality (or whatever is the right reconstruction) and hence does not care, or he is mortal and ready to fight heroically.

8–9 ἀθάνατος] ... καὶ ἀγή[ραος: the restoration is almost certain; the pairing is formulaic in early hexameter, with an occurrence also in Sarpedon's speech (12.323). See also Sa. 58b.7–8n.

10 ἐν Ὀλύμπ[ωι evokes a contrast with Geryon's opponent Heracles, whose arrival on Olympus was a popular topic in mid and late sixth-century iconography; see Boardman 1990.

11–12 ἐ]|λεγχέα 'contemptible' or 'reproachful'. The accent is in the papyrus, indicating that this is the adjective ἐλεγχής, not the neuter noun ἔλεγχος.

16–24 *Scenario 2: Geryon mortal.* The two scenarios are contrasted pointedly: ageing rather than agelessness (16–17 vs 9), a life among humans rather than gods (18–19 vs 9–10), avoiding rather than accepting opprobrium (22 vs 11–12).

16–19 E.g. αἰ δ' ὦ φί[λε χρὴ στυγερόν μ' ἐπὶ γῆ]|ρας [ἱκ]έςθαι, | ζώ[ει]ν τ' ἐν ἐ[παμερίοις ἀπάτερ]|θε θ[ε]ῶν μακάρω[ν ... (Page, Barrett). ἐπαμερίοις ~ ἐφημερίοις.

16 ὦ φί[λ(ε) may be picking up ὦ φίλε in fr. 13: a dialogue of φίλοι. Placed here, the address lends emphasis to the second scenario. The masculine termination is made certain by the metrically determined need for a short syllable.

20–4 E.g. νῦν μοι πολὺ κά[λλιον ἐστι παθεῖν] (Page) | ὅ τι μόρσιμ[ον ἦι, μὴ δυσκλεῖα] | καὶ ὀνείδε' [ἐμοί τε γένηται] (Barrett) | καὶ παντὶ γέ[νει παρ' ἀεισομένων (West) ἐξ]|οπίσω Χρυσ[άο]ρο[ς υ]ἱόν ('As it is, it is much better for me to endure whatever is my fate, so as to avoid ill repute and opprobrium for me and my whole race, from those who will in future sing of the son of Chrysaor'). The first part of the statement may be echoed by Pindar at fr. 169a.16–17 (of Diomedes, robbed by Heracles of his mares; Geryon appearing in lines 6–8).

20 νῦν: more likely to mean 'as it is' (LSJ s.v. 1.4) than 'now', which would have point only if placed with the infinitive (to endure my fate now). πολὺ κά[λλιον occurs in epic: *Od.* 6.39, etc.

23–4 ἐξ|οπίσω rather than ὀπίσω is made likely by avoidance of word-break at this point in all surviving strophes and antistrophes; see Haslam 1974: 22, 56.

Χρυσ[άο]ρο[ς υ]ἱόν: Geryon ends with an emphatic reference to himself. The use of his father's rather than his own name suits the genealogical focus throughout the fragment. West's παρ' ἀεισομένων in 23 would create a construction for the accusative, and Geryon's consciousness of future song would be reminiscent of Hector's words when facing his fate at *Il.* 22. 303–5. The future participle would, however, make for odd phrasing. For the audience, Geryon's interest in his reputation after death is justified by the *Geryoneis* itself as well as the other poetic or iconographic treatments of his story.

25–6 'May that (= future ill repute) not be dear to the blessed gods.' Geryon continues with scenario 2.

29]κλεος could be either κλέος or Ἡρα]κλέος.

Fr. 17 Finglass (S13 SLG)

A distressed woman beseeches Geryon. This can only be his mother Callirhoe, who tries to prevent him from facing Heracles, probably by reminding him of the time when she nursed him as a baby.

Stes. portrays a mother pleading with her grown-up children also in fr. 97 (the mother of Eteocles and Polynices), but the motif is already Homeric. Callirhoe's speech echoes Thetis' and Hecuba's grief at the predicament of Achilles and Hector, respectively. Particularly close is Hecuba's vain attempt to persuade Hector to avoid battle with Achilles by exposing her breast and asking him to remember how she nursed him long ago (*Il.* 22.79–89); on epic scenes between mothers and sons, see Murnaghan 1992. Stes. inserts the monster Geryon into a pointedly human scene.

Several late sixth-century Attic depictions of Geryon's battle with Heracles include a woman (never named) who looks on or flees; see Brize 1990: 83.

Callirhoe seems to be starting her pleas to Geryon in the even more fragmentary fr. 16 (not included in this selection). The speech in 17 may begin in line 2, or continue either the speech in 16 or a separate speech within the same dialogue. In any case, the encounter of mother and son was given considerable space, over seventy lines, since frs. 16 and 17 must be two columns apart in Π; see Page 1973: 147 and cf. above, pp. 154–5.

We cannot be sure whether Callirhoe's appeal precedes or follows the exchange with the male *philos* (fr. 15). In favour of the majority view, *philos* before Callirhoe, is the consideration that Geryon needs to learn of Heracles' presence first (from the *philos*) and that the mother's appeal makes for a natural climax. See Castellaneta 2005: 21–30 for an argument for the order 12 (possibly: Geryon learns of Heracles' presence), 16–17 (Callirhoe), 13 and 15 (justification to male *philos*). Either way, the narrative focuses on Geryon's decisions and interactions with those who care for him.

Source: *P.Oxy.* XXXII.2617 fr. 11.

Discussions (in addition to those on p. 158): Xanthou 2015: 38–45.

2–3 Callirhoe is giving voice to her suffering, probably fearing that Geryon will die. Even if construed with 4 γωνάζομα[ι or another verb, ἐγών and the adjective(s) and participle(s) amount to an exclamation. The supplements in the apparatus produce 'miserable me, who gave birth to a dismal son and who suffers dismally', a loose reminiscence of Thetis' lament of her mortal son Achilles at *Il.* 18.54, likewise before the event, ὤ μοι ἐγὼ δειλή, ὤ μοι δυσαριστοτόκεια; see further Prest 1989: 71–3, who points to the possible manipulation of Callirhoe's words at Eur. *El.* 1186–8, and Castellaneta 2005: 34–9.

3 ἄλ[ασ]τὰ πᾳθοῖσα: for the expression, cf. Alcm. 1.34–5(n.). Homer repeatedly uses the adjective in the context of parental grief; see *Il.* 24.105, *Od.* 14.174, 24.423, *h.Aphr.* 207.

4–9 Callirhoe makes an emotional and formal appeal: address by name (vocative Γ]αρυόνα), a verb of supplication (γωνάζομα[ι), a reminder of what she did for Geryon when he was little. It is likely that a specific request is lost somewhere in her speech, and that this request was for Geryon to abandon his plan to fight.

4 γωνάζομα[ι: for ω rather than ου, see fr. 15.1n.

5 With the supplements in the apparatus the line translates: 'If ever I offered (aor. act.) you (τιν ~ σοι) my breast.' It is modelled on Hecuba's εἴ ποτέ τοι λαθικηδέα μαζὸν ἐπέσχον (*Il.* 22.83).

8–9 With Barrett's παρὰ ματρί] φίλαι, we get 'by your dear mother, gladdened ... by good cheer'. Callirhoe would be continuing to remind Geryon of feeding from her breast. The elaboration of the image of the baby at the mother's breast foreshadows Clytemnestra's appeal to Orestes at Aesch. *Cho.* 896–8. Stes. may have been the creative intermediary between Homer and Aeschylus.

8 γανυθ[ε: nom. γανυθ[είς (Lobel) or acc. γανυθ[έντα (Barrett) depending on the construction. The aorist of γάνυμαι is otherwise only attested as an emendation at Libanius *ep.* 216.2, but hard to avoid.

9 εὐφ]ροσύναις is redolent with human sociability and striking in its application to a monster.

10–13 Callirhoe may be opening her robe to display her breast, as Hecuba does at *Il.* 22.80. Alternatively, her speech continues. The adjective in 10 could be e.g. θυώ]δεα 'fragrant' (Barrett).

Fr. 18 Finglass (S14 SLG)

A divine assembly ends; subsequently Athena addresses Poseidon on the matter of Geryon's impending death.

Divine gatherings are common in epic. Two in particular offer points of comparison: (i) the exchange at *Il.* 22.166–85, in which Zeus contemplates saving Hector but yields when Athena insists that he is mortal and fated to die, and (ii) the assembly at the beginning of the *Odyssey*, in which Zeus assures Athena that her protégé Odysseus will return home despite Poseidon's anger at the blinding of his son Polyphemus. Perhaps Stes., like Homer, pitted Athena and an Athena-supported hero against Poseidon and a Poseidon-related monster.

The scene would make sense either early in the work, as our first fragment, or (as printed here) shortly before Geryon's death, corresponding on the divine plane to the human exchanges that highlight his mortality in frs. 15 and 17. In the latter case, the combination of metre and the layout of the papyrus indicates a gap of seventy-three lines between the end of fr. 18 and the beginning of fr. 19; see Barrett 2007a [1968]: 17–18. **Source:** *P.Oxy.* XXXII.2617 fr. 3.

1–2 None (or possibly one) of the gods remained by Zeus' side. They are either leaving Olympus, perhaps to watch proceedings in Erytheia, or rising from their seats for some reason. For the phrasing, cf. *h.Apol.* 5 Λητὼ δ' οἴη μίμνε παραὶ Διί (as the others jump in fear).

2 παμ[βασιλῆα: an epithet of Zeus at Alc. 308.4, and a much better fit than other known adjectives starting with παμ-.

3–5 Athena reminds a male god, who is a 'driver of horses' as well as somehow related to her (ὄν 'her...'), of something to do with Geryon's death. This must be Poseidon, who will take an interest in his grandson Geryon (see 15.8–24n. for Geryon's ancestry). Thus πάτρω(α) 'uncle' is a likely supplement. A past tense verb of speaking is probably lost in 4, e.g. φάτ' ἐϋφραδέω]ς (Page, Barrett).

κρατερό|[φρονα: the only attested κρατερο- compound that is suitable. As an epithet of a god it is first attested at Ibyc. 298.

6–8 Athena speaks about Geryon's death, possibly warning Poseidon against trying to save him. What does she ask him to remember? Page thinks it is a promise, supplying ἄγ' ὑποσχέσιο]ς μεμναμένος ἅ[ν|περ ὑπέστας, but Geryon's mortal status or a command from Zeus is at least as likely.

Fr. 19 Finglass (S15 + ?S21 SLG)

The most substantial fragment of the *Geryoneis*, from the early stages of the battle between Heracles and Geryon. Heracles first ponders what tactic to adopt (?5–9), and then begins his attack (10–17). After a lacuna, the second part (31–47) describes in detail an arrow launched by Heracles, its trajectory, and the wounds it inflicts on Geryon's first head. The text gives out partway into a simile that likens the drooping of the head to a poppy that sheds its petals (44–7). The fragment gives us a sense of the level of detail of Stes.'s narrative at a climactic moment.

Stes. borrows phrasing and motifs from epic battle narrative, but makes Heracles adopt modes of fighting that deviate sharply from open hand-to-hand combat. Not only does he resolve to fight by stealth, but he probably dislodges Geryon's helmet with a missile of some sort before shooting him in his forehead and uses poisoned arrows, methods that are rare or unparalleled in Homer. The propriety of Heracles' tactics is difficult to assess. Homer presents the use of trickery and ambushing as appropriate against overwhelming opposition, see Edwards 1985: 18–41. Unconventional means of one sort or other are standard in early Greek accounts of overcoming monsters; see e.g. Bellerophon's shooting of the Chimera from mid-air (Pind. *Ol.* 13.86–90) or Perseus' use of a set of special accoutrements in his encounter with Medusa ([Hes.] *Scut.* 216–37, Pherecydes, *FGrHist* 3 F 11). Geryon certainly is one such monster, but he is also a noble hero with a shield and, especially in the poppy simile, a pathetic victim. Heracles' stealth is such that Geryon's head is fatally injured before he even gets the chance to defend himself. It is likely that Stes. is aiming for ethical and emotional complexity.

Source: The substantial *P.Oxy.* xxxii.2617 fr. 4, which consists of the lower parts of two columns, supplemented with the tiny fr. 5. See 18–22n. on whether fr. 1 should be inserted at the top of the second column of fr. 4 (i.e. after line 17).

Discussions (in addition to those on p. 158): Curti 1995, Tsitsibakou-Vasalos 1990, Maingon 1980.

3 δοιῳ: δοιώ or some other form of 'two'.

5–9 *Heracles considers how best to attack Geryon and settles on stealth.* The verb in 5–6 may be διελέ[ξ|ατο 'spoke (to his mind)'. At the beginning of 7 Diggle suggests ἐδοάσσατό οἱ], modelled on the epic formula ὧδε δέ οἱ φρονέοντι δοάσσατο κέρδιον εἶναι (e.g. *Od.* 18.93). Thus: 'It seemed to him to be much better ... to fight by stealth ... against the strong man' (Page's φωτί vel sim. in 9).

7 εἶν ~ εἶναι. The form is attested in Euboean, and therefore perhaps local to Himera, which was founded by settlers from the Chalcidian (i.e. Euboean) colony Zankle, and with which Stes. is associated in the testimonia; see Willi 2008: 54–5, 68.

9 κραταιῶι underlines the need for stealth.

10–17 *Heracles ambushes Geryon and (probably) knocks the helmet off one of his heads.*

10–11 Heracles '... devised ... bitter death for him', probably from a hiding place. At the beginning of the sentence εὑρ]άξ (probably 'to one side') is attractive, preceded by a nom. ptcpl. such as Page's βεβαὼς δ'. The adverb occurs twice in Homer, both times in connection with stealth in battle: στῆ δ' εὑράξ σὺν δουρὶ λαθών (*Il.* 11.251, 15.541).

11 πι]κρόν is an epithet especially of arrows in early hexameter, and never of death. There may be a foreshadowing of the weapon Heracles is planning to use.

12–13 Probably 'he held the shield before him', with the supplement πρόσ]θεν or πρόσ|θ(ε); cf. Iliadic phrases such as πρόσθεν δ' ἔχεν ἀσπίδα (13.157, 13.803). The subject is almost certainly Geryon, who is regularly portrayed with a shield in his encounter with Heracles, while Heracles is not.

13–17 Page's reconstruction (1973: 151) is as likely as any: Heracles hits Geryon with a rock or some other missile, Geryon's horse-plumed helmet (ἱπ]πόκομος τρυφάλει') comes off his head (ἀπὸ κρα|τός), and it sits or rolls on the ground. Thus the head is exposed to the arrow-shot that is described when the text resumes in 31. On the options for supplementation, see Lazzeri 2008: 205–15, but too little is left for more than speculation.

If Page is broadly right, Heracles adopts a technique – stripping an enemy of his helmet to make him vulnerable – that occurs neither in ordinary epic battle action, nor probably in the iconographic record of the Geryon–Heracles encounter; see Brize 1980: 59–61. Closest comes Apollo's attack on Patroclus at *Il.* 16.786–806, stunning him with a blow from behind and striking off his helmet to enable Euphorbus and Hector to finish him off; see Lerza 1979.

18–22 The text printed in smaller type is a separate papyrus scrap (*P.Oxy.* xxxii.2617 fr. 1). It is, papyrologically, the remnant of the beginning of a column as well as, metrically, the remnant of the first five lines of an epode, a combination that recurs only every 390 lines yet suits the position here; see Page 1973: 154, and in general p. 154–5 above. This coincidence, together with the potential relevance both of something falling to the ground (20) and of κεφαλά (21), has prompted several scholars to place this piece of text here. The argument has very considerable force but the resulting text is difficult to reconstruct. Who are the female swift-flying creatures? And what is falling to the ground? The most obvious approach is to have the helmet (18 τὰ]ν μέν, Lerza) knocked (20 ἐπ[λ]άξαν < πλήσσω, Lobel) to the ground; see Lerza 1978. However, the helmet has already fallen (16–17), and it is hard to see what effect Stes. would have tried to create with the repetition. It is best to keep an open mind about the placing of this scrap. For other approaches, arguably even more difficult, see Irvine 1997 and Ercoles 2011.

31–6 *A description of Heracles' poisonous arrow.* The arrow is probably already in mid-air; see 36–43n. The main verb is lost. See apparatus for credible supplements otherwise: '... <bringing> the <end> that is hateful death, having <?doom> around its head, and befouled with blood and <adjective> gall, the pain of the man-killing shimmer-necked Hydra'. Hexameter poetry often gives prominence to an important weapon, though not usually to arrows. The only instance is [Hes.] *Scut.* 130–4, which shares some motifs and phrasing with this passage.

31–2 στυγε[ρ]οῦ | [θανάτοι]ο . .[: the reconstruction is secure because of a marginal note, στυγεροῖο τὸ [ ]· στυγεροῦ θανάτ[(στυγεροῖο is presumably a textual variant or a quotation from another text). The best candidate for the word lost at the end is τέλος; cf. Stes. 97.213 θανάτου τέλος στυγερο[ῖο], with Hutchinson *ad loc.* (= S211b.213).

33 κ]έφ[αλ]ᾶι: the metaphor 'arrow-head' is much more startling in Greek than in English, investing Heracles' arrow with an almost demonic force; the closest parallel is Bacch. 5.74–5 χαλκεόκρανον . . . ἰόν, 'bronze-headed arrow'.

33–4 πεφορυ|[γ]μένος . . . Ὕδρας: the killing of the Lernaean Hydra was another of Heracles' labours, popular in vase-painting and mentioned in poetry from early on; see Hes. *Th.* 313–18, Alc. 443. This is the first attestation of Heracles' use of the Hydra's blood as poison for his arrows. The Hydra story has a twofold thematic connection with the main narrative. (i) It adds to the sense that Heracles uses every means at his disposal. Poisoned arrows appear only once in Homeric epic, and with a strong hint of ethical transgression (*Od.* 1.260–4, of Odysseus). (ii) The killing of the Hydra serves as a doublet that presages the subsequent killing of Geryon: both are many-headed monsters, both have their blood splattered, both have their suffering brought into focus (ὀδύναισιν).

πεφορυ|[γ]μένος: φορύσσειν and cognate words express visible dirtying with fresh blood in Homer (*Od.* 18.336, 20.348), and as such this verb is strikingly gory when used here to refer to dipping in poison. The phrasing is taken up by 42 ἐμίαινε . . . αἵματι, of Geryon. The bile as the source of the Hydra's poison is standard in later literature and may or may not have been Stes.'s invention; see e.g. Soph. *Trach.* 573–4, Ap. Rh. 4.1403–5, Diod. Sic. 4.11.6. The lost adjective in 34 could be e.g. πικροτάτα]ι (Lerza 1979).

35 ὀλεσάνορος: a variation on epic φθινσήνωρ, φθισίμβροτος, ἀνδροφόνος.

αἰολοδε[ίρ]ου 'with shimmering neck(s)': a rare word, which evokes both variegated colouring and the swirling mass of necks and heads that characterises the Hydra in art as early as the seventh and sixth centuries. For the semantics of αἰόλος – colour and movement – see West 1966b on Hes. *Th.* 300, where the term describes the snake-like Echidna, and for the iconography of the Hydra, Kokkorou-Alewras 1990.

36 ὀδύναισιν is best taken in apposition to 34 αἵματ[ι and χολᾶι. The 'pains' can be understood as either the Hydra's own as she died and thus yielded her blood and gall, or as those she inflicts on others, above all Geryon, indirectly through her poison. For fuller discussion, see Lazzeri 2008: 242–4.

36 (ὅ γ')–43 *The arrow's trajectory into and through the head.* The anatomical detail makes this an immensely physical and gory sequence, as well as slowing down the narrative pace at the moment of climax. ὅ γ' is the arrow rather than Heracles: for ὅ γε taking up the previous subject, to the exclusion of other possible referents ('this same arrow'), see *Il.* 21.455, *Od.* 10.214–15, and the discussion of Bertrand 2015. Heracles probably shoots the arrow in the lines lost before 31, and the arrow then remains the grammatical subject until 43. If this analysis is correct, the arrow is invested with agency. The head is probably still the one that lost its helmet some twenty lines earlier, and is thus now exposed to the arrow; see 13–17n. The passage shares motifs with Homeric battle narrative; see in particular *Il.* 4.122–40 and 5.95–100.

36–7 σιγᾶι ... ἐπι|κλοπάδαν: the references to stealth are emphatic, picking up 8 λάθραι. The entire fragment is characterised by an eerie silence: the episode is visualised graphically, but no sound accompanies the execution-like killing.

37 ἐνέρεισε 'smashed into': intransitive (ἐν)ερείδειν + dat. is unusual, but cf. Aristoph. *Clouds* 558 ἐρείδουσιν εἰς.

38–9 δαί|μονος: in early hexameter a δαίμων tends to bring harm rather than benefit. The term often expresses the viewpoint of a character, ignorant of which god is at work, e.g. Elpenor's δαίμονος αἶσα κακή at *Od.* 11.61; see de Jong 2001 on *Od.* 5.421. Thus the phrase may not just refer (objectively) to divine dispensation guiding the arrow but also (subjectively) suggest Geryon's ignorance.

40 σχέθεν: aor. act. (~ ἔσχεν).

40–1 ἐπ' ἀ|κροτάταν κορυφάν 'to the very top of the head'. For the language, cf. *Il.* 8.83, where Nestor's horse is hit by an arrow ἄκρην κὰκ κορυφήν. For a weapon (here a lance) passing through the head, cf. *Il.* 5. 290–3. On the mid-sixth century amphora Louvre F53 an arrow sticks out on both sides of the head of Geryon's herdsman Eurytion; see Brize 1980: 61 with plate 2.2.

42 ἐμίαινε: another emotive word, fairly rare before the fifth century. Homer uses it of defilement with blood for two sympathetic characters, Menelaus (*Il.* 4.146) and Patroclus (16.795, cf. 13–17n.).

πορφ[υρέωι primarily denotes colour ('purple'), possibly also suggesting movement ('gushing'?); cf. Alcm. 89.5n.

43 βροτόεντ['gory': the missing noun is more likely to be μέλεα than ἔναρα ('spoils', Lobel), which would overlap with θώρακα. The blood spills from his head to his chest and then limbs. Even so, the strong association of βροτόεντα with ἔναρα (formulaic in Homer) goes some way towards creating the impression that Geryon is already dead.

44–7 *Simile (lacking its ending).* This is the first of several surviving adaptations of the poppy simile at *Il.* 8.306–8, μήκων δ' ὡς ἑτέρωσε κάρη βάλεν, ἥ τ' ἐνὶ κήπωι, | καρπῶι βριθομένη νοτίηισί τε εἰαρινῆισιν, | ὡς ἑτέρωσ' ἤμυσε κάρη πήληκι βαρυνθέν; cf. Ap. Rh. 3.1399–1401, Verg. *Aen.* 9.433–7, Ov. *Met.* 10.190–5. As in Homer, the point of comparison is the tilting of the head in death, here the head of Geryon, there that of Priam's son Gorgythion, who is killed by an arrow aimed at Hector. Also as in Homer, the simile creates a moment of stillness within intense battle action and shifts the focus from attacker to victim (nom. Γαρ[υόνας in 44). At the same time Stes. pointedly deviates from Homer in two ways. (i) Homer's poppy remains intact, bowing its head in the spring rain. The image is a closed blossom, appropriate for the helmeted head of a warrior. By contrast, Stes.'s image is one of disfigurement (46 καταισχύνοισ', picking up 42 ἐμίαινε ... αἵματι πορφ[υρέωι). The poppy turns ugly as it loses its petals, and their redness invokes the blood dripping from Geryon's head-wound.

(ii) Gorgythion is one of many victims of battle introduced by Homer at the point of death; his fate, elaborated by a mini-biography and the simile, illustrates the frailty of human life. By contrast, Geryon is a monster who suffers fatal injuries to one of several heads, and so the pathos of the comparison with the drooping, beautiful and tender poppy is extraordinary (but in line with Stes.'s strategy elsewhere). For further discussion, see Garner 1990: 14–18, Herzhoff 1994, Salvador Castillo 1994, and 'Discussions' p. 167 above.

45 ἐπικάρσιον 'at an angle': the head has turned into a lifeless thing. Several pots depict Geryon with one or two heads drooping and the other(s) still fighting; see Brize 1980: plates 3.2, 4.1, 4.2, 5 and Shapiro 1994: 75–6.

ὡς ὅκα (~ ὅτε) 'like', without verb, as often in poetry, e.g. *Od.* 5.281, Pind. *Ol.* 6.1–3; see *CGCG* §47.17.

46 ἅ τε 'who': the 'epic' τε accompanies the relative pronoun in statements of permanent validity. The usage is frequent in epic, and occurs also in lyric; see Ruijgh 1971: chs. 10 and 32. A finite verb is probably lost, governing both participles.

καταισχύνοισ' 'defiling'. This primarily aesthetic usage ('make ugly') is ocasionally attested for simple αἰσχύνω (e.g. *Il.* 18.24, Pind. *Pyth.* 4.264). In so far as a moral connotation is felt ('dishonour'), the verb reinforces what doubts there are about Heracles' actions.

ἁπαλόν: in Homer usually of humans, gods and animals, and often describing the neck. Whatever noun is lost at the end of the line (perhaps δέμας), the adjective looks beyond the simile.

47 αἶψ': poppies blossom only briefly and shed their petals quickly, as was noted already by ancient botanists; see Dioscorides 4.63 (vol. II, p. 217 Wellmann). Stes.'s simile therefore need not have continued with a specific event affecting the poppy, equivalent to Homer's spring showers.

φύλλα 'petals', a very rare meaning, but close to certain in this context.

IBYCUS

The poetry of Ibycus (probably seven books in the Alexandrian edition) is poorly preserved, and therefore difficult to assess. Many of the texts celebrate individuals, in particular male youths. Many feature now often very fragmentary mythical narratives. The themes of beauty and desire are prominent, both in statements of praise and admiration, and in the myths.

Ibycus was known in antiquity for his love poetry addressed to boys (e.g. *AP* 7.714, Cic. *Tusc.* 4.71 = testt. 6, 12 Campbell). On the surviving evidence a distinction suggests itself. On the one hand, there are more formal praise songs, probably commissioned by influential individuals and families, which foreshadow the *enkomia* and even victory odes of the professional poets Simonides, Pindar and Bacchylides; see S151 (presented here), S166 (attribution to Ibycus uncertain), S221. On the other hand, we find expressions of desire which in their foregrounding of the speaker's state of mind are closer to the love songs of Sappho and Anacreon; see 286, 287, 288 (all presented here), S257a *PMGF* (attribution uncertain). However, the preserved corpus is too small to treat the distinction as certain; see further Cingano 1990.

According to ancient tradition, Ibycus came from Rhegium on the Strait of Messina. Some texts treat myths and other subjects specific to localities in Magna Graecia, e.g. S220 (Leontini), 321 (Ortygia ~ Syracuse). Others point elsewhere. S151 was composed for Polycrates, almost certainly the tyrant of Samos, and it is possible (though hardly certain) that S166 was composed for a Spartan patron, and that the use of local Sicyonian myth (308, 322) reflects links with that Peloponnesian *polis*. Even though the detail is a matter for speculation, it is clear that Ibycus operated well beyond his native region. He may have lived for sustained periods in different places, like Anacreon, or may have undertaken individual commissions, like Pindar. See further Bowie 2009: 122–7.

The most reliable indicator of Ibycus' date is the address to an apparently youthful Polycrates in S151 (see p. 174), which puts him roughly into the middle of the sixth century (for Polycrates' – very uncertain – dates see Carty 2015: 75–89). Ancient scholars seem to have pegged Ibycus' dates to those of Polycrates' father (esp. *Suda* 180 = test. 1 Campbell), and Anacreon's to those of Polycrates himself; see Ornaghi 2008, also Woodbury 1985: 207–20. It is unclear whether they had relevant evidence beyond fr. S151 (cf. p. 174).

The papyri exhibit the dialect mix characteristic of choral poetry (pp. 24–5); see Nöthiger 1971, and below, p. 182. The rhythmical structure of many of the texts is triadic. For the question of performance, see on the individual fragments.

Wilkinson 2013 is a commentary on the substantive fragments. In general on erotic lyric addressed to young males, and its cultural contexts, see Breitenberger 2007: ch. 8, Stehle 2009: 66–8, Davidson 2013.

Ibycus S151 SLG (282a PMG)

A lengthy manipulation of epic narratives of the Trojan War culminates in an encomiastic address to Polycrates. Praise and self-conscious reworking of the poetic tradition are equally important to Ibycus' intents, and reinforce one another.

After a summary treatment of the war and sack of Troy in what remains of triad 1, the next two triads name major Trojans and then Greeks. These three stanzas are cast as a *recusatio*: the poet claims he will not sing about these topics (10–12, ?15, 23–6), even though he obviously does. Triad 4 continues to name participants in the war, but shifts from images of destruction to the celebration of beauty. The poem ends with Polycrates, whose future fame is proclaimed and linked to that of the poet himself. At least one stanza is missing at the beginning (to complete the triad). The poem may have opened, as it concludes, with Polycrates, at least briefly.

Ibycus' engagement with the epic tradition has two separate goals. On the one hand, he treats the epic topic *par excellence*, adopting an allusive style that relies on extensive knowledge of the epic tradition, more so than any other surviving text of this period. On the other hand, he develops his own, poetically distinctive, treatment, distancing himself from epic explicitly as well as implicitly. This dual objective is manifest at various levels. (i) Epic phrases occur throughout yet are strung together in untraditional ways. (ii) The rhythm is dactylic but more varied than the epic hexameter (cf. p. 157 on Stes.). (iii) The narrative recalls the Trojan War in comprehensive fashion but is starkly compressed and deviates sharply from canonical accounts when it eventually turns from fighting to beauty and gives prominence to minor, perhaps even untraditional, figures in the final triad. (iv) The speaker accepts the superiority of the Muses but does not invoke them, and rather than consistently maintaining the third person characteristic of epic he introduces his own first person, which he uses to state his rejection of epic subjects, and he concludes the poem with the fanfare of ἐμὸν κλέος. (v) Finally, the poem is self-consciously wide-ranging in its engagement with epic traditions. Several major hexameter poems and genres are harnessed within the confines of Ibycus' short lyric poem: there are allusions not just to the *Iliad*, but also to Hesiod, the *Cypria* and other 'cyclic' epic, and (probably) the *Homeric Hymns*. On lyric and epic in general, see pp. 16–18.

Ibycus' encomiastic strategy is to attach Polycrates' name to the famous names of epic. The strong voice he develops, and above all the introduction of (other) less familiar characters immediately before the address to Polycrates, support this manoeuvre. The confident latter-day poet Ibycus is able to enhance the fame not just of three second-generation heroes but also of his latter-day patron. His own fame is produced as evidence.

Depending on the punctuation, the final lines either hint or state that Polycrates will be famed specifically for his beauty (46–7n.). Beauty and warlike myth are regularly juxtaposed in the lyric corpus; e.g. Sa. 16.

The pairing derives its effectiveness from symmetry as well as contrast. Both war and beauty are frequent objects of celebration but not usually on the same occasion. Like Sappho, Ibycus transfers the renown of martial achievement to beauty.

It is often argued that the celebration of beauty, and the absence of other encomiastic topoi (such as military prowess), indicate that Polycrates was still a boy, and that the song was therefore commissioned by his father; cf. p. 172 on the ancient tradition. This is possible. However, it is also possible that he was a young adult, and that he had already seized power. Beauty is a relatively uncontroversial topic of praise, which may appeal to a tyrant. Alcibiades, tyrant-like in many ways, is often called 'beautiful' (e.g. Antisthenes fr. 32a Caizzi, Xen. *Mem.* 1.2.24, Pl. *Prt.* 316a4), and twelve pots painted by Epiktetos (active *c.* 520–490) bear the inscription ΙΠΠΑΡΧΟΣ ΚΑΛΟΣ or similar (*ARV²* p. 1584), one of them depicting the carving of a herm and hence clearly associated with Hipparchus the brother of the tyrant Hippias. The establishment in Athens of an altar of Eros probably under Pisistratus suggests a public association of the tyrants with the god and what he stood for (Kleidemos, *FGrHist* 323 F 15; Shapiro 1989: ch. 8). Further on the question of Polycrates' age, see Hutchinson 2001: 231–3, who argues that he was a boy. On erotic motifs in large-scale encomiastic poetry, including Ibycus, see Nicholson 2000.

Scale, triadic metre (cf. p. 23) and 'choral' dialect (pp. 24–5) may suggest a choral premiere, whether at a select or public occasion, but the matter is highly uncertain. See Cingano 2003.

Source: *P.Oxy.* xv.1790 (late 2nd/early 1st cent. BC), edited by Hunt in 1922. Minor scraps were published separately as *P.Oxy.* xvii.2081f in 1927, again by Hunt. Two pieces were correctly placed only by Cockle, and first included in a complete edition in Barron 1969, which prompted Page to re-edit what was *PMG* 282a as S151 in *SLG*. Attribution to Ibycus rests in part on the address to Polycrates, with whom Ibycus is connected in the ancient tradition (p. 172); see further Barron 1969: 132–3.

Metre:

str./ant.

– ⏑⏑ – ⏑⏑ – ⏑⏑ – ⏑ ⏑   *4da*
– ⏑⏑ – ⏑ ⏑ – ⏑⏑ – ⏑ ⏑   *4da*
– ⏑⏑ – ⏑⏑ –   *(D)*
⏑⏑ – ⏑ ⏑ – ⏑ – –   ‖ *(hag)*

ep.

– – ⏑ ⏑ – ⏑ ⏑ – –   ?‖ *paroemiac*   18 –φοῖ ἐλ–
– – ⏑ ⏑ – ⏑ ⏑ – –   ?‖ *paroemiac*   19 ἥρωας
⏑⏑ – ⏑⏑ – ⏑ ⏑ – –   ‖ *paroemiac*
– ⏑ – ⏑ ⏑ – ⏑ ⏑ – ⏑ – –   ?‖ *pher²ᵈᵃ*
– ⏑ ⏑ – – ⏑ ⏑ – ⏑ –   ‖ *dodᶜʰ*   48 καὶ ἐμὸν

A predominantly dactylic triad, with aeolic elements at the end. The strophe starts with a sequence of dactyls. The colometry of the papyrus (reproduced here) disguises the continuation of that sequence in the second half: str. 3 + str. 4 might be better articulated as a further set of four dactyls, closed off by – ᴗ – –. The epode also opens with a continuous, broadly dactylic sequence, but the pendant close (– –) of the paroemiacs gives this stanza a rather different character from the outset. The last two lines have an aeolic quality. Sentences often run across stanza-ends; only the end of the epode regularly coincides with a strong syntactic break.

Discussions: Spelman 2018: 164–6, Hardie 2013, Sbardella 2012: 229–36, Natale 2009, *Bonanno 2004, Giannini 2004: 56–9, Mueller-Goldingen 2001, Nicholson 2000, Goldhill 1991: 116–19, Buongiovanni 1990: 121–9, *Woodbury 1985, Péron 1982, Simonini 1979, Gianotti 1973, *Barron 1969, Sisti 1967, Maehler 1963: 75–7, Page 1951b.

1–9   *The destruction of Troy and its causes* (Zeus's will, Helen, Aphrodite). 8–9 correspond to 1–2 in ring composition. This would make a suitable beginning of the myth section. In epic similarly concise statements summarise a bard's song (*Od.* 1.326–7, 8.489–90); here the statement turns out to describe the song the speaker will not sing. Aphrodite's actions that led to the war (in particular the Judgement of Paris), and the departure of the Greek fleet, were narrated (*inter alia*) in the *Cypria* (arg. 1–8 West).

1 Δαρδανίδα: Iliadic epithet of Priam, here invoking Troy's ancient heritage. Gen. -ᾱ (< -ᾱο) is Doric.

2 περικλεές: a variant of the metrically identical Homeric περικλυτόν, and the first reference to fame, one of the major themes of the text; cf. 6, 46–8.

ἤναρον 'slayed'; a brutal word. Like ὄλβιος, the verb is normally associated with people rather than impersonal objects. This is one of several instances of 'Doric' accentuation in the papyrus (Attic–Ionic ἤναρον); cf. 18 πολυγόμφοι, 23 Μοῖσαι, 24 ἐμβαίεν, 29 ἠλύθο[ν, 47 ἑξῆς. Further such accents are introduced by modern editors for consistency (13 παῖδας). See in general p. 63.

3 ὀρνυμένοι 'rushing': the likeliest supplement for the preceding word is Ἄργ]οθεν, which would be picked up at 28 and 36.

4 Ζηνὸς ... βουλαῖς: such compressed statements of divine causation are an epic motif; e.g. in the opening sections of the *Cypria* (fr. 1.7 West) and *Iliad* (1.5).

5 Ἑλένας περὶ εἴδει 'the form of Helen' amounts to 'beautiful Helen', on the model of βίη Διομήδεος, etc. Even so, beauty receives emphasis since fighting is usually over something concrete. For the compressed reference to Helen as the object of the conflict, cf. Alc. 42.15 ἀμφ' Ἐ[λέναι with n.

6 πολύυμνον: an explicit reference to earlier song traditions.

7 πό]λεμον κατὰ δακρ[υό]εντα occurs already at *Il.* 17.512.

8 ἄ]τα replaces the personal subject in otherwise similar phrases, e.g. *Il.* 24.699–700 Κασσάνδρη, ἰκέλη χρυσέηι Ἀφροδίτῃι, | Πέγραμον εἰσαναβᾶσα. The effect is enhanced by the use of ταλαπείριο[ν, which usually qualifies persons, as an emotive epithet of the city; cf. 2 ὄλβιον. ἄ]τα is the 'destruction' of Troy, but may also allude to Paris' and the Trojans' 'delusion' in bringing Helen into the city.

10–22 *A statement of refusal, followed by Greek and Trojan names.* Despite the refusal, the speaker effectively proceeds to flesh out his account. The structure is balanced. A Trojan section (10–15) continues to foreground the erotic theme by singling out Paris and Cassandra before culminating with (again) the destruction of Troy. By contrast, the Greek section (15–22) is centred on warlike qualities and on Agamemnon.

10 νῦ]ν δέ marks the sharp shift from mythical narrative to the speaker's own stance.

ξειναπάταν 'cheating his host', an epithet of Paris also at Alc. 283.5, its only earlier attestation. Paris' abduction of Helen was narrated (*inter alia*) in the *Cypria* (arg. 2b West).

11 ἐπιθύμιον 'it was my wish to' (together with 10 μοι and the likely supplement ἦν]). The adjective occurs only here in early Greek, but the θυμός often prompts a particular speech or song; e.g. the epic formula ὄφρ' εἴπω τά με θυμός ἐνὶ στήθεσσι κελεύει (*Il.* 7.68, etc.), and Alc. 308.1–2 σὲ γάρ μοι | θῦμος ὔμνην. The (likely) past tense probably refers to the account so far: even though it may appear otherwise, the speaker did not intend to sing about the Trojan War.

τανίσφυρ[ον: the epithet highlights Cassandra's attractiveness; cf. [Hes.] *Scut.* 35, fr. 43a.37. She was the object of Apollo's, Agamemnon's and the Lesser Ajax's desire. Also relevant are her warnings against Paris' voyage to Sparta in the *Cypria* and against the Wooden Horse in the *Little Iliad*; see West 2013: 83–5, 205.

12 ὑμ]νῆν ~ ὑμνεῖν 'sing of', echoing 6 πολυύμνον. ὔμνος is often a song that invokes a god, e.g. in Alc. 308.2 (to Hermes, cited in 11n.), but the range of uses is broad from early on; cf. p. 12.

14–15 rework *Il.* 16.698 = 21.544 ἔνθα κεν ὑψίπυλον Τροίην ἕλον υἷες Ἀχαιῶν (or the tradition behind it), as well as the epic trope of the 'day' on which Troy falls, e.g. *Il.* 4.164. Ibycus may or may not have known Stes. 100.11 εὐρυ]χόρο[ο]υ Τροίας ἁλώσι[μον ἆμαρ. The fall of Troy was narrated (*inter alia*) in the *Iliupersis*.

15 ἀνώνυμον: the primary sentiment is horror ('unspeakable'); cf. Homer's δυσώνυμος (*Od.* 19.571, etc.) and οὐκ ὀνομαστός (*Od.* 19.260, etc.). There is also the sense that the poet, who refuses to sing of this topic, will leave it 'unspoken'; cf. νώνυμ(ν)ος 'destined to be forgotten' (*Il.* 12.70, etc., often of people perishing).

οὐδεπ[: something like 'nor do/will I sing of' seems most likely, e.g. Wilamowitz's οὐδ' ἐπ[ελεύσομαι, 'nor shall I recount'.

16 ἥρ]ώων: one of the terms epic uses for figures of the past.

17 ὑπ]εράφανον expresses pride out of the ordinary (ὑπερ-). Such pride can be the object of admiration (e.g. Bacch. 17.48), but it is usually negative (e.g. Hes. *Th.* 149). A negative tinge here would be in keeping with the speaker's negative tone elsewhere in the list of topics he chooses to omit.

17–19 οὕς τε . . . ἐσθ[λούς: the motif of the ships that bring suffering to Troy is common in the *Iliad*; both the Greek ships as here (13.453–4) and Paris' νῆας . . . ἀρχεκάκους (5.62–3). The juxtaposition κακόν . . . ἐσθ[λούς adds poignancy.

17 οὕς τε: 'epic' τε typically occurs in relative clauses that express a permanent state (see Stes. 19.46n.), which this does not. The force of τε here may therefore be stylistic (epic tone) more than semantic.

18 πολυγόμφοι survives in earlier texts only at Hes. *WD* 660 νηῶν . . . πολυγόμφων. It thus constitutes the first of several allusions to Hesiod's sea journey from Aulis to Euboea; see 23–31n.

ἐλεύσα[ν 'brought', aor. of the rare ἐλεύθω.

20–2 Agamemnon is singled out before the allusion to the Iliadic Catalogue of Ships (23–31n.), just as he is before the Catalogue itself (*Il.* 2. 477–83).

20 τῶν] μέν: three times in the fragment, μέν with demonstrative pronoun has a 'quasi-connective, progressive, force' (Denniston 1954: 360, not citing Ibycus): 20, 32, 46. The usage probably recalls the Catalogue of Ships, where there are seven occurrences of τῶν μέν (out of eleven in the *Iliad* overall), several of them, as here, without corresponding δέ.

κρείων: one of Agamemnon's standard epithets, also in the Catalogue (2.576).

21 ἆ]ρχε 'the leader was'. Both verb and tense are frequent in the Catalogue.

Πλεισθε[νί]δας 'descendant of Pleisthenes'. Agamemnon was known variously as son of Atreus (throughout Homer) or Pleisthenes (e.g. [Hes.] fr. 194 MW); see Gantz 1993: 552–6. Ibycus may be making a point of combining Homeric and Hesiodic mythology in his comprehensive account.

ἀγὸς ἀνδρῶν is Iliadic (4.519, etc.), and Agamemnon is frequently ἄναξ ἀνδρῶν, e.g. in the Catalogue at 2.612.

22 ἐσθ[λός]: much more likely than ἐσθ[λοῦ], since the second-declension genitive throughout the fragment is -οιο.

23–31 *A second, fuller statement of refusal.* The Muses might narrate those things; no mortal man could enumerate all the Greeks who sailed to Troy. The passage is heavily intertextual, with a number of clear verbal allusions to the Iliadic Catalogue of Ships, in particular its preamble (*Il.* 2.484–93), and to Hesiod's description of his journey to Euboea (*WD* 646–62). Homer invokes the Muses, and professes that without them he 'could not narrate and name the multitude' of the Greek leaders even if he had ten tongues and mouths. Ibycus paraphrases this denial, but unlike Homer he does not ask the Muses for help and does not enumerate the Greeks; instead, he provides a compressed and selective account, and then moves on. In his avoidance of the Homeric scale Ibycus is Hesiodic. Hesiod pointedly mentions the departure of the Greek host from Aulis in the context of reporting the only occasion on which he travelled by ship, his – minuscule – journey from Aulis to Euboea to sing in a competition. For further discussion of the connections between the three passages, see Dougherty 2001: 20–7 and Steiner 2005. More generally on the *Nachleben* of the Hesiod passage see Hunter 2014: 52–8, and on the partial independence from the Muse that is affected by much lyric, Finkelberg 1998: ch. 6 and Ledbetter 2003: ch. 3.

23 σεσοφι[σ]μέναι ('skilled') recalls *WD* 649 οὔτε ... σεσοφισμένος, from Hesiod's profession of inexperience in seafaring. Here the term may allude to earlier treatments of the Trojan War: the Muses have acquired skills (perfect) to sing about these topics in so far as they have done so before.

24 Ἑλικωνίδε[ς]: these are Hesiod's Muses (658); Homer's are Olympian.

ἐμβαίεν λόγω[ι: lit. 'embark on their tale', a seafaring metaphor that amounts to 'narrate'; hence the accusative τά is probably best understood as a direct object. Whatever the syntax, this is a further piece of intertextual distancing: Hesiod recalls how the Muses 'made me embark on song', ἐπέβησαν ἀοιδῆς (659), while Ibycus suggests the Muses themselves embark.

25–6 There are two textual problems:

25 θνατός: the second line of the strophe should end with a short syllable (*pace* Gentili 1967: 177–8, Gostoli 1979). The simplest emendation would be to replace θνατός with a word starting with a vowel, creating correption λόγωι. (θνατός might be explained as a gloss on 26 διερ[ός that intruded into the text). West's αὐτός may be considered, but 'no man on his own' produces a weaker contrast with the Muses than 'no mortal man'.

26 διερ [. . . . . .] is often restored as διερ[ός]. The extra space may have contained erroneous letters, cancelled out by the scribe. However, διερός is difficult. 'Moist', the usual post-Homeric meaning, is inappropriate here. In Homer (*Od.* 6.201, 9.43) 'alive', 'vigorous' seems most likely, which would make for a concessive expression here: '(not) even a vigorous man . . .'; see Bonanno 1990: 79–83 and Pitotto 2011. Together, the unwanted space and the problematic meaning raise serious questions about the text.

τὰ ἕκαστα: the Muses allow Homer to catalogue νῆας ... προπάσας (*Il.* 2.493).

27 ναῶν ὄ[σσος ἀρι]θμός 'all the many ships'. The supplement ἀριθμός is virtually certain, which in turn makes ὄ[σσος highly likely.

ἀπ' Αὐλίδος: the departure from Aulis was narrated in the *Cypria* (arg. 6–8 West), and as a flashback at *Il.* 2.303–30.

28 Αἰγαῖον ... **[πό]ντον:** the only occurrence of the 'Aegean Sea' before the fifth century, but epic locates Poseidon's palace in the sea in the mythical Aigai; see esp. *Il.* 13.21–2. On ancient interpretations of the name 'Aegean', see Ceccarelli 2012.

ἀπ' Ἄργεος: the combination with ἀπ' Αὐλίδος has raised suspicion, but probably alludes to Hes. *WD* 651–3 ἐξ Αὐλίδος, ἧι ... Ἀχαιοί ... Ἑλλάδος ἐξ ἱερῆς.

30 ἱπποτρόφο[ν: Homer has ἱππόδαμος as a formulaic epithet of the Trojans.

31 υἷ]ες Ἀχα[ι]ῶν: the Greeks in general, an epic usage.

32–45 *More Greeks: famous figures of war, followed by little-known figures of beauty.* The professed inability to provide a comprehensive catalogue does not prevent the speaker from listing individuals. By singling out Achilles and Ajax, he jumps straight to the end of the Catalogue of Ships, where Homer names Achilles as πόλυ φέρτατος and Ajax as the best of men in his absence (2.768–9). Unlike Homer, Ibycus explicitly limits Achilles' field of excellence to fighting (32 πρ[οφ]ερέστατος α[ἰ]χμᾶι) and omits to acknowledge his beauty (*Il.* 2.674). Deviating from the theme of excellence in battle, he then proceeds to celebrate three lesser figures for their beauty.

33 A verb is missing at the beginning, such as Hutchinson's ἦνθε]ν 'came'.

34–5 Probably both verses are about Ajax: either a verbless nominal expression, parallel to Ἀχιλλεύς, or a new clause with a new verb, parallel to that lost in 33. The apparent mention of fire may be a reference to Ajax's prominence in the defence of the ships.

36 κάλλι]στος: a reasonably certain supplement because of 41–5. The accolade will have gained point from the prominence of pederasty in mid and late Archaic elite ideology. *Kalos*-inscriptions appear on pots from the mid-sixth century onwards; see Lissarrague 1999. Ibycus uses similar language at S166.25 and S173.7.

37 Κυάνι]ππ[ο]ς: an Argive king, absent from surviving texts of the period. Later texts know him variously as Adrastus' son ([Apollod.] 1.9.13) or grandson (Paus. 2.18.4); see further Cingano 1989. A marginal scholion (which is the basis of the restoration) shows that Kyanippos' lineage was the subject of scholarship already in antiquity. Sbardella 2014 speculates that Ibycus adopted Kyanippos and Zeuxippos from a (now lost) epic tradition propagated by the Samian rhapsode guild of the Kreophyleioi.

40 Barron 1961 identified the missing person as Zeuxippos, on the basis of Paus. 2.6.7, where he is named as king of Sicyon, son of Apollo and the Argive nymph Hyllis (Hyllis in Pausanias' text is restored from Callim. fr. 712 Pfeiffer). He too is not attested in early texts.

χρυσόστροφ[ος 'with golden breast–band'.

41–5 A distinction is made, but the beauty of both Troilus and Zeuxippos is stressed through 45 μάλ'... ὅμοιον; cf. Alcm. 1.58–9(n.) for a similar kind of comparison. The agreement of Trojans and Greeks further adds to the sense of harmony. Beauty is no longer destructive: contrast 5–8, 11(n.).

41 Τρωΐλον: mentioned only briefly in Homer (*Il.* 24.257), but a major figure elsewhere. Troilus' death at the hands of Achilles is narrated in the *Cypria* (arg. 11 West) and in Ibyc. S224, and was one of the most popular Trojan scenes in sixth-century iconography. The story of Achilles' desire for him is not attested in literature before the Hellenistic period, but his representation as a boy on most images makes it unlikely that Ibycus invented the tradition of his beauty. See further Kossatz-Deissmann 1997.

42–3 ὀρει|χάλκωι 'mountain-copper', a mythical precious metal, mentioned in the same breath as gold at *h.* 6.9 and [Hes.] *Scut.* 122.

43 τρὶς ἄπεφθο[ν] ἤδη: refining makes the gold even more brilliant; cf. Pind. *Nem.* 4.82–3. τρίς and ἤδη lend emphasis. Refined metals are often used to express a person's true worth; see Thgn. 449, 1106, and the discussion of Kurke 1999: 41–60.

45 εἴσκον: a verb often used for comparison with extraordinary looks; e.g. *Od.* 6.152 (Artemis), Sa. 23.5 (Helen). The imperfect is chosen because (Ibycus says) the Trojans and Greeks often made this comparison; cf. Pind. *Ol.* 13.60 for a similarly repeated scene from the epic past.

46–8 *The glory of Polycrates and the poet.* Statements of a fundamental connection between poet and addressee occur in a number of Archaic texts; see in particular the endings of the Delian part of *h.Apol.* (165–78), Pind. *Ol.* 1 and Bacch. 3, and Theognis' 'seal' (237–54). The syntax, and thus the sentiment, is very uncertain in two places: see 46–7, 48nn.

46–7 The punctuation is disputed. (i) As printed here, the text translates: 'Among them (πέδα ~ μέτα), you, too, Polycrates, will on account of your beauty always have undying fame ...' Polycrates is admired explicitly for his beauty, and imagined as existing among the beautiful figures of the past; cf. *Il.* 20.235, where the human Ganymede is said to have been made to pour wine for Zeus κάλλεος εἵνεκα οἷο, ἵν' ἀθανάτοισι μετείη. For the non-preparatory μέν see 20–2n.; κάλλεος is probably best understood as a loose causal genitive, rather than as governed by κλέος, which would produce a strained hyperbaton. (ii) Alternatively, 46 may be treated as a complete clause, with punctuation at line end: 'They will always have a share in beauty. You too, Polycrates, will have undying fame …' On this construction of the text, Polycrates is loosely associated with the beautiful youths rather than explicitly termed beautiful. καὶ σύ would give the praise a strong hymnic note (47n.). It is normal to 'have beauty' (*Od.* 6.18 etc.), but the abstract τοῖς … πέδα (~ μέτεστι) κάλλεος is difficult. Presumably, the point would be to emphasise again that Troilus, Zeuxippos and perhaps Kyanippos are equals. Arguably, version (i) is a little less difficult, but the punctuation in the papyrus shows that this was a problematic passage already for ancient readers. See further Woodbury 1985: 203–5, who argues for version (i).

46 αἰέν: this poem, which is itself preserved and reperformed, can preserve even something as transient as beauty. The earlier sections are relevant: Troy was destroyed but is now famous.

47 καὶ σύ is hymnic in register, especially so if it introduces a new sentence after punctuation at the end of 46. The phrase opens the penultimate verse of many *Homeric Hymns*, often – as here – coupled with a vocative and in the final verse a first-person statement about song; e.g. *h.Apol.* 545–6 καὶ σὺ μὲν οὕτω χαῖρε Διὸς καὶ Λητοῦς υἱέ· | αὐτὰρ ἐγὼ καὶ σεῖο καὶ ἄλλης μνήσομ' ἀοιδῆς.

Πο⟨υ⟩λύκρατες is emphatic: the final name and the only address in the fragment, unadorned by epithets. For the metrical lengthening, cf. Alcm. 1.1 Πωλυδεύκης.

κλέος ἄφθιτον: like Sa. 44.4 (n.) and Thgn. 245–7, Ibycus repurposes the language of heroic achievement for his different purpose. ἄφθιτον echoes 46 αἰέν.

48 The construction is uncertain. Probably, (i) '…just as my own fame too is dependent on my singing'. Ibycus' own fame, which is (presumably) already an established fact, depends on his singing. It follows (he says) that his singing will also be able to bestow fame on Polycrates. Or, (ii) '…as far as my singing and my own fame make possible'. But ὡς has little point, and the parallelism ἐμὸν κλέος/σύ … κλέος is lost.

ἐμὸν κλέος: for the notion of fame of a poet or a poem, see *Od.* 8.73–4, Timocreon 728 (5th cent. BC) and probably Sa. 65.9.

A *coronis* indicates end of poem.

Ibycus 286 PMG

An expression of the pain of love, couched as a pair of contrasting images, each of them rich in associations.

The lush, pure and sheltered garden of the maidens in spring (1–6) offsets the speaker's subsequent account of the assault of Eros: parching, violent and without regard to season (6–13). The lines vividly convey the sense of ceaseless amorous affliction but different interpretations are possible of what precisely the speaker cries out against: ἔρος *per se* (contrasted with innocence), a debilitating type of ἔρος (contrasted with gentle eroticism and promise of fertility), or unseasonal and incessant ἔρος (contrasted with intermittent bouts of ἔρος, or ἔρος confined to one's youth). The images linger, and resist conversion into a simple underlying proposition.

Ibycus draws on the *locus amoenus*, as a generic trope and possibly also with reference to specific texts. Particularly close is the grove of Sa. 2, with which the garden of the maidens shares apple-trees, water, spring and (probably) a group of females. However, whereas in Sappho Aphrodite is welcome, the breezes are gentle and sleep descends onto those present, Ibycus' ἔρος never rests, and both ἔρος and the north wind are forces of harm. What is a single, pleasant scene in Sappho turns into a contrast of the pleasant and the unpleasant. Also worth comparing is Alcinous' orchard at *Od.* 7.112–31. As in Ibycus, there are apple-trees, vines and water, but in contrast to Ibycus the wind is beneficial, and it is the garden, not ἔρος, that knows no seasons. (A different kind of comparison is offered by 'Thgn.' 1275–8, probably post-dating Ibycus.)

We may well have the beginning of the poem. The metre makes it very likely that we do not have the end. The lost portion may have included an address to a youth (cf. 'Source'). The subject matter suggests that the piece will have been sung by (individual) symposiasts. Ibyc. 287 is remarkably similar in structure.

Source: Athen. 13.601b, who quotes the fragment in the context of discussing songs about love for boys. The transmitted text exhibits several Ionic forms, in particular η rather than the Doric α that was apparently standard in the Alexandrian edition. These are kept here despite the obvious case for emendation; see Ucciardello 2005: 30–45, who discusses the possibility that the Ionic forms go back to a divergent pre-Alexandrian tradition.

Metre:

$- \cup \cup - \cup \cup - \cup -$?‖ dod^d ($= 2da - \cup -$)
$- \cup \cup - \cup \cup - \cup -$?‖ dod^d
$- \cup \cup - \cup \cup - \cup -$?‖ dod^d
$- \cup \cup - \cup \cup - - \cup \cup$ $4da$
$- \cup \cup - \cup \cup - \cup \cup - \cup \cup$ $4da$ 5
$- \cup \cup - \cup \cup - \cup \cup - \cup \cup$ $4da$
$- \cup \cup - \cup \cup - \cup - -$?‖‖ ar^d ($= 2da - \cup - -$)
$\dagger \cup \dagger \cup - \cup \cup - \cup -$?‖
$- \cup \cup - \cup \cup -$?‖ D
$- - - \cup \cup - \cup \cup - \cup \cup$ $4da$ ἀΐσσων   10
$- \cup \cup - \cup \cup - \cup \cup - -$ $4da$

‒ ◡ ◡ ‒ ◡ ◡ ‒ ◡ ‒ ‒   ᵖ‖   *ar*ᵈ
‒ ◡ ◡ ‒ ◡ ◡ ...   *2da* ...

Fast-moving dactylic rhythms with aeolic elements (*dod, ar*) are characteristic of Ibycus; the dodrans with dactylic expansion that is repeated at the beginning is also known as 'ibycean'. However, the overall shape raises doubts, as one does not expect such a long stanza (thirteen lines) in this kind of poem. It is possible that lines 1–7 form a complete stanza: they constitute a sense unit, and 7 would make a suitable closing line (cf. the metre of Alcm. 1). The implication would be either that the song is triadic (1–7 ep. or ant., 8–13 str. or ep.), or that there is major corruption in 8–13. The most persuasive attempt to create responsion by transposing text and positing lacunae is that of West 1966a: 153–4. Less attractive metrically and poetically (though less interventionist) are the approaches of Gallavotti 1981: 121–2 and Tortorelli 2004, which end the stanza after line 6 and establish responsion between 1–6 and 7–13 (or 12).

The transmitted text is maintained here, with considerable misgivings. If there are indeed no lacunae, at least a few syllables are likely to be missing at the end since the dodrans (‒ ◡ ◡ ‒ ◡ ‒) would be unexpected as a closural phrase in this largely dactylic context. (Alternatively, one could obtain a closural pattern by emendation; Palumbo Stracca 1981, for example, proposes transposing ἡμετέρας φρένας before ἐγκρατέως, thus replacing the blunt close with a pendant one).

Discussions: *Cazzato 2013, Cavallini 2000: 188–93, Giannini 2000, Bonanno 1990: 73–9, Mariotti 1987, *Davies 1986b: 399–401, Jenkyns 1982: 32–6, Gallavotti 1981, Trumpf 1960.

1–6 *A fertile and sheltered garden in spring.* See headnote for other poetic gardens, esp. Sa. 2. Gardens often have erotic connotations: Aphrodite had gardens sacred to her in various *poleis*, Eros was conceived in the garden of Zeus according to Pl. *Symp.* 203bc, and Boreas abducts the nymph Oreithyia to Apollo's garden (Soph. fr. 956 *TrGF*); see further Calame 1999 [1992]: 153–74, esp. 168–9, who however stresses the difference from the meadow as the more regular place of love-making. The eroticism here is merely hinted at.

1 ἦρι μέν creates the expectation of a subsequent contrast. The particular contrast will turn out a surprise.

Κυδώνιαι: the Cydonian apple is probably the quince. It appears in erotic contexts at e.g. Stes. 88 and Aristoph. *Ach.* 1199. Cf. Sa. 2.3n.

2 μηλίδες 'apple-trees'. The common term is μηλέη, but the ending -ίς is common in tree-types.

2–3 ἀρδόμεναι ῥοᾶν | ἐκ ποταμῶν 'watered from (ἐκ) the streams of rivers'. For ἐκ following its noun, cf. *Od.* 11.346, 17.518. Much the same meaning is yielded if ῥοᾶν is construed with ἀρδόμεναι, followed by an explanatory ἐκ ποταμῶν, but ῥοαὶ ποταμῶν is an established phrase, e.g. *Od.* 9.450.

3–4 παρθένων | κῆπος ἀκήρατος: nymphs come to mind; they roam springs, meadows and trees, and possess gardens (e.g. Sa. 215, *IG* i³.977). However, Ibycus uses the παρθένοι to foreground purity, seclusion, and sacredness as such, and does not give them a specific identity. Whether this purity harbours the promise (or threat) of inevitable future erotic activity is a matter of interpretation; cf. Hippolytus' insistence that Artemis' meadow is ἀκήρατος (Eur. *Hipp.* 73, 76).

4–6 αἱ ... οἰναρέοις 'and the flowers that grow below the shade-giving leafy shoots of the vines': the adj. οἰνάρεος is formed from οἴναρον 'vine-leaf', perhaps ad hoc by Ibycus. The imagery of young growth picks up παρθένων, and the reference to wine would suit the *symposion*.

6–7 *The speaker's predicament stated: ceaseless ἔρος.* Unless some text is lost at the beginning, it is only at this point that the first person enters the poem, that the erotic theme becomes explicit, and that the garden assumes its full symbolic force. As often, it is hard to decide whether ἔρος is abstract 'love/desire' or a personified Eros. Personification becomes more obvious as the image develops.

7 οὐδεμίαν κατάκοιτος ὥραν 'at rest in no season'; a sign of abnormality. The phrase plays with the dual meaning of ὥρη, 'season' (as here; cf. 1 ἦρι) and 'time of day'. It recalls Homeric expressions for 'time to sleep', notably κοίτοιο ... ὥρη (*Od.* 19.510). Mimn. 2 compares the loss of youth to the passing of the season of spring (1–2 ὥρη | ἔαρος), and one might indeed imagine Ibycus' speaker as old; cf. the comparison with the old race horse in 287. The notion of rest resonates with the subsequent image: winds can 'sleep', e.g. Boreas at *Il.* 5.524; on metaphors of sleep, see Alcm. 89.1n.

8–13 *The speaker's predicament expanded: Eros assaults him like the north wind.* Unexpectedly, a second image illustrates Eros' impact. Syntactically, 8 ὑπὸ στεροπᾶς φλέγων goes with 9 Βορέας, whereas everything from ἀΐσσων onwards characterises Eros, but vehicle and tenor interact to create an image of total onslaught. Some of the language evidently describes Eros: Κύπριδος, μανίαισιν (cf. Anacr. 398, Thgn. 1231), ἀθαμβής ('reckless'; cf. similar notions at Alcm. 58 and Thgn. 1234). Other terms, however, are at least as appropriate for a stormy wind: ἀΐσσων ('rushing', cf. *Il.* 2.146), ἀζαλέ|αις ('parching'), ἐρεμνός ('dark', cf. *Il.* 12.375, 20.51); see also 12n. (φυλάσσει). Vice versa, φλέγων suits not just Boreas but also Eros, since love can burn; see Sa. 31.9–10n. After the controlled syntactic parallelism in the depiction of the garden (1–6), the sentence about Eros is characterised by a less orderly piling up of attributes.

8 †τε†: a word meaning 'like' needs to be restored (like Boreas, Eros inflicts harm on me), e.g. ἀλλ᾽ ἅθ᾽. An apposition would be awkward (a Boreas, Eros inflicts harm on me).

9 Βορέας: northerly, cold and fierce, Boreas 'burns' (8 φλέγων) by means of his violent strength and the lightning he brings (8 στεροπᾶς). At *Il.* 21.346–7 he quickly dries a watered orchard. The personified Boreas of myth commits erotic violence; see 1–6n. For the comparison of Eros' impact with that of a fierce wind, cf. Sa. 47 Ἔρος δ᾽ ἐτίναξέ <μοι> | φρένας, ὡς ἄνεμος κὰτ ὄρος δρύσιν ἐμπέτων.

12 πεδόθεν 'from the bottom, completely'. The transmitted παῖδ᾽ ὅθεν (i.e. παιδόθεν 'since childhood'?) is problematic in sense and metre, *pace* Pavese 1992b.

†φυλάσσει† is almost certainly corrupt: 'guarding' does not suit a wind and is at odds with the sense of violence in these lines; contra Gentili 1984, Bonanno 1990: 73–9, Luginbill 1995. The most promising emendation is Naeke's τινάσσει ('shakes'), which suits both Eros and Boreas, and cf. Sa. 47 (cited above). ταράσσει (Hutchinson and Poole *apud* Cazzato 2013: 269) produces a similar meaning ('stirs'). West's paleographically simpler λαφύσσει ('devours') creates the wrong image for Boreas, *pace* Borthwick 1979.

13 ἡμετέρας: poetic plural.

Ibycus 287 PMG

The onset of Eros is met knowingly, helplessly and with reluctance.

The sentiment and the two-part structure (Eros' attack; the speaker's attitude) are simple, but the text is remarkable for its exuberant play with what are individually well-established images. Different constructions of the 'reality' behind the images are possible: is Eros with his dark eyelids a metaphor for love, or is a desirable youth looking at the speaker? What is the youth's intent? Is only the horse ageing, or the speaker too? Is the image of the prize-winning horse a boast about past erotic prowess?

The fragment bears obvious resemblance to Ibyc. 286. αὖτε suggests that we have the beginning of the poem (see 1n.), but we probably do not have the end (see 'Metre').

Source: Σ vet. (p. 49 Greene) and Proclus (1028 Cousin) on Pl. *Parm.* 137a. Plato himself summarises and briefly interprets the text.

Metre:

∪∪–∪∪–∪∪–∪∪–	2an	κ̄ῠ–
∪∪–∪∪–∪∪–∪∪– ?‖	2an	
––∪∪–∪∪–∪∪–	2an	
∪∪–∪∪–∪∪––– ‖	2an	
––∪∪–∪∪–∪∪– ‖	2an	

‒ ∪ ∪ ‒ ∪ ∪ ‒ ∪ ∪ ‒ ∪ ∪ ‒ ∪ ∪ ‒ ‒ ‖ *6da*
∪ ∪ ‒ ∪ ∪ ‒ ∪ ∪ ‒ ∪ ∪ ‒   *2an*
∪ ∪ ‒

A mostly anapaestic sequence, interrupted by more lively dactyls in the reference to the prize horse. The interruption is even more marked if the first four lines are perceived as two tetrameters: expectations of a third tetrameter in 5–6 are disappointed when the metre changes halfway through. Lines 7–8 are unlikely to be complete as they stand: an anapaestic dimeter plus ∪ ∪ ‒ would be surprising. Line 4 is emended twice, for metrical reasons. <ἐσ>βάλλει (or something like it) is necessary to create a colon-end that fits the surroundings. Many editors keep ἄπειρα unemended, but regular anapaests seem preferable in what is otherwise a run of anapaests; see further Gentili 1966. **Discussions:** Papadimitropoulos 2016, Breitenberger 2007: 186–8, Tsomis 2003: 238–42, Davies 1980.

1–2 The gaze that kindles desire is a frequent motif; cf. Alcm. 3.61–2 (τακερώτερα ... ποτιδέρκεται), Pind. fr. 123, Sim. fr. eleg. 22.9–12 *IEG*², and see Cairns 2011 and Calame 2016.

1 αὖτε: see Anacr. 358.1n. on this multi-functional erotic cliché, used often at the beginning of a poem.

1–2 κυανέοισιν ὑπὸ | βλεφάροις 'below dark eyelids', suggesting perhaps seductively half-closed eyes.

2 τακέρ' 'meltingly' (neut. adv.). The word has strong erotic connotations; apart from Alcm. 3.61, see Ibyc.(?) 282C (xiv) Campbell = S257a fr. 29 + 31 *PMGF*, Anacr. 459.

3 κηλήμασι 'enchantments', a strong metaphor for the psychagogic power of love. Cf. *Od.* 18.212 ἔρωι δ' ἄρα θυμὸν ἔθελχθεν, and Sa. 1.2n.

3–4 ἐς ἀπεί|ρ<ον>α ... <ἐσ>βάλλει: hunters, often ephebes, used nets to ensnare hares. The motif of erotic pursuit conceived as a hunt becomes popular only in the Classical period, e.g. Ariphron 813.4–5 *PMG*, Aeschin. 1.195, and Eros-as-hunter iconography. However, the broader connection between hunting and amorous activity goes back a long way; cf. e.g. the use of animals as love gifts on sixth-century pots (see Schnapp 1997, Barringer 2001: ch. 2). For the emendations, see 'Metre'.

ἀπεί|ρ<ον>α 'inextricable'. Cf. Aesch. *Ag.* 1382 ἄπειρον ἀμφίβληστρον with Fraenkel 1950 *ad loc.*, and probably already *Od.* 8.340 δεσμοὶ ... ἀπείρονες, the bonds with which Hermes imagines himself tied while in bed with Aphrodite.

4 Κύπριδος: Eros acts as Aphrodite's agent, as often, e.g. Alcm. 59a.

5 τρομέω introduces the speaker's perspective: he trembles with fear. ἦ μάν asserts the truth of this hyperbole. His fear is illustrated and explained by the subsequent simile, but trembling also continues the image of the prey.

6–8 The image of the ageing horse plays on the erotic associations of horses and horsemanship, for which see headnotes to Alcm. 1 and Anacr. 417. The motif is variously developed in later authors, e.g. Soph. *El.* 25–7, Hor. *Ep.* 1.1.8–9; see Perelli 1993.

6 φερέζυγος 'bearing the yoke'. The word occurs otherwise only at Alc. 249.3, of a ship 'with benches'. For Eros' yoke, cf. Thgn. 1357–8. **ποτὶ γήραι** 'at the threshold of old age'.

7 ἀέκων: unlike Iliadic teams of horses, which formulaically run οὐκ ἀέκοντε (5.768, etc.). Sappho 1.24(n.) has κωὐκ ἐθέλοισα of a woman yielding to desire against her wish.

8 ἔβα: the aorist denotes a typical action, as often in Homeric similes; see Chantraine 1942–53: ii.185–6.

Ibycus 288 PMG

The speaker expresses the erotic appeal of one Euryalos by addressing him as the nursling of Aphrodite and her cortège, thus endowing him with their attributes: grace, beauty and seductiveness in general, and blue eyes, beautiful hair and teasing glances in particular. The conceit approximates Euryalos to Eros, while drawing on the role of various female deities as nurturers of children (*kourotrophoi*) in cult and myth; see Archil. 112, Pind. *Pyth.* 9.59–65, and for discussion and documentation Price 1978. If 282C(i) Campbell = S257a fr. 1 *PMGF* is correctly attributed to Ibycus, he uses a similar image there, a boy nurtured by Charis at Aphrodite's temple.

The fragment seems to allude to Hes. *WD* 72–5: γλαυκῶπις Athena dresses Pandora, the Charites and Peitho give her necklaces, and the καλλίκομοι Horai garland her with spring flowers. The formal address suggests that this was the opening of the poem. In what followed, the text may have moved on to the speaker's own longing for Euryalos; cf. 286, 287. A dark continuation (the pain of love) would tinge the allusion to Pandora with darkness, too.

Source: Athen. 13.564f, who quotes the fragment among other amatory pieces about boys. Eustathius (*Od.* p. 1558.17–18) in turn quotes the Athenaeus passage.

Metre:

− ∪ ∪ − − − ∪ ∪ − ∪ ∪ < > ?*5da* γλαυκέ͜ων

− ∪ ∪ − ∪ ∪ − ∪ ∪ − ∪ ∪ *4da*

− ∪ ∪ − ∪ ∪ − − *3da*

− ∪ ∪ − ∪ ∪ − ∪ ∪ − − *4da*

A flowing dactylic sequence.

Discussions: Cavallini 2000: 193–5, Brillante 1998, Bernardini 1990, Davies 1986b: 404–5, Barron 1984: 15–16.

1 **Εὐρύαλε:** not otherwise known. There may be resonances from myth: the Odyssean Euryalos is exceptionally good-looking (8.115–17). **γλαυκέων** 'bright-eyed', 'blue-eyed', as probably at Xenophanes 18.2 GP, Hdt. 4.108.1. The model is Athena's epithet γλαυκῶπις (whatever its real etymology), which appears in the *Works and Days* passage (see headnote) and which Ibyc. 303a.1 applies to Cassandra. Further on the adjective, see Leumann 1950: 148–54, Pötscher 1998. There is no need to adopt Jacobs' and Fiorillo's γλυκέων. **Χαρίτων:** the Graces regularly accompany Aphrodite; e.g. *Od.* 8.364–6, *h.Aphr* 61–3. **θάλος** 'scion'.

2 **μελέδημα** 'darling', 'object of care'. A noun in the gen. pl., qualified by καλλικόμων, evidently dropped out. The *WD* passage suggests the Horai (= Seasons).

3 **ἀγανοβλέφαρος** 'soft-eyed'.

3–4 **Πει|θώ** is often erotic, as here and probably in the *WD* passage. In Pind. fr. 123.13–15, for example, Peitho and Charis 'reside in' the boy Theoxenos; see further Buxton 1982: 31–48, Breitenberger 2007: 117–35. 4 **ῥοδέοισιν ἐν ἄνθεσι:** see Sa. 2.6n.

ANACREON

Even more clearly than Ibycus, Anacreon was a mobile poet, whose presence and services were sought by several prominent individuals. He originated in Teos on the coast of Asia Minor, and moved to Abdera in Thrace with the rest of the Teian population when their city was conquered by the Persians, probably sometime between 546 and 540 BC; see Strabo 14.1.30 ~ Anacr. 505a. He spent a period of time in Samos, in the surroundings of Polycrates. Probably towards the end of his life he lived in Athens, where he is linked above all with the Pisistratid Hipparchus, but not exclusively so. He also celebrated Critias, the grandfather of the better-known fifth-century politician and poet of the same name. For Polycrates, see Hdt. 3.121.1, and for his broader cultural ambitions, Shipley 1987: 69–99. For Hipparchus, see [Pl.] *Hipparch.* 228b–c (test. 6 Campbell), and regarding his cultural programme *carm. conv.* 893.3n. For Critias, see Pl. *Charm.* 157e = Anacr. 495, cf. 412, 500. Further on Anacr.'s life and dates, see Hutchinson 2001: 256–60, and above, p. 172.

The Hellenistic poet Antipater of Sidon calls Anacr. the 'glory of the Ionians' (*AP* 7.27 = test. 12 Campbell). The *poleis* in which he was active all had claims to being Ionian. Alone among the canonical lyricists, Anacr. composed in (a mix of literary and vernacular) Ionic. His Ionian credentials are manifest also in his composition of elegiac and iambic poems, alongside his apparently more substantive lyric oeuvre; these genres seem first to have come to prominence in Ionia and adopt an Ionic-dominated poetic language.

Anacr.'s poems are typically short, simple in metre and expression, and often witty. Almost everything that survives is, more or less obviously, intended for the *symposion*. Anacr.'s reputation as an easy-going poet of love and wine is, however, too narrow, and derives in part from the *Anacreontea* (see p. 190). He also produced invective (represented here by 388; see headnote), made reference to politics and wars (e.g. 353, 391, 419, 426; closest in this selection comes 348), and composed what might broadly be called wisdom poetry (represented here by 395). There is some reason to think that he also wrote *partheneia* (see 500, 501). Myth, though much less prominent than in many other lyric poets, was not altogether absent (355, 501; and see Bernsdorff 2016).

Despite this variety, erotic and convivial themes were doubtless hallmarks of Anacr.'s poetry. They dominate what survives. It is noteworthy, moreover, that no transmitted text adopts an obviously partisan perspective in the manner of Alcaeus' political poetry, or constitutes a large-scale encomium in the manner of Ibyc. S151 or Pindaric epinician. We do not know to what degree this is the result of a biased transmission process: according to Strabo (14.1.16 ~ Anacr. 483), Anacr.'s poetry was 'full of' references to Polycrates. In any case, it is significant that almost everything we have is generic in the sense that we can relate only very few individual texts to particular patrons or locales.

One factor affecting these poetic choices may have been be the circumstances in which Anacr. operated. The tyrants who hosted him may have been keen not to accentuate divisions, and as a poet who had arrived from elsewhere Anacr. may not have belonged to any particular faction in Polycrates' Samos or the Pisistratids' Athens; see Kantzios 2005 and 2010. Both the distinctiveness and the extensive afterlife of Anacr.'s poetry, however, suggest that his own poetic preferences played an important role too. Anacr. created a brand of poetry that must have appealed for what it offered – neatness, sophistication and elegance – as much as for what it avoided.

This sophistication was not purely aesthetic but could, in certain quarters, take on an ideological charge. In Athens, Anacr. was both admired and caricatured as a representative of a world of ease and luxury associated with Ionia and the east; see pp. 196–7 (on the 'Anacreontic' vases), Aristoph. *Thesm.* 160–3, Critias 8 GP = 1 Gerber, and the discussions of

Wilson 2003 and Shapiro 2012, as well as Kurke 1992 on the associations of ἁβροσύνη in different contexts.
Uniquely among the lyric poets, Anacr. gave rise to a poetic tradition. The *Anacreontea* are a body of some sixty poems in imitation of Anacr., composed between the first century BC and the sixth century AD, and transmitted alongside the *Palatine Anthology*; for discussion, see Rosenmeyer 1992, Lambin 2002 and Baumbach and Dümmler 2014. It is these poems above all that shaped perceptions of Anacr. in later times.
There is some reason to think that the Hellenistic edition of Anacr. was organised metrically. It probably contained fewer books (but not fewer poems) than those of the other poets. References survive to books 1, 2 and 3, respectively. An epigram by Crinagoras (*AP* 9.239 = test. 13 Campbell, 1st cent. BC) may be referring to a five-book edition, but both text and interpretation are uncertain. See Acosta-Hughes 2010: 160–3.
Gentili 1958 provides a critical edition, Leo 2015 an edition with commentary of the erotic fragments. A complete edition and commentary by Bernsdorff is in preparation; see also Rozokoki 2006. References to discussions of erotic lyric are given on p. 172; for Anacr. specifically, see Williamson 1998.

Anacreon 348 PMG

An address to Artemis, which formed the first stanza of a poem of at least two stanzas (see 'Source'). The next stanza probably included a request.
Line 4 identifies Artemis as Artemis Leukophryene, who was worshipped in a temple on the river Lethaios, a branch of the Meander. The πόλις in 6 must therefore be Magnesia, nearby in the Lethaios plain.
The poem moves from wild nature to first the out-of-town sanctuary, and then the city and its citizens: ἀγρίων | δέσποιν'... θηρῶν (wild animals) is taken up by θρασυκαρδίων | ἀνδρῶν ... πόλιν (suggestions of wildness, but also a city) and οὐ ... ἀνημέρους | ποιμαίνεις πολιήτας (city again, and language of animal husbandry). For Artemis as a goddess both of the wild and of cities and cultivation, see Bacch. 11.37–9 Ἄρτεμις ἀγροτέρα ... Ἡμ]έρα and *h.Aphr.* 18–20, and the discussions of Cole 2004: 178–230 and Kowalzig 2007: 271–97.
It is very possible that the poem was performed at *symposia*, like much of Anacr.'s output. Anacr. 357 is a sympotic hymn to Dionysus; in general on the religious dimension of the *symposion*, see Hobden 2011.
Like Anacr.'s Teos (p. 188), Magnesia was conquered by the Persians in the years immediately following 547/546 BC (Hdt. 1.161). We do not know whether the poem predates these events. If it does not (and possibly even if it does), Anacr. will be imagining Magnesia from afar. One may suppose

that celebration of the Magnesians – Greeks under Persian rule – would be well received both among the Teans who, Anacr. among them, settled in Abdera when their own city fell to the Persians, and in the surroundings of Polycrates, who had ambitions to rule all Ionia (Hdt. 3.122.2). Vetta 2000 suggests that Anacr. evokes for audiences elsewhere (he thinks Samos) a Magnesian Artemis festival taking place at the same time: νῦν. (The Leukophryneia were a major event in the Hellenistic era, but little is known about the early history of the festival.) Page 1960 argues for a connection with Polycrates' journey to Magnesia which ended with his death at the behest of the Persian governor Oroites. For other similarly small-scale and potentially sympotic prayers that invoke geographies with which the author is not otherwise associated, see Alc. 45 (the Thracian river Hebrus), 307 (Delphian Apollo) and 325 (Athena Itonia at Coronea in Boeotia; cf. 4n.).

 Source: The complete eight lines are quoted in the A scholia (p. 172 Consbruch) on ?Hephaestion's *On Poems* 4.8 (p. 68 Consbruch), which itself quotes lines 1–3. *On Poems* identifies the text as 'the first song of Anacreon', viz. the opening poem in the Alexandrian edition. Songs addressed to gods are placed first also in the Attic *skolia* collection (*carm. conv.* 884–7) and the *Theognidea* (1–18), and opened the Alexandrian editions of Sappho (fr. 1) and Alcaeus (fr. 307, mentioned above).

 On Poems further shows that our text is one stanza in a song of at least two stanzas. It describes the song as composed κατὰ σχέσιν ('in [strophic] correspondence'; cf. Aristid. Quint. 1.29), and speaks of a 'strophe of eight cola'. (When further calling the whole song μονοστροφικόν, the author must therefore mean that just one strophic pattern is repeated rather than that there was only one stanza. Further on the terminology and analysis in *On Poems*, see Kehrhahn 1914: 481–94.)

 Several other scholarly texts quote shorter sections: see Page's, Gentili's or Rozokoki's editions.

 Metre:

– – – ⌣ ⌣ – ⌣ –	*gl*	
– – – ⌣ ⌣ – ⌣ –	*gl*	
– – – ⌣ ⌣ – – [?]∥	*ph*	
– – – ⌣ ⌣ – ⌣ –	*gl*	Ληθαίου
– – – ⌣ ⌣ – ⌣ –	*gl*	
– – – ⌣ ⌣ – ⌣ –	*gl*	5
– – – ⌣ ⌣ – ⌣ –	*gl*	
– – – ⌣ ⌣ – – ∥∥	*ph*	

A flowing, regular aeolic sequence. In each line, the aeolic base is constituted by two longs, and there are no instances of *brevis in longo* or hiatus. Already *On Poems* (see 'Source') points out that the stanza may be divided into two sequences, of three and five lines respectively. Each consists of a sequence of glyconics closed off by a catalectic glyconic (= pherecratean), and forms a sense unit. For a detailed discussion of the metre, see Morantin 2009. Cf. also 358. **Discussions:** Furley and Bremer 2001: 1.178–9 and 11.128–31, Tsomis 2001: 62–5, *Vetta 2000, Bonanno 1983, Page 1960.

1 γουνοῦμαι: used mostly for supplicating humans, but also for invoking gods; see *Od.* 4.433, Archil. 108.1, Anacr. 357.6.

ἐλαφηβόλε 'deer-shooter'. For this common epithet of Artemis', see e.g. *h.* 27.2, [Hes.] fr. 23a.21 MW, *carm. conv.* 886.3.

3 δέσποιν' ... **θηρῶν** is a variation on the Homeric πότνια θηρῶν (*Il.* 21.470).

4 ἤ κου: the expression of uncertainty befits a human statement about a deity's actions. Cf. Alc. 325.2 ἄ ποι, in an address to Athena. For references to the deity's location as a standard feature of prayers, see Sa. 1. 7–13n. κου, κως etc. for που, πως etc. is a feature of literary Ionic.

νῦν: sympotic songs often create a scene that unfolds now and here, see e.g. Xenophanes 1.1. It is possible that in this case a connection is made with an event that is taking place now but not here: see headnote.

4–5 ἐπὶ Ληθαίου | δίνῃσι: sanctuaries of Artemis were often situated near flowing water; see Cole 2004: 191–4.

5–8 convey Artemis' status as the deity presiding over the city of Magnesia.

5 θρασυκαρδίων: a marked adjective, usually singling out individuals, and even more marked if Magnesia was already under Persian control.

6 ἐσκατορᾷς ('you look down at') ... **χαίρουσ':** Artemis' delight in viewing men from on high recalls the Iliadic gods, e.g. 7.58–61, 8.51–2, 14. 153–6 (with χαίρειν); but she delights in civilised citizens, not battle action. Concern with a deity's pleasure is a common expression of (hoped for) reciprocity between divinity and worshippers. It is usually framed as a wish, e.g. *CEG* 227 χαίροσα διδοίες; but cf. *h.Apol.* 146 ἐπιτέρπεαι of the pleasure Apollo takes in the festival at Delos.

ἐσκατορᾷς: East Ionic (the dialect of Anacr.'s hometown Teos, and of Samos) does not have initial aspirates (i.e. it has no rough breathings), but does seem to maintain aspiration within compounds (viz. καθορᾷς); see Stüber 1996: 75–8. The practice of the Alexandrian editors of Anacr. is difficult to reconstruct from the relatively few papyri. In the texts edited here (all of which are preserved as quotations in other authors), cf. 388.10 καθέρματα, 395.3 οὐκέτ' ἤβη (an emendation), 395.11 κάτοδος (κάθοδος also transmitted).

7 οὐ ... ἀνημέρους: the emphatic double negative marks a climactic contrast at several levels. The citizens are 'not untamed', viz. 'civilised', even though: (i) Artemis' animals are wild, (ii) they are θρασυκάρδιοι, (iii) Magnesia was (perhaps) controlled by Persia, (iv) Magnesia was famous for acts of ὕβρις in the past; see Thgn. 603–4, 1103–4 and West's apparatus for Archil. 20.

8 ποιμαίνεις expresses solicitous care. It adapts epic ποιμένα (-μένι) λαῶν: Homer's 'shepherds' are not usually divine and his λαοί not civic.

Anacreon 358 PMG

One of Anacr.'s many variations on the theme of unrequited desire; cf. 360, 376, 378, 417, 445, and see Rosenmeyer 1992: 41–9. A ball thrown by Eros challenges the speaker to play with a girl (1–4), but it turns out the girl is not interested in him (5–8). The poem appears to be complete.

In a stylised manner the two stanzas mimic the speaker's consciousness: onset of desire is followed by accounting for lack of reciprocation. Listeners are playfully subjected to their own gradual realisation process. The second stanza first insinuates a younger, more attractive (male) rival, until the last line (probably: see 5–8n.) springs a surprise: the girl has eyes only for another girl. As Eros has his way with the speaker, so the speaker has his way with the audience. Cf. the less pronounced twists at the end of Anacr. 388 and 395.

Sympotic performance is highly likely. Whether the imaginary scene itself should be mapped onto the *symposion* is left to the audience's discretion. The girl *may* be imagined as a *hetaira* performing with a ball and flirting with the speaker: upmarket prostitutes were often presented as companions, bestowing their favours as a gift; see Davidson 1997: 120–7, Kurke 1997 ~ 1999: 175–219; cf. 388.5n. Yet like much of Anacr.'s poetry, the text hovers between the concrete and the metaphorical. There are no deictic pronouns.

Source: Athen. 13.599 c–d. In the context of a discussion of Anacr.'s and Sappho's relative dates, Athenaeus' character Myrtilos quotes the text and cites the fourth- to third-century Peripatetic scholar Chamaeleon (fr. 26 Wehrli). According to some authorities, Chamaeleon claims, Anacr. addressed the lines to Sappho. Sappho's alleged reply is also quoted (fr. adesp. 953 *PMG*). This scenario is chronologically impossible, but the reference to Sappho may have a point: see 5–6n.

Metre:

– – – ⏑ ⏑ – ⏑ –	*gl*	1 πορφυρέῃι (see 417.2n. (δοκέεις))
– – – ⏑ ⏑ – ⏑ –	*gl*	
– × – ⏑ ⏑ – ⏑ –	*gl*	
– – – ⏑ ⏑ – – |||	*ph*	

Two stanzas, each formed of a run of three glyconics, rounded off by a catalectic glyconic (= pherecratean). This type of metre is characteristic of Anacr.; cf. 348 above.

Discussions: Gellar-Goad 2017, Bowie 2013: 35–6, *Yatromanolakis 2007: 142–3, 174–83, 355–8, *Pfeijffer 2000a, Williamson 1998: 78–81, Pace 1996, Pelliccia 1995a, *Pelliccia 1991, Davidson 1987, Goldhill 1987: 16–18, Renehan 1984, Marcovich 1983, *Woodbury 1979, Gentili 1973, Giangrande 1973, Davison 1959.

1–4 *Desire aroused.* The image is simple yet evocative. The ball may be real or symbolic of desire. It may be thrown by a personified Eros or by girls playing ball. The girl may be misdirecting the ball flirtatiously or accidentally. Females playing with balls appear on pots in both more and less clearly erotic contexts from the late sixth century; see Pfisterer-Haas 2003: 168–74.

The scene evokes Odysseus' encounter with Nausicaa in *Od.* 6. Odysseus is woken by a ball that Nausicaa meant to aim at one of her female companions (110–18). There too the ball game is choreographed by a deity (Athena), who moreover enhances Odysseus' appearance (112–14, 229–35). Nausicaa (it is hinted) comes to desire Odysseus (esp. 244–5). In lines 5–8, both the speaker's looks and the girl's attitude will turn the implied comparison with Odysseus against the speaker.

1 δηὖτε: characteristic of the lyric of love and desire, and very rare in other kinds of poetry. The word typically appears in the opening lines, which often take the form, 'Eros . . . me, again!'; in this edition, see Ibyc. 287.1 (αὖτε) and cf. Sa. 1 (δηὖτε 3x), and for further discussion Mace 1993, LeVen 2018: 225–32. δη- amounts to 'voilà'. The notion of repetition (-αυτε) creates a connection with other songs of Anacr. (a poet of, and in, love), and/or with other pieces performed at the same *symposion* (an occasion for eroticised discourse). It takes on a further dimension when it becomes clear that the speaker is old.

πορφυρέηι: cf. *Od.* 8.372–3 σφαῖραν . . . πορφυρέην.

2 χρυσοκόμης carries connotations of divinity and eroticism; cf. Hes. *Th.* 947 (Dionysus, sleeping with Ariadne), Alc. 327 (Zephyrus, begetting Eros), Eur. *IA* 548 (of Eros himself).

3 νήνι (Ion.) ~ νεάνιδι, 'girl', 'young woman'.

ποικιλοσαμβάλωι draws attention to her feet and hence movements. The hint of sophistication in ποικιλο- prepares for 5–6.

4 συμπαίζειν refers to the playing with balls; cf. παίζειν of Nausicaa and her companions at *Od.* 6.100. It is also suggestive erotically; see Anacr. 417.5n.

προκαλεῖται 'challenges'; an agonistic term appropriate not just to the battlefield but also the *symposion*; cf. Critias 6.6–7.

5–8 *Accounting for rejection.* In two parentheses the speaker provides two separate reasons why the girl is not interested in him, as though searching for explanations. When he finally turns to the person she *is* interested in, he is dismissively vague (8 ἄλλην τινά). The vagueness has made interpretation controversial. (a) Probably (the majority view): the girl looks at 'some other girl', perhaps a fellow ball-player, if the picture of 1–4(n.) is still felt. (b) Syntactically, πρὸς δ' ἄλλην τινα could mean 'some other hair', picking up τὴν ἐμὴν κόμην; thus Woodbury 1979. But this makes for a weaker punchline, and for an unnecessarily difficult expression: 'some other hair' is not an obvious shorthand for '(the hair of) some other man'. (c) The same objection (difficult shorthand) applies to the idea that Anacr. invokes the reputation of Lesbian women for oral sex (well attested in the fifth century): 'some other (i.e. pubic) hair' of some other man; thus esp. Gentili 1973. (d) Giangrande 1973 (and in several subsequent articles, the last of which is Giangrande 1995) proposes 'some other (i.e. pubic) hair' of the speaker, but the train of thought 'does not want to play with me and instead gawps at my pubic hair' is far-fetched.

5–6 ἔστιν γάρ ἀπ' εὐκτίτου | Λέσβου: the significance of her Lesbian origin is left for the listeners to supply. Lesbian women are beautiful at *Il.* 9.129–30 (~ 271–2), 'Lesbian women, whom I [Agamemnon] chose when [Achilles] captured well-settled Lesbos (Λέσβον ἐϋκτιμένην), and who surpassed the tribes of women in beauty'. Beautiful Lesbian women appear again at Alc. 130b.17–20(n.). The implication of the girl's beauty is presumably that the speaker is not a suitable match: she is too beautiful for the white-haired man. However, when it emerges that the girl is interested in another girl, Lesbos probably becomes a reference to Sappho's poetry of love and desire between women. This kind of allusion is unparalleled but easily understood. It does not require the (much later) notion of 'lesbian' as a sexual orientation.

7 λευκή contrasts with the purple ball, Eros' golden hair, the girl's elaborate sandals, as well as (probably) the beauty of the Lesbian women. For Anacr.'s old speaker, see 395 (headnote), with white hair in lines 1–2(n.), and for old age as incompatible with sex, Mimn. 1, Sa. 58b; further Bertman 1989. Anacr. is unusual in stressing the asymmetry of the desiring but undesirable old man.

8 χάσκει 'gawps'. The tone is slightly contemptuous, matching the dismissive 'some other'; cf. Aristoph. *Clouds* 996–7. Rhetorically at least, the speaker gets his own back. The verb need not be erotic, as West 1970b: 209 and others emphasise, but in the context an erotic interpretation is invited.

Anacreon 388 PMG

A satirical sketch of a transformation from rags to riches, in which both rags and riches are grotesque and disreputable. Artemon then (1–9) was uncouth and criminal; Artemon now (10–12) is effeminate in his over-enthusiastic adoption of a luxurious, Eastern lifestyle. The expected second part, announced by the very first word (1 πρίν) but then delayed for three stanzas, is eventually delivered with deflating punch. Further stanzas may or may not have followed.

This is one of several invective texts in Anacr.'s corpus; see in particular 424 (fr. iamb. 7 *IEG²*), 427 and 432, and the discussion of Brown 1983: 2–5. Like many forms of satire, the poem attacks its target by focusing on his appearance. Some of the vocabulary is notably rare in the higher-register texts that dominate the surviving record.

Artemon appears also in the brief fr. 372 ξανθῆι δ' Εὐρυπύληι μέλει | ὁ περιφόρητος Ἀρτέμων 'blonde Eurypyle ("Wide-Gate") cares for that litter-rider Artemon (or "that notorious Artemon")'. It seems likely that Anacr. was caricaturing a known individual, but the possibility that he invented a fictional exemplar of louche, parvenu behaviour cannot altogether be excluded. Either way, he shaped a recognisable character in its own right: Aristophanes alludes to Anacr.'s Artemon (5, 7–9nn.), and ὁ περιφόρητος Ἀρτέμων becomes proverbial (see Gentili 1958: 9).

Social and economic change, and with it the rise of once marginalised groups, caused resentment among established elites throughout the Archaic period. In some of the detail (2–3n.), as well as its ideology, Anacr.'s poem resembles Theognis' complaint (53–68) that those who used to be poor and criminal now hold the position of the 'good' yet have not really changed their ways. Both texts adopt the same conservative stance according to which new-found wealth cannot turn a lowly and base man into a genuine aristocrat.

Artemon's outfit in the final stanza resembles that of a distinctive type of komast and symposiast found on a set of some fifty Attic pots of the late sixth and early fifth centuries. In deviation from the standard iconography, these figures are not partially nude but wear a chiton and himation, and some of them also sport headgear, earrings and/or parasols. How these images relate to actual fashions is disputed. They certainly testify to an interest in luxurious and vaguely Eastern ways of life in the Athens of Anacr.'s day. The inscription 'Anacreon' on one of the pots creates an apparent contradiction. In 388 Anacr. mocks Artemon's new, luxurious life; and yet, as a poet from the east of the Aegean who celebrated the good life of the *symposion*, he himself could evidently be associated with such luxuries. This apparent contradiction makes most sense if one considers that notorious cultural trends often give rises to complex attitudes.

Whether Eastern luxuriousness was approved or disapproved of depended on perspective, and was a matter of context and indeed degree. What is wrong with Artemon (according to Anacr.) is not the fashionable luxuries as such but the excess he displays in adopting such a way of life, an excess that is all the more objectionable in a man of his background. It is noteworthy that the figures on the pots never ride a carriage, unlike Artemon, and are always pictured within the demarcated context of the komos and *symposion*. For divergent interpretations of the iconography, see Frontisi-Ducroux and Lissarrague 1990 [1983], Boardman 1986, Delavaud-Roux 1995, Yatromanolakis 2007: 110–40, Bing 2014: 27–33.
   Source: Athen. 12.533f–34b, who quotes frs. 372 and 388, citing Chamaeleon as his source (fr. 36 Wehrli); cf. 358 'Source'.
   Metre:

¹ $- \cup \cup - \quad - \cup \cup - \quad \times - \cup - \times - \cup - \quad \| \quad$ 10 σατινέων χρύσεα φορέων
      $or - \cup \cup -$
² $- \cup \cup - \quad - \cup \cup - \quad - \cup \cup - \times - \cup - \ ^?\| \quad$ 5 ὁμιλέων
   $or - - \cup - \ or \cup - \cup -$
³ $\times - \cup - \quad \times - \cup - \quad \||\|$

Four three-verse iambo-choriambic stanzas, each formed of two tetrameters followed by a dimeter. A sense of regularity is created by the choriambic opening and iambic close of each of the tetrameters and by the consistently iambic dimeters at stanza-end. Patterns vary considerably at the centre of the tetrameters.
   Discussions: Bruce 2011, Lambin 2002: 113–20, Kurke 1999: 187–91 ~ Kurke 1997: 119–23, Steinrück 1995: 183–90, Lenz 1994, *Brown 1983, Davies 1981, Slater 1978.

1–9 *Artemon past.* He was low in means, status and standards of behaviour.
   1 βερβέριον '?hat'. The term is otherwise unknown, and no doubt pointed. Since κάλυμμα is typically a veil, and since the description in 1–4 moves from the head downwards, βερβέριον is probably a floppy hat. καλύμματ' (in apposition) abusively exaggerates its shapelessness. Soft hats are characteristic of labourers, who need protection against the sun; see Pipili 2000, with a striped hat in fig. 6 and hats with protuberances at the top in figs. 7 and 10.
   ἐσφηκωμένα: lit. 'wasped', either striped or (more likely) pinched. Cf. σφήκωμα of the thin point of a helmet where the plume is attached, for which see Pearson 1917 on Soph. fr. 341. Both associations are present at *Il.* 17.52, 'hair that is "wasped" with gold and silver'.
   2 ξυλίνους ἀστραγάλους: a mark of Artemon's poverty, and probably also of his effeminate tendencies already back then. Bruce 2011: 307 points to the archaeological evidence for jewellery made from knucklebones, and for *astragalos*-shaped jewellery made from precious materials.

2–3 ψιλόν ... **βοός:** a noun meaning 'skin' is evidently lost. There may also have been a verb, e.g. ἤιει 'he went'. Animal skins are the clothes of those who cannot afford wool; cf. Thgn. 55 ἀμφὶ πλευραῖσι δορὰς αἰγῶν κατέτριβον, Aristoph. *Clouds* 72, Pl. *Crito* 53d.

4 νήπλυτον ... **ἀσπίδος** 'the unwashed wrapping of a poor shield'. The skin he wears is not even new, but had been used for a different purpose.

ἀρτοπώλισιν: women who had to work in public were of low status. Bread-women are a byword for loud-mouthed quarrelling at Aristoph. *Frogs* 857–8.

5 κἀθελοπόρνοισιν 'voluntary prostitutes' (masc./fem.). This is a double insult. Unlike ἑταίρα, the term πόρνη emphasises sex for pay (< πέρνημι 'sell') and is often abusive; see Kurke 1997 ~ 1999: 175–219 and Cohen 2015: 31–8. ἐθελο- indicates the voluntary pursuit of something one should not voluntarily do; cf. ἐθελόδουλος.

ὁμιλέων may insinuate sex (LSJ s.v. IV), but is more general; Artemon keeps bad company. Cf. Alc. 117.29 π[όρν]αισιν ὁμίλλει.

ὁ πονηρὸς Ἀρτέμων 'the miserable Artemon', delayed for effect. Aristoph. *Ach.* 850 ὁ περιπόνηρος Ἀρτέμων amalgamates this phrase with Anacr. 372.2 ὁ περιφόρητος Ἀρτέμων, unless Anacr. himself varied the epithet of his standard target. The article treats Artemon as familiar to the audience; cf. 427.2–3 τῆι πολυκρότηι | σὺν Γαστροδώρηι, and *carm. conv.* 892.1n.

6 κίβδηλον εὑρίσκων βίον 'making a fraudulent living'. Unlike an aristocrat, Artemon had to find a living, and he did so by crime. κίβδηλος carries with it the metaphor of counterfeit coinage, and was a charged term in an age in which the established elites had to adapt to the increased circulation of money; see Thgn. 117–24, 963–6, and the discussion of Kurke 1999: 53–7. Artemon was 'fake' even before his transformation.

7–9 Repeated corporal punishment demonstrates Artemon's criminal habit, and probably also his low status. Certainly in democratic Athens, free citizens were largely protected from torture and whipping; see Hunter 1994: 154–84 and Allen 2000: 197–242.

7 πολλά 'often'.

δουρί ('plank') is a reference to either the stocks or the pillory, a wooden collar weighing down the head; cf. Cratinus, *PCG* fr. 123 ἐν τῶι κύφωνι ('pillory') τὸν αὐχέν' ἔχων.

τροχῶι: victims were tied onto the 'wheel', where their limbs were stretched and broken. See Aristoph. *Lys.* 845–6 (with Henderson 1987 *ad loc.*) and *Peace* 452.

8 θωμιχθείς 'flogged'; only here and in the lexica.

8–9 κόμην ... **ἐκτετιλμένος:** plucking or shaving of hair of one sort or other is referred to as a treatment inflicted on adulterers in Aristophanes;

see *Ach.* 849 (possibly alluding to Artemon), *Clouds* 1083, *Wealth* 168.
Carey 1993 defends the view that this reflects actual practice, aimed at
humiliation.

10–12 *Artemon now.* His new life constitutes a like-for-like improvement
on the poverty of the first stanza: more luxurious protection against the
sun (1 vs 11), more luxurious earrings (2 vs 10), more luxurious transport
(3? vs 10). The cause of Artemon's rise is irrelevant to the thrust of the
poem.

10 σατινέων 'carriage', a female means of transport, possibly with
Eastern associations, to judge from its three other occurrences. See *h.
Aphr.* 13 with Faulkner 2008 *ad loc.*, Sa. 44.13, Eur. *Hel.* 1311. The term
is attested only in the plural.

χρύσεα . . . καθέρματα: in mainland Greece earrings were normally worn
only by women. Boardman 1986: 61–2 interprets their appearance on two
of the pots referred to in the headnote as an East Greek adoption of Lydian
customs.

11 †παῖς Κύκης† is difficult. The transmitted text is a syllable short.
The crux could be cured e.g. with Hermann's παῖς <ὁ> Κύκης, but the
corruption may be wider. The name Κύκη is unusual. Perhaps Anacr.
coined it from κυκάω ('mix'): the newly grand Artemon would be the
'child of Hotchpotch', not a man of decent lineage.

σκιαδίσκην: parasols were a status symbol in the Near East and probably
also in Greece, where however they were mostly carried by women; see in
general Miller 1992. The diminutive exacerbates any inherently feminine
connotations.

12 γυναιξὶν αὔτως – ◡ – : a final swipe makes it clear how Artemon's
new luxury is to be understood; cf. 358 headnote for punchy closing lines
in Anacr. Since αὔτως does not normally combine with the dative to mean
'like' many editors favour Schömann's supplement ἐμφερής, but the exception is less problematic in view of ὡσαύτως + dat. at Soph. *Trach.* 372, Hdt.
2.67. An adjective qualifying γυναιξίν is just as likely.

Anacreon 395 PMG

A stanza about old age, followed by a stanza about death. Both are common themes in early Greek poetry. The originality of the poem rests in the
effect Anacr. achieves by combining them.

Despite the graphically sketched physical deterioration that comes
with old age, life has not lost its sweetness, and what makes ageing
miserable is in fact fear of death. This is a deviation from the sentiment,
common in particular in elegy, according to which death is preferable to
the wretchedness of old age: see Mimn. 1 and 2, and the proverbial

notion that dying early is second-best only to never being born (Thgn. 425–8, Bacch. 5.160–2). Anacr. seems to be using (the twelve-line version of) Sa. 58b as an intertextual foil. Both texts divide into two halves, the first dominated by symptoms of old age and centred on the contrast between then and now, the second opening with the attention-grabbing †τα† στεναχίζω (Sa.) / διὰ ταῦτ᾽ ἀνασταλύζω (Anacr.). Whereas Sappho, however, laments the ineluctability of old age (ἀγήραον ἄνθρωπον ἔοντ᾽ οὐ δύνατον γένεσθαι), in Anacr. it is death that cannot be escaped. For a less specific invocation of Sappho, see Anacr. 358.5–6n., and in general Yatromanolakis 2007: 216–20. In treating death as the greatest evil, Anacr. 395 may recall the perspective of Achilles in the underworld, who would rather be a serf on earth than a ruler in Hades (*Od.* 11.488–91).

The song holds the potential for both grave and flamboyant delivery; cf. 'Metre'. The neat pairing of the two stanzas, together with the likely intertextuality with Sa. 58b, suggests that the text is complete. Even so, the loss of further stanzas, featuring e.g. an exhortation to make merry, cannot altogether be ruled out.

Anacr. uses an old speaker in several other surviving poems, notably 358, 379 and 418, and there is little reason to doubt that the poet was indeed old when he composed them. The old 'Anacreon' seems to have been characterised by a continued desire to enjoy himself. 358 presents him as still interested in love-making, as may 379 and 418.

Source: Stobaeus 4.51.12 (vol. v, p. 1068 Hense). The fifth(?)-century AD anthologist quotes the fragment in a section 'on death and its ineluctability', and attributes it to Anacr. Two MSS are cited here, S (Vindobonensis Phil. gr. 67, 11th cent.) and A (Parisinus gr. 1984, 14th cent.). The opening four words are included in the third/second-century BC list of lyric and tragic incipits in Michigan papyrus inv. 3250c recto (col. i.7); see Borges and Sampson 2012: 27.

Metre:

◡ ◡ – ◡ – ◡ – –		$2io^{+}$	
◡ ◡ – ◡ – ◡ – –	?‖	$2io^{+}$	
◡ ◡ – ◡ – ◡ – –		$2io^{+}$	Ἀίδεω
◡ ◡ – ◡ – ◡ – –	?‖	$2io^{+}$	γηραλέοι, ἀργαλέη
◡ ◡ – – ◡ ◡ – –		$2io$	
◡ ◡ – ◡ – ◡ – –	‖‖	$2io^{+}$	μὴ ἀνα-

Anacr. uses the same pattern of anaclastic and non-anaclastic ionics in 356, for a light-hearted drinking theme. In 395, he may be seeking a clash between jolly metre and grave theme.

The text is printed here as a set of six dimeters only to preserve the conventional line numbering. It would be better articulated as three tetrameters; the non-anaclastic opening of the final tetrameter is a closural technique.

Discussions: Burzacchini 1995: 104–6, *Preisshofen 1977: 74–7, Coletti 1972, Pereira 1961; see also 12n. On old age in Greek poetry, see Falkner 1995, and on death Sourvinou-Inwood 1983 and Vermeule 1979.

1–6 *Old age.* The symmetry created by 1 ἤδη – 3 οὐκέτι – 5 οὐκέτι conceals a development: lines 5–6 move from past (youth) and present (old age) to future (impending death), thus preparing for 7–12.

1–2 rework traditional markers of old age; cf. *Il.* 8.518 and Hes. *WD* 181 πολιοκρόταφος and Tyrt. 10.23 ἤδη λευκὸν ἔχοντα κάρη πολιόν τε γένειον. The speaker's hair is λευκός also at Anacr. 358.6–7 (designating loss of erotic appeal).

1 ἡμῖν: poetic pl., but the audience may choose to feel included; cf. Anacr. 357.7, 396.1.

ἤδη: lyric, elegy and iambus often present old age in terms of youth that is lost 'now/already'; see Archil. 188.1, Tyrt. 10.23, Sa. 21.6, 58b.3, Alc. 119.9, Xenophanes 8.1.

3 χαρίεσσα refers in the first place to appearance, as at *Od.* 10.278–9 (of Hermes), νεηνίηι ἀνδρὶ ἐοικώς, | ... τοῦ περ χαριέστατη ἤβη. **ἤβη** is often contrasted with old age, e.g. Mimn. 1, 2 and 5, Thgn. 527–8, 1131–2. Anacr. puts less emphasis than many such texts on the pleasures of being young, thus preparing for 5–6.

4 πάρα ~ πάρεστι.

γηραλέοι ... ὀδόντες: graphic and physical, evoking difficulty with eating. Teeth are not normally part of physical descriptions in early Greek poetry, nor are they normally 'aged'.

5–6 γλυκεροῦ ... βιότου: it is usual for 'sweet life' to be transient (*Od.* 5.152, [Hes.] *Scut.* 331), but unusual for life still to be 'sweet' in old age.

7–12 *Fear of death.* This both is and is not a suitable topic for sympotic song: the joys of the *symposion* are often opposed to the ineluctability and grimness of death; see Alc. 38a, Thgn. 973–8, fr. adesp. 1009 *PMG*; further Murray 1988.

7 ἀνασταλύζω 'well up (with tears)' (?): the speaker uses a vivid *hapax* and shifts from plural (1 ἡμῖν) to singular, to express his response to his predicament. There is a sense of theatricality and self-mockery. The hyperbolic improvement on Sa. 58b.7 (n.) στεναχίζω contributes to the effect. Tears are rarer in lyric, elegy and iambus than in epic (cf. Archil. 13.10 γυναικεῖον πένθος), and even in Homer heroes do not cry because they will die some day. On weeping, see Arnould 1990: esp. 22–5, 191–3, van Wees 1998a, Föllinger 2009: esp. 33–5. ἀνασταλύζειν seems to be related to σταλάσσειν 'drip, let drop'. Hesych. α7813 glosses ἀσταλύζειν (MSS ἀσταλύχειν) with ἀναβλύζειν ('make gush forth') and κλαίειν.

8 Τάρταρον is here much the same as Hades; cf. the similarly unspecific use at Thgn. 1036, and contrast *Il.* 8.13–16, where Tartarus is below Hades.

9–10 Ἀΐδεω ... | μυχός ('recess of Hades') evokes obscuring darkness. For the phrasing, cf. Hes. *Th.* 119 Τάρταρά τ' ἠερόεντα μυχῶι χθονὸς εὐρυοδείης, and the common 'house of Hades'.

10–12 The irreversibility of death is a truism. The phrasing in terms of descent and ascent evokes heroic katabasis myths, and may draw an implicit contrast with heroes such as Odysseus and Heracles for whom, unlike for ordinary humans, return *is* possible.

10 ἀργαλέη: the speaker is afraid of death as well as dying. Journeys (*Od.* 4.393, 4.483), disease (*Il.* 13.667, Sol. 13.37, 13.61) and old age (Mimn. 1.10, 2.6, 5.5) can all be described as ἀργαλέος.

11 κάτοδος 'the journey down'. The notion of the soul 'descending' to Hades is traditional (e.g. *Il.* 6.284 κατελθόντ' Ἄϊδος εἴσω); but the noun usually means 'return' (from exile, etc.) in early Greek, and the literal usage here is therefore vivid. For the (uncertain) unaspirated κατ-, see 348.6n.

11–12 καὶ ... ἀναβῆναι: the stanza culminates in the irrevocability of death, which supremely explains its terror.

11 καὶ γάρ 'in fact'. The sentence will elaborate (καί) as well as explain (γάρ) the preceding statement. Cf. Thgn. 177, where καὶ γάρ introduces a similarly climactic generality.

ἑτοῖμον 'certain'. Cf. Sol. 4.7–8 οἷσιν ἑτοῖμον ... ἄλγεα πολλὰ παθεῖν, and Bond on Eur. *HF* 86 ('apparently always of death or other unpleasantness'). There is a contrast with 10 ἀργαλέη: the one thing that is not difficult is the certainty that death is forever.

12 ἀναβῆναι: neither the context (a literal journey down, then up), nor the intransitive construction (contrast Aristoph., *PCG* fr. 344 ἀναβῆναι τὴν γυναῖκα 'mount the woman'), points to a sexual *double entendre*, as Giangrande 1968: 109–11 and 2011: 31–3 maintains; contra Campbell 1989 and Bain 1990: 258–9. Of course performers may choose to render the phrase with innuendo.

Anacreon 417 PMG

A variation on the theme of unrequited male desire (cf. 358 headnote), which takes the shape of an address to a frolicking filly who shows no interest in her would-be rider. Each stanza comprises a unit of thought: 1–2 complaining question ('why do you ... ?'), 3–4 attempt at persuasion/ fantasising ('I would ...'), 5–6 accusatory assessment ('as it is, you ...'). The text seems complete.

On the one hand, the poem is an elegantly simple yet impressively sustained piece of erotic allegorising. The allegory exploits the well-established associations of horses with beautiful young women, with erotics, with aristocratic pursuits, and with male mastery (teasingly undermined); see p. 60. In Anacr.'s corpus cf. esp. 360, where the situation is reversed: the speaker is the horse, the reins of his soul held by the object of his desire (who significantly is male). See also Thgn. 257–60: a horse complains about its rider.

On the other hand, from the first sentence ('Thracian filly, why do you flee from me?'), this is a poem about mental states. The filly may be interpreted as either an unmarried girl or a prostitute (see *ad loc.*). If she is a *parthenos*, her rejection of erotic overtures would be expected, and could be constructed as innocence, a sense of decorum or disdain. The speaker would be engaged in fantasising about what might be, but in lyric, as in reality, hardly ever will be (in contrast e.g. to the sexual encounter in Archil. 196a, which the speaker presents as real). If she is a prostitute, the speaker might have reason to hope, or even to expect, that her refusal is a temporary and playful pretence (cf. 358 headnote). Or indeed she might be already otherwise engaged in erotic 'play' (line 5; cf. again 358).

Source: Heraclitus, *Homeric Problems* 5.10–11 (*c.* 1st cent. AD), who is illustrating the concept of allegory: 'Anacreon of Teos, attacking the attitude of *hetairai* (ἑταιρικὸν φρόνημα), and the arrogance of a haughty woman, used the allegory of a horse to describe her skittish disposition, as follows.' Geißler 2011 suggests that Heraclitus' reading is influenced by an exegetical tradition, manifest also in the reworking of Anacr. 417 in [Theoc.] 20.11–18, in which the woman is a *hetaira*. (She is an immature girl in Horace's adaptation in *Odes* 2.5.)

Metre:

```
− ∪ − × − ∪ − × − ∪ − × − ∪ − − ?‖  4 tr        βόσκεαι
− ∪ − × − ∪ − × − ∪ − × − ∪ −  ‖‖  4 tr‸       δοκέεις
```
Three trochaic mini-stanzas.

Discussions: Hullinger 2016, Giangrande 2011: 29–30, Griffith 2006: 325–6, *Rosenmeyer 2004: 170–3, Kurke 1999: 183–4 ~ 1997: 113–14, Pretagostini 1993a, Silk 1974: 124–6, Wilamowitz-Moellendorff 1913: 117–20.

1 πῶλε Θρηικίη: the status of the woman is ambiguous. If she is Thracian and hence a foreigner, she is likely to be a slave and/or prostitute. But Θρηικίη would be sufficiently motivated by the fame of Thracian horses; see Hes. WD 507 Θρήικης ἱπποτρόφου with West 1978 *ad loc.* See also headnote and 'Source'.

λοξόν ... βλέπουσα 'looking askance', a sign variously of anger and hostility (Sol. 34.4–5), contempt ([Theoc.] 20.13) or shyness (Ap. Rh. 3. 444–5). The speaker is right to wonder (and makes the audience wonder) about the reason, but wrong in the way he subsequently narrows down the possibilities. με is governed by 2 φεύγεις.

2 νηλεῶς 'without pity'. In the *Iliad* it is Achilles who is repeatedly νηλεής when he refuses to yield to pleas; *Il.* 9.497, etc., *LfgrE* s.v. 1a. Here the word is inappropriately solemn, mocking the addressee and/or possibly the speaker; see further Harvey 1957: 211–13.

δοκέεις ... σοφόν 'and (why) do you think that I know no skill'. This supposed misapprehension is what the speaker addresses in the remainder of the text; cf. 3 καλῶς, 6 δεξιόν, and the superior tone of ἴσθι τοι. Inasmuch as the speaker is understood as (the witty poet) Anacr., σοφόν carries additional irony.

δοκέεις: this epic form is maintained here as the apparent choice of the Alexandrian editors: cf. δοκέει at 346.4, a papyrus text. In the texts edited here, a similar issue occurs at 358.1 (πορφυρέηι) and 395.10 (ἀργαλέη). One could legitimately adopt the contracted form, which is standard in Ionic inscriptions; see Stüber 1996: 59–60.

3–4 It is left to the listener whether to translate the envisaged actions into sexual detail.

3 τὸν χαλινὸν ἐμβάλοιμι 'insert the bit', rather than 'put on the rein'. This is standard terminology of horsemanship; cf. *Il.* 19. 393–4, Eur. *Alc.* 492 and Xen. *Eq.* 6.7. The first τοι in the verse is the particle, the second the personal pronoun (Attic σοι).

4 τέρματα 'turning-posts'. Understood as a genuine plural, with one post at each end, this suggests a race of several laps. But the plural can be used for just one post, e.g. *Il.* 23.333, 23.358.

5 νῦν δέ 'as it is', 'instead'.

λειμῶνας: instead of racing on a man-made course, the filly grazes in a meadow. The meadow may symbolise the girl's inexperience and lack of interest in men, but is also, in literature, myth and religion, a place of erotic encounters; e.g. Hes. *Th.* 278–9, *h.Dem.* 2–20. See further Calame 1999 [1992]: 153–74, and cf. Ibyc. 286.1–6n.

κοῦφα 'lightly', i.e. nimbly as well as light-heartedly.

παίζεις: the young horse is playful. It is left open with whom the girl is playing, but it is not the speaker. The verb can denote both innocuous and erotic play, an ambiguity exploited elsewhere by Anacr.; see 357.4, 358.4, and the discussion of Rosenmeyer 2004.

6 ἱπποπείρην: a *hapax*, meaning 'expert in horses', but also suggesting 'one who tries it on with a horse'. Cf. μονοπείρας 'hunting alone', and the erotic/sexual meaning of πειρᾶν, for which see Pind. *Pyth.* 2.34, Lys. 1.12, and Henderson 1975: 158.

ἐπεμβάτην 'rider': ἐπεμβαίνειν does not of itself carry sexual connotations, unlike ἐπιβαίνειν and ἐπαμβαίνειν. However, as in 3–4, a sexual reading is invited; see Henderson 1975: 164–5 on obscene uses of riding imagery in comedy. 'Climbing on *in*' suggests a charioteer more than a rider, but in the absence of a chariot and of another horse, horseback riding is the default image; for this usage, see Eur. *Ba.* 782 ἵππων … ἐπεμβάτας.

SIMONIDES

Simonides (late 6th/early 5th cent: see below) composed in a striking range of genres and styles. His lyric work comprised epinicians (see fr. 511 headnote), *threnoi, enkomia,* paeans, dithyrambs and poems about the Persian Wars (see fr. 531 headnote); several other lyric genres are attested with less certainty. Many of the surviving texts, including the substantial frs. 542 and 543 presented here, are difficult to classify – a consequence, one may assume, not just of the fluidity of lyric genres but also of Sim.'s poetic adventurousness. More extensively than the other canonical lyricists, Sim. also composed (longer as well as shorter) elegiac poems. The 45-line fragment of his Plataea poem (fr. eleg. 11 *IEG*²) is the most substantive example of narrative elegy to survive from the Archaic or early Classical period; on this text, see Boedeker and Sider 2001. Finally, a large number of epigrams were attributed to Sim. in antiquity, most but not all of them spurious; among the stronger candidates for Simonidean authorship are the three texts inscribed at Thermopylae according to Hdt. 7.228 ('Sim.' VI, XXIIa and b *FGE*). On the epigrams, see Bravi 2006 and Petrovic 2007. For what is known of the Alexandrian edition of Sim., see Obbink 2001: 74–81 and Poltera 2008: 11–14, and cf. on 511 fr. 1a Title below.

Sim. was a native of the Ionic-speaking island of Ceos (60 km south-east of Athens), but his dialect choices exemplify the overriding importance of genre. While his elegies display the Ionic-dominated language typical of the genre, the lyric compositions are couched in the traditional dialect of choral lyric, Doric mixed with epic and other forms; see Poltera 1997: 524–38; cf. 531.6n. (σακός). (It does not necessarily follow that all of Sim.'s lyric songs were composed for choruses, but in many cases it is clear that they were.)

Sim. is part of a development which may have its first beginnings as early as Ibycus but reaches maturity only with Sim. and his younger contemporaries Pindar and Bacchylides: the emergence of the professional poet who receives one-off commissions from individuals, families and (especially in Sim.'s case) *poleis.* Sim. composed poems for patrons as far apart as Thessaly (p. 206), Euboea (518, 530), Magna Graecia (515, 580) and Athens (probably: see 519 fr. 35 and cf. next paragraph). In the wake of

the Persian invasions, Sim. was commissioned to commemorate the majority of the principal battles. With professionalism came a new form of poetic
self-consciousness, which is reflected in Sim.'s repeated references to
other poets and poems (see p. 227).

Sim.'s poetry about the Persian Wars shows that he was active as late as
the third decade of the fifth century. We do not know when his career
began. The veracity of ancient reports of his association with Hipparchus,
who was killed in 514 BC, is disputed (test. 10 Campbell), and attempts to
date fr. 509 to 520 BC are uncertain. Ancient chronography put his birth to
556/552 or 532/528 BC. For the reconstruction of Sim.'s life, see
Molyneux 1992 and more cautiously Hutchinson 2001: 286–8.

Sim. remained well known beyond his lifetime. Pindar (*Ol.* 9.48–9,
cf. Sim. 602), Aristophanes (*Knights* 405–6, cf. Sim. 512; *Clouds*
1355–6, cf. Sim. 507; probably *Peace* 736–7, cf. Sim. fr. eleg. 86 *IEG²*)
and Timotheus (791.204n.) all assume some familiarity with particular
works. Plato chooses one of Sim.'s poems for a lengthy display of
purposefully misguided literary criticism; see fr. 542 headnote and
'Source'. Several Hellenistic texts enter into dialogue with Sim., esp.
Theoc. 16 and Callim. *Aitia* (fr. 64 Pfeiffer), and Latin poets also refer
to him. As many as six copies of Sim.'s work survived at Oxyrhynchus,
and we know of several scholarly treatises devoted to him (testt. 30–2
Campbell). Already in the Classical period, Sim. was the subject of an
unusually rich anecdotal tradition; see Bell 1978. Like Sappho, he
generated interest as a biographical figure no less than as a poet. He
was seen, above all, as a celebrity poet who worked for money, and as
a wise man who coined aphorisms and spoke truth to power (see esp.
the imaginary dialogue with Hiero in Xenophon's *Hiero*). These traditions are responses to Sim.'s authorial persona, and reflect an aware-
ness that the nature of poet–patron relationships changed at the end
of the Archaic period.

The standard commentary on Sim.'s lyric fragments is Poltera 2008.
Although dated, Bowra 1961: 308–72 is still a valuable overview. Carson
1999 is an imaginative engagement with Sim.'s poetry.

Simonides 511 PMG (7 Poltera)

The beginning and a further fragment of an epinician ode celebrating
a victory in the single-horse race. The patrons are Thessalian; the occasion
of the victory is almost certainly the Pythian games, date unknown.

A number of more or less clearly epinician fragments suggest that Sim.
composed with some frequency in the genre; see 506–19 *PMG* and, more
comprehensively, 1–99 Poltera. This is the most substantial of them.
Various features, esp. the grand opening and the allusive reference to

the victory (fr. 1a), as well as what seems to be an account of local early history/myth (fr. 1b), suggest strong continuities with Pindar's and Bacchylides' epinician poetics. For potential discontinuities, see Title n., and beyond this poem Bowra 1961: 311–17 and Rawles 2012.

Prominent individuals from out-of-the-way but wealthy Thessaly competed at the panhellenic festivals and employed composers of panhellenic status in much the same manner as their counterparts elsewhere; see Stamatopoulou 2007. Sim. in particular worked regularly for Thessalian patrons: 510, 521, 528, 529, 542, possibly 22 *IEG*² and *FGE* LXXXVIII = 25 *IEG*²; cf. testt. 14, 21 Campbell, and for discussion Molyneux 1992: 117–45.

Source: *P.Oxy.* XXV.2431 (2nd cent. AD), ed. Lobel. For the attribution to Sim., see on Title below.

Metre: No schema is provided here because of the fragmentary state of the text. Gentili 1960: 118–20, 123 and Poltera 2008: 285–7 attempt analysis of what is left.

Discussions (apart from Lobel's *editio princeps*): Rawles 2013: 199–200, Molyneux 1992: 129–30, Gentili 1960.

fr. 1a Title 'For the victory in the single-horse race, for the sons of Aeatius': the title in the Hellenistic edition. Joint victories occur occasionally in equestrian events, as horses can be co-owned: the 'sons of Pheidolas' were victorious in the horse race at Olympia in 508 (Paus. 6.13.10 ~ anon. XCVII *FGE*), and what appears to be a publicly owned (δημόσιος) racehorse and chariot from Argos won at Olympia in 480 and 472, respectively (*P.Oxy.* II.222 col. i.6 and 31). The word order and the omission of the venue (Olympia, Nemea, etc.) suggest an edition arranged by event (single-horse race, pentathlon, etc.) rather than venue. This principle of classification is characteristic of the Hellenistic edition of Sim., but not Pindar or Bacchylides, and supports the attribution of this fragment to him; see Callim. fr. 441 Pfeiffer and the sources preserving Sim. 506 (δρομέσι), 508 (πεντάθλοις), 512 (τεθρίπποις), and the discussions of D'Alessio 1997: 52–3, Obbink 2001: 75–8 and Poltera 2008: 12–13.

1–7 Probably two parallel clauses, connected by καί. (i) Zeus <verb> the race of Aiatios. For the lost verb (]ται) Spelman 2018: 187 n.13 suggests δέρκε]ται 'looks with favour upon', cf. Pind. *Pyth.* 3.85–6. (ii) Apollo, Delphi (?and horse races) ?mark it out. The second clause announces the victory in the Pythian Games, presided over by Apollo. Zeus in the first clause is unlikely to allude to a separate victory at Olympia or Nemea since only Delphi (Πυθ[ώ) is mentioned. He may be referred to as ancestor of the race of Aiatios: as a Heraclid, the mythical Aiatios descended from Zeus; see 2n. and cf. the opening of Pind. *Pyth.* 10, 'Fortunate is

Lakedaimon, blessed is Thessaly. For both are ruled by a γένος descended from a single father, Heracles, excellent in battle.'

1]α: probably an epithet of Kronos, in the genitive, e.g. Lobel's Οὐρανίδ]α.

2 Ạίατίου γενεάν 'race of Aiatios'. Two meanings seem to merge suggestively: (i) the victorious brothers and their immediate family; (ii) all generations of that family or even all Thessalians. Aiatios is not just (i) the name of the victor's father but probably also (ii) that of the mythical first settler of Thessaly and early king, a Heraclid and father of Thessalos; see Polyaen. 8.44 and Charax, *FGrHist* 103 F 6. His name is transmitted as Aiatos in those sources (and as Aratios at Photius θ147 and *Suda* θ291), but this papyrus suggests that it was in fact Aiatios. Both the spelling and the significance of the mythical Aiatios are supported by Αιατιιο in *SEG* 52.561, an inscription on a seventh/sixth-century BC roof tile found at a sanctuary near Metropolis in central Thrace, perhaps a hero shrine of Aiatios.

3 χρυσοφ[όρ]μι[γξ is a *hapax*, but the notion of Apollo's – often golden – lyre is traditional; cf. Pind. *Pyth.* 1.1 and Austin and Olson 2004 on Aristoph. *Thesm.* 315.

4 ἑκαταβόλο[ς: standard for Apollo, but particularly apposite at Delphi, where he shot the serpent Python.

5 σαμαίνει: either 'marks it (= Ạίατίου γενεάν) out', or 'orders', with the object or dependent construction lost, e.g. 'that I sing'; cf. Pind. *Nem.* 9.4 αὐδὰν μανύει 'signals for a song'. In either case the verb plays with Apollo's oracular function; cf. Heraclitus DK 22 B93 ὁ ἄναξ, οὗ τὸ μαντεῖόν ἐστι τὸ ἐν Δελφοῖς, οὔτε λέγει οὔτε κρύπτει ἀλλὰ σημαίνει, and LSJ s.v. 1.3.

λιπαρά 'shining', often of cities, esp. in Pindar; see LSJ s.v. v.

6 . θ' ἱπποδρ[ο]μ : the traces suggest αἱ (rather than τὸ) θ' ἱπποδρ[ο]μι-. Since fr. 1a is the top of a column and fr. 1b the bottom (of the same or a different column), a good number of lines are lost in between. The tiny fr. 2, which may be from the centre of the column, is not edited here.

fr. 1b describes a major ruler in Thessaly. On our knowledge the best candidate is Aleuas the Red (ὁ Πυρρός), the mythical or historical figure credited with organising the Thessalian commonwealth into four tetrads (Aristot. fr. 497 Rose). According to a tradition preserved only later, he was declared king by the Delphic oracle (Plut. *Mor.* 492a–b). **7** Πυρ<ρ>ίδαν would be punning on his cognomen. However, a figure unknown to us, or even the Aiatios of fr. 1a, are also possible. For our scarce knowledge of early Thessalian history, see Sordi 1958: chs. 1–4, Helly 1995, Hall 2002: 134–54.

5–7 '... pronounced the son of Pyrrhos king with full authority over those dwelling around'.

5 βασιλῆα [τ]ελεσφόρον: βασιλεύς is used repeatedly of Thessalian rulers; see Pind. *Pyth.* 10.3, Hdt. 5.63.3, 7.6.2. In Sim.'s day there was probably more than one; see Helly 1995: 101–30, with the review by Sordi 1998: 419.

6 ἀμφικ[τιό]νων: a loose term. Whoever the king, Sim.'s Thessalian audience will probably have made out a reference to what later texts call the *perioikoi*, communities under Thessalian influence in the areas surrounding the Thessalian heartland; see esp. Xen. *Hell.* 6.1.19. **ἔχρησαν:** LSJ s.v. χράω B.1 fits the context best, 'pronounced (in prophecy)'. The subject would have to be a plural expression amounting to 'the oracle'.

7 Πυρ<ρ>ίδαν: a highly likely restoration. The name Pyrrhos is common in Thessaly (see *LGPN* III.B s.v.). Pyrrhos = Neoptolemus is at least indirectly linked to Thessaly through his father Achilles, the most famous Thessalian of all. For later evidence for direct links, see Gentili 1960: 120–1 and Aston 2012: 50–1, and for speculation about the putative exploitation of such links by Aleuas Sordi 1958: 71–80.

7–8 ἅμα ... δάμωι: perhaps: 'At the same time... with good fortune also for the whole Thessalian people.' A good king brings blessings to his subjects. Pind. *Pyth.* 10.70 has a different set of Thessalians, Thorax and his brothers, uphold the νόμος Θεσσαλῶν. Such apparently pan-Thessalian notions gloss over the reality of competition between the major Thessalian families. Sentence-break, and a new sentence starting with ἅμα δ(έ), are likely, but the next word(s) are difficult. One wants γένοιτο, but the letter before the ο does not look like a τ.

The remaining scraps are too small to add much to our understanding of the poem, and are not printed here.

Simonides 531 PMG (261 Poltera)

A celebration of the select group of Greeks under the command of the Spartan king Leonidas who died at Thermopylae in 480 BC after fighting a vastly more numerous Persian army. Neither the battle nor the dead men's achievements are elaborated. Instead the text adopts a poetics of reconfiguration: the realities of death and burial, as well as the here and now, are all explicitly transformed into something else.

The central proposition is that unlike ordinary deaths, which are commemorated with lament and gifts but eventually forgotten, the deaths of these men have given rise to everlasting glory and even cult. Several terms hint at the memorialising power of poetry (κλέος, μνᾶστις, ἔπαινος, κόσμος), yet no overt claim is made for the contribution this poem makes to the glory of Leonidas' men. Sim. glorifies and transforms the dead by treating their fate as famous already, their grave an altar already, and Leonidas as 'having left behind' glory already (perfect λελοιπώς, 8).

This objective stance is a poetic fiction only in part. It also exploits the very considerable poetic and material programme of commemoration for the dead of the Persian Wars in general, and the dead of Thermopylae in particular, as well as Sim.'s own extensive contributions to both. The text achieves glorification now by harnessing glorification in the past. For Sim.'s poetry about the Persian Wars, which included longer compositions that treated Plataea, Artemisium and possibly Salamis (frs. eleg. 1–18 IEG^2, frs. 532–6 PMG), as well as inscribed epigrams, see Molyneux 1992: 147–210, Rutherford 2001a, Kowerski 2005.

Place, too, and occasion, are manipulated for the purpose of celebration. Herodotus reports that the dead were buried on the battlefield, where various epigrams were inscribed (7.228), but this is not where the text situates itself: 'those who died at Thermopylae' rather than (as often in epigram) 'these men', 'the(ir) tomb' rather than 'this tomb', etc. The only clearly deictic expression is ὁ ἀνδρῶν ἀγαθῶν ὅδε σακός. What is 'this precinct'? As far as we know, only Leonidas had a tomb and precinct in Sparta (and received rites there), whereas the other Thermopylae-fighters shared this precinct at best in the sense of being commemorated with a *stele* that may have been erected in the proximity of Leonidas' tomb; see 6n. (ὅδε σακός). If the song was performed at that site it will have transformed what was primarily Leonidas' shrine into a 'precinct of the excellent men', and transformed the men into cult heroes in the mould of Leonidas. When performed anywhere else, the song would conjure 'this precinct' poetically. The occasion, whatever it is, becomes an encounter with the war dead, imagined as more-than-human heroes. (Going further, Steiner 1999: 387–8 and esp. Wiater 2005: 51–3 suggest that 'this precinct' refers to the song itself. On this interpretation, one should not deprive the deictic ὅδε of its concrete force: it points to the whole occasion, the site transformed by the song as well as the song itself.)

The prominence of Leonidas makes it very likely that the song originated in Sparta, but it is not a narrowly inward-looking composition: see 6–7 εὐδοξίαν | Ἑλλάδος and 7–8n. This combination of a city-specific focus with a consciousness of Greece at large is characteristic also of other poetry commemorating the Persian Wars, e.g. Sim.'s Plataea elegy (Sparta/Greece), 'Sim.' XVI *FGE* (Megara/Greece) and Aeschylus' *Persians* (Athens/Greece).

The stark and balanced phrasing recalls commemorative epigram, as do several tropes, yet Sim. manipulates these tropes for his own purposes; see notes below and Steiner 1999. There are points of contact also with (later) Athenian funeral orations, which probably reflect a broader shared tradition rather than constitute imitation of this poem in particular.

The text is probably fragmentary, extracted from a longer, choral work. However, neither point (extract, choral) is certain, and nothing definite can be concluded from the language Diodorus ('Source' below) uses to introduce the quotation: ἄξιον τῆς ἀρετῆς ποιήσας ἐγκώμιον ἐν ὧι λέγει ('composing an *enkomion* worthy of the valour (of the Greek fighters), in which he says …'). The absence of a connecting particle in line 1 would suit the opening of a song. The suggestion that fr. 594 was part of the same poem, developed most fully by Burzacchini 1977, is rightly criticised by Citti 1987 and Poltera 2008: 550–1.

Source: The text is quoted by the first-century BC historian Diodorus Siculus (11.11.6), and also included in the florilegium of Arsenius (15th/16th cent.), s.v. Λεωνίδου (p. 342 Walz).

Metre:

```
---∪∪-∪∪-- ?‖  --D-
-∪-∪-∪-∪-- ?‖  E² -
--∪∪-†∪∪-†×-∪∪-∪∪-- ?‖  -D×D-
-∪∪-∪∪-∪-- ?‖  D∪--    τοιοῦτον
-∪-∪∪-∪---∪-‖  e∪∪E                         5
--∪∪-∪∪-∪-∪----∪- ?‖  -D∪E
-∪∪-∪∪-∪-∪∪-∪- ?‖  D∪d∪-
---∪∪-∪∪-∪-∪-- ?‖  --D∪e-
-∪-∪∪-∪∪- ?‖  -∪D
```

An unusual rhythm, which cannot be pressed into either a rigid dactylo-epitrite or a rigid aeolic framework. The analysis adopted here assumes free dactylo-epitrites; see Dale 1969 [1951]: 81, and for an aeolic interpretation Gentili and Catenacci 2007: 303.

Discussions: Ferrarini 2014, Fearn 2013: 235–9, Wiater 2005, Ford 2002: 110–12, *Steiner 1999, Palmisciano 1996, Carson 1999: 52–5 ~ Carson 1992b: 55–7, West 1970b: 210–11, Podlecki 1968: 258–62, Kierdorf 1966: 24–9, Fränkel 1975 [1962]: 319–21, *Bowra 1961: 346–9.

1–3 The underlying ideas, but not the starkly paradoxical phrasing, were traditional in Sparta and beyond, not least so the notion that death in battle, together with the subsequent burial, gives rise to fame; see esp. Tyrt. 12.27–34.

1 τῶν ἐν Θερμοπύλαισι θανόντων is placed before the clause proper (which starts εὐκλεὴς μέν, 2), to announce the topic of the sentence and the whole fragment. For this word order, see Allan 2014: 189–93. West 1975: 308–9 and Poltera 2008: 468–9 regard these four words as a title added at a later stage, but the case is not conclusive; see Page 1971 and Lloyd-Jones 1974.

2 καλός … πότμος invokes the trope of the 'beautiful' death in battle, which goes back to Homer and probably had particular currency in Sparta, e.g. Tyrt. 10.1, 10.30; see further Vernant 1991 [1979] and Clarke 2002.

3 βωμός ... τάφος invokes hero cult. This is a metaphor rather than reality; see headnote and 6n. (ὅδε σακός).

†προγόνων† δὲ μνᾶστις interrupts the flow of the sentence and must be corrupt, even though ancestral achievements are a topos of commemoration (Thuc. 2.36, Lys. 2.3ff.). The most popular emendation is πρὸ γόων, intended to yield 'instead of lamentation they have remembrance'. However, the rest of the sentence makes one expect 'lamentation is/amounts to remembrance', rather than 'is replaced by remembrance'; and πρό = 'instead of' normally occurs in the context of choosing or preferring one thing over another (e.g. Pind. *Pyth.* 4.140 κέρδος αἰνῆσαι πρὸ δίκας). For arguments in favour of προγόνων, see Palmisciano 1996 and Inglese 2002, for arguments against, Napolitano 2000.

ὁ δ' οἶ<κ>τος ἔπαινος 'the lament they receive is praise'. Versions of the conceit recur in Athenian funeral orations; e.g. Thuc. 2.44.1, Lys. 2.77–81. The emendation removes the problematic 'their doom is praise'; for a defence of οἶτος, see Poltera *ad loc.*

4–5 'Such a funerary offering neither mould nor all-conquering time shall obscure.' Memory is indestructible. There is an implied contrast between the permanence of commemoration in song (Homer's κλέος ἄφθιτον; cf. 9 ἀέναον ... κλέος) and the transience of physical tokens of remembrance. Sim. develops this *topos* most fully in 581; see also 594. τοιοῦτον refers to the series of reconfigurations in 2–3 in general, and to the immediately preceding μνᾶστις and οἶ<κ>τος in particular. For the omission of the first οὔτε, common in lyric, see KG II.291. The deletion creates a more regular metrical shape, but the metre is too unusual to allow for certainty; an alternative intervention would be οὐ τις (West 1967b).

4 ἐντάφιον: any item used in a burial, viz. something like 'funerary offering'. The more specific 'shroud' (LSJ s.v. II.1) would produce good sense but the evidence for such a meaning is uncertain. Sim.'s conceit may have given rise to a tradition; see Isocr. 6.45, *AP* 7.435.

5 πανδαμάτωρ ... χρόνος: Sim. may be drawing on Bacch. 13.205–7, the first attestation of this phrase, in a comparable context. Cf. also Sim. fr. eleg. 20.14–15 *IEG²*.

6–7 'This precinct of excellent men obtained as its inhabitant the high esteem of Greece.' A daring expression, playing with two different 'inhabitants' of the precinct, both of them metaphorical: the dead men and half-personified εὐδοξία; see Thuc. 2.43.2 for a broadly similar conceit. In addition, the precinct is invested with agency. It does not just 'hold' the dead (the formulaic (κατ)έχειν, e.g. *Il.* 16.629, *CEG* 131), but actively 'chose' (εἵλετο) the glory that resides in it.

6 ἀνδρῶν ἀγαθῶν: common phraseology in commemoration and celebration of patriotic bravery; e.g. *CEG* 13 and 136, Tyrt. 10.2, 12.10, 12.20.

ὅδε σακός: as with 3 βωμός, the war-dead are accorded more-than-human status. Sim. is probably reshaping reality in two respects: the status of the dead and their place in 'this precinct'. Several Greek cities had forms of collective cult for the dead, e.g. Plataea and Megara; see Currie 2005: 89–102. The practice is less certain for Sparta. As a king, Leonidas received cultic honours at his tomb in Sparta. His body was brought home only some decades after the battle, but an *eidolon* was probably buried early on; see Hdt. 6.58.3, Paus. 3.14.1, Förtsch 2001: 56–60, esp. n. 515, and Richer 2012: 182–6. The other Thermopylae deaths were also commemorated, but not in the same manner. Above all, those men had no tombs in Sparta, and had a 'precinct' at best by extension: according to Paus. 3.14.1, their names were inscribed on a *stele* near Leonidas' tomb, very possibly within the same precinct. The date of the *stele* is unknown, but the comparable casualty list erected in the Marathon precinct soon after the battle (*SEG* 16.430), and Herodotus' claim to have learned the names of the 300 as well as others (7.224.1), make an early date at least a possibility. Cf. headnote.

ὅδε: with the MSS ὁ δέ, marking the beginning of a new sentence, ἀνδρῶν ἀγαθῶν would be governed by ἐντάφιον. Word order makes that very unlikely.

σακός: MSS σηκός. Doric alpha is hesitantly adopted here and elsewhere in Simonides because the papyri predominantly (but not quite always: Poltera 1997: 534–6) have alpha, and because the change from putative alpha to eta is easily attributed to the quoting authors and their copyists. (Certainly in a performance at a Spartan precinct, Ionic ὅδε σηκός is difficult to imagine.)

οἰκέταν: for the meaning 'inhabitant', see Aesch. *Ag.* 733.

6–7 εὐδοξίαν Ἑλλάδος: the context suggests the 'high repute accorded by Greece' to the dead fighters, rather than the 'high repute of Greece' created by the battle of Thermopylae. For this genitive, cf. Pind. *Isthm.* 3.3 εὐλογίαις ἀστῶν, Pl. *Mx.* 238d μετ' εὐδοξίας πλήθους.

7–9 μαρτυρεῖ ... κλέος: famed as he is himself, Leonidas bears persuasive testimony to the excellence and glory of those he commanded at Thermopylae and with whom he is now (imagined to be) sharing a precinct. He thus provides support for everything that has been said before. κλέος looks back to 2 εὐκλεής, ἀρετᾶς to 6 ἀγαθῶν, κόσμον to 4 ἐντάφιον, ἀέναον to 5 πανδαμάτωρ ἀμαυρώσει χρόνος.

7 μαρτυρεῖ: witnessing is a trope in commemoration; e.g. *CEG* 82 and Sim. fr. eleg. 16.1 *IEG²*. The καί transmitted after μαρτυρεῖ δέ in Arsenius' text (see 'Source') is necessary neither for the metre nor the sense.

7–8 Λεωνίδας | ὁ Σπάρτας βασιλεύς: the formal identification aggrandises both Leonidas and Sparta. 'King of Sparta' rather than e.g. 'Agiad' may suggest that a panhellenic audience is (ultimately) intended; cf. 7

Ἑλλάδος. Some editors delete the article, but it is idiomatic and creates metrical correspondence with the first verse.

9 κόσμον 'adornment'. Leonidas' achievement is itself a κόσμος, and so is the material as well as the literary programme of commemoration. Similar uses of κόσμος are common in Pindar, e.g. *Nem.* 2.8, *Isthm.* 6.69. For the poetic associations of the term, see already Sol. 1.2, and cf. Sim. fr. eleg. 11.23 *IEG²*.

ἀέναον ... κλέος 'ever-flowing glory'. The topos goes back to the Iliadic κλέος ἄφθιτον (9.413) and is common in the celebration of those who died in the Persian Wars; see Sim. fr. eleg. 11.28 *IEG²*, 'Sim.' ix.1 and xxa.1 *FGE*, and *CEG* 2(ii).1.

Simonides 542 PMG (260 Poltera)

A sustained treatment of a single nexus of concepts, the good man and the difficulty of being a good man. The text is reconstructed from Plato's *Protagoras*: Socrates cites it piecemeal in the course of an extended discussion of the poem; see 'Source'.

We may have most of the poem; see 1–3, 39–40nn. It is structured as follows:

Str. 1: It is difficult to be a completely good man. (Rest of strophe missing.)

Str. 2: 'It is difficult to be good', the sage Pittacus says, but that sounds wrong to me. Men unlike gods will always be wretched when struck with misfortune. Being ἀγαθός or κακός is a matter of circumstance. (Two lines missing at the end.)

Str. 3: I will not look for a completely blameless man. Rather, I praise anyone who avoids willingly doing something shameful.

Str. 4: (Beginning missing.) I am content with a sound man. All things are good that have nothing shameful mixed in.

The question as to what constitutes a good person is one of perennial interest. In the sixth and early fifth centuries, it was coloured by widespread and sometimes rapid changes in wealth and status, and the attendant debates over values and class; see Morris 1996, Morgan 2008. Individual sentiments in the poem can be paralleled more or less closely in other Archaic and early Classical poetry; see Dickie 1978, Most 1994. What is, however, notable is the way in which Sim. combines them in a lengthy and demanding argument.

This argument takes the form of a shifting train of thought rather than of a formally structured case. Fundamentally, the poem moves from emphasising, negatively, the difficulty and even impossibility of perfection, to affirming, positively, the merit of what is realistically achievable.

The opening and closing positions in this argument are both clear and compatible, but parts of the intervening sequence aim to surprise. In particular, the salient discrepancy between the first and second stanzas has prompted debate. The second stanza resumes the statement that opened the first (attributing it now to Pittacus), but only to reject it. It soon turns out that what is rejected is in fact a particularly exacting (and probably tendentious) understanding of Pittacus' *gnome*, along the lines of, 'It is difficult <but perfectly possible> to be good.' This exacting position serves as the foil against which the speaker presents his stance of realistic expectations: 'It is not just difficult but impossible to be good; therefore I will be content with a more moderate standard of goodness.' The realistic stance could have been arrived at without introducing and then critiquing the (mis)reading of Pittacus; e.g., 'It is difficult to be good; therefore I am realistic in what I expect.' Instead, the speaker sets himself off against Pittacus, and creates a display of intense engagement with a difficult subject, adjusting his position as his thoughts unfold. This mingling of moral reasoning and self-presentation is characteristic of the often overtly competitive intellectual discourse of late Archaic and early Classical Greece, for which see Griffith 1990, Payne 2006, Burton 2011; also pp. 227–8 below.

In a manner familiar (later on) from tragedy and indeed Plato, Sim. explores the question of the 'good' man by shifting between different nuances of goodness. In the opening statement, the ἀνήρ ἀγαθός is a man of both mental and bodily perfection, an established idea with aristocratic overtones. ἐσθλός (a near-synonym of ἀγαθός) in the resumption of that statement in 13 is likely to have been understood similarly. By contrast, the argument about the influence of circumstance in 14–18 foregrounds in both ἀγαθός and its opposite κακός ideas of success and standing that were not previously emphasised. In the second half of the text (21–40), ἀγαθός is dropped for predominantly ethical phrasing: 24 πανάμωμον, 29 αἰσχρόν, 40 αἰσχρά. These different nuances are not mutually exclusive, but the shifts in emphasis compound the sense of a mobile train of thought, and impress the need to ponder what constitutes the 'good man'.

According to Plato, the song is addressed to the Thessalian aristocrat Scopas (λέγει ... πρὸς Σκόπαν, 339a6–7), for whom Sim. seems to have composed further songs (see 510 and 529), as indeed he composed songs for other Thessalians (see the headnote to 511). It is likely that Scopas was addressed in the poem, probably in the large gap in str. 1. We do not know how elaborate this address, and thus how properly encomiastic the poem, was. The rejection of the ideal of the perfect man, with first-person plural phrasing (25), certainly does not suggest an epinician or sympotic *enkomion* in the manner of Pindar or Bacchylides.

Close thematic (as well as certain metrical) parallels are offered by fr. 541, including the statement that 'it is not easy to be good'.

Source: The text is pieced together from separate quotations in Plato's *Protagoras* (339b1–3, 339c3–5, 341e2, 344c4–5, 344e7–8, 345c6–11, 345d3–5, 346c4–6, 346c8, 346c11). With the exception of the three gaps it is reasonably secure, and has been printed in broadly the same form in most editions since Wilamowitz-Moellendorff 1913: 159–65. Editors generally think that Plato quoted the extracts in the sequence in which they occur in the poem. (The reordering proposed by Beresford 2008 is unconvincing; see Manuwald 2010.)

The philosophical purpose of this section of the dialogue is disputed (and not the subject of this commentary), but it is clear that Socrates' interpretation of the poem is distorting and not intended to be taken at face value. For a diverse set of discussions focused on Plato rather than Sim., see Frede 1986, Scodel 1986, Ledbetter 2003: 99–114, Andolfi 2014.

Because of the *Protagoras*, the poem was well known in antiquity. Numerous later texts cite individual passages, but none of the citations can be shown to be independent of Plato, and they contribute little to the establishment of the text. For lists, see Poltera's and Hutchinson's editions.

Metre:

1 – ⏑ ⏑ – ⏑ ⏑ – ⏑ – ⏑ – – ⏑ ⏑ – *dod*^{d} *dod*¨ (?) μοῖ ἐμ-
2 – – ⏑ – ⏑ ⏑ – ⏑ – – *gl*
3 – ⏑ – ⏑ ⏑ – ⏑ – × – ⏑ – ?|| *gl ia* βαλέω
4 ⏑ ⏑ – ⏑ – – ⏑ – ⏑ ⏑ – ⏑ – *ia? gl* εὐρυεδέος
5 – ⏑ – ⏑ ⏑ – ⏑ – || *gl* μὴ οὐ
6 ⏑ ⏑ – ⏑ – – ⏑ – ⏑ ⏑ – ?|| *ia? dod*¨
7 – – ⏑ – – ⏑ – ⏑ ⏑ – ?|| *ia dod*¨
8 ⏑ – – ⏑ – – *2ia*$_{\wedge}$
9 – ⏑ – ⏑ ⏑ – – *ph* (= *gl*$_{\wedge}$)
10 – ⏑ – ⏑ – – ||| *ith* θεοί

A largely aeolic strophe. Its complexity makes the labelling of individual cola more than usually arbitrary. Especially hard to interpret is the first line, which is recognisable as aeolic only with hindsight. The analysis above, essentially that of West 1982a: 66, aims to indicate the elements of repetition, especially from one line to the next. Particularly frequent are the glyconic, together with the related dodrans (Lat. *dodrans* = 'three quarters' of *gl*), and the iamb. Lidov 2010 points out that a more regular structure, built around six glyconics and three pherecrateans, can be produced by accepting a colometry that takes little account of word-divisions and punctuation.

Discussions: Porter 2010: 459–62, *Scodel 1996: 69–71, *Most 1994, Carson 1992a, Schütrumpf 1987, Gentili 1988 [1984]: 64–71, Vernant

1991 [1979], *Dickie 1978, Svenbro 1976: 141–72, Babut 1975, Easterling 1974: 41–3, Donlan 1969, Parry 1965, Gentili 1964, Adkins 1960: 165–7, 196–7, 355–9, Woodbury 1953.

1–3 The difficulty of achieving excellence is conventional; e.g. Hes. *WD* 289–92, Thgn. 336, Phoc. 13 GP/Gerber. But the exacting qualifications ἀλαθέως and χερσίν ... τετυγμένον prepare for the attention to questions of degree and nuance in what follows. Plato's Socrates is probably trustworthy when he calls this the beginning of the song: *Prt.* 343c7, cf. 339a6–b4.

1 ἄνδρ' ἀγαθόν announces as the topic of this poem what is a standard subject of reflection in gnomic poetry, as exemplified by ten occurrences in the *Theognidea*.

μέν: a corresponding δέ may be lost in 4–10.

ἀλαθέως qualifies ἀγαθόν, not χαλεπόν, as Socrates purports at *Prt.* 343d1–44a7.

γενέσθαι will probably be understood as 'be' rather than 'come to be' or 'become'. In any case, there is nothing to support a contrast with 13 ἔμμεναι, as Socrates suggests at *Prt.* 340c2–d4. Neither verb carries emphasis.

χαλεπόν 'it is hard to'. The word is often used rhetorically in the sense of 'it is impossible to'; see *Il.* 16.620, Thgn. 1075, and further Most 1994: 137–8. However, it is only in 13–16 that the audience is prompted to determine its precise nuance.

2–3 χερσίν ... τετυγμένον 'fashioned four-square and without fault in hands, feet and mind': Sim. creates an image of bodily and mental perfection by developing epic expressions such as *Od.* 20.365–6 εἰσί μοι ὀφθαλμοί τε καὶ οὔατα καὶ πόδες ἄμφω, | καὶ νόος ἐν στήθεσσι τετυγμένος, οὐδὲν ἀεικής. Helped by ἄνευ ψόγου, the term τετράγωνος is readily comprehensible as an expression of completeness, perhaps beyond what is natural (not many squares in nature). If there is a reference to sculpture-making, as Svenbro 1976: 154–6, Steiner 2001: 42–3 and Johnston and Mulroy 2004 argue, it is probably remote.

3 ἄνευ ψόγου will subsequently turn out to prepare for the language of praise and blame.

4–10 It is impossible to tell what, or how much, has been lost (and hence what is the precise force of 11 οὐδέ). An address to Scopas is a possibility (cf. headnote), as is further elaboration of the theme of lines 1–3.

11–20 For the contradiction between 1–3 and 11–13, and the critique of Pittacus, see the headnote. The argumentative tone is reinforced by the use of the first person (11 μοι, 'in my opinion') and two consecutive asyndeta (13, 14).

11 οὐδέ ... **ἐμμελέως** 'out of tune', viz. 'jarringly'; cf. Pind. *Nem.* 7.69 πὰρ μέλος ... ἐννέπων, and the later πλημμελής. The metaphor will still have been felt as such in this period, esp. so since Sim.'s piece was sung.

τὸ Πιττάκειον 'Pittacus' saying': names and the authority they convey are important in discourse on wisdom; cf. the tag καὶ τόδε Φωκυλίδεω (or Δημοδόκου), which opens many elegiac and hexametric *gnomai*. On Sim.'s references to other authors, see p. 227. On Pittacus, see p. 94.

νέμεται: meaning uncertain; perhaps 'is being broadcast', 'is widely cited', as an extension of the core meaning 'is being distributed'. For a discussion of the term in the context of the shift from a predominantly oral to a predominantly literate culture, see Svenbro 1993 [1988]: 109–22. We do not know how familiar Pittacus' saying in fact was.

12 σοφοῦ: the canon of the Seven Sages (σοφοί), which usually includes Pittacus, is first properly attested in the *Protagoras* passage (343a1–5, cf. Pl. *Hp.Ma.* 281c), but the treatment of Pittacus here and of Cleobulus in Sim. 581 (see esp. 7n.), as well as references in Herodotus, suggest that individual figures developed special status much earlier; see further Martin 1993, Busine 2002: 15–46, Asper 2006: 85–96. In attacking 'wise' Pittacus, Sim. is staking a claim for his own, greater, σοφία.

13 χαλεπόν: emphatically placed, to prepare for the focus of the subsequent critique on this word specifically.

14–18 state the speaker's objection to Pittacus. The passage aims to startle in two ways. First, one expects 'it is difficult' to be contradicted by 'it is easy': 'it is impossible' (οὐκ | ἔστι) comes as a surprise. Secondly, 14–15 seem at first to make the provocative claim that to be ἐσθλός is a divine privilege, and that humans cannot help being κακός. Only in 16–18 does the proposition turn out to be much more traditional: it is a matter of good or bad fortune whether a person is ἀγαθός or κακός; cf. the common theme of the fragility of human affairs, and the notion that wealth makes a man ἀγαθός and vice versa, e.g. Alc. 360, Thgn. 1117–18, Bacch. 10.49–51.

16 καθέληι vividly expresses human lack of control. Subjunctive without ἄν in a conditional relative clause expressing a general supposition is poetic; see Goodwin 1887: §540.

17–18 The point is made in a pointedly logical, almost tautological, form.

17 πράξας ... **εὖ** 'when he meets with good fortune', the usual meaning (e.g. Bacch. 3.94), and not 'doing good'.

{μὲν} γάρ: the metre requires deletion of one syllable. There is little to choose between deleting μέν or γάρ.

18–20 Socrates' statement at 345c3, shortly before the quotation of 21–6, would provide continuity of thought for the lacuna: ἐπὶ πλεῖστον δὲ καὶ ἄριστοί εἰσιν οὓς ἂν οἱ θεοὶ φιλῶσιν, 'in general, those that the gods love the most are also the most ἀγαθοί'. But the phrasing would need alteration to fit language and metre, and it is not clear that Socrates is drawing on Sim.'s text at that point. Cf. 31–4n.

21–30 The speaker shifts from predominantly third- to predominantly first- (and even second-)person phrasing, and from criticism to praise. In the course of this stanza and the next, he builds up the persona of an encomiastic poet, who bestows praise where praise is due, and does not blame unnecessarily; see e.g. Pind. *Pyth.* 2.52–6, *Nem.* 7.61–3, and the discussions of Nagy 1979: 222–42 and Morgan 2015: 188–94. However, whereas Pindar praises individuals, Sim. adopts an encomiastic persona in order to continue the exploration of the generic good man. (For the possibility of an address to Scopas earlier in the poem, see headnote.)

21–4 τοὔνεκεν . . . ἄνθρωπον 'Therefore I shall never, in search of what cannot be, throw away the lifetime apportioned to me on an empty, unachievable hope: an altogether irreproachable human being.' The abstract phrasing creates an emphatic declaration. The motif of searching in vain for an ideal person occurs elsewhere (e.g. Thgn. 83–6, 415–18), but is given especial elaboration here, culminating in the ironical flourish of 26.

21 τοὔνεκεν: more markedly logical language.
ἐγώ insinuates that Pittacus is less sensible.

24–5 εὐρυεδέος . . . χθονός: traditional language is used to make a non-traditional point. Eating the fruit of the earth distinguishes humans from gods also elsewhere (e.g. [Hes.] fr. 211.13 MW χθονὸ[ς ὅσ[σ]ο̣[ι καρ]πὸν [ἔ]δ̣ουσι), χθονὸς εὐρυοδείης is formulaic (but here εὐρυεδέος . . . χθονός pointedly expresses the extent of the fruitless search), and αἴνυσθαι is epic vocabulary. 'Empty hope' in 22–3 goes back to Hesiod (*WD* 498).

24 ὅσοι 'among all of us who'.

25 αἰνύμεθα: the only first person plural in the fragment. It aligns the speaker with imperfect mortals, and with the audience.

26 'When I find (ἐπί . . . εὑρών, tmesis) one I shall report to you.' ἐπὶ δ᾽ ὔμμιν is one of several possible emendations of the MSS' unmetrical ἔπειθ᾽ ὑμῖν. Sauppe suggests the even more sarcastic ἐπὶ δή μιν.

27 ἐπαίνημι: an originally Aeolic form, as Socrates points out at *Prt.* 346d9, already found in early hexameter; cf. Hes. *WD* 683 αἴνημι.

28 ἑκών 'willingly', in the sense of not just 'purposefully' but also 'gladly'. The qualification is emphatically placed and important. It excuses inadvertent and reluctant flawed behaviour. Vocabulary of volition is used in assessing wrongdoing already in epic (e.g. *Il.* 23.585, *Od.* 22.351, Hes. *Th.* 232), and was important in early legal thought; see esp. *IG* i³.104 = Draco's law. Further on ἑκών, see Rickert 1989: 145–7.

29–30 ἀνάγκαι . . . μάχονται: ἀνάγκαι contrasts with 28 ἑκών, and the clause as a whole serves to justifiy the preceding assertion. If the *gnome* was not proverbial already, it became so later; e.g. Diog. Laert. 1.77 (with attribution to Pittacus), Zenob. 1.85, and variants at [Aesch.] *PV* 105, Pl. *Laws* 7.818b. The supreme role of necessity was certainly a topic in contemporary thought; e.g. Thales, DK 11 A1 (Diog. Laert. 1.35); Parmenides, DK 28 B8.30–1.

31–40 The surviving portion of the stanza is an elaboration of the abstract statement of 27–30. The speaker continues the first-person stance of the poet who praises (and does not blame); cf. 21–30n.

31–4 According to Socrates, Sim. says ἐγώ, ὦ Πιττακέ, οὐ διὰ ταῦτά σε ψέγω, ὅτι εἰμὶ φιλόψογος, ἐπεὶ ἔμοιγ᾿ ἐξαρκεῖ ὃς ἂν μὴ κακὸς ἦι μηδ᾿ ἄγαν ἀπάλαμνος ... ('Pittacus, I censure you not because I am a faultfinder; for I am content with whoever is not bad and not too shiftless ...', 346c). The sentiment suits the context, but the quotation fits the metre only from μηδ᾿ ἄγαν onwards, and it is unclear how closely Plato paraphrases Sim. in the earlier part of the sentence, and what he omits. Cf. 18–20n.

34 μηδ᾿ ἄγαν: again the demands are pointedly moderate.

ἀπάλαμνος: meaning uncertain, lit. 'un-handy'. Both 'shiftless' (*Il.* 5.597, Pind. *Ol.* 1.59) and 'unrestrained' (Sol. 27.12, Thgn. 481) suit the context. Whatever its precise import, ἀπάλαμνος creates a foil for the positive expressions that follow. Further on ἀπάλαμνος, see Gerber 1982: 98–9.

34–5 εἰ|δώς τ᾿ ... **δίκαν:** after two double negatives, this is the first positive description of the man the speaker praises. It introduces a civic frame. τ᾿ is an emendation. With the MSS᾿ γ᾿, the rhetoric would be: a slightly shiftless man is Ok, *as long as* he knows the justice that benefits the city.

35 ὀνησίπολιν: probably invented for this passage, but ἐρυσίπτολις is epic and the connection of δίκη and πόλις commonplace; e.g. Hes. *WD* 220–4, 267–9, Sol. 4.14–17.

36 ὑγιὴς ἀνήρ: all the *polis* needs is a 'sound man', not an unattainable ideal. The expression may or may not be novel. If it is, it provides an emphatic climax to the sentence. For related, slightly later, expressions, see e.g. Aesch. *Eum.* 535–6 ('health of mind') and Soph. *Phil.* 1006.

†οὐ μήν†: the metre demands – ⏑ – ⏑. Various reconstructions are possible, e.g. οὐδὲ μή μιν (Bergk), οὔ μιν ὦ φίλ᾿ (Maas).

37 μωμήσομαι: the future extends the refusal to blame beyond this moment and beyond (this performance of) this song. On such futures, see in the first instance Pelliccia 1995b: 317–34.

37–8 τῶν ... **ἀλιθίων** ... **γενέθλα** mockingly adapts the language of race in expressions such as γένος γυναικῶν (e.g. Hes. *Th.* 590), θηρῶν ... γενέθλην (*h.* 27.10); cf. Pind. *Pyth.* 3.21 ἔστι δὲ φῦλον ἐν ἀνθρώποισι ματαιότατον.

39–40 This is probably the end of the poem, both because of Socrates᾿ earlier declaration that he will 'go through the whole shape/character (τὸν τύπον ... τὸν ὅλον) <of the song>' (344b4–5), and because of the sense of closure the statement creates. The poem, which had begun with a *gnome*, ends with a *gnome*, one that is compatible but altogether different in emphasis. In contrast to 1–3, and as in 27–30, the focus is not on the ideal standard of goodness but on the absence of badness. The asyndeton is adversative ('but'), and lends emphasis to this capping statement.

39 πάντα ... καλά: a catchphrase in ethical statements, but used to very different ends: πάντα ... καλά when a young man dies in battle (*Il.* 22.73 and often alluded to; cf. Sim. 531.2n.); the κακός ἀνήρ can easily do ἀπάλαμνα things, and thinks that καλὰ πάντα (Thgn. 279–82); σὺν δ' ἀνάγκαι πᾶν καλόν (Pind. fr. 122.12).

40 τ': 'epic' τε; see Stes. 19.46n.

Simonides 543 PMG (271 Poltera)

A vivid and emotive portrayal of the predicament of Danae and her baby son Perseus, shut into a chest and tossing helplessly on the sea. The metre shows that the poem is severely incomplete, and the surviving portion gives no clue about its genre and about what is lost before and after.

The main elements of the myth of Danae and Perseus are as follows. Acrisius, ruler of Argos, locks away his daughter Danae because an oracle had prophesied that her son would kill him. When Zeus enters her prison in the form of golden rain and Danae gives birth to a son (Perseus), Acrisius shuts mother and baby into a chest and puts them out to sea. The chest drifts to the Cycladic island of Seriphos, where Danae is rescued by the fisherman Dictys. Perseus eventually grows up to become the hero who frees and marries Andromeda and kills Medusa.

Danae appears already in the *Iliad* (14.319–20) and the Hesiodic *Catalogue of Women* (frs. 129 and 135 MW), but seems to have been particularly popular in the early fifth century. Several pots survive, as do treatments by Pindar (*Pyth.* 12) and the mythographer Pherecydes (*FGrHist* 3 F 10). For the iconographic record, see *LIMC* s.vv. 'Akrisios' and 'Danae' and Reeder 1995: 267–76, and on the myth in general, Gantz 1993: 299–311 and Ogden 2008: 13–26.

Sim. creates an effect of unusual immediacy by allowing his audience to overhear Danae as she speaks to her baby. Twenty lines long (7–27), the speech dominates the fragment, and assumes functions that might otherwise have been fulfilled by authorial narrative. The tableau of mother and baby in the chest is introduced by narrative (1–7, in what survives), but is then developed further by Danae's own words, rich in visual and even acoustic detail. The audience does not just listen to Danae, but comes to witness the scene through her eyes and ears, and as inflected by her emotions.

Danae's speech is not static. Resigned despair addressed to the sleeping baby (7–20) gives way to something like a lullaby (21–2) and a prayer to Zeus (23–7). Throughout, Sim. creates a form of dramatic irony. The audience knows that the anxious Danae and her serenely sleeping baby will both survive, and that the baby is destined for future greatness. **Source:** Dion. Hal. *Comp.* 26.15. Dionysius (1st cent. BC) quotes the fragment as one of several pieces which (he claims) illustrate poetry that resembles prose. He makes a point of setting out the text as prose, without colometry, and challenges his readers: 'the rhythm of the ode will escape you, and you will not be able to make out strophe, antistrophe or epode'. This challenge has set the agenda for much of the modern scholarly reception of the fragment.

Since F preserves *Comp.* only up to ch. 25, the principal MSS are not P and F, as for Sa. 1, which is also cited in *Comp.* (see p. 116), but P and the relatively late M (*Marcianus* gr. 508, *c.* 1330). For M's relationship with P and F, see Aujac and Lebel 1981: 50. Athenaeus quotes lines 7–9 ὦ τέκος . . . κυ(ο)ώσσεις for the use of the word γαλαθηνός (9.396e). Both Dionysius and Athenaeus attribute the text to Sim.

Metre:

```
   ... ᴗ ᴗ – ᴗ – ‖
 – – ᴗ ᴗ –  ‖  ₍dod¨
 ᴗ ᴗ – ᴗ – –   pe    πνέων
 – – – ᴗ ᴗ – – – ᴗ –  ‖  ph ₍ia
 ᴗ – ᴗ – ᴗ ᴗ – – ᴗ ᴗ – – ?‖  ia ph                        5
 – ᴗ ᴗ – ᴗ ᴗ – ᴗ ᴗ – ᴗ –  ‖  glᵈ
 – – – – ᴗ ᴗ – ᴗ ᴗ – ᴗ – ?‖‖  glᵈ

 ᴗ ᴗ ᴗ – – ᴗ ᴗ – – – ᴗ – ?‖  ph ₍ia                      ?ep.
 ᴗ – – – ᴗ ᴗ – –  ph
 – ᴗ ᴗ – – ᴗ ᴗ – –  ph                                    10
 † ᴗ – ᴗ – – †
 – ᴗ ᴗ – – – ᴗ – † ᴗ – † ?‖
 – – ᴗ – ᴗ ᴗ – ᴗ –  enn
 ᴗ – – ᴗ ᴗ – – ?‖  ph
 – ᴗ ᴗ – ᴗ ᴗ – – ᴗ ᴗ –  dod¨ cho                          15
 – – – ᴗ ᴗ –  dod¨
 – ᴗ ᴗ – ᴗ ᴗ – ᴗ – – ᴗ –  ‖  gl ₍ia
 – ᴗ – – – ᴗ ᴗ – ᴗ – ?‖  ₍ia tl
 – ᴗ ᴗ – – ᴗ –  cho ₍ia
 – ᴗ ᴗ – ᴗ – – ?‖‖  ar                                     20

 ᴗ ᴗ – ᴗ ᴗ – ‖  dod¨                                       ?str.
```

– ⏑ – ⏑ – ⏑ – ⏑ – ⏑ ⏑ – ⏑ – ?|| ‸*ia ia tl*
⏑ ⏑ – ⏑ – ⏑ – ⏑ – – – ⏑ ⏑ – ⏑ – || *ia ia tl* 23–4
⏑ ⏑ – – ⏑ ⏑ – ⏑ ⏑ – ⏑ – || *gl*[d] -έο̄ν (ϝ)έπος 25
– – ⏑ ⏑ – ?|| ‸*dod*¨
– – ⏑ – . . .

Dionysius appears to have chosen an extract with minimal responsion. As a result, the colometry is highly uncertain. The schema above is for the most part that of West 1981. It is based on the (rather uncertain) assumption that the very end (25–7) responds to the very beginning (1–3), with a loose responsion between ἄνε- (⏑ ⏑) and σύγγ- (–). If that assumption is correct, it follows that the quotation starts some way into the antistrophe, contains the whole epode, and ends some way into the strophe.

The rhythm is fundamentally aeolic, with some iambic elements. More or less strict forms of the pherecratean, glyconic and anaclastic dodrans give it some regularity, but there is considerable variation. The analysis adopted here avoids ionics as on the whole alien to the aeolic lyrics of Sim., Pindar and Bacchylides. Especially in Danae's address to her baby (the presumed epode) the rhythm is free-flowing, and indication of pauses becomes a matter of guesswork. For discussion of the metre, often in conjunction with the text, see apart from West 1981: Poltera 2008: 498–502, Führer 1976, Page 1951c: 133–40, Wilamowitz-Moellendorff 1886: 144–50.

Discussions: Peponi 2016: 9–10, Pelliccia 2009: 250–2, Carson 1999: 55–60 ~ Carson 1992b: 57–60, Rosenmeyer 1991, Burnett 1985: 11–14, Bowra 1961: 337–40.

1–7 sketch a picture of the frightened Danae in the chest, holding the baby. The sense is clear, but the syntax is uncertain: as printed here, the fragment starts with a subordinate clause ('when . . .'), and the preceding main clause is lost. Since Danae (3 μιν) must have been identified earlier on, this is probably not the beginning of the narrative. Poltera 2008: 497 argues that the quotation starts only with λάρνακι, introduced in Dionysius by ὅτι (both ὅτε and ὅτι are transmitted).

1–2 λάρνακι | ἐν δαιδαλέαι introduces an image of evocative incongruity: an 'elaborate chest' out of place in the stormy sea, carrying human cargo. Danae and Perseus travel in a λάρναξ also at [Hes.] fr. 135.3–5 MW and Pherecydes, *FGrHist* 3 F 10. Women who survive being cast out to sea inside a box, together with their (often illegitimate) children, form a pattern in Greek myth, e.g. Auge and Telephus; see Beaulieu 2016: 90–118. More widely on myths of female imprisonment, see Seaford 1990, and on the symbolism of women and boxes Lissarrague 1995.

3 μιν: object of 5 ἔρειπεν, referring to Danae, who must have been identified earlier on. The transmitted μήν has no obvious point.

4–5 δείματι | ἔρειπεν 'were laying low in terror': the verb has both literal and metaphorical force. The (augmentless) imperfects ἔρειπεν and (6) βάλλε create a sustained backdrop against which Danae's speech is set (aor. εἶπεν).

5 οὐδ' ἀδιάντοισι παρειαῖς: lit. 'with cheeks not unwetted'. A visually poignant elaboration of expressions such as οὐδ'... ἀδακρύτω ... ὄσσε (*Od.* 4.186) and οὐδέ ... ἄκλαυτον (*Od.* 4.493–4). The double negative intensifies.

6 ἀμφί ... βάλλε ... χέρα: an intimate gesture. Danae seeks comfort as much as she gives it.

7–27 *Danae's speech* falls into two sections, one lamentatory and addressed to the sleeping baby (7–20), the other more composed and dominated by a prayer to Zeus (21–7).

7–20 Danae's love for her child combines with a sharp sense of despondency about her own situation. The despondency is reinforced by the lack of response from the sleeping baby. Sim. develops the motif of the lone wakeful person, who is anxious while others sleep; see p. 84. Children are often seen as innocent of the adult world, e.g. *Il.* 2.337–8, Soph. *Aj.* 552–5, Eur. *IA* 621–4.

8 σὺ δ' ἀωτεῖς emphatically introduces what will be a major theme of the stanza. The verb must mean something like 'slumber'. In its other two occurrences it is addressed to people who sleep when they should be awake; *Il.* 10.159 and *Od.* 10.548. To avoid the sequence 'you slumber, you sleep/snore' (9 κνοώσσεις (n.)), some editors adopt Schneidewin's ἀωρεῖς (poorly attested, perhaps 'you do not care'). However, the repetition is appropriate: Perseus' sleep preoccupies Danae.

γαλαθηνῶι δ' ἤτορι: lit. 'with suckling heart'. The adjective suits an infant; cf. Sim. 553.2 γαλαθηνὸν τέκος. The presumably novel transfer to the heart develops the notion of the baby's characteristic oblivion, and creates a contrast with Homeric epithets of ἦτορ, such as ἄλκιμον and νηλεές. Some editors print ἤθεϊ ('character'), reconstructed from the corrupt Dionysius MSS. Here Athenaeus' ἤτορι is preferred as the more expressive and more easily corrupted reading: inflected ἦτορ is rare (but attested, see esp. Pind. fr. 52f.12 ἤτορι).

9 κνοώσσεις is preferred as *lectio difficilior*, and because it creates a pherecratean, which suits the context. Sim. artificially lengthens κνώσσεις, perhaps to express the sound of snoring; see West 1980: 153–5, who also argues that κνώσσειν itself is an onomatopoeic word meaning 'snore'.

10 δούρατι: one of the earliest instances of the meaning 'boat'. In so far as the base meaning 'stem, plank' is still felt, it creates an appropriate usage for a wooden chest employed as a boat.

χαλκεογόμφωι 'with brazen pegs'. The *hapax* may link Danae's confinement in the chest with her previous confinement in a bronze-fastened or bronze-clad room, designed to prevent her from conceiving a son; cf. Soph.

Ant. 946 ἐν χαλκοδέτοις αὐλαῖς, Pherecydes, *FGrHist*, 3 F 10 θάλαμον ...
χαλκοῦν. γόμφος is chosen for its associations with ships; e.g. Hes. *WD* 660,
Hdt. 2.96.2. Pegs were normally made of wood. Danae's two confinements
are juxtaposed on the two sides of an early fifth-century calyx crater, *LIMC*
s.v. 'Danae' 1 and 48.

11–12 The text cannot be restored with any confidence. One promis-
ing restoration is {δὲ} νυκτί <τ' ἀ>λαμπεῖ | κυανέωι τε δνόφωι σταλείς 'sent forth
in the unlit night and the dark murk' (Bergk, developing earlier proposals). The heavy emphasis on darkness suits Danae's sorrow; see further
Poltera *ad loc.* (who prefers Schneidewin's ταθείς 'stretched out'), and for
other approaches, see West 1981: 31, Ivanov 2010 and Hutchinson *ad loc.*

12 κυανέωι ('dark', 'dark-blue') is particularly appropriate for the sea-
setting, cf. Sim. 567.4 κυανέου 'ξ ὕδατος.

13–14 ἄχναν ... βαθεῖαν 'deep ... foam', acc. obj. of οὐκ ἀλέγεις.
The transmitted text is corrupt (see apparatus). The restoration receives
some support from *Il.* 15.623–8, a simile in which a ship is hidden under
foam (ἄχνη) after being struck by a wave. Other reconstructions are
possible: (a) gen. pl. βαθειᾶν qualifying κομᾶν, and/or (b) ἅλμαν instead
of ἄχναν ('seawater' washing over them).

13 ὕπερθε 'above' (+ gen.).

14–15 παριόντος | κύματος: the absolute genitive elaborates on βαθεῖαν:
'deep, as a wave passes'.

15 οὐκ ἀλέγεις 'you are taking no notice of'.

16 φθόγγον: the wind has a 'voice', and yet Perseus is not listening.

16–17 πορφυρέαι ... χλανίδι contrasts Perseus' surroundings with his
divine lineage, and perhaps his future glory. Purple is a marker of status
from Homer onwards, and the χλανίς, a fine woollen cloak, is often a token
of luxury, cf. Aristoph. *Peace* 1002, *Lys.* 1189.

17 πρόσωπον καλόν creates an intimate vignette as the culmination of
the sentence. The face that Danae looks at, or all that she can see of her
wrapped-up sleeping baby. It makes little difference whether πρόσωπον is
understood as a nominative loosely following on from κείμενος ἐν χλανίδι, or
as a vocative. Some editors print καλὸν πρόσωπον, citing the parallel Sa. 4.7
and Sim.'s broad preference for adjectives preceding nouns; see Führer
1976: 118–23. However, the MSS point to πρόσωπον καλόν (see Poltera
2008: 496), as probably does the metre.

18–20 Unaware of the danger, Perseus is not listening to Danae. Unlike
Perseus, the audience is listening. But unlike Danae, the audience knows
that, paradoxically, Perseus is right not to regard τὸ δεινόν as δεινόν, since he
and Danae are destined to survive.

18 τοι ~ σοι.

19 καί lends emphasis by strengthening the connection between if-
clause and main clause; see Denniston 1954: 308.

ἐμῶν ῥημάτων: genitive because λέπτον ὑπεῖχες οὖας ('lend your delicate ear') syntactically amounts to a verb of hearing ('listen to').

21–7 Danae ceases to address Perseus, and ceases to lament. She lulls her baby to sleep, hopes for an improvement in their predicament, and diffidently prays to Zeus. All seven verb forms express requests, whereas none did in 7–20.

21–2 The repetitive conjuring of sleep recalls lullabies. On lullabies, see Colesanti 2014: 102–6 and Karanika 2014: 160–4, and for the metaphorical use of εὕδειν, Alcm. 89.1n.

21 κέλομ' ('I ask') marks the shift from description to appeal. The asyndeton lends force to the request, as often; cf. Maehler 2000: 423–4 and Poltera *ad loc.* There is no syntactic reason to remove it by printing Bergk's κέλομαι <δ'>, as many editors do. If κέλομαι is preferred rhythmically, one might consider <σ'> (D'Angour *per litt.*). For the combination κέλομαι + imperative, cf. Pind. *Pyth.* 1.71 λίσσομαι νεῦσον.

22 ἄμετρον κακόν reworks epic ἀμέτρητος πόνος (*Od.* 23.249) and πένθος ἀμέτρητον (*Od.* 19.512).

23–4 Lit.: 'May some change of plan manifest itself, father Zeus, from you.' Danae continues with third-person phrasing even as she turns to Zeus, and adds ἐκ σέο only at the end. She is concerned to bring about an end to her suffering, not to hold Zeus to account.

μεταβουλία: Zeus's βουλή shapes events in epic. μεταβουλία is a *hapax*, but the cognate verb is used to describe a divine change of plan already at *Od.* 5.286 (μετεβούλευσαν).

Ζεῦ πάτερ: not a merely conventional address since Zeus is the father of Perseus.

25–7 'Whatever prayer I utter that is either too bold or without justice, I ask for your understanding.' Danae's anxiety about the propriety of her prayer is sufficiently motivated by her attempt, however indirect, to change Zeus's βουλή. Further, more daring requests may of course have followed.

25 ὅτι δ' ἤ reinterprets the MSS' ὅτι δή, which does not make sense here. An alternative would be ὅττι δέ (ὅτι δέ is problematic metrically). The epicism ὅττι might be acceptable in a line that is altogether epic in tone: cf. the epic prosody -έον (ϝ)έπος and the near-formulaic combination of ὅτ(τ)ι and ἔπος (e.g. *Il.* 1.543, 2.361, 24.92).

27 σύγγνωθί μοι: this kind of request is often accompanied by reasons that account for the potentially offensive act; e.g. Soph. *Ant.* 65–7, Aristoph. *Wasps* 1001. Danae gives no such explanations (unless they followed), but the whole text portrays her state of mind as desperate, and σύγγνωθί μοι reinforces the portrayal.

It is impossible to tell whether the speech ended here.

Simonides *581* PMG *(262 Poltera)*

An intertextual critique of an epigram Sim. attributes to the sage Cleobulus, as well as an intervention in contemporary poetic discourses about monuments and memorialisation. The text is either complete or a self-contained section of a longer poem; cf. 7n.

References by name to other authors and their texts are rare in earlier lyric but increase sharply in the late sixth and early fifth centuries, testimony perhaps to a growing circulation of written texts, as well as to the competitive attitude of panhellenic composers like Sim. and Pindar. Sim. quotes Pittacus in 542, names Homer and Stesichorus in 564, and quotes Homer (as 'the Chian') in fr. eleg. 19 *IEG²*. 579 manipulates a passage from Hesiod without naming him. Here Sim. names Cleobulus and attacks him for a funerary epigram. He gives a paraphrase of the epigram that is detailed but not precise, and not wholly fair. See 'Source' below for the epigram, p. 215 for the competitive nature of early Greek intellectual discourse, and West 1999: 378–9 for poets naming poets. Also relevant are vase-paintings of named poets, which first appear in this period; see p. 16 n. 29.

Beyond the intertextual quarrel with Cleobulus, the piece is a self-standing engagement with an established topos. The paraphrase makes the text fully comprehensible without knowledge of the epigram, and the notion that is the target of Sim.'s broadside – an everlasting funerary monument – goes back to Homer (*Il.* 17.434–5) and appears on various inscribed epitaphs; see esp. *CEG* 108 (mid-5th cent.), 'an unwearying *stele*, which will speak to passers-by for all days'. The epigram Sim. attacks may be remarkable for its confident tone, but its fundamental sentiment is not exceptional.

Two historical developments provide relevant context to Sim.'s poem. One is the widespread appearance of inscribed grave markers in the course of the sixth century; see Sourvinou-Inwood 1995: 278–94. The other (depending on the date of the poem) is the major programmes of commemoration in the wake of the Persian Wars, which are documented across (and beyond) mainland Greece and which prominently involved poetry, monuments, and poetry on monuments. These developments prompted a sustained interest among poets in material monuments, and in the mutual dependency as well as rivalry that characterised the relationship between poetry and monuments. For Sim., see fr. 531, testt. 47a–c Campbell; for Pindar, e.g. *Ol.* 6.1–4, *Nem.* 5.1–3; and for discussion, Steiner 2001: ch. 5, Ford 2002: 93–130, Porter 2010: ch. 9, Fearn 2013.

Sim. 581 confronts this relationship by intricately entangling poem and material object. A poet who himself composed epigrams inscribed on monuments (p. 205) manipulates and attacks an epigram that purports to be inscribed on a monument. The monument in question is probably an imaginary verbal creation, and in any case, the epigram was known independently of it. Moreover, this epigram, unlike ordinary inscribed epigrams, is presented as furthering (or failing to further) the reputation not of the dead man (whose name is omitted in Sim.'s poem), but of its alleged author. The criticism of Cleobulus in fr. 581 is more aggressive than that of Pittacus in fr. 542, but as often with invective the tone is hard to judge. This is a very self-conscious piece of writing, at least as invested in the witty manipulation of an established text and an established topos as in denigrating Cleobulus or establishing a truth about the limitation of monuments.

Source: Diog. Laert. 1.90. Diogenes (probably 3rd cent. AD) quotes the song in the Cleobulus section of his history of Greek philosophy (for Cleobulus, see 1n.). Diogenes introduces the quotation as evidence (according to some) for Cleobulus' authorship of a hexameter epigram, which he cites immediately before. The epigram purports to be inscribed on the tomb of Midas, the legendary king of Phrygia, and is put in the mouth of the sculpture of a 'maiden' (a sphinx?) on top of the tomb:

χαλκῆ παρθένος εἰμί, Μίδου δ' ἐπὶ σήματι κεῖμαι.
ἔστ' ἂν ὕδωρ τε ῥέηι καὶ δένδρεα μακρὰ τεθήληι,
ἠελιός τ' ἀνιὼν λάμπηι, λαμπρά τε σελήνη,
καὶ ποταμοί γε ῥέωσιν, ἀνακλύζηι δὲ θάλασσα,
αὐτοῦ τῆιδε μένουσα πολυκλαύτωι ἐπὶ τύμβωι,   5
ἀγγελέω παριοῦσι Μίδας ὅτι τῆιδε τέθαπται.

I am a bronze maiden and I rest upon the tomb of Midas. So long as water shall flow and tall trees flourish, and the sun and the bright moon rise and shine, and rivers flow and the sea washes on the coast – I shall remain here upon this tomb rich in tears, and shall announce to passers-by that Midas is buried here.

The epigram is quoted by different sources in different versions (some of them shorter) and under different names (usually Homer's, not Cleobulus'). It is therefore uncertain what text was known to Sim. and his audience, but the extent of the similarities leaves no doubt that at the very least he knew lines 2–3 in a version similar to that quoted by Diogenes. For the different versions of the epigram, see Markwald 1986: 34–83, and for a broader treatment Ford 2002: 101–5.

Metre:

$- \cup - - - \cup \cup - \cup \cup - - - \cup \cup - \cup \cup - - \parallel \quad e - D - D -$
$- \cup \cup - \cup \cup - - \cup \cup - \cup \cup - \quad D\ D$
$- \cup \cup - \cup \cup - - - \cup \cup - - \quad D - d - \quad$ χρυσέας
$- \cup - - - \cup - - - \cup \cup - \cup \cup - - - ^? \parallel \quad E - D\ e_\wedge$
$\cup - \cup \cup - \cup \cup - - - \cup - \cup ^? \parallel \quad \cup D - e \cup$ 5

− ⏑ ⏑ − ⏑ ⏑ −   *D*

− − ⏑ − − − − ⏑ − ⏑ − − ‖   − *E* ⏑ *e*ₓ

The dactylic hexameters of the epigram are answered by dactylo-epitrites (and indeed by epic phraseology). The first period soon turns into what sounds like a hexameter, with Λίνδου ναέταν Κλεόβουλον occupying the characteristic position of an epithet–name formula at the end. The dactylo-epitrites of this poem are more regular than those of 531, but here too different interpretations are possible, in particular in the second half (e.g. *ith* for the final − ⏑ − ⏑ − −). See Dale 1969 [1951]: 80–1 and West 1982a: 71.

Discussions: Fearn 2013: 233–5, Porter 2010: 479–81, Ford 2002: 101–9, Fränkel 1975 [1962]: 306–7.

1 The language is belligerent. Nobody who 'trusts his wits' (νόωι πίσυνος) would praise Cleobulus – who presumably was a widely admired figure.

Λίνδου ναέταν Κλεόβουλον: Cleobulus (7th–6th cent.) was ruler of Lindus on Rhodes, and came to be considered one of the canonical sages (cf. 7n.), as well as a composer of songs and riddles amounting to 3,000 hexameter lines (Diog. Laert. 1.89). Sim. omits to make reference to any such tokens of distinction.

2–4 correspond closely to lines 2–4, or in any case 2–3, of the 'Midas epigram' (line 4 of the epigram may be a late addition). The changes in the phrasing are not merely poetic variation but subtly undermine the epigram. ἀντι<τι>θέντα ('setting against') hints at a confrontation of statue and nature, even though the epigram made a purely temporal statement ('as long as . . .'). The description of nature emphasises what the *stele* does not have, permanence (ἀεναοῖς, perhaps also the – ever-reappearing – 'spring flowers'), movement (ἀεναοῖς, δίναις) and energy (φλογί).

2 ἄνθεσι ... εἰαρινοῖς: formulaic in early hexameter, including lengthened εἰ-; e.g. *Il.* 2.89, Hes. *Th.* 279.

4 ἀντι<τι>θέντα: the loss of a syllable is suggested by the metre, and the present tense suits the reference to an enduring poem. Bergk's ἀντία θέντα would also be possible.

μένος στάλας 'power of a *stele*'. The paradoxical culmination of the sentence is underscored by the slowing rhythm. It is living beings and natural forces such as rivers (*Il.* 12.18) and the sun (*Il.* 23.190) that have μένος, not a *stele*, viz. an (inscribed or uninscribed) slab of stone. In addition, μένος acoustically echoes yet distorts μένουσα in the epigram. Sim. makes no reference to the extravagant 'bronze maiden' of the epigram, which suits the famously rich Midas but is out of line with the standard practice of using stone for funerary monuments and would therefore have narrowed the reference of the piece. 5 λίθον reinforces the point. It is unnecessary to hypothesise that Sim. did not know the first line of the epigram, which is missing from some versions (see Markwald 1986: 58–9, 82).

5–7 Formally, the contrast of gods and humans serves to express the fragility of stone: even humans can break it. However, it has the effect of insinuating that Cleobulus overstepped human limits.

7 μωροῦ φωτός: this pointed put-down strongly suggests that Cleobulus was already in Sim.'s day known as a sage; cf. 1 and 542.12nn. The asyndeton adds force.

βουλά: chosen probably for the pun on Cleobulus' name, and as a reference to the wisdom poetry with which he was credited. The ring composition creates a sense of completeness.

TIMOTHEUS

According to the testimonia, Timotheus lived from *c.* 450 to *c.* 360 BC. He was born in Miletus on the coast of Asia Minor, was at one point active in Athens, perhaps for a considerable period, and became well known across the Greek world. The *Suda* speaks of nineteen nomes (narrative songs, performed by a soloist who also plays the kithara), eighteen dithyrambs, thirty-six *prooimia*, twenty-one hymns, as well as other works (τ620). Many of Tim.'s compositions were very lengthy, but the only substantial fragment is fr. 791, from the nome *Persians*, sections of which are selected here. *Persians* is unusual in treating a historical subject: Tim. otherwise composed, *inter alia*, nomes entitled *Cyclops*, *Niobe*, *Nauplios*, and chorally performed dithyrambs named *Madness of Ajax*, *Birthpangs of Semele*, *Scylla* (classification tentative in some cases). Timotheus' dialect, as transmitted, is the literary mix characteristic of the choral tradition, but the Doric component is less prominent than in Stesichorus or Simonides, and does not extend much beyond the use of Doric ᾱ (alongside instances of η).

Tim. is one of the most prominent figures of the 'New Music', a musical and poetic trend of the last three decades of the fifth and the beginning of the fourth century. It centred on Athens, and encompassed several genres, not least dithyramb, nome and tragedy. Other well-known names include Euripides, Agathon and Philoxenus.

'New Music' is a modern term, but novelty was central already to these poets' own self-presentation, and defined the way they were perceived. Tim. declares, 'I do not sing the old songs, for my new ones are better ... May the old Muse depart' (796; cf. Eur. *Tro.* 512, and Tim. 791.202–40 below). The comic poets readily seized on the New Music's conspicuous departures from tradition as material for parody, e.g. Aristoph. *Birds* 1372–1409 (Cinesias), *Thesm.* 100–29 (Agathon), *Wealth* 290–301 (Philoxenus), Pherecrates, *PCG* fr. 155 (see below, p. 245). Later

scholarship regularly highlights novelty, often with disapproval; for Tim.
specifically, see e.g. Aristoxenus fr. 76 Wehrli, [Plut.] *De mus.* 4 and 12.
The innovations of the New Music encompass many aspects of musical
and poetic practice. Most obvious on the page is a verbal style that seeks
out elaborate and unparalleled forms of expression, is markedly mimetic
and sometimes densely intertextual; see more fully below, p. 233.
The metrical design is often astrophic, abandoning strophic and triadic
patterning, and there are quick shifts between different types of rhythm.
Rhythms are less tightly determined by the syllabic quantities of the verbal
text than in earlier composers; most notable is the occurrence of
melisma (several notes to one syllable). Further on metre and rhythm,
see pp. 235–6. Instruments too underwent elaboration. Particularly notorious was the addition of several strings to the traditional lyre, which
increased the range of pitch and the capacity for harmonic modulation;
see 791.225–6, 229–31nn. Further on this gamut of innovations, see
D'Angour 2006, Wallace 2009, and the more technical treatments of
Hagel 2010: esp. 444–50 and Franklin 2013.

The New Music, then, was certainly new, but because of the loss of
almost all lyric music, 'New' and otherwise, it is difficult to assess precisely
how radical its musical innovations were. Some of the poets' own boasts
are exaggerations (see Tim. 791.229–31n.), and some of the hostility in
musical scholarship will stem from conservatism. More traditional lyric
features, which can certainly be made out in the texts, and which will
have extended to the music, are at risk of getting lost because poets,
parodists and detractors alike highlight above all what is new. Such
features include traditional metres at the end of *Persians* (see 'Metre')
and the use of compound adjectives and periphrasis as markers of poetic
style. On the blend of tradition and innovation in the New Music, see
LeVen 2014.

In a different way, however, the frequency of comic treatments and
the stridency of later critics are reliable evidence. They are testimony to
the popularity and notoriety of Tim. and his peers. The New Music was
not just a set of developments in musical practice but also a major
cultural phenomenon. Tim. was a star musician who performed (and
had his work performed) before large audiences, and who elicited
strong responses.

Hordern 2002 provides a full commentary. For a brief introduction to
Tim. and the New Music, see Csapo and Wilson 2009. Csapo 2004 analyses
the economics, poetics and politics of the New Music, Power 2010 is
a book-length treatment of kitharodes (incl. Tim. and the genre of the
nome), and LeVen 2014 a monograph about late Classical lyric (incl.
Tim.). For Tim.'s dialect, see Brussich 1970 and Hordern 2002: 43–50.

Persians

A kitharodic nome on the theme of the Persian defeat at Salamis.
The papyrus fragment 791 *PMG* preserves the last 240 lines of the poem,
in several columns. The legible portion is structured as follows:

1–39: Battle narrative.

40–195: Four consecutive mini-scenes, centred on four different individuals or groups among the Persians and their allies, the fourth of
   them Xerxes. Each mini-scene contains at least one speech.

196–201: Greek celebrations.

202–36: Tim. delivers a statement about the nature of his poetry, much
   of it in the first person (the '*sphragis*').

237–40: A prayer on behalf of 'this city', which concludes the poem.

We cannot tell the original extent of the poem because the left-hand
part of the papyrus is missing. A different fragment gives us what may be
the opening line (fr. 788, below), and we have two further isolated lines,
of which certainly one, and probably both, come from a speech
addressed to the Greeks (frs. 789 and 790, the latter translated in 791.
191–5n.). It is possible therefore that the focus on the defeated Persians
in the bulk of 791 was matched by a similarly extensive focus on the
Greeks in what preceded. Alternatively, the Greeks may have appeared
briefly near the beginning, just as they appear only briefly in lines
196–201 towards the end. The (ancient) title suggests predominance
of the Persians.

 By Tim.'s day, the Persian Wars of the early fifth century were well
established as a canonical subject in which both poets and prose authors
strove to distinguish themselves. In the immediate aftermath of the
Persian invasions, Simonides had assumed the status of a national poet
by commemorating victories and losses in epigrams as well as lyric and
elegiac works; see p. 210. Aeschylus' *Persians* was first performed in
472 BC, and subsequently became a classic; for quotations and allusions,
see Hdt. 8.68γ, Aristoph. *Frogs* 1026–7, Eupolis, *PCG* fr. 207 and Plato
Comicus, *PCG* fr. 226, and for discussion Rosenbloom 2006: 161–2 and
Garvie 2009: liii–lvii. Herodotus himself chose the Persian invasions for
his historiographic project that rivalled epic accounts of the Trojan War.
The epic poet Choerilus of Samos composed a *Persika*, the first known
historical epic (late 5th cent.). Part of the reason for this interest in the
past was the present. Persia remained a dominant presence in Greece
during the Peloponnesian War and beyond, politically, culturally, finan-
cially and militarily.

Tim. recalls this long-standing tradition throughout the surviving text. A particularly frequent point of reference is Aeschylus' *Persians*: verbal allusions are pervasive, and the narrative develops Aeschylus' portrayal of the battle through Persian eyes (and mouths), as well as the climactic appearance of Xerxes. Homer, too, is omnipresent, and there are some points of contact also with Persian War-related works of Simonides, Pindar and Herodotus. In a different, more explicit, manner the nome's self-conscious interest in the poetic tradition is continued in the *sphragis* at the end.

The unusually intense reuse of other texts is part and parcel of the novel poetic style of the nome, which constantly tests the limits of the language and seeks new forms of expression for an old topic. (There are very broad similarities in this respect with the narrative lyric of Stesichorus.) The distinctive features of Tim.'s poetics may be grouped under two headings. First, the style of *Persians* is highly *mimetic* in specific ways. Speeches expressing extremes of emotion provide rich opportunities for enactment by the performer. One of them, in the mouth of a man from Phrygia, even imitates the linguistic errors of a non-Greek speaker (791.150–61). Sensory and visual language gives a mimetic quality also to the descriptive passages. The effect is enhanced by certain absences: no intervention by the narrator in the description of the battle, limited narrative progression and a privileging of the physical over the ethical. The audience is transported into the midst of the Persians' struggle. See also 791.68n. on tense.

Secondly, the style is pointedly *combinatory*. Along with allusions to an array of earlier texts, it incorporates various genres and modes. The tone alters from speaker to speaker, and there are no transitional passages as the narrative cuts from one scene to the next. The metre changes rapidly. The extensive metaphorical phrasing draws on a range of different domains, often several at the same time. There are numerous compounds, many of them not previously attested. Critics both ancient and modern have varied between perceiving this style as one of suggestive blending or of disturbing incongruity. In any case, it is a style of showy artifice, which nevertheless invites listeners to enter into a simulated world. See further Csapo 2004: 216–29, LeVen 2014: chs. 4 and 5, Budelmann and LeVen 2014.

Performances of *Persians* must have been emotionally uplifting. The old Salamis theme was ever-satisfying as a reminder of the glorious past, and so were the barbarian stereotypes that Tim. draws on in his portrayal of the Persians and their allies; on these stereotypes (which are even more marked than in Aeschylus), see Hutzfeldt 1999: 171–205 and Hall 2006: ch. 9. Frs. 788, 789 and 790 suggest that some passages were stridently patriotic in tone. Less strident, but still upbeat, is the ending with the prayer for the well-being of city and populace.

There are good reasons to believe that *Persians* was premiered in Athens. Above all, Salamis was an obvious choice of topic for the Athenians, who regarded this as very much their victory, while it would be an unlikely choice for the Ionian cities, which fought on the Persian side (e.g. Hdt. 7.94, 8.22), or for land-locked Sparta. There are also potential connections with Euripides. The polymetric monody of the Phrygian slave in *Orestes* resembles the equally polymetric (sung) speech by the Phrygian in *Persians* (791.150–61); see Porter 1994: 199–207, and cf. below. A later anecdote, according to which Euripides helped Tim. with the proem, is unlikely to be historical but may nevertheless be based on evidence for the Athenian origin of the nome (Satyrus *Vit. Eur.* = Eur. test. 87a *TrGF* = Tim. test. 6 Campbell). The occasion will have been the kitharodic competitions at the Panathenaia, held in the Odeion (adjacent to the Theatre of Dionysus), which during this period was the most high-profile contest of its kind in the Greek world.

The likelihood of an Athenian premiere makes it noteworthy that nothing in the text points explicitly to Athens. Outside the *sphragis*, 'Greece' and 'Greeks' appear only as a unit (frs. 788, 790 and 791.118, 143, 146 and 188). Athens is not named, nor are any individuals. The description of the battle is generic, and even Xerxes is referred to only as 'the (viz. Persian) king'. In fact the identification of the battle as Salamis is only an inference, on the basis of Salamis' status as *the* naval battle against Persia, the allusions to Aeschylus' Salamis play, and the presence and flight of the Persian king. The generic quality of the narrative is too systematic to be solely a consequence of the loss of part of the poem. Two intended effects may be considered. First, the rarity of specific historic features adds to the fantastic quality that the style also otherwise creates: the nome is only weakly tethered to reality. This is the opposite of e.g. Herodotus' narrative style. Secondly, the absence of divisive Athenian propaganda will have broadened the appeal of the nome. For Tim. as a classic, in and beyond his lifetime, see Hordern 2002: 73–9, Power 2010: 549–54. Regarding *Persians* specifically, Plutarch reports that after the defeat of a Persian army in Phrygia in 395 BC, many of the victorious Ionians quoted in triumph the line that is now fr. 790 (*Agesil.* 14.4). Elsewhere he relates a rabble-rousing performance of the nome in Nemea in 205 BC (see fr. 788 headnote).

Plutarch's report makes 395 BC the *terminus ante quem* for the first performance. More specific suggestions are speculative. The most noteworthy is the argument for 412–408 BC by Bassett 1931. In 412/411 Sparta concluded three treaties with Persia (Thuc. 8.18, 8.37, 8.58), and 408 is the date of *Orestes*. The proposal has a certain appeal, and is also compatible with Tim.'s (*b.* mid-fifth cent.; see above) apparent claim in line 214 that he is neither old nor young. However, Salamis was always resonant as a political and not least a literary theme in Athens; and even though the polymetric Phrygian is more remarkable in tragedy than in a nome, it is not beyond Euripides to have conceived him first. Hansen 1984 lists other theories about both date and place of performance.

The *sphragis* is discussed in 791.202–40n.

Metre: The metre of *Persians* differs from that of all other texts in this anthology in two respects, both of them shared with other compositions of the 'New Music'. First, the nome is neither strophic nor stichic: the metre progresses continuously, without the kind of patterning imposed by responsion; cf. Heph. *Poem.* iii (3), pp. 64–5 Consbruch. Secondly, it is polymetric: iambo-trochaic rhythms dominate, but aeolic, choriambic, dactylic and dochmiac shapes also appear, with fluid shifts from one kind of rhythm to another. The variation is remarkable.

Certain patterns can be made out:

- A dactylic hexameter creates a traditional opening (fr. 788).
- Lines 66–9 are dochmiac in character (though the deviation from the iambo-trochaic pattern of the surroundings is minor). This agitated metre suits the struggles of the deranged drowning man.
- The king's speech (178–95) introduces a greater number of aeolic cola. Changes are for the most part seamless. The iambo-trochaics of 173–8 continue into 179; then the double short of the final choriamb of 179 introduces the shift to a 'double-short' form of trochaic dimeter in 180, which creates a glyconic and thus begins the aeolic section (180–6).
- The Greek celebrations (196–201) are introduced by a dactylic line.
- The rhythm changes fundamentally as Tim. embarks on self-presentation in the *sphragis* (202). Polymetric variation gives way to a much more uniform pattern of glyconics and pherecrateans (= glyconics catalectic). For an attempt to detect structuring within this regular run, see Ercoles 2010: 115–20.
- As the end approaches, a different aeolic form comes to dominate (hipponacteans). The final line slows down the pace with a sequence of long syllables, but then gives emphasis to the concluding pun (εὐνομίαι) with a blunt clausula (⌣ ⌣ –).

For the most part, the analysis adopted here follows Page in *PMG*, West 1982b: 1–5 and Hordern 2002. Multiple labels aim to bring out underlying rhythmical continuities. The variation and lack of responsion create greater than usual uncertainty in establishing a colometry (the pre-Alexandrian papyrus presents a continuous text), and in labelling individual cola. In performance, moreover, the music, which was a core feature of Tim.'s acts, is likely to have changed some of the quantities. Such musical adjustments are irrecoverable, and the schema here necessarily assumes standard syllabic quantities. Because of the even greater-than-usual uncertainty about the articulation of the rhythm, the text is printed without indication of putative period-ends. For the shortening and lengthening of quantities in musical performance, see in general Dion. Hal. *Comp.* 11.22–3, and for the New Music in particular Aristoph. *Frogs* 1314, 1349. Further on the metre of *Persians*, see (apart from the items cited above): Lambin 2013: 165–85, West 1982a: 138–9, Korzeniewski 1974, Wilamowitz-Moellendorff 1903: 29–38.

Discussions: Gurd 2016: 114–23, *LeVen 2014: 90–101, 178–87, 193–220, Lambin 2013: 109–85, *Power 2010: 516–49, Hall 2006: ch. 9, Rosenbloom 2006: 148–54, Huber 2002, Gambetti 2001, Hutzfeldt 1999: 171–205, van Minnen 1997, *Herington 1985: 151–60, Bassett 1931, *Wilamowitz-Moellendorff 1903.

Commentaries: Sevieri 2011, *Hordern 2002: 121–248, Janssen 1984.

Fr. 788 PMG

Plut. *Philopoem.* 11 and Paus. 8.50.3 quote the verse as the beginning of a rendition of Tim.'s *Persians* by the kitharode Pylades at Nemea in 205 BC. It will be the first line either of the nome proper or of the proem that typically preceded the nome; for kitharodic proems, see Power 2010: 187–200.

The line introduces the subject of *Persians*. The phraseology places Tim.'s work in the tradition of public praise poetry; cf. Sim. 531.8–9 ἀρετᾶς μέγαν λελοιπώς | κόσμον ἀέναόν τε κλέος (preceded by 6–7 εὐδοξίαν | Ἑλλάδος), and Pind. fr. 77 ὅθι παῖδες Ἀθηναίων ἐβάλοντο φαεννάν | κρηπῖδ' ἐλευθερίας, both from poems about the Persian Wars (though perhaps not alluded to specifically).

For two reasons, the grammatical subject is more likely to be either the army at Salamis or Themistocles (creating through their action an adornment that consists in freedom) than Tim. himself (creating a poetic adornment for the freedom achieved at Salamis). (i) The latter would make the genitive ἐλευθερίας more difficult. (ii) Both Plutarch and (more briefly) Pausanias suggest a military rather than poetic feat: Pylades' audience, buoyed by this reminder of the former glory of Greece, clapped to signal that the song applied to the Greek general Philopoemen. κόσμον would still have metapoetic overtones, as often (see Sim. 531.9n.).

ἐλευθερίας: an important concept in Greek accounts of the Persian Wars from early on, e.g. 'Sim.' xxa *FGE*, Pind. fr. 77 (above), Aesch. *Pers.* 402–5. Subsequently, the Athenian empire had made 'freedom' contentious. Sparta presented itself as the liberator of Greece from Athenian domination. Athens used its contribution to the panhellenic struggle for freedom in the Persian Wars as a line of defence. See e.g. Thuc. 6.76–7 and 82–3, and the discussion of Raaflaub 2004.

Fr. 791 PMG

Source: Berlin papyrus inv. 9875 (= Π), alongside the Derveni papyrus our oldest literary papyrus, dating to the fourth century BC. The first edition is Wilamowitz-Moellendorff 1903. On the papyrus, see van Minnen 1997: 247–50 and Hordern 2002: 62–73.

60–85 *The drowning man.* Π becomes legible in the middle of a narrative of death and destruction. Ships are rammed, damaged, sunk, men injured and killed (1–39). In line 40 the focus narrows to one shipwrecked sailor. He seems to be of high standing (42 ἄναξ), but it is unclear whether he is a Persian or a Persian ally (40–2, with Hordern *ad loc.*; 45–6). In the excerpt edited here, a speech (72–81) is preceded and rounded off by accounts of the man's struggles (60–71, 82–5). The narrative stops short of his death, as it does with subsequent speakers. The effect is one of abrupt changes of focus.

In Greek ideology, the inability to swim marks out barbarians; see Hdt. 8.89 and the discussion of Hall 2006: ch. 9. Here drowning is also a concrete manifestation of the abstract notion that the Persians are defeated by the sea itself; for which see 79–80n.

The language creates an ever-fluctuating visual stream, blending elements from the domains of the sea and seafaring, the human body, madness and sympotic conviviality. Connections between these domains are well established, but some of Tim.'s images have a grotesque quality. See further Gargiulo 1996, Budelmann and LeVen 2014: 198–201.

60–1 ὅ]τε … ἐπεισέπιπτον 'Whenever the winds let off in one place, they would attack in another.' τᾶι … τᾶι δ᾽ amounts to τᾶι μέν … τᾶι δ᾽ (cf. LSJ s.v. ὁ A viii 1d), with the two coordinated expressions distributed between sub- and main clause rather than (as is usual) two parallel clauses; cf. Denniston 1954: 179, 378–9.

61 ἐπεισέπιπτον: for winds 'falling' upon land or sea, see e.g. Hes. *Th.* 873, Sa. 47. The ἐπεισ- compound is particularly aggressive.

61–2 †ἀφρωισ|δε†: a dot underneath the σ may indicate deletion, viz. ἀφρωι|δε. The general sense must be that water was foaming. It is likely that a verb in the imperfect is lost. An attractive option is ἀφρῶι δ᾽ ἔ<ζε᾽> 'boiled with foam' (ἔζε᾽ ~ ἔζεε); for the sea seething, see Hes. *Th.* 695–6 and 847 (both ἔζεε), Hdt. 7.188.2. Hordern *ad loc.* discusses further emendations, arguing for ἄφρει δ᾽ (impf., 'foamed').

62 βακχίωτος ὄμβρος 'unbacchic water', a riddling phrase. The context of ingesting eventually makes it clear that the liquid is 'unbacchic' in the sense of 'not wine', viz. unsuitable for drinking and joyless. The context also suggests that ὄμβρος refers to the foaming high sea. Even so the core meaning 'rainstorm' remains active; the drowning man is overwhelmed by an indistinguishable mass of water.

63 τρόφιμον ἄγγος 'alimentary vessel', viz. the stomach, but the phrasing continues the irony of ἀβακχίωτος. The seawater is the opposite of nourishing; the notion of 'pouring (ἐχεῖτο < χέω) into a vessel', unremarkable when wine is poured at the *symposion*, here evokes the masses of water pouring unhindered down the man's throat and into the inappropriate and small 'vessel'.

64–5 'When the surging brine was boiling over from his mouth . . .' He vomits the seawater he just swallowed.

64 ἀμβόλιμος ἅλμα: seawater 'boils' elsewhere (61–2n.), but the phrasing continues the ironical alimentary theme since ἅλμη is also the 'brine' in which food is boiled; e.g. Antiphanes, *PCG* 221.2, Mnesimachus, *PCG* 4.13. The rare ἀμβόλιμος usually means 'adjourned', but 'bubbling up' is attested for the cognate adverb ἀμβολάδην; see esp. *Il.* 21.361–5, a passage that is recalled here. There may be play with ἀναβολή = 'instrumental prelude' of a kitharodic performance: the water spurts from the mouth as a non-vocal prelude to his (sung) speech that follows.

66 ὀξυπαραυδήτωι ('shrilly raving') combines two ideas: (i) Shrill shouts; cf. *Il.* 17.89 ὀξὺ βοήσας and related Homeric phrases. (ii) Senselessness; cf. παραλέγω and παραληρέω 'talk nonsense'. Tim. uses the grander root αὐδ-, deviating from the usual meaning of παραυδάω, 'console'.

67 παρακόπωι τε δόξαι φρενῶν: lit. 'and with the notions of his mind deranged', viz. hallucinating. The phrase has a tragic ring; cf. esp. Aesch. *Ag.* 222–3.

68 κατακορής 'excessive, unrestrained': cf. Pl. *Phdr.* 240e and Aristot. *Rh.* 3.1406a13, who use the word of speech and language. But applied to the drowning man rather than adverbially to his speech, κατακορής also suggests the literal sense of κόρος: the man had a 'surfeit' of water.

ἀπείλει: the imperfect is the chosen narrative tense throughout the long battle narrative. The aorist occurs only in two temporal sub-clauses (163, 173–4) and once at the end (198). The effect is one of (spatially organised) visual description, as opposed to (temporally organised) sequential narrative. The narrator acts as 'painter' (imperfects), rather than 'chronicler' (mix of tenses) or 'eye-witness' (historic presents); see Allan 2013 for these distinctions.

69–71 The general sense is clear: he gnashes his teeth at the sea which is maltreating him. But there are three problems, which can be resolved only speculatively. (i) One would normally expect an accusative with ἐμπρίων ('gnashing together'). (ii) θαλάσσας is impossible to construe. (iii) μιμούμενος is difficult to make sense of: the verb is potentially relevant to Tim.'s mimetic poetics (p. 233), but what is the man imitating? The first two problems can be resolved by emending to acc. γόμφους and dat. θαλάσσαι, 'gnashing his pegs (viz. teeth) at the sea, the destroyer of his body', but as long as μιμούμενος raises questions it is impossible to be confident about the rest of the sentence. Collard proposes δινούμενος 'whirled about'; see Hordern *ad loc.* for further proposals.

69 γόμφοις 'pegs'. The drowning man's body is described in vocabulary appropriate for a boat. The meaning 'tooth' is standard for γομφίος.

72–81 The drowning man's speech. He reminds the sea that Xerxes has tamed it in the past, ἤδη ... καὶ πάρος (72–4); threatens that he will do so again now, νῦν δέ (75–8); then descends into abuse (79–81). Some of what he says about the sea applies to himself: he is overbold (72 θρασεῖα), impetuous (74 λάβρον), roused to a frenzy (75 ἀναταράξει) and maddened (79 οἰστρομανές).

72–4 'Already on a previous occasion, because (or "in spite") of your audacity, you were yoked and had your violent neck in a shackle bound with flax.' Xerxes crossed the Hellespont on a bridge of boats en route to Greece. The phrasing recalls two passages of Aeschylus' *Persians*. (i) The army crossed the Hellespont 'on a floating bridge bound with flaxen ropes (λινοδέσμωι σχεδίαι), yoking the neck of the sea (ζυγὸν ἀμφιβαλὼν αὐχένι πόντου) with a roadway bolted together' (69–71, trans. Hall 1996). (ii) Xerxes cast the Hellespont in 'hammered shackles (πέδαις)' (747–8). Cf. Aesch. *Pers.* 112–14, and Hdt. 7.34–6. It is an indication of progressing calamity that Tim.'s next speaker will wish that Xerxes had never built the bridge (114–16).

72 θρασεῖα: a storm destroyed earlier bridging work. Xerxes had the Hellespont lashed as a punishment, according to Hdt. 7.35.

73 αὐχέν': the metaphor was clichéd; apart from the Aeschylus passage, see Hdt. 4.85.3 and 118.1. It pertains to the elongated shape of the Hellespont, as well as to the image of yoking.

ἐμ: Π contains several instances of -μ for -ν in assimilation to the opening consonant of the next word. This phenomenon is common in Classical inscriptions, and reflects pronunciation.

74 πέδαι ... λινοδέτωι: the bridge of boats, tied together with cables. For its construction, see Hammond and Roseman 1996.

75 ἀναταράξει: a sign of folly. A yet more tumultuous sea is not what a drowning man needs.

76 ἐμὸς ἄναξ ἐμός: the man's emphatic faith in his master, even at the point of death, is an expression of barbarian subservience; cf. 152 ἐμὸς δεσπότης. It contrasts with the indomitable sea and the indomitable Greeks. The repetition conveys emotion.

76–7 πεύ|καισιν ὀριγόνοισιν 'mountain-born pines'. In 13 πεῦκαι are probably 'boats', but here 'stir up' suggests oars. The phrase is picked up by 90–1 ὀρεί|ους πόδας ναός 'the ship's mountain feet' = oars.

77–8 ἐγ|κλήισει: Aeschylus' Darius 'closes up' (κλῆισαι, *Pers.* 723) the Bosporus, but to 'shut in' the (whole) sea is another misguided notion.

78 πεδία . . . ναύταις: an elaborate version of the familiar 'plain of the sea'; cf. Aesch. fr. 150 *TrGF* πεδίον πόντου, and see Mastronarde 1994 on Eur. *Phoen.* 208–10.

79–81 The man concludes by hurling a pair of abusive neuter nominal phrases at the sea. Nouns in -μα are often contemptuous when applied to a person (or here a personification); see Long 1968: 114–20.

79–80 οἰστρομανὲς παλαιομί|σημ' 'you gadfly-maddened long-standing object of hatred'. The topos of the sea as inimical to the Persians is developed by Aeschylus and Herodotus; see Pelling 1997: 6–9 and 1991: 136–9, respectively. Storms destroy the first bridge, and parts of the fleet at Mt Athos; further losses are incurred at Artemisium. παλαιο- may refer to the long-standing topos in addition to the long-standing hate. The 'gadfly' is a reference to Io, who was tormented and driven mad by the gadfly sent by Zeus. The same metaphor occurs at Aristoph. *Thesm.* 325 οἰστροδόνητον, also of the sea.

80–1 ἄπιστον . . . αὔρας: lit. 'treacherous object of the embraces of the wind, which rushes to submerge one'. The phrasing aims at surprise. An ἄπιστον ἀγκάλισμα would normally be an unfaithful lover; cf. Soph. *Ant.* 650 ψυχρὸν παραγκάλισμα (of a bad wife). Yet the sea is unfaithful not to the wind that embraces her but to the sailors.

81 κλυσιδρομάδος: an unusual formation, from κλύζειν ('dash over', of the sea) and δρομάς ('running').

82–5 'Said he, labouring under his choking, and spat out ?horrifying foam, vomiting up from his mouth the deep-sea brine.' Cf. *Od.* 5.322–3 στόματος δ' ἐξέπτυσεν ἅλμην | πικρήν. Ring composition with 64–5 frames the speech. The man's stuggles continue without change.

82 βλοσυράν: 'horrifying' fits here and in several other occurrences, but the meaning is uncertain; see Leumann 1950: 141–8.

84 ἐπανερευγόμενος: the double prefix ἐπαν- makes ἐρεύγομαι more graphic.

85 βρύχιον ἅλμαν: a quotation of Aesch. *Pers.* 397 ἅλμην βρύχιον.

The next two sections centre on a group of Mysians who lament their plight in the midst of the general rout (86–139), and a terrified Phrygian who supplicates one of the Greeks (140–61). The final section in the sequence is dominated by Xerxes (162–95). It begins with a further account of defeat and lamentation, and culminates (in the portion presented here) with Xerxes' own response.

173–95 *Xerxes.*

173–7 Xerxes' show of despair mirrors his surroundings. The army has just been described as lacerating their faces, tearing their clothes and wailing (166–70). Xerxes' entourage laments as it is 'observing (εἰσορώμενοι) the suffering to come' (172). The scene of Xerxes watching the battle from on high was famous: see Aesch. *Pers.* 465–70 and Hdt.

8.90.4. Tim. strips it of what (temporary) grandeur it had, and uses it to
represent the peak of Xerxes' misfortune.

173 ὁ δέ refers back to 171 βασιλέως ('and he'), and is then clarified by
174 βασιλεύς. For such clarifying noun phrases late in the clause, see Allan
2014: 202–4.

173–4 παλινπόρευτον … εἰς φυγήν recaps the earlier narrative of universal flight, as the focus shifts to the king's reaction; cf. 162–3 παλίμπορον
φυ|γὴν … ταχύπορον, and later 182–3 ὀπισσοπόρευ|τον.

174 βασιλεύς: the Persian king, a common usage. On the avoidance of
names, see p. 234.

175 παμμιγῆ: ethnic variation, perhaps also confusion. Different ethnicities were on display in the three earlier speeches (see 60–85n. and the
paragraph before 173–95n.), and the ethnic mix is highlighted in
Aeschylus and especially Herodotus; e.g. Aesch. *Pers.* 53, Hdt. 7.55.2.

176 γονυπετής 'falling to his knees', in despair. An ironical manipulation of the stereotype according to which kneeling before a master is
characteristically non-Greek; see esp. Eur. *Phoen.* 293, the only other pre-
Hellenistic instance of γονυπετής.

αἴκιζε σῶμα: at 70–1, the sea maltreated the body of the drowning sailor.
Now Xerxes maltreats his own body, while metaphorically in a sea of
trouble.

177 κυμαίνων τύχαισιν: lit. 'heaving in his misfortunes'. Two ideas are
combined: (i) swelling emotion; cf. Aesch. *Sept.* 443, LSJ s.v. κυμαίνω 1.2;
(ii) the sea of trouble; see LSJ s.v. κῦμα 1.2b.

178–95 Xerxes' speech falls into two sections: lament of the defeat and
losses (178–88), and preparation for immediate retreat (189–95). The first
part begins and ends with exclamations introduced by ἰώ and followed by
relative clauses. In Aeschylus, the same two-part response is reported by the
Messenger (*Pers.* 465–70). In its place in the work as a whole, however, the
speech is the equivalent of Xerxes' long onstage lament in Aeschylus'
exodus. Like Aeschylus, Tim. has built up expectations through references
to Xerxes (76, 116, 152), while delaying his appearance till the end.
The speech presents an unsympathetic Xerxes. He is narrowly preoccu-
pied with his personal plight and (unlike Aeschylus' Xerxes) sees himself
as a wholly innocent victim of fate.

178 ἰὼ κατασκαφαὶ δόμων quotes Aesch. *Cho.* 50. Charitably read, the
exclamation is concerned with the losses of all Persian families
('houses') rather than narrowly Xerxes' own ('house'). Even then it
strikes an inappropriate note if one recalls that the chorus of *Choephori*
lament the death of their former master, whereas Xerxes is himself the
leader in control.

179 σείριαι 'Sirius-like'. Sirius betokens destruction and heat; see
Alcm. 1.62, Alc. 347.1nn. The Greek ships are a devastating force of

nature in Xerxes' eyes. More specifically, the burning missiles used by the Greeks at 26–8 may come to mind; cf. 183–5(n.).

179–81 αἵ ... πολύανδρον 'which wiped out the many young men in their prime, my contemporaries'. Tim. combines several pieces of phrasing from Aeschylus' *Persians*. (i) 669–70 νεολαία ... κατὰ πᾶσ' ὄλωλεν 'all the young people have been wiped out' (the only other Classical attestation of the rare κατόλλυμι). The death of Persia's young men is a persistent theme throughout the play. (ii) 681 ἥλικες ... ἥβης ἐμῆς 'contemporaries of my youth', Darius' address to the elderly chorus. (iii) 72, 533, 896 πολύανδρος, always of the Persians or their subjects.

180 μέν corresponds to 182 δ(έ), even though the constructions are not parallel.

ἥλικ' has more point if understood as 'contemporary (to me)' than as 'contemporary (to one another)'. Xerxes' errors are attributed to his youth by Darius at Aesch. *Pers.* 744 and 782, and by Xerxes himself at Hdt. 7.13.2.

181 νέων ('of the young men') is preferable to Page's νεῶν or Mazon's ναῶν ('of my ships'), despite the pleonasm. 'Youth of the ships' would be an odd expression; and the transition from the Greek ships in 179 to the Persian ships is rhetorically stronger when it coincides with the nominative νᾶες and the new sentence in 182.

182–3 ἄξουσιμ requires an object and the adjective ὀπισσοπόρευ|τον a noun. The simplest solution is to write οὖ νιν<ν> for οὐκί: the ships will not bring home the young men (νιν = ἥβαν). See Hordern *ad loc.* for other suggestions.

183–5 πυρός ... φλέξει 'but the scorching energy of the fire will burn ?them with its savage body'. Again the Persians are struggling with an elemental force (cf. esp. 79–81). μένος is common of fire, but σῶμα is not; in this very physical poem, rich in suffering bodies (σῶμα at 71, 109, 176), even fire has a body. Fire appears also at 26–7 (burning missiles); and cf. 179n. No other source documents the use of fire at Salamis, but according to Hdt. 9.106.1 the Greeks burned the Persian fleet a year later at Mycale, after killing the men. Tim. may be compressing the two battles into one.

185 στονόεντα δ' ἄλγη: probably 'sorrows rich in groaning', viz. 'sorrows and groaning', rather than 'lamentable sorrows'. The pain and lament of those back home are dramatised by Aeschylus.

187 Again Xerxes sees responsibility elsewhere. The tone is tragic, even without the easy change from ὤ to the characteristically tragic ἰώ (cf. ἰώ in 105 and 178).

188 ἅ ... ἤγαγες: at 152–3 the Phrygian had said that 'my master (viz. Xerxes) brought me here'.

189–95 Abandoning the lament, Xerxes urgently calls on those around him, splitting them up and allocating separate tasks (190–1 μὲν ... οἱ δ'). The final image of the Persians is one of preparation for mass retreat.

190–1 τετράορον ἵπ|πων ὄχημ': according to Hdt. 7.140, an oracle advised the Athenians to flee from 'fire, keen Ares, and the driver of the Syrian chariot'; cf. Aesch. *Pers.* 84–5. Now Xerxes uses the chariot to flee himself.

191–5 οἱ δ' ... πλούτου: an isolated line survives from earlier in the nome: 'Ares is lord; Greece does not fear gold' (fr. 790). The uselessness of Persia's famous wealth proves true here. The destruction of Persia's prosperity through Xerxes' campaign is a theme in Aeschylus; Tim. has Xerxes himself set fire to his possessions.

191–2 ἀνάριθμον ὄλ|βον: ὄλβος often has a material dimension ('wealth', not just 'happiness'), but even so Xerxes' notion that he can preserve his ὄλβος in the midst of general catastrophe is misguided. In Aeschylus, the loss of the mass of men and the loss of the mass of wealth are interlinked; see esp. *Pers.* 166–7, 250–2. Cf. 238 ὄλβωι.

192 ἀπήνας 'carts', probably pulled by mules. Cf. Sa. 44.13n.

193 πίμπρατε δὲ σκηνάς: at sea the Greeks burn Xerxes' navy; on land Xerxes plans to burn the camp. He failed at least in part, and the Greeks came to 'benefit from the wealth'. Mardonius' luxurious tent, believed by some to be passed on to him by Xerxes, was captured at Plataea; see Hdt. 9.70.3, 9.82. Xerxes may have failed also in a metaphorical sense: according to Plut. *Per.* 13.5 and Paus. 1.20.4, the Athenian Odeion, in which Tim. probably premiered *Persians*, was modelled on Xerxes' tent, though it is unclear whether that tradition originated in the fifth century; see further Miller 1997: 218–42 and Power 2010: 545–9.

194 ἡμετέρου: *our* wealth should not fall into *their* hands.

196–201 *The victorious Greeks set up a trophy and sing a paean.* After Xerxes' distraught solo speech in the midst of mass flight, the Greeks act as a community and perform measured choruses. Xerxes is concerned about his riches, while the Greeks give thanks to the gods. In its brevity and sparseness, this section stands apart from the main narrative. The description of the paean creates a fluid transition to Tim.'s own (very different) paean in the *sphragis*; see 202–5n., and cf. Bacch. 17.128–32.

196 οἱ δέ 'the others', viz. the Greeks. The change in metre helps to mark the beginning of a new section.

196–7 τροπαῖα ... τέμενος: lit. 'setting up a trophy as a most holy precinct of Zeus'. The phrasing is very difficult. If there is no corruption, the trophy (Tim. says) is more than a victory-marker; it constitutes a sacred precinct. For trophies as gifts to the gods, cf. Gorgias, *Epitaphios*, DK 82 B6 τρόπαια ἐστήσαντο ..., Διὸς μὲν ἀγάλματα, ἑαυτῶν δὲ ἀναθήματα. The original temporary Salamis trophy was eventually replaced with a permanent stone construction, and a regular ephebic cult for Zeus Tropaios was established at the trophy, but none of the evidence is pre-Hellenistic; see e.g. *IG* II².1028.27–8 (100/99 BC), and further West 1969 and Clairmont 1983: 1.117–18. The text would become easier with Hutchinson's insertion (*apud* Hordern) of καί before Διός: 'setting up a trophy *and* a precinct'.

196 Διός: Zeus (Tropaios) was regularly invoked in connection with trophies; e.g. Eur. *Hcld.* 936–7, *Suppl.* 647–8.

196–9 Παιᾶν' . . . **ἄνακτα:** to 'call on Lord Ieios Paian' is to perform a paean. Victory celebrations were a common occasion for paeans; see Xen. *Hell.* 7.2.15, Rutherford 2001b: 45–7.

199 σύμμετροι must be 'in time'. Cf. σύμμετρον = 'compliant with the metre' at Soph. (1) fr. eleg. 1 *IEG²*.

199–200 ἐπε|κτύπεον 'stamped'. The imperfect expresses sustained dancing after the one-off invocation of Paian (aor. ἐκελάδησαν, 198).

201 ὑψικρότοις 'high-pounding', viz. raising the feet high and stamping them down. The implication must be joyful exuberance, but an olden-day performance style may also be suggested; see *h.Apol.* 516 (Apollo dances ὕψι βίβας), and Aristoph. *Wasps* 1492 and 1524–5, where high kicks seem to be treated as characteristic of the early tragedian Phrynichus.

202–40 *The sphragis.* A *paragraphos* and a *coronis* after 201 mark a new section. The battle narrative ends, and Tim. sings about himself and his mode of composition. The metre grows more uniform (see 'Metre'). In contrast to the main narrative, there are numerous names, of cities as well as individuals. The conventional label *sphragis* ('seal') is derived from the list of structural elements of a nome in Pollux 4.66 (2nd cent. AD).

The central theme is poetic tradition and innovation: Tim.'s work is *both* new *and* traditional. The structure is as follows:

202–5: Appeal for help from Paian-Apollo, supporter of new music. (This follows on from the Greeks' paean just before.)
206–12: This help is needed because Tim. is attacked by the Spartans for composing novel and anti-traditional music.
213–20: Such attacks are unfair because Tim. makes music for everybody; he excludes only those who themselves maltreat the Muse.
221–36: Tim. continues a tradition started by Orpheus and Terpander. It is a tradition of innovation.
237–40: Another invocation of Apollo, now on behalf of the city, ends the nome. On Pollux's scheme these final lines are the 'epilogue', separate from the *sphragis*.

Three considerations help to place Tim.'s self-presentation in context. (i) Composers of all periods sought and sometimes flaunted novelty; for lyric, see Alcm. 14, Bacch. 19.8–10, [Terpander] fr. 4 Gostoli (undatable), and on pre-fourth-century discourses of newness, D'Angour 2011: ch. 8.

(ii) So did Tim. and other composers of the New Music; see above, p. 230. (iii) The New Music did indeed introduce major changes to melodic range, harmonic structure, rhythm and the specification of the musical instruments, and Tim. in particular was considered an innovator in antiquity; see p. 231. What Tim.'s *sphragis* does, then, is reinforce and polemically promote a sense of an unheard level of newness, while pointing to the constant presence of change in the musical tradition.

The tone is elusive. The mode of Tim.'s self-presentation changes continuously: prayer, autobiographical narrative of persecution, explication of his position, abuse, musical history, prayer again (ending with a pun). As in the main narrative, metaphor abounds and some phrases are hyperbolic or provocative. Despite the clear break, there are several verbal and thematic echoes of the main narrative – this is not an altogether detached statement. In all these respects, the *sphragis* is reminiscent of some Aristophanic parabases. Like those parabases it raises (and probably raised already then) questions about the factual accuracy, the sincerity, and even the precise proposition of the claims. As much as anything, the *sphragis* is the culmination of Tim.'s bravura performance. Instead of the voices of others, he now performs his own.

Tim.'s mesmerising self-portrayal draws on a long tradition of complex true-and-false self-presentation not just in lyric, but also epic, iambus, comedy and other genres. In turn, the *sphragis* influenced later texts, notably Callimachus' *Aitia* prologue and *Hymn* 2. It may have stood in dialogue also with *sphragides* of other nomes; cf. the short fr. 796, in which (unlike here) Tim. postures as hostile to the 'old Muse'.

There is a specific intertextual relationship with Pherecrates, *PCG* fr. 155, a comic complaint by the Muse who has been maltreated by the composers of the New Music. Both texts present musical history through a sequence of musicians and their innovations, the last of them Tim., both refer to the polychordic kithara (for which see 229–31n.), and both share the conceit of the abuse of the Muse. We do not know which text is older: either Tim.'s passage is an implicit response to Pherecrates' accusation, or Pherecrates attacks Tim. through a combination of direct insult and parody.

The *sphragis* is the most widely discussed text of the New Music. See in particular: LeVen 2014: 90–101 and 219–20, *Power 2010: 534–45, Csapo and Wilson 2009: 284–6, Wilson 2004: 303–6, Brussich 1999, Nieddu 1993.

202–5 *Appeal to Paian.* As a supporter of new music, Paian (Apollo) is asked to come to Tim.'s aid. The call for help prepares for the account of the altercation with Sparta, and introduces the traditional-and-new Timotheus: traditional in that he aligns himself with Apollo the kitharode, new in that the Muse is new. In invoking Paian, Tim. continues the tradition of the Salamis-paean of yesteryear (197 Παιᾶν', 205 Παιάν), but he manipulates that tradition by asking Paian for assistance in musical rather than martial battles; cf. Ford 2006: 293–4. The background to the lines is the New Musicians' adoption of the customarily aristocratic lyre for performances before broad audiences; see Wilson 2004 and Bundrick 2005: 144–50 and 172, who illustrates how the once popular iconography of Apollo the kitharode became rare and marked.

202 ἀλλ' marks the shift from narrative to prayer; for similar passages, see Denniston 1954: 16.

χρυσεοκίθαριν: the golden lyre is Apollo's traditional instrument; see Sim. 511 fr. 1a.3n.

203 Μοῦσαν νεοτευχῆ 'newly fashioned Muse'. Tim. creates a clash by amalgamating two normally separate models of musical creation (the latter of them more recent): (i) inspiration by the immortal Muses, (ii) 'making' by a human ποιητής, for which see Ford 2002: 131–57.

204 ἐμοῖς: after the army's prayer to you (197–9), here follows mine. **ἔλθ':** cf. Sa. 1.5n. (τυίδ' ἔλθ').

ἐπίκουρος recalls Simonides' appeal for poetic assistance in the Plataea elegy; fr. eleg. 11.20–1 *IEG*² αὐτὰρ ἐγώ[... | κικλήισκω] σ' ἐπίκουρον ἐμοί, ... Μοῦσα; see Rutherford 2007: 634–5.

204–5 ὕμ|νοις: the plural may be poetic ('song'), or may be taken to extend the request to Tim.'s entire output ('songs'); cf. 212 and 215.

205 ἰήϊε signals the genre paean. It may be (as printed here) articulated as the vocative of the cult name Ieios ('invoked by cries') or as the cry itself, ἰὴ ἰέ.

206–12 *Timotheus is attacked by the Spartans.* Lit.: 'For the high-born and long-lived great leader of Sparta, the people, teeming with the flowers of youth, buffets and scorches me, and harasses me with fiery blame, (saying) that I dishonour the older Muse with new songs.' The use of (real, exaggerated or imaginary) criticism as a foil for self-presentation is an established strategy; cf. Aristoph. *Ach.* 630–64 and *Clouds* 518–62. Tim. uses it to advertise his newness: he is so innovative that he suffers persecution. The historicity of the criticism is impossible to assess, and Tim.'s language is vague. For later anecdotes about the musically conservative Spartans' hostility to Tim., see Csapo 2004: 241–5, Prauscello 2009: 172–88.

The accusation that Tim. dishonours traditional music was already pre-empted by Apollo's own championship of the new in 202–3, and is now further discredited by the identity of the accusers. Not only are they Spartans, viz. Athens' enemy, but they themselves mix old (206–7 μακραί|ων) and young (208 ἥβας). Moreover, their political identity is cast as paradoxical. 'The high-born and long-lived great leader of Sparta' will first be understood as an individual commander or king, but turns out to qualify 'the people'. As a whole, the expression suggests the Spartiates, the high-born (206 εὐγενέτας) group of citizens of ancient descent (μακραίων) who formed the core of the Spartan army (cf. 208–9 βρύων ἄνθεσιν ἥβας ... λαός) and dominated a large non-citizen population (207 ἀγεμών). Yet the absurdity, certainly in Sparta, of the notion of the λαός as ἀγεμών, and as old yet youthful, makes fun of Tim.'s (alleged) critics. The grand language is ironical.

206 γάρ: this is why Tim. needs the support of Paian.

206–7 μακραί|ων: if the sentence as a whole refers to the Spartiates, the allusion here is to their claim to descend from Heracles (e.g. Tyrt. 11.1, Xen. *Hell.* 6.3.6). Alternatively, the Gerousia may be suggested, Sparta's council of old men.

208–9 βρύων ἄνθεσιν ἥβας | δονεῖ rearranges the elements of a Homeric simile into a violent and incoherent image: *Il.* 17.55–6 τὸ δέ τε πνοιαὶ δονέουσι | παντοίων ἀνέμων, καί τε βρύει ἄνθεϊ λευκῶι 'the blasts of every kind of wind shake (the young tree), and it teems with white blossoms'. For 'flowers of youth' denoting vigour and fighting spirit, cf. *Il.* 13.484.

209 λαός: often of armies from Homer on, and thus appropriate for the Spartiates, but a λαός always has a leader. ἀγεμών ... λαός is more paradoxical than δημοκρατία.

ἐπιφλέγων: a further change of metaphor. The fire imagery takes up 26–7, 179(n.) and 183–5(n.). It continues with 210 αἴθοπι.

211–12 ὅτι ... ἀτιμῶ: indirect speech; 210 ἐλᾶι ... μώμωι amounts to a verb of blaming.

213–20 *Timotheus denies the accusation.*

213–15 Unlike the Spartans, Tim. (ἐγώ δ') is inclusive. His music is for everybody.

214 ἰσήβαν: a *hapax*, probably 'in their prime, like me'. See p. 234 for Tim.'s age, but the context suggests (also) a metaphorical reading: he occupies a middling position, is not extreme. νέος and ἥβη are usually aligned rather than contrasted, but neither is fixed in its age range. The language echoes 180–1 ἥλικ' ... ἥ|βαν.

215 εἴργω ... ἑκάς: the language grandly inverts the kind of requests to stay away that are associated with ritual language; cf. Callim. *Apol.* 2. ἑκὰς ἑκὰς ὅστις ἀλιτρός, and Horace's adapation for metapoetic scene-setting, *Odes* 3.1 *odi profanum uulgus et arceo.*

216–20 Despite his inclusiveness, there is one group Tim. does exclude (217 ἀπερύκω ~ 215 εἴργω ... ἑκάς): 'the old (i.e. old-fashioned and/or long-standing) violators of the Muse'. The Old Comedy-style compound μουσοπαλαιολύ|μας (216–17) manipulates the charge of 'dishonouring the παλαιοτέραν Μοῦσαν', to throw it back at the traditionalists. The rest of the sentence expands on how those people have been abusing the Muse: through monotony and lack of musicality. The alternative translation 'violators of the old Muse' would also provide good sense, as abuse of

Tim.'s rivals. But Greek compounds tend to place the element that is modified on the right (here λύμαι), with elements on the left modifying everything to their right, viz. μουσο(παλαιολύμας) rather than (μουσοπαλαιο)λύμας; see in general Risch 1974: 189–212.

217 τούτους δ': 'resumptive' δέ. See Denniston 1954: 185.

218 λωβητῆρας ἀοιδᾶν ('debauchers of songs') essentially restates 216–17 μουσοπαλαιολύ|μας, without the qualifier -παλαιο-.

219–20 κηρύκων … ἰυγάς: lit. 'stretching out shouts of shrill- and loud-voiced heralds', viz. shouting rather than singing. For the loud shout of the herald, see e.g. Thgn. 887–8, and for the opposition of herald and singer, Sol. 1. In so far as the insult is specific, it refers to the lesser degree of melodic variation prior to the New Music; cf. the unrefined, shouting Aeschylus at Aristoph. *Frogs* 840–59.

λιγυμακροφώ|νων turns epic λιγύφωνος and λιγύφθογγος into abuse, the former sometimes describing singers and music, the latter an epithet of κήρυκες.

220 τείνοντας: uncertain. Duration ('stretching out') suits the abusive tone better than pitch ('make taut, raise high'). Cf. Aesch. *Pers.* 575, Eur. *Med.* 201 and perhaps Pind. fr. 70b.1, and see Rocconi 2003: 15, 143–4.

ἰυγάς: emphatically not a musical kind of utterance. Cf. Soph. *Phil.* 752 (Philoctetes in pain), Hdt. 9.43.2 (barbarians).

221–36 *A selective history of kitharodic song: Orpheus, Terpander, Timotheus.* This musical tradition is one of constant innovation, Tim. implies, and he himself is not the only innovator. Each entry provides (an allusive expression of) one kitharode's major musical achievement and place of origin. Tim.'s own entry is twice as long as the other two. The numerical sequence 225 δέκα – 230 ἑνδεκακρουμάτοις – 235 δυωδεκατειχέος enhances the sense of continuous and seamless progress.

See 202–40n. for the intertextually related multi-poet musical history in Pherecrates. Interest in early musical history was lively in this period, and was exploited also by other poets of the New Music; cf. Telestes frs. 806 and 810. For discussion, see (apart from the items in 202–40n.) Ercoles 2008 and 2010, Power 2010: 336–45, 350–5, Barker 2014: 29–55; and on the topos of the πρῶτος εὑρετής, Kleingünther 1933.

221–4 Orpheus. He regularly appears as kitharode, e.g. Eur. fr. 752g. 6–14 *TrGF, Ba.* 562. Both his potential as a legitimating model and his psychagogic powers will have appealed to the composers of the New Music.

221 πρῶτος introduces the originator-theme of the passage, and is followed by 225 ἐπὶ τῶι and 229 νῦν δέ. The change of topic, without connective, is abrupt, like some shifts in the main narrative.

ποικιλόμουσος 'varied in his music'. Music is ποικίλος ('elaborate', 'variegated') already in Pindar, e.g. *Ol.* 3.8, *Nem.* 4.14, but ποικιλία was also a watchword for the distinctive style of the New Music, e.g. Aristoxenus fr.

76 Wehrli, and see LeVen 2014: 97–105. Some editors print accusative -μουσον to put the emphasis on the (otherwise unqualified) instrument, perhaps rightly. However, the adjective suits Orpheus sufficiently well to justify Π's text.

222 <χέλ>υν: the supplement is hard to avoid. It preserves Π's -υν and introduces the lyre, in preparation for 231 κίθαριν ἐξανατέλλει. See further Ercoles 2010: 112–14. For Tim., the tortoise-lyre was a traditional instrument, smaller than the kithara he himself would have played, and with fewer strings.

ἐτέκνωσεν: the language of procreation and nurturing contrasts with the terminology of abuse in the previous lines; cf. 228, 231, 235. Orpheus is φορμιγκτὰς ἀοιδᾶν πατήρ ('lyre-player, father of songs') at Pind. *Pyth.* 4. 176–7.

223 υἱὸς Καλλιόπα<ς>: Orpheus' standard parentage, which traces the tradition ultimately back to the Muses. The metre suggests that some text has been lost here. Ercoles 2010: 120–2 suggests Οἰάγρου τε; Oeagrus was Orpheus' father in one tradition.

224 Πιερίαθεν is the most economical emendation of πιεριασενι. 'From' rather than 'in' Pieria because Orpheus passes the lyre on to Terpander in Lesbos; cf. the story of Orpheus' lyre which travelled the sea from Thrace to Lesbos after his death, attested in Phanocles, *CA* fr. 1 and Nicomachus p. 266 Jan.

225–8 Terpander. He is the semi-legendary founder of kitharodic song and inventor of the nome, usually dated to the early seventh century. See Gostoli for testimonia and (dubious) fragments, and Power 2010: part III for his place in the Greek musical imagination.

225–6 'After him, Terpander fashioned the Muse in ten songs.' A difficult sentence, and the text may be corrupt. 'Fashioning the Muse' takes up 203 Μοῦσαν νεοτευχῆ, but 'in ten songs' is riddling. The sandwiching between Orpheus' lyre and Tim.'s eleven-string kithara, together with Terpander's fame as a kitharode, may suggest 'ten strings'. On this interpretation, Tim. subtly casts him as the originator of the polychordic instrument that he himself uses – except that Tim. outdoes him by one string. Elsewhere Terpander invents the *seven*-string lyre, e.g. Strabo 13.2.4 ~ [Terpander] fr. 4 Gostoli, *Suda* τ354. Various emendations have been suggested. The most popular, ζεῦξε for τεῦξε ('yoked the Muse'), would introduce an allusion to the lyre (ζυγόν = crossbar of a lyre, *Il.* 9.187) but does not resolve the fundamental problem of the 'ten songs'.

227–8 'Aeolian Lesbos brought him forth as an object of fame for Antissa.' For the construction, cf. Eur. *HF* 1263–4. Lesbos, and often specifically Antissa, is Terpander's traditional birthplace. Tim. is silent about Terpander's strong connections with Sparta, where he is said *inter* *alia* to have been victorious at the original Karneia festival and to have cured civic tension; see e.g. Hellanicus, *FGrHist* 4 F 85a and *Suda* μ701.

229–36 Timotheus.

229–31 This passage is the likely origin of the later (incorrect) tradition according to which Tim. created the eleven-string kithara; e.g. Nicomachus p. 274 Jan, Paus. 3.12.10. He almost certainly used that instrument to perform *Persians*, and these lines do indeed serve to make it his own, but the phrasing is flexible and best interpreted as the (still hyperbolic but less falsifiable) claim that he gave a new lease of life to the art of kitharody by what he did with rhythms, metres and sounds. For the polychordic kithara pre-Timotheus, see Ion of Chios fr. 32, Pherecrates, *PCG* fr. 155, and several pots listed by West 1992b: 62–4.

229 Τιμόθεος: Tim. names himself and his home town Miletus also in fr. 802. The insistent self-reference is probably a product of the competitiveness of the kitharodic contests as well as Tim.'s poetic self-consciousness. Here the name also continues the third-person catalogue form. In general on self-naming in ancient literature, see Kranz 1961 (Tim. on pp. 27–8).

229–30 μέτροις | ῥυθμοῖς τ': the distinction, such as it is, is probably between the individual 'measures' and the general patterning (iambic, etc); cf. Aristot. *Poet.* 1448b21–2 'μέτρα are parts of ῥυθμοί'. But the point is Tim.'s accomplishments in both.

230 ἑνδεκακρουμάτοις: lit. 'eleven-struck', suggesting 'with eleven notes', and in the context alluding in non-technical language to the polychordic kithara. κρούειν is used for 'striking' a string instrument with a plectrum (LSJ s.v. 5); thus κροῦμα is 'sound', 'note'; cf. Aristoph. *Thesm.* 120 'κρούματα of the Asian (kithara)'. For a different interpretation, and references, see LeVen 2011.

231 κίθαριν: Classical kitharodes played a large lyre with a square body, normally referred to as κιθάρα. The epic term κίθαρις is used here for its traditional ring rather than to suggest a different shape. Cf. 202 χρυσεοκίθαριν.

ἐξανατέλλει 'makes rise up'. For the usage, cf. Aesch. fr. 300.7 *TrGF*, Ap. Rh. 4.1423. The metaphors of human procreation are succeeded by one of natural growth and creation.

232–3 Unlike Xerxes, who at 191–5 tries to take away his wealth with him, Tim. opens up the Muses' treasure. There is a contrast also with the possible model Pind. *Pyth.* 6.7–8 ἑτοῖμος ὕμνων | θησαυρός 'a treasure-house of songs has been prepared' (but not 'opened').

232 πολύυμνον 'rich in song'. Together with 233 Μουσᾶν, the adjective picks up 221 ποικιλόμουσος and 225–6 δέκα ... Μοῦσαν ἐν ὠιδαῖς.

233 θαλαμευτόν 'chambered', 'tucked away', a *hapax*. The θάλαμος is the most secluded room of a house or temple. The adjective gives θησαυρός the nuance 'treasure-trunk', 'safe', rather than 'treasure-house', as in Pindar.

234–6 'Miletus is the city that nurtured him, the city of the twelve-walled people, pre-eminent chief among the Achaeans.' Tim.'s home town of Miletus was a member of the Athenian-controlled Delian League. After one or more failed uprisings, it wrestled free in 412, and then fought on the Spartan side until the end of the Peloponnesian War; see Rubinstein 2004: 1085–6. Tim. avoids these divisive events. Instead he alludes to the uncontentious, ancient *dodekapolis*. This grouping of twelve Ionian cities took joint military and political action against Persia during the Ionian revolt of the 490s, but appears only in its ethnic and religious roles in our sources for the later fifth century; see Hdt. 1.141–6, 6.7.

235–6 δυωδεκατειχέος | λαοῦ: the twelve walls are unlikely to be the walls of Miletus alone. In combination with 'Achaeans', 'twelve' evokes the Ionian *dodekapolis*, cf. Hdt. 7.95.1 δυωδεκαπόλιες Ἴωνες. It is uncertain whether Miletus even had walls when *Persians* was first performed: see Thuc. 3.33.2 with Hornblower 1991–2008 *ad loc.*, Gerkan 1935: 122.

236 πρωτέος: possibly corrupt. If correct, it must be a gen. sg. of πρωτεύς ('pre-eminent chief'), in apposition to λαοῦ. The otherwise unattested noun πρωτεύς relates to πρῶτος as the common ἀριστεύς does to ἄριστος. For the use of the noun (rather than the adjective πρῶτος) as a form of superlative, cf. Dem. 60.10 οἱ μὲν ἐξ ἁπάσης τῆς Ἑλλάδος ὄντες ἀριστεῖς (of the Greeks at Troy). For superlative + ἐξ ('among', 'of'), cf. Hdt. 1.196.2 τὴν εὐειδεστάτην ἐκ πασέων.

Ἀχαιῶν: Hdt. 1.145 reports that the *dodekapolis* traced its descent from twelve cities in Achaea (in the northern Peloponnese). Tim. avoids the term 'Ionian', possibly because Athens, self-proclaimed mother-city of the Ionians, would not have wanted to yield the position of 'pre-eminence among the Ionians' to Miletus, cf. Hdt. 1.147.

237–40 *Epilogue: prayer on behalf of the city.* Ring composition rounds off the *sphragis*: a further invocation of Apollo, and 237–8 ἀλλ' ... ἔλθοις repeats 202–4 ἀλλ' ... ἔλθ'. But now the request is on behalf of the community. It thus harks back also to the victory paean of 197–9. In the course of the *sphragis* Tim. has morphed from a poet persecuted by a city and its λαός (209) into one who represents and helps a (different) city and its λαός. The motif of the foreign poet who benefits a community is common; see D'Alessio 2009a.

Prayers are a regular closural device in Greek lyric; see Rutherford 1997: 44–6. The sense of closure is enhanced by the conventionality of the blessings; for related phrasing, see esp. Pind. *Paeans* 1.9–10 (fr. 52a) and 9. 8–9 (fr. 52k), Bacch. 15.53–6, fr. adesp. 1018b.5–9 *PMG*. Despite this conventionality, the prayer for the city's well-being may have had a specific resonance in war-torn Athens, as similar themes in late fifth-century texts such as Aristoph. *Frogs* and Soph. *OC* suggest. The conventionality is punctured by a pun in the final word.

237 ἁγνάν: for the motif of the sacred city, see Alc. 42.4n., and with reference to Athens, Pind. fr. 75.4 and Bacch. 18.1. There may also be a proleptic note: Apollo's arrival will make the city sacred.

238 τάνδε πόλιν could be applied to any city in which the nome was reperformed. There is also a contrast between 'this' and the cities named before: come here, not there. The same is true for 239–40 λαῶι | τῶιδ'. After the panhellenic vista of the opening (*PMG* 788), the nome closes with a narrower focus.

ὄλβωι 'prosperity': a contrast with Xerxes at 191–2.

239 ἀπήμονι: proleptic, more clearly so than ἁγνάν. The people will be free, or even freed, from suffering.

λαῶι: the populace celebrating the Athenian Panathenaia was variously referred to as λεώς (~ λαός); see Haubold 2000: 183–8.

240 εὐνομίαι 'good order', 'obedience to the laws'. A characteristically flamboyant usage creates a final flourish. εὐνομία was associated with Sparta (e.g. Hdt. 1.65.2, Thuc.1.18.1), and within Athens with oligarchs (e.g. Thuc. 8.64.5, [Xen.] *Ath. pol.* 1.8); see further Ostwald 1969: 62–85 and Smith 2011: 72–6. Tim. provocatively appropriates the term by punning on two meanings of νόμος, 'law' and 'nome'. In this sense a community with εὐνομία is a community that has good nomes, and Tim.'s prayer for this community is a further prayer for his own music and a further self-advertisement. For the dual meaning of νόμος, see Pl. *Laws* 4.722d–e, 7. 799e–800a, [Aristot.] *Probl.* 19.28; and further Power 2010: 215–24.

A *paragraphos* in Π, as well as blank space, indicate that this is the end of the text.

ANONYMOUS SONG

The texts gathered in this section are drawn from what are two very different corpora, popular song (*carmina popularia*: 848, 853, 869 *PMG*) and Attic *skolia* (*carmina convivalia*: 892–6 *PMG*). They share, however, a crucial quality which sets them apart from the other poems in this volume: they are not ascribed to named authors. Both types of song, moreover, focus our attention on the binary of low and high in aesthetics, cultural practice and social stratification.

The modern notion of popular song originated in the Enlightenment, and its articulation since then has been shaped by changing attitudes and scholarly approaches to popular and 'folk' culture in general. There is no equivalent Greek term, and it is not certain that the Greeks would recognise the modern corpus of *carmina popularia* as a coherent genre. This corpus was assembled in the nineteenth century and is marked by considerable variation in subject matter (work songs, begging songs, love songs, cult songs, etc.), tone, geographic origin, dialect and date (often impossible to determine). Nevertheless, it is clear that already in the Classical period what we call popular song was considered distinct from the work of well-known poets. In Aristophanes' *Frogs* Dionysus accuses 'Aeschylus' of creating 'rope-winders' songs' (1297), and in *Clouds* Pheidippides mockingly compares the sympotic practice of singing Simonides to the singing of a woman grinding barley (1358): in both cases, the joke depends upon a recognised difference between the two types of song.

An important characteristic of popular song is its anonymity. In a culture which, from very early on, associated many lyric pieces with named authors, anonymous song sits in a different category; cf. p. 5. Beyond anonymity, the question of what sets popular song apart becomes more difficult, but at least a partial answer is provided by a set of formal features that recur throughout the corpus: brevity, straightforward modes of verbal expression, short sentences, simple rhythms, repetition and parallel structures, avoidance of enjambment, second-person address. Together these features amount to a particular kind of simplicity, which goes a certain way towards distinguishing popular song from what over time became canonical lyric, and vice versa.

However, not only do all of these features occur also in the canonical lyricists (though not with the same frequency and rarely in the same concentration), but side by side with them we find in some popular songs reminiscences of high genres like tragedy; see esp. on 853 below, also e.g. the high choral idioms in the Cretan hymn to Zeus (Furley and Bremer 2001: no. 1.1). Popular song (like much popular culture across the ages) can be markedly polyphonal, and by no means everything about it is 'simple'. A boundary exists between popular song and canonical lyric, but it is porous.

This porousness extends from form to use. More often than not, popular songs will have been sung in what might indeed be classified as 'popular' settings and will have performed a traditional function. Labourers sing while they work (see on 869), children sing as they knock at doors to collect gifts (see on 848). But in the song culture of early Greece, in which poetry was commonly reperformed and repurposed, and in which literary and musical ambition did not exclude social function, the distinction between popular and non-popular settings is fragile. Civic festivals were occasions for both the premiere of Pindaric odes and the rendition of traditional songs (e.g. *carm. pop.* 871, a cletic appeal to Dionysus from Elis). Symposiasts too could sing classics by the famous poets of the past and anonymous pieces alike. With several of the *carmina popularia* it is difficult to determine a typical performance setting altogether, popular or otherwise (see on 853), and some were taken up in other, more formal, poetry (see on 848: Aristophanes, possibly Phoenix of Colophon).

Unlike popular song, *skolion* is an ancient category. The great majority of our Attic *skolia*, including the five selected here, are transmitted as a group by Athenaeus, who describes them as 'those (i.e. the famous) Attic *skolia*', while also providing a discussion of the genre (15.693f–696a). They are short texts of typically 2–4 lines, sung at *symposia*, and include prayers (cf. p. 191), proverbial wisdom, witticism, amorous fantasies and songs celebrating Athenian history and ideology. Most scholars date them to the late sixth and the fifth century, and Athenaeus' collection itself may well derive from a fifth-century songbook put together for sympotic use, rather than from a later scholarly edition. Some impression of how these songs could be performed may be gained from a comically distorted *symposion* scene in Aristophanes' *Wasps* (1219–49, the term σκόλια at 1222). Symposiasts take turns singing to the accompaniment of an *aulos*-player, and part of the fun lies in 'capping' one another's lines with a wittily appropriate continuation.

The strong ties to the *symposion* may suggest that *skolia* were an elite pursuit more than a form of popular culture. However, for the *skolia* about the tyrannicides in particular there are good reasons to posit non-elite performances (893–6, p. 266), and only very few of the pieces point to an exclusively elite ideology. The brevity of the *skolia*, moreover, and the accompanying *aulos*-player, who removes the need for the singers themselves to play the lyre, make the Attic *skolia* accessible to performers with minimal musical education. If popular song could cross the boundary from popular to elite, *skolia* could cross the boundary from elite to popular.

Athenaeus' collection is anonymous, but the anonymity of *skolia* is less absolute than that of popular song. A character in Aristophanes requests 'a *skolion* from Alcaeus or Anacreon' (*PCG* fr. 235; what these *skolia* are we do not know). Three of Athenaeus' *skolia*, 890, 893 and 897, are in other (post-Classical) sources attributed, respectively, to Simonides, Epicharmus or Aristotle, to Kallistratos, and to Alcaeus, Sappho or Praxilla. Another, 891, is a reduced version of a song of Alcaeus (fr. 249), which cuts a single stanza out of Alcaeus' longer composition, thus converting it into a self-standing piece of gnomic thought, and changes most of Alcaeus' Aeolic forms to the Attic with which performers were familiar. Even though this may be an exceptional case, two conclusions suggest themselves. On the one hand, the Alcaean origin supports the notion that *skolia* have strong ties with an elite sympotic performance culture. On the other, the textual adjustments demonstrate that a form of simplification can come with the loss of author. In their own way, Attic *skolia* differ from the poetry of named poets.

Beyond the anonymous Attic *skolia*, much remains unknown about the genre. The term first occurs in a rather more elaborate and substantial Pindaric composition for a Corinthian patron (fr. 122), and separately Pindar is reported to have named Terpander as the originator of the genre ([Plut.] *De mus.* 28.1140f); clearly, for Pindar *skolia* were not a lesser genre. Two further fragments of Pindar (125, 128) are cited as *skolia* in later sources, and there was a debate over whether Aristotle's song for Hermias (Aristot. 842 *PMG*) was a *skolion* or a paean; see Athen. 15.696a–b. The genre must either have been considerably more capacious than the anonymous Attic *skolia* lead one to believe, or the meaning of the term was not stable; on this question, see Harvey 1955: 162–3, Jones 2016.

Even less clear is the origin of the term σκόλιον: what is 'crooked' about the genre? An ancient debate is reported by Σ Pl. *Gorg.* 451e (= *scol.* test. 2 Campbell, cf. 893.1n.); one view reported there is that the term points to the crooked, viz. non-linear, order in which symposiasts took turns singing these songs. Numerous further theories have been put forward by modern scholars; see Liberman 2016: 51–60 for references. Particularly noteworthy is that of Martin 2017, who suggests that a song becomes a *skolion* when it is performed 'slant-wise', viz. avoiding direct comment on other symposiasts. It is unlikely that the matter will be settled.

Yatromanolakis 2009 provides a brief account of both popular song and *skolia*. Lambin 1992 is a book-length treatment. For the Attic *skolia*, see the commentary of Fabbro 1995 and the general discussion of Vetta 1983. Capping is discussed by Collins 2004: 84–134. The *carmina popularia* lack a full commentary. Neri 2003 provides an edition, and Magnani 2013a studies the modern history of the collection. For methodologically relevant discussion of issues of high and low in other ancient genres, see Hunter 2002, Avlamis 2011: 65–86, Grig 2017, and beyond antiquity Burke 2009.

carm. pop. *848* PMG

Conventionally labelled 'swallow song', the piece seems to have been performed by children (19) as they went from house to house, celebrating and enacting the arrival of the first swallow of the year, and collecting gifts. The text is probably complete.

PMG 848 is what is best called a begging-and-blessing song. Other examples include: (i) the *Samian Eiresione*, Hom. *epigr.* 15 = *Vita Homeri Herodotea* 33 West, attributed to Homer (an *eiresione* is a branch hung with first fruits and carried in procession); (ii) the *Kiln*, Hom. *epigr.* 14 = *Vit. Hom. Her.* 32, likewise attributed to Homer; (iii) the crow-song by the Hellenistic poet Phoenix of Colophon, *CA* fr. 2. All these songs, *PMG* 848 included, act out a reciprocity of taking and bestowing, of prosperity gained and prosperity shared. See Schönberger 1980 and Lambin 1992: 351–75.

The swallow was a potent symbol in Greek culture, exploited in poetry, iconography and ritual practice. Above all, it is a harbinger of spring; e.g. Hes. *WD* 568–9, Sim. 597, Aristoph. *Knights* 419 and the late sixth-century pot *ARV*² 1594/48. Like many portents, the swallow was often accorded agency and efficacy. According to a proverb, 'one swallow does not make (ποιεῖ) a spring' (Cratinus, *PCG* fr. 35; Aristot. *NE* 1.1098a), and Hippon. 172 speaks of 'a remedy against swallows'. In *PMG* 848 the swallow 'brings' fine spring and a fine year (2 ἄγουσα), and poses a threat.

Athenaeus and his source Theognis (see 'Source') maintain that the song is performed annually at Lindus on Rhodes, and was first introduced by Cleobulus, the seventh- or sixth-century ruler of Lindus and frequent member of the canon of the Seven Sages. The *aition* is probably fictional, but the notion of *PMG* 848 as an institution with a fixed place in the community's calendar is plausible; for children, women and men collecting on behalf of the community and its deities, see Burkert 1985: 101–2.

Similarities of phrasing with the *Samian Eiresione* suggest that the song belongs to a tradition that reached beyond Rhodes (1–5, 13, 19nn.). The earliest reference to *PMG* 848 may be in Aristophanes (1–5n.), which would provide a *terminus ante quem* for the existence of the song, and its circulation in Attica.

The language of the transmitted text blends forms characteristic of Doric and thus in keeping with a Rhodian origin of the song, with forms characteristic of Attic and *koine* Greek. Almost all of the distinctively Doric or Attic forms are metrically neutral and therefore not guaranteed: on the one hand, Doric α in λευκά and τάν, as well as two instances of the 1st pers. pl. ending -μες; on the other, Attic/Ionic εἰ (rather than αἰ) and μιν (rather than νιν), as well as three instances of the 1st pers. pl. ending -μεν. Only one change from Attic to Doric, ἄν > αἴ κα in 17, would affect the metre, but the line is metrically uncertain. The strongest candidate for a metrically guaranteed Doric form is often thought to be the short fem. acc. pl. -ᾱς in 2, but see 'Metre'.

As a consequence of these uncertainties, we do not know whether (i) the song does indeed go back to Archaic Rhodes and was composed in Doric, or whether (ii) it was composed in the Classical period or even later, in a mix of Attic and Doric, like for example Theocritus' *Idylls*. If it was originally Doric, the Attic forms will have entered the text gradually as it was performed and copied by speakers of *koine* Greek. However, one can also envisage, conversely, Doricising pressures as performers and writers wanted to strengthen the supposed Archaic and Rhodian character of the song. The text is printed here for the most part as transmitted (and conjectures designed to produce a homogeneous dialect are omitted from the apparatus), even though it is unlikely that it was ever performed exactly like this. The mixed-dialect text acknowledges the impossibility of restoring a putative original version with any degree of confidence and serves as a reminder that this was a changing song that reflected the language of its (Classical and later) users while audibly carrying with it a (real or imagined) earlier tradition.

The tradition of swallow songs continued into Late Antiquity and then Byzantine and modern Greece; see Herzfeld 1977 and 2004, Alexiou 2002: 87–94.

Source: Athen. 8.360b–d, with reference to an otherwise unknown scholar by the name of Theognis, on whom see *BNJ* 526. The text is transmitted both in A (Marcianus gr. 447, probably 10th cent.), which has the full text of Athenaeus, and in C (Parisinus suppl. gr. 841) and E (Laurentianus LX.2), which preserve an Epitome. It is disputed whether superior readings in CE, as in line 9 of the text adopted here, are conjectures or stem from an independent witness; see Arnott 2000. B (Laurentianus LX.1), a late MS dependent on A, is cited only once (in 9), where its deviation from A, though almost certainly either a conjecture or error, deserves consideration. Lines 1–5, 11–15 and 18–19 are also cited by Eustathius (*Od.* p. 1914.45–9), whose text deviates from CE only in error.

Metre:

```
— —        ∪ ∪ — — ?‖
∪ ∪ —      ∪ ∪ — —  ‖   or ∪ — —   — ∪ — —  ‖
— ∪ —      ∪ ∪ — — ?‖
∪ ∪ —      ∪ ∪ — — ?‖
— ∪ —      ∪ ∪ — —  ‖                                5
∪ ∪ — —    ∪ ∪ — ?‖
— —          ∪ ∪ — —  ‖
— —          ∪ ∪ — — ?‖
— —          ∪ ∪ — — ?‖
— —          ∪ ∪ — — ?‖                             10
— ∪ ∪ —  — — ∪ —  — — ?‖ ch ia ia∧∧ ?
∪ ∪ ∪ ∪ —  ∪ — ∪ —  ∪ —  ‖ ia ia ia∧∧ ?
```

13–19 each line *3ia*, except 17 †— —∪— ∪∪∪—∪∪—† (13 μή,͜ οὐκ 14 τὸ͜ ὑπ–)

Rhythmically, the song falls into two parts, each consisting of a fairly regular run of simple rhythms: 1 to 10 and 13–19, with uncertainty over 11–12.

The interpretation of the first part is difficult. The analysis above, as a sequence of loose ionic dimeters, is broadly that of West 1982a: 147. The alternative would be to establish a sequence of reiziana (× – ∪ ∪ – ×), more or less uniform, depending on the degree of emendation. The ionic interpretation presumes considerable variation on the ionic base rhythm

(˘ ˘ – –): often one or more elements are omitted, especially from the verse-initial metra, and the opening biceps is often contracted (– for ˘ ˘). The extent of this variation suggests that the shorter metra may be best analysed as 'syncopated' versions of the standard ionic; i.e. elements are amalgamated rather than elided, and the metron as a whole retains its standard duration. Such syncopation would give the rhythm a marked regularity.

Line 2 is often analysed with the short 1st decl. acc. pl. endings that are characteristic of certain forms of Doric (καλᾶς, ὥρᾶς). But the line does not lose its basic ionic shape if the alphas are pronounced long. No such ambiguity affects the 2nd decl. acc. pl. in 3, where the metre makes long -ους more likely than short -ος. (Acc. in short -ος is parallel to acc. in short -ᾱς in the development of the language, but literary dialects can adopt one without the other; see West 1966b: 85 for Hesiod.)

The second part consists of iambic trimeters. The exception is 17, which is impossible to analyse in keeping with its surroundings and must be corrupt.

The transitional lines 11 and 12 are difficult. The analysis tentatively suggested above presumes double syncopation at line-end, which slows down the song in the shift from one type of rhythm to another.

Discussions: *Palumbo Stracca 2014, Magnani 2013b: 51–6, Griffith 2000, Martín Vásquez 1999, *Stehle 1997: 39–41, *Lambin 1992: 361–6, Schönberger 1980: 17–42, Adrados 1974, Morelli 1963.

1–5 *Arrival of the swallow.* In performance, it is not just the swallow that has arrived but also the swallow-singers who enact its arrival, a connection made explicit in the *Samian Eiresione* (v. 11), νεῦμαί τοι νεῦμαι ('I will return') ἐνιαύσιος ὥστε χελιδών. The first line may be alluded to at Aristoph. *Birds* 679–80 ἀηδοῖ, | ἦλθες ἦλθες; see Dunbar 1995 *ad loc.* The arrival motif is shared with literary choruses: e.g. Alcm. 3.8, Pind. *Parth.* 2.39–41.

2–3 ὥρας ... ἐνιαυτούς: along with the fine season (viz. spring), the singers, who perform only once a year, promise a fine year. The plurals are either poetic or express the annual recurrence.

4–5 If the singers are costumed as swallows or carry a replica swallow, the attention to the appearance of the swallow invites a performance routine. At the same time, the reference to the swallow's white breast and black back may symbolise its power to do both good and harm.

6–11 *Request for gifts of food.* A range of traditional and affordable foods are named, as is common at many Greek festivals (Parker 2005: 184–6), and as suits the request of beggars. Cf. Phoenix, *CA* fr. 2 and the Athenian *eiresione* poem transmitted by Plut. *Thes.* 22.5 (= *carm. pop.* 2 Diehl). Some of the vocabulary is rare, perhaps because the food items are too humble for most surviving genres, or else because the song derives ritual overtones from hints of obscurity.

6 παλάθαν: a pressed fruit cake, often made with figs. A παλάθη was carried at the head of the Athenian Plynteria procession, symbolising the original cultivated food; see Hesych. η68 and Photius η37. According to the historian Menecles (*FGrHist* 270 F 8) the Athenian *eiresione* included cakes baked in various round shapes.

οὐ προκυκλεῖς 'won't you roll out?' The verb occurs only here. The hyperbolic image expresses the alleged vast wealth of the house, and perhaps plays with the shape of the cakes. The tone is blunt. For οὐ + pres. indic. in questions that amount to commands, see Aristoph. *Knights* 728, Pl. *Lys.* 203b3; further Rijksbaron 2002: §5.2.

8 δέπαστρον: a rare variant of δέπας 'cup'.

9 τυροῦ: in view of 8 οἴνου, sg. τυροῦ or τυρῶ ('severe' Doric) is more likely than pl. τυρῶν.

κάνυστρον: a rare variant of κάνεον 'basket'. There is a case for emending to the slightly better attested κάναστρον, to strengthen the rhyme with 8 δέπαστρον.

10 πύρνα 'wheat-breads': an emendation of πυρῶν ἁ. If the MS reading is kept, sentence-end moves from the end of 9 to after πυρῶν ('basket of cheese and wheat'), but the sentence-break mid-verse would be awkward. An alternative emendation is πυρῶνα (acc., also 'wheat-bread'?), which is sg. like λεκιθίταν and an even simpler change, but the word is attested only once and with uncertain meaning (see LSJ s.v.). Palumbo Stracca 2014: 69–70 proposes καὶ πυρῶν ... καὶ λεκιθιτᾶν οὐκ ἀπωθεῖται, but the partitive genitives ('some of the wheat and of the breads') are difficult with ἀπωθεῖται.

11 λεκιθίταν: probably 'pulse bread', *sc.* ἄρτον. For ἄρτος λεκιθίτης, see e.g. Athen. 3.111b and 114b.

12–17 *Threats, increasingly specific and hyperbolic.* The addressee misses various imaginary opportunities to respond.

12 'Are we to leave <without getting anything>, or will we get <something>?'

13 εἰ μέν τι δώσεις: at least verbally, the apodosis is left unexpressed ('then all is well', 'then we shall leave you in peace'). The emphasis is on the threat. The *Samian Eiresione* uses similar language, εἰ μέν τι δώσεις· εἰ δὲ μή, οὐχ ἑστήξομεν (14); and cf. *Il.* 1.135–9.

οὐ ἐάσομεν 'we shan't leave you in peace'.

14–16 The threat of violence against home and wife is a threat to the addressee's honour. Hyperbolically, and in the mouths of children incongruously, the song develops the komastic topos of forcing entrance and behaving transgressively towards the women in the house; cf. Lysias 3.6

and fr. 279.5 Carey, Herodas 2.34–7 with Headlam 1922 *ad loc.*
The questions pick up from 12: '... Or shall we carry off ...?'
14 ὑπέρθυρον 'lintel' and/or 'architrave'. At Herodas 2.65 the door
seems to be forced by singeing τὰ ὑπέρθυρα. Complete removal, as threa-
tened here, would bring the wall down. **16 μικρά:** not a compliment. Tall women were admired.
17 resumes the request of 13, and reverses the language of 16: *you bring*
something big. For the cruces, see 'Metre' above.
18–19 *Coda.*
18 Repetition of the verb, followed by χελιδόνι, echoes line 1, to round
off the song. The verse may be understood as a continuation of the request
for gifts or as a return to the celebration of the swallow's coming that
opened the song: the two themes coalesce. Cf. Phoenix, *CA* fr. 2.8.
19 Self-referential statements are a well-established closural device in
lyric; e.g. Ibyc. S151.47–8, Bacch. 17.130–2. Here, the singers' identity as
children propitiously deflates the earlier threats. The *Samian Eiresione* ends
with a similar line: οὐ γὰρ συνοικήσοντες ἐνθάδ' ἤλθομεν.

carm. pop. *853* PMG

A woman tries to wake her lover before they are discovered. The song may
or may not be complete.

The song adopts the tone of tragic lament, but the theme of the
unfaithful woman belongs to comedy and 'adultery mime'; cf. Aristoph.
Thesm. 467–519, Herodas 1 and 5; further Trenkner 1958: 80–4,
McKeown 1979. The language mixes high and low. Men might perform
the piece at the *symposion*, women might sing it while working, or it might
be taken up by more elaborate performers, such as the lewd, cross-dressing
magodoi, whose acts included adulterous women according to Athen.
14.621c–d.

Athenaeus cites *PMG* 853, without author, as one of the 'Locrian songs',
which he characterises as μοιχικαί, 'adulterous' (see 'Source'). Elsewhere
he cites Clearchus, a pupil of Aristotle's, as saying that 'the erotic and so-
called Locrian songs are no different from those of Sappho and Anacreon'
(14.639a = fr. 33 Wehrli). It follows that 'Locrian songs' go back to at least
the fourth century and were somehow racy, but little else is known about
them; see further Lambin 1992: 33–7 and De Martino 2006: 272–6.
Epizephyrian Locris, on the south-eastern coast of modern Calabria, had
a rich song-making tradition; see Bellia 2012. It is also possible that Locris
gave its name to the songs not because they originated there but because
Locrian women were associated with adultery and sexual licence; for these
associations, see Aristot. fr. 547 Rose, Justin 21.3, and further Redfield
2003: ch. 7.

Beyond the 'Locrian songs', *PMG* 853 belongs to a tradition of high and low lyric treatments of female amorous voices. See in particular the amorous song exchange between a girl inside and a man outside at Aristoph. *Eccl.* 952–75, and two anonymous Hellenistic texts, the song by the abandoned woman in the *Fragmentum Grenfellianum* and the fragmentary lyric exchange between two lovers inscribed in Marisa in Judaea (*CA* p. 184), with the discussions of Hunter 2005 and Esposito 2005: 59–70. More distantly related are aubades, songs of lovers parting at dawn, which are traditional in many cultures and are reflected in Hellenistic epigram; cf. *AP* 5.3, 5.172, 12.136–7, and see Hatto 1965, Klinck 2002: 21–5. The persistence of such traditions makes it is impossible to tell whether *PMG* 853 predates Clearchus' account of 'Locrian songs' in the fourth century, or is Hellenistic.

As with *carm. pop.* 848 (pp. 256–7), we do not know in what (vernacular or literary) dialect the text was first composed, and it is therefore best not to standardise the text. The Epizephyrian Locrians spoke a form of Doric (see Blomquist 1975), and the transmitted text does indeed contain the Doric forms ἀμέρα and τᾶς. On the other hand ἄμμ' is Aeolic, and μολεῖν (MS μολιν), κεῖνον (see n.) and τήν are Ionic, though easily amended to Doric.

Source: Quoted by Athenaeus' character Cynulcus at 15.697b–c, in the context of talking of 'sensuous songs'. He notes that 'the so-called Locrian songs, which have to do with illicit sex, belong in this category' (trans. Olson), and gives *PMG* 853 as an example, adding that Phoenicia is 'full of such songs'.

Metre

```
‒ ◡ ‒ ‒   ‒ ◡ ‒ ‒   ◡ ◡ ‒ ‒  ?‖    3 io
‒ ‒ ◡ ‒ ‒   ◡ ◡ ‒ ‒  ?‖   ‒ 2 io
‒ ◡ ‒ ◡ ◡   ◡ ◡ ‒ ‒  ?‖   2 io
‒ ◡ ‒   ‒ ◡ ‒  ?‖   ∧ia ∧ia
‒ ◡ ‒   ‒ ‒ ◡ ‒   ◡ ‒ ◡ ◡ ◡   ‒ ‒ ‒ ◡ ‒  ?‖   ∧ia 3 ia (διά sung as a single syllable)
```

As analysed here the overall pattern is ionic and iambic, but text (3–4n.) and analysis are uncertain because there is only one stanza. An overall trochaic analysis might be thought more satisfactory, but would involve heavier emendation. The metre is discussed by Wilamowitz-Moellendorff 1889–90: 22 and 1921: 344, and West 1982a: 149.

Discussions: Yatromanolakis 2007: 291–3, De Martino 2006: 272–6, *Petropoulos 2003: 131–3, *Lambin 1992: 33–7.

1 τί πάσχεις; 'what's wrong with you?', in the sense of 'why are you being stupid?' The phrase tends towards the colloquial; see e.g. Aristoph. *Wasps* 1 (waking up a sleeper for fear of being caught), and further Stevens 1976: 41.

ἱκετεύω can cover the full range from formal supplication to everyday 'please', and gains its nuance from the context.

2 καί lends emphasis to the whole clause: before 'it even gets to the point that' he comes home.

μολεῖν: the register of high poetry, especially tragedy; e.g. Eur. *Ion* 332 πρὶν πόσιν μολεῖν.

κεῖνον: for the lovers, the husband is just 'he'. Cf. Herodas 1.42 κεῖνος ἦν ἔλθηι, of the potential return of the legitimate partner. After μολεῖν, the Ionic form of the word (Attic ἐκεῖνον) may continue the tragic tone.

ἀνίστω ~ ἀνίστασο: imperative.

3–4 μή ... κἀμέ 'lest you do a great harm to yourself and me'. Α σε to accompany κἀμέ is likely to be lost somewhere in the sentence as transmitted. Placing it after κακόν produces (on an ionic analysis) the most regular metre, but this is guesswork. For the reflexive σε, cf. Eur. *Phoen.* 437 παῦσαι πόνων σὲ κἀμὲ καὶ πᾶσαν πόλιν, Aesch. *Sept.* 254, and *CGCG* §29.17. Most editors emend to third person ποιήσηι, which produces good sense ('lest he does great harm to you and me'), but there is no reason to break the run of second persons.

4 δειλάκραν ('miserable') as well as δειλακρίων otherwise only occur in comedy.

5 καὶ δή: 'look'; see Denniston 1954: 250–1. More dramatic than the transmitted καὶ ἤδη, but the difference is small.

carm. pop. *869* PMG

A very brief but quite possibly complete grinding song, which could be repeated continuously to accompany the monotonous task of working the mill. It could be sung by women or men. Grinding will often have been an individual task but in larger households workers might grind (and sing) as a group; cf. the twelve grinding women at *Od.* 20.105–8, and the late sixth-century BC terracotta Louvre B116, which depicts four bakers kneading bread to the sound of an *aulos* (photograph in Mollard-Besques 1954: vol. I, plate xv).

Grinding songs were sufficiently common for ancient scholars to include them in taxonomies of musical genres (Athen. 14.618c–d, Pollux 4.53), and songs accompanying various aspects of food preparation are mentioned in comedy, e.g. winnowing at Aristoph., *PCG* fr. 352 and hulling at Aristoph. *Clouds* 1358. Closest among surviving texts are *carm. pop.* 849 ('Let me have the largest sheaf, a sheaf, let me have a sheaf') and the fragmentary *P.Ryl.* 1.34, on which see Gronewald 1988. For a collection of grinding songs from other cultures, see Bücher 1899: 60–77, and for the uses and significance of work songs, Gioia 2006.

The logic is: 'Even grand Pittacus milled his own flour; hence so must you/I.' Pittacus' willingness to do humble work chimes with his status as a sage (for which see p. 94 above). Some singers may have given the exemplum an abusive slant: Pittacus as a 'grinding' ruler, who crushed his opposition and exploited his people; cf. Alcaeus' Pittacus who 'devours' his people (129.23–4n.). There is also room for sexual innuendo: ἀλεῖν 'grind' = 'screw'; cf. the synonymous μύλλειν at Theoc. 4.58–9.

It is very possible that the song originated in Lesbos, whether or not in Pittacus' day. Much of the dialect is compatible with the language of Alcaeus and Sappho, esp. the first-declension endings with alpha, -α, -ας (but Μυτιλήνας is an emendation). A likely *terminus ante quem* is provided by Clearchus, who in the late fourth century BC records a story, attested also in later writers, according to which Pittacus ground corn to take exercise (fr. 71 Wehrli = Diog. Laert. 1.81).

Source. Plutarch's Thales cites the text in *The Dinner of the Seven Wise Men* (*Mor.* 157e), claiming that he had heard his hostess sing it when he stayed in the Lesbian city of Eresos. Pittacus, who is present, does not comment.

Metre:

⏑ – ⏑ – ⏑ – ?‖
– – – ⏑ ⏑ – – ?‖
⏑ ⏑ – ∧ ⏑ ⏑ – – ⏑ ⏑ – – ‖

The metre is very uncertain. As set out here, lines 2 and 3 are ionic. The analysis of line 1 assumes hiatus without shortening after μύλᾱ, so as to create the regularity that one might expect in a grinding song. For the same reason, it is tempting to think that the final syllable of μεγάλας was protracted, thus creating rhythmical regularity also in lines 2–3. After the brisk base unit ⏑ –, lines 2 and 3 would change to the longer ⏑ ⏑ – – (and then the singers return to the opening).

Discussions: Karanika 2014: 144–53 ~ Karanika 2007: 138–45, Lambin 1992: 170–1, Bowra 1961: 131–2, Blumenthal 1940, Wilamowitz-Moellendorff 1890: 225–7.

1 'Grind, mill, grind.' The apostrophe turns arduous use of an inanimate tool into a dialogue. The repetition mirrors the repetitiveness of the grinding.

μύλα: in the Archaic and Classical periods mills were probably not yet rotary and required laborious rubbing of the upper stone to and fro across the lower stone; see Moritz 1958: esp. chs. 1, 6–8.

2 ἄλει: the imperfect is metrically easier. However, (timeless) present ἀλεῖ cannot be ruled out.

3 μεγάλας need not be conventional: Pittacus too (καί) did his own grinding, despite ruling over a great city.

Μυτιλήνας: gen. sg. The MSS' Μιτυ- may have been in Plutarch's text, but will not go back to the Classical period or earlier. It first appears around 300 BC, e.g. *Syll.*³ 344.30.

βασιλεύων: value-neutral. Alcaeus calls Pittacus a 'tyrant' in fr. 348 (but established in that position by the people) and probably also fr. 75, and may call him a βασιλεύς at fr. 5.14. Cf. p. 87.

carm. conv. *892* PMG

This Athenian *skolion* turns on a pun: the notoriously cunning and twisting snake is threatened with becoming 'straight' in death. The song exemplifies the appetite for wordplay at the *symposion*.

The moralising statement and the use of animal protagonists are reminiscent of fables, and indeed a related fable survives under Aesop's name in a collection from the Roman period (no. 196 Perry). A snake and a crab are living together. The snake does not repay the crab's decent and sincere behaviour, despite the crab's exhortations. Angered, the crab grabs and kills the snake, and makes a comparable (though less punning) statement about the need to be sincere. The fable ends with a moral about the need for proper behaviour towards friends.

The *skolion* is self-standing, but the narrative compression suggests that some version of the fable was already current; cf. 1n. Fables and fable-like narratives were popular in Athens certainly as early as Aeschylus; cf. Aesch. fr. 139 *TrGF*, and see further Nøjgaard 1964–7: 1.454–63, Jedrkiewicz 1989: 346–94. The potential that fables present for indirect moralising and attack is sometimes exploited in poetry, e.g. Hes. *WD* 202–12 (nightingale and hawk), Archil. frs. 172–81 (eagle and fox). Further on the genre fable, see Holzberg 2002 and Kurke 2011: esp. ch. 3.

The sparseness of the *skolion*'s narrative, lacking both the full account of the snake's earlier misbehaviour and the concluding authorial statement of the fable, makes this a more open-ended piece (cf. already Hesiod's use of the fable of the nightingale and the hawk). (i) The song makes an ethical statement yet is also humorous. (ii) It is unclear whether, as in the fable, the snake deserves its death, and the accusation of crookedness may also be levelled at the crab, which is known for its sideways walk. (iii) The attack on the snake's σκολιός disposition is delivered in a song that was classified as a *skolion* in later periods and may well have been known as one already then (on the term see above, p. 255).

As transmitted, the language is markedly non-Attic in two places: χαλᾶι (Attic–Ionic χηλῆι) and ἔμμεν (εἶναι), an Aeolic form used in Homer and choral lyric but very rare even in tragedy. Together with a metrical pattern which unlike that of 893–6 does not reappear in other *skolia*, these forms raise the possibility that the song originated elsewhere and was adapted or even excerpted for use in Athens. A parallel would be provided by *carm. conv.* 891: see above, p. 254. (In addition, most editors emend ἔφη to ἔφα, but it is perfectly possible that Athenian singers adopted ἔφη as the familiar form of this common verb, while preserving χαλᾶι and ἔμμεν.)

Source: For Athenaeus' collection, see p. 254. This is the ninth song in the sequence. The text is also cited by Eustath. *Od.* p. 1574.15–17, as a *skolion* teaching upright behaviour among friends.

Metre:

```
∪ ∪ − ∪ ∪ − ∪ −  ?‖  gl
− − ∪ ∪ − ∪ −  ?‖  tl (= ∧gl)
− − − ∪ ∪ − ∪ −  gl
− − − ∪ ∪ − ∪ −  ‖‖  gl
```

A simple glyconic stanza.

Discussions: Davies 2015, Collins 2004: 127–9, van Dijk 1997: 150–2, Fabbro 1995: 130–7, Lambin 1992: 297–9.

1–2 The pattern 'this is what X said, as s/he was doing Y' frames a pointed message also in other fables; see Hes. *WD* 203–4, further Davies 2015: 79.

1 ὁ: animals in fables are not usually given an article when they are first introduced ('a crab' lives with 'a snake'). 'The crab/snake' is a consequence of narrative compression. The *skolion* (accurately or rhetorically) assumes familiarity with the fable. Cf. 'the eagle' at Aesch. fr. 139.

δέ occurs at the beginning of several shorter texts that may have been sung at *symposia*. See Archil. 1 with Campbell 1982 *ad loc.*, Mimn. 1, 2; also Michigan papyrus inv. 3250a recto col. iii.2 τηνίκα δ' ἔαρ, in a list of lyric and tragic incipits (Borges and Sampson 2012: 34). The effect may be to encourage the audience to make a connection with whatever piece is sung before.

3–4 pun on a commonplace. Cf. Hes. *WD* 7 (Zeus 'straightens the crooked man', ἰθύνει σκολιόν), Sol. 4.36. More generally, the insincere friend is a frequent motif in sympotic poetry; closest among the *skolia* are 889, 908 and 912a.

carm. conv. *893–6* PMG

Four, interrelated, Athenian *skolia* about the so-called tyrannicides Harmodios and Aristogeiton.

At the Panathenaia of 514 BC Aristogeiton and Harmodios, Aristogeiton's *eromenos* according to some sources, killed the Pisistratid Hipparchus, who together with his brother Hippias was tyrant of Athens (see 893.3n. on Hipparchus' status). Hippias continued to reign as tyrant until 511/510 and Cleisthenes' democratic reforms date only to 508/507, but even so Harmodios and Aristogeiton were soon celebrated as tyrannicides and became figureheads of the democracy. A bronze statue group by Antenor was erected for them in the agora, the first human statues in this central public space (possibly as early as 510). They were replaced in 477/476 with a group by Kritios and Nesiotes after Xerxes removed the original statues when he plundered Athens (*Marmor Parium* α54). At some point, the tyrannicides were given a tomb in the Kerameikos (Paus. 1.29.15) and started receiving public cult ([Aristot.] *Ath. Pol.* 58), and their descendants were able to dine at public expense in the Prytaneion (*IG* I³.131.5–9, and various references in the orators). The main early sources for the tyrannicides are Hdt. 5.55–6, Thuc. 6. 53–9, [Aristot.] *Ath. Pol.* 18.

In view of the prominent place the tyrannicides occupied in the self-image of the democracy it is unsurprising that diverging accounts circulated, and that there were also traditions of dissent. In particular their motives – political or personal? – were disputed. Nevertheless, Harmodios and Aristogeiton were on the whole integrating figures. Their story conveniently sidelines the Spartan involvement in the expulsion of Hippias, as well as the reforms of Cleisthenes, both divisive topics. Despite their appropriation by the democracy, Harmodios and Aristogeiton were aristocrats, and many of the values that they came to represent reach across different political ideologies: freedom, discipline, responsibility, solidarity.

The four *skolia* express democratic ideals but the anti-tyrannical rather than anti-aristocratic phrasing, certainly of 894 and 895 (for ἰσονομία in 893 and 896, see 893.4n.), may well have extended their appeal beyond fervently democratic circles. Political allegiance apart, we should reckon with performance at both elite and non-elite *symposia* (on the latter, see Fisher 2000), and indeed at *polis*-sponsored events, such as the tyrannicide cult or commensality in the Prytaneion (cf. Arethas' scholion on Pl. *Gorg.* 451e, p. 462 Greene); see further Jones 2014. A column-krater of about 470 BC (Boston 1970.567) seems to show symposiasts enacting the postures of Kritios and Nesiotes' statues: suggestive evidence for one – theatrical – mode of rendition. Cf. the old men's comic Harmodios stance at Aristoph. *Lys.* 634.

893 and **895** begin identically, with the declaration that 'I shall carry my sword like Harmodios and Aristogeiton.' They differ only in what they say about the killing in their respective lines 3–4: 893 foregrounds the outcome (ἰσονομία), 895 the event itself (at the Panathenaia, Hipparchus named). The phrasing of the first line enables light-hearted or even satirical renditions (893.1n.).

With its focus on the eternal glory of the dead as well as its Homeric phrasing, **896** evokes the tone of commemorative epigram. In particular, there are points of contact with 'Sim.' 1 *FGE* = *CEG* 430, which was probably inscribed on the base of Kritios and Nesiotes', and possibly already

Antenor's, statue groups: 'Certainly it was a great light for the Athenians when Aristogeiton and Harmodios killed Hipparchus. [1.5 lines missing] the two made their fatherland ...' Cf. also the speculatively reconstructed epigram *SEG* 46.949. However, in 896 the address to 'dearest Harmodios and Aristogeiton' creates a personal relationship that is absent from those inscriptions.

894 is focused on just Harmodios. Like 896, it blends reminiscence of public commemoration and indeed cult (immortal Harmodios) with an address to the dead man. But the tone is different: the address is more emotional and more personal, while the notion of Harmodios in the Isles of the Blest contains a degree of wishful thinking. The song may have parodic potential, but can certainly be performed 'straight'.

The *skolia* were sufficiently popular for comedy to refer to them: the 'Harmodios-song' appears at Aristoph. *Ach.* 980 and *PCG* fr. 444, as well as Antiphanes, *PCG* fr. 85. The beginnings of 893 and 895 are alluded to at Aristoph. *Lys.* 631–2. Aristoph. *Ach.* 1093 plays with the beginning, and Plato Com., *PCG* fr. 216 with the end, of 894.

Aristoph. *Wasps* 1226 quotes a line that does not feature in 893–6 as the beginning of the 'Harmodios-song' (= *carm. conv.* 911). Undoubtedly further versions circulated. The shared lines and phrases in what survives point to the role of improvisation in the creation and performance of these songs. (Hesych. α7317 attributes the 'Harmodios-song' to one Kallistratos, but it is doubtful that he had reliable information; see also p. 254).

The four versions cannot be dated with confidence either absolutely or relatively to one another. All that is certain is that they circulated in Aristophanes' day, but they may well have originated soon after the end of the tyranny. Though unlikely, it is conceivable that 894 and 895, which do not say that ἰσονομία has been established, go back to Hippias' reign, when they would have expressed resistance. The prosody of Ἁρμόδιε (see 'Metre') suggests that 896 was developed out of 893 rather than vice versa.

Source: See p. 254. The four texts are numbers 10–13 in Athenaeus' sequence.

Excerpts from the openings of 893, 894 and 895 are also quoted elsewhere, mostly in scholarly texts. See the apparatus of 894.1 for a correct reading preserved only in an Aristophanes scholion, and see the apparatuses in *PMG* and Fabbro for full documentation.

Metre:

$- \times - \cup \cup - \cup - \cup - - \; \| \quad phal$

$- \times - \cup \cup - \cup - \cup - - \; \| \quad phal$

$\cup \cup - \cup - - \cup \cup - \quad 2\,chor \; (= {}_\wedge dod\; chor)$

$- \cup \cup - \cup - - \cup \cup - \cup - \; \| \| \quad 2\,dod$

This largely aeolic stanza, with a shift in metre after the first half, is used in several other *skolia*. There is corruption in 893.4 = 896.4 ἐποιησάτην. 893.2 = 895.2 = 896.2 καὶ Ἀρ- must be pronounced as one short syllable in synecphonesis, with καί rendered as half-consonant (since synecphonesis with καί is unusual some editors print κ' Ἀρι-). The last syllable of 896.2 Ἁρμόδιε is irregularly lengthened. Performers will not have had a problem fitting unusual word shapes to a rhythm and tune they sang so frequently.

Discussions specifically of the four *skolia*: Collins 2004: 112–14 and 126, *Fabbro 1995: 137–52, *Lambin 1992: 273–85, *Taylor 1991: esp. 22–35, Ostwald 1969: 121–36, Podlecki 1966: 139–40, Bowra 1961: 391–6, Ehrenberg 1956. The bibliography on the tyrannicides is large. For the historical events, see Lewis 1988; cf. the revisionist account of Anderson 2003: 197–211. Later oral traditions: Thomas 1989: 238–82. Fifth-century ideological negotiations: Ober 2003, Raaflaub 2003, Neer 2002: 168–81 (who covers especially pots), Monoson 2000: 21–50. Statues: Fehr 1984, Brunnsåker 1971. References in comedy: apart from the commentaries, Lambin 1998 and Vetta 1983. Thucydides: Hornblower 1991–2008: III.433–53 and Wohl 1999.

893

1 ἐν μύρτου κλαδί is difficult. The most likely interpretation is 'equipped with / wearing a sprig of myrtle'; for this use of ἐν, cf. [Aesch.] *PV* 424 ἐν αἰχμαῖς, Eur. *El.* 321. The expression would amount to 'at the *symposion*'. Singers of *skolia* sometimes passed around a sprig of myrtle as they handed off to one another; see esp. Aristoph., *PCG* fr. 444 (the 'Admetus-' and 'Harmodios-songs' performed 'to the myrtle-sprig'), and the fuller accounts Σ Aristoph. *Wasps* 1222a and Σ Pl. *Gorg.* 451e (= *scol.* testt. 1 and 2 Campbell). The point would probably be a clash between the martial Harmodios stance and the topos of the *symposion* as a space in which there should be no fighting; for this topos, see e.g. Anacr. fr. eleg. 2 *IEG²*. The tone can be serious or humorous. A humorous rendition would be able to exploit the obscene meaning of ξίφος and μύρτος = male and female genitals, as Aristophanes may be doing when playing with the line at *Lys.* 632; for documentation, see Henderson 1975: 122, 134–5. Some ancient (and modern) scholars thought that Harmodios and Aristogeiton carried the sword hidden in a myrtle-branch; e.g. Σ Aristoph. *Lys.* 632, *Suda* φ592. This notion is unsupported by the surviving literary and iconographic treatments of the tyrannicides, and is also intrinsically unlikely. See further Ostwald 1969: 182–5, Lambin 1992: 280–3, Pavese 1995: 337–8.

ξίφος: the tyrannicides almost certainly wielded swords in the statue by Kritios and Nesiotes; see e.g. Neer 2002: figs. 82–3. The sword is more heroic than the dagger in the account at Thuc. 6.57–8, in which personal motives are to the fore.

φορήσω: an iterative verb. The stance will be habitual.

2 In 893, 895 and 896, Harmodios and Aristogeiton are treated as equal and given no distinguishing characteristics. This makes them suitable representatives of democracy.

3 τὸν τύραννον: '*the* tyrant' rhetorically exaggerates Hipparchus' status, neglecting his brother Hippias. Thuc. 6.54.2 asserts that in fact Hippias was the sole inheritor of Pisistratus' tyrant role, but he overstates his case; see Lewis 1988: 287–8. Hipparchus certainly was in the public eye, as he had herms bearing his name erected throughout Attica, played a leading role in reorganising the literary contests at the Panathenaia, and attracted high-profile poets such as Anacreon (p. 188); see [Pl.] *Hipparch.* 228b–229d, and further Shapiro 1989: index s.v. 'Hipparchos'. As Hipparchus is not named, Harmodios and Aristogeiton alone are memorialised; cf. Kritios and Nesiotes' statue group, which altogether omits Hipparchus.

4 ἰσονόμους: 'equality of rights' best captures the suggestively vague concept of ἰσονομία. Like ἰσηγορία, ἰσονομία is strongly associated with democracy; see esp. the use of it by Herodotus' Otanes when advocating democracy at 3.80.6, 3.83.1. For a democrat, this line therefore celebrates the establishment of a new constitution. However, with only some ten surviving instances from the fifth century, almost exclusively post-450 BC, ἰσονομία never became an entrenched slogan, and its early history is uncertain. Unlike 'rule of the *demos*', equality need not in itself be off-putting for an aristocrat. If the song originated soon after the end of the tyranny, aristocrats may well have been able to use it to celebrate the end of submission to somebody who should be their equal. In any case, equality is central to the ethos of the *symposion*. Further on ἰσονομία, see Ostwald 1969: 96–136, Fornara 1970: 171–80, Hansen 1991: 81–5.

Ἀθήνας, rather than anonymous 'the city', as often in the *Theognidea*. However the statement was originally intended, it lent itself to expressing pride in democracy as an Athenian achievement.

894

1 φίλταθ' Ἁρμόδι': the apostrophe expresses very strong affection, and a sense of both absence (death) and presence (continued existence). Cf. Teucer's address to the dead Ajax at Soph. *Aj.* 977, 996, 1015. A homoerotic tinge is possible, but not necessary.

οὔ τί που 'surely not', 'an incredulous half question, which is in effect an exclamation' (Braswell on Pind. *Pyth.* 4.87).

τέθνηκας 'you are (not) dead': the question is not whether he died, but what his state is now. The line refers to the topos of immortality conferred by achievement, but treats it literally. Cf. Sim. 531 and 'Sim.' ix.3 *FGE* οὐδὲ τεθνᾶσι θανόντες, with Page's note; and contrast the reference to κλέος rather than immortality at 896.1.

2 νήσοις δ' ἐν μακάρων: the Isles of the Blest combine the notions of a blissful continued existence, exclusivness and divine reward, all of which are relevant here; see *Od.* 4.561–9, Hes. *WD* 166–73, Pind. *Ol.* 2.68–80, Pl. *Gorg.* 523a–24a. The motif is one of heroic myth rather than cult, as is underlined by 3–4(n.). In later periods the motif appears in sepulchral epigram, e.g. *GVI* 1830.2 and 1990.9.

φασιν: attribution to anonymous speakers is common in relaying received stories, e.g. *carm. conv.* 898 and 899, Pind. *Pyth.* 1.52, Thgn. 1287, Thuc. 2.102.5–6. Such expressions can be authorising (a traditional account) or distancing (not an account to which the speaker commits). Here either option is available to the performer. We have no evidence for the existence of such a story.

3–4 Achilles, who chose death and glory over life, is an obvious paradigm. He is in Hades in *Od.* 11 but comes to live on the Isles of the Blest also at Pind. *Ol.* 2.79–80 and later Pl. *Symp.* 179e. Two figures are needed to match the two tyrannicides, and Diomedes may be chosen as the fighter whom the first half of the *Iliad* portrays as almost Achilles' equal. He is immortalised in some stories, and is occasionally placed on the island of Diomedeia, as an object of worship; see Pind. *Nem.* 10.7, and Σ *ad loc.* (Drachmann iii.167–8) ~ Ibyc. 294. The formulaic ποδώκης and Τυδεΐδην again point to epic myth more than cult.

4 is unmetrical and cannot be restored with confidence. Manzoni's Τυδεΐδην παρ' ἐσθλὸν Διομήδεα would be grammatically more straightforward than Lowth's Τυδεΐδην τέ φασιν Διομήδεα, which (like the transmitted text) gives different constructions to Ἀχιλεύς (*sc.* ἐστίν) and Διομήδεα (acc. + inf. after φασι).

895

3 The 'festival of Athena' is the Panathenaia. Sacrifices and the feasting that follows are so central to Greek festivals that θυσία can stand for the festival in general (LSJ s.v. 1.3). The phrasing makes a connection between the sacred killing of animals and the killing of Hipparchus.

4 ἐκαινέτην 'they were killing'. The imperfect suits the focus on the enterprise itself and its circumstances. Contrast the aorist in 893.3 = 896.3, where the focus is on the outcome.

896

1 κλέος ἔσσεται is epic; see esp. *Od.* 24.93–4 (in the underworld), ἀλλά τοι αἰεί | πάντας ἐπ' ἀνθρώπους κλέος ἔσσεται ἐσθλόν, Ἀχιλλεῦ. Epic κλέος is often a reward after death for what a hero achieved while alive. The form αἶαν, rather than γαῖαν, adds to the epic tone.

3–4 κτανέτην and ἐποιησάτην must be 2nd pers. here (they are 3rd pers. in 893). The usual 2nd pers. ending of the historical tenses is -τον, but -την is attested in several Athenian texts, e.g. Soph. *OT* 1511 (metrically guaranteed). See further Page 1938 on Eur. *Med.* 1073.

WORKS CITED

Acosta-Hughes, B. 2010. *Arion's lyre: Archaic lyric into Hellenistic poetry*, Princeton

Adkins, A. W. H. 1960. *Merit and responsibility: a study in Greek values*, Oxford

Adrados, F. R. 1974. 'La canción rodia de la golondrina y la cerámica de Tera', *Emerita* 42: 47–68

Agócs, P. 2012. 'Performance and genre: reading Pindar's κῶμοι', in P. Agócs *et al.*, eds. *Reading the victory ode* (Cambridge) 191–223

Aldrete, G. S., *et al.* 2013. *Reconstructing ancient linen body armor: unraveling the linothorax mystery*, Baltimore, MD

Alexiou, M. 2002. *After antiquity: Greek language, myth, and metaphor*, Ithaca, NY

Alfageme, I. R. 1978. 'El sueño de la naturaleza: Alcmán fr. 89 Page', *CFC* 15: 13–52

Allan, R. J. 2013. 'History as presence: time, tense and narrative mode in Thucydides', in A. Tsakmakis and M. Tamiolaki, eds. *Thucydides between history and literature* (Leiden) 371–89

2014. 'Changing the topic: topic position in ancient Greek word order', *Mnemosyne* 67: 181–213

Allen, A. 1993. *The fragments of Mimnermus: text and commentary*, Stuttgart

Allen, D. S. 2000. *The world of Prometheus: the politics of punishing in democratic Athens*, Princeton

Aloni, A. 1986. *Tradizioni arcaiche della Troade e composizione dell'Iliade*, Milan

1997. *Saffo: frammenti*, Florence

2001. 'What is that man doing in Sappho, fr. 31 V.?', in Cavarzere *et al.* 2001: 29–40

(ed.) 2008. *Nuove acquisizioni di Saffo e della lirica greca: per il testo di P.Köln inv. 21351 + 21376 e P.Oxy. 1787*, Alessandria

Aloni, A., and A. Iannucci 2007. *L'elegia greca e l'epigramma dalle origini al v secolo*, Florence

Amigues, S. 2005. 'Végétaux et aromates de l'Orient dans le monde antique', *Topoi orient-occident* 12–13: 359–83

Anderson, G. 2003. *The Athenian experiment: building an imagined political community in ancient Attica, 508–490 BC*, Ann Arbor

2005. 'Before *turannoi* were tyrants: rethinking a chapter of early Greek history', *ClAnt* 24: 173–222

Andolfi, I. 2014. 'Una vetrina esegetica per tre sofisti: il carme di Simonide nel *Protagora* di Platone', *SemRom* n. s. 3: 117–49

Andrisano, A. M. 1994. 'Alcae. fr. 129, 21ss. V. (L'eroe e il tiranno: una comunicazione impossibile)', *MCr* 29: 59–73

2001. 'Iambic motifs in Alcaeus' lyrics', in Cavarzere *et al.* 2001: 41–63

Arnott, G. 2000. 'Athenaeus and the epitome: texts, manuscripts and early editions', in D. Braund and J. Wilkins, eds. *Athenaeus and his world: reading Greek culture in the Roman empire* (Exeter) 41–52

Arnould, D. 1990. *Le rire et les larmes dans la littérature grecque d'Homère à Platon*, Paris

Asheri, D., *et al.* 2007. *A commentary on Herodotus Books I–IV*, trans. B. Graziosi *et al.*, Oxford

Asper, M. 2006. '"Literatursoziologisches" zu den Sprüchen der Sieben Weisen', in J. Althoff and D. Zeller, eds. *Die Worte der Sieben Weisen* (Darmstadt) 85–103

Aston, E. M. 2012. 'Thessaly and Macedon at Delphi', *Electrum* 19: 41–60

Athanassaki, L., and E. Bowie (eds.) 2011. *Archaic and Classical choral song: performance, politics and dissemination*, Berlin

Aubriot-Sévin, D. 1992. *Prière et conceptions religieuses en Grèce ancienne jusqu'à la fin du VE siècle av. J.-C.*, Paris

Aujac, G., and M. Lebel 1981. *Denys d'Halicarnasse: opuscules rhétoriques*, vol. III : *La composition stylistique*, Paris

Austin, C. 2007. 'Nuits chaudes à Lesbos: buvons avec Alcée, aimons avec Sappho', in G. Bastianini and A. Casanova, eds. *I papiri di Saffo e di Alceo* (Florence) 115–26

Austin, C., and S. D. Olson 2004. *Aristophanes: Thesmophoriazusae*, Oxford

Austin, N. 1994. *Helen of Troy and her shameless phantom*, Ithaca, NY

Avlamis, P. 2011. 'Isis and the people in the *Life of Aesop*', in P. Townsend and M. Vidas, eds. *Revelation, literature, and community in Late Antiquity* (Tübingen) 65–101

Babut, D. 1975. 'Simonide moraliste', *REG* 88: 20–62

Bachvarova, M. R. 2007. 'Oath and allusion in Alcaeus fr. 129', in A. H. Sommerstein and J. Fletcher, eds. *Horkos: the oath in Greek society* (Exeter) 179–88, 258–64

Bain, D. 1990. 'Greek verbs for animal intercourse used of human beings', *Sileno* 16: 253–61

Bakhuizen, S. C. 1977. 'Greek steel', *World Archaeology* 9: 220–34

Bakker, E. J. (ed.) 2017. *Authorship and Greek song: authority, authenticity, and performance*, Leiden

Bakker, S. 2002. 'Futura zonder toekomst', *Lampas* 35: 199–214

Ballabriga, A. 1986. *Le soleil et le tartare: l'image mythique du monde en Grèce archaïque*, Paris

Barbantani, S. 2009. 'Lyric in the Hellenistic period and beyond', in Budelmann 2009: 297–318

Barker, A. 2014. *Ancient Greek writers on their musical past: studies in Greek musical historiography*, Pisa

Barkhuizen, J. H. 1983. 'Alcaeus 42 LP, 5', *Mnemosyne* 36: 151

Barrett, W. S. 2007a [1968]. 'Stesichoros and the story of Geryon', in Barrett 2007c: 1–24

2007b [1978]. 'Stesichoros, *Geryoneis*, *SLG* 11', in Barrett 2007c: 25–37

2007c. *Greek lyric, tragedy, and textual criticism: collected papers*, Oxford

Barringer, J. M. 2001. *The hunt in ancient Greece*, Baltimore, MD

Barron, J. P. 1961. 'The son of Hyllis', *CR* 11: 185–7

1969. 'Ibycus: *To Polycrates*', *BICS* 16: 119–49

1984. 'Ibycus: *Gorgias* and other poems', *BICS* 31: 13–24

Bassett, S. E. 1931. 'The place and date of the first performance of the *Persians* of Timotheus', *CPh* 26: 153–65

Battezzato, L. 2009. 'Metre and music', in Budelmann 2009: 130–46

Baumbach, M., and N. Dümmler (eds.) 2014. *Imitate Anacreon! Mimesis, poiesis and the poetic inspiration in the Carmina Anacreontea*, Berlin

Beaulieu, M.-C. 2016. *The sea in the Greek imagination*, Philadelphia

Bell, J. M. 1978. 'Κίμβιξ καὶ σοφός: Simonides in the anecdotal tradition', *QUCC* 28: 29–86

Bellia, A. 2012. *Il canto delle vergini locresi: la musica a Locri Epizefirii nelle fonti scritte e nella documentazione archeologica (secoli VI–III a. C.)*, Pisa

Beresford, A. 2008. 'Nobody's perfect: a new text and interpretation of Simonides *PMG* 542', *CPh* 103: 237–56

Bernardini, P. A. 1990. 'La bellezza dell'amato: Ibico frr. 288 e 289 P.', *AION(filol)* 12: 69–80

Bernsdorff, H. 2004. 'Schwermut des Alters im neuen Kölner Sappho-Papyrus', *ZPE* 150: 27–35

2005. 'Offene Gedichtschlüsse', *ZPE* 153: 1–6

2016. 'Anacreon and Athens', *ZPE* 198: 1–13

Bertman, S. 1989. 'The ashes and the flame: passion and aging in classical poetry', in T. M. Falkner and J. de Luce, eds. *Old age in Greek and Latin literature* (Albany, NY) 157–71

Bertrand, N. 2015. 'Le pronom anaphorique ὅγε chez Homère', *Gaia* 18: 275–91

Bettarini, L. 2005. 'Note linguistiche alla nuova Saffo', *ZPE* 154: 33–9

Bierl, A. 2003. '"Ich aber (sage), das Schönste ist, was einer liebt!": eine pragmatische Deutung von Sappho Fr. 16 LP/V', *QUCC* n. s. 74: 91–124

2016. 'Visualizing the Cologne Sappho: mental imagery through chorality, the sun, and Orpheus', in Cazzato and Lardinois 2016: 307–42

Bierl, A., and A. Lardinois (eds.) 2016. *The newest Sappho: P.Sapph. Obbink and P.GC inv. 105, frs. 1–4*, Leiden

Bing, P. 2014. '*Anacreontea* avant la lettre: Euripides' *Cyclops* 495–518', in Baumbach and Dümmler 2014: 25–45

Blomquist, J. 1975. 'The dialect of Epizephyrian Locri', *OAth* 11: 17–35

Blondell, R. 2010. 'Refractions of Homer's Helen in Archaic lyric', *AJPh* 131: 349–91

2013. *Helen of Troy: beauty, myth, devastation*, Oxford

Blümel, W. 1982. *Die aiolischen Dialekte: Phonologie und Morphologie der inschriftlichen Texte aus generativer Sicht*, Göttingen

Blumenthal, A. v. 1940. 'Das Lied der Müllerin von Eresos', *Hermes* 75: 125–7

Boardman, J. 1986. 'Booners. Part 2: the boon companions', *Greek vases in the J. Paul Getty Museum* 3: 47–70

1990. 'Herakles: VIII. Herakles' death and apotheosis', *LIMC* v.1: 121–32

Boedeker, D. 2009. 'No way out? Aging in the New (and old) Sappho', in Greene and Skinner 2009: 71–83

2016. 'Hera and the return of Charaxos', in Bierl and Lardinois 2016: 188–207

Boedeker, D., and D. Sider (eds.) 2001. *The New Simonides: contexts of praise and desire*, Oxford

Boehringer, S. 2013. '"Je suis Tithon, je suis Aurore": performance et éroticisme dans le "nouveau" fr. 58 de Sappho', *QUCC* n. s. 104: 23–44

Bonanno, M. G. 1973. 'Osservazioni sul tema della "giusta" reciprocità amorosa da Saffo ai comici', *QUCC* 16: 110–20

1976. 'Alcaeus fr. 140 V.', *Philologus* 120: 1–11

1983. 'Anacr. fr. 3 P.', *MCr* 18: 23–7

1990. *L'allusione necessaria: ricerche intertestuali sulla poesia greca e latina*, Rome

1991. 'Nota ad Alcmane (fr. 3,3 Cal.)', *Eikasmos* 2: 9–11

1993. 'Saffo 31,9 V.: γλῶσσα ἔαγε', *QUCC* n. s. 43: 61–8

2004. 'Come guarire dal complesso epico: l'*Ode a Policrate* di Ibico', in E. Cavallini, ed. *Samo: storia, letteratura, scienza* (Pisa) 67–96

Bonifazi, A. 2012. *Homer's versicolored fabric: the evocative power of ancient Greek epic word-making*, Washington, DC

Bonnechere, P. 2007. 'The place of the sacred grove (*alsos*) in the mantic rituals of Greece: the example of the *alsos* of Trophonios at Lebadeia (Boeotia)', in M. Conan, ed. *Sacred gardens and landscapes: ritual and agency* (Washington, DC) 17–41

Borges, C., and C. M. Sampson 2012. *New literary papyri from the Michigan collection: mythographic lyric and a catalogue of poetic first lines*, Ann Arbor

Bornmann, F. 1978. 'Zur Geryoneis des Stesichoros und Pindars Herakles-Dithyrambos', *ZPE* 31: 33–5

Borthwick, E. K. 1979. 'Φυλάσσω or λαφύσσω? A note on two emendations', *Eranos* 77: 79–83

Bowie, A. M. 1981. *The poetic dialect of Sappho and Alcaeus*, Salem, NH

Bowie, E. L. 2007. 'Early expatriates: displacement and exile in Archaic poetry', in J. F. Gaertner, ed. *Writing exile: the discourse of displacement in Greco-Roman antiquity and beyond* (Leiden) 21–49

2009. 'Wandering poets, Archaic style', in Hunter and Rutherford 2009: 105–36

2010. 'The Trojan War's reception in early Greek lyric, iambic and elegiac poetry', in L. Foxhall and H.-J. Gehrke, eds. *Intentional history: spinning time in ancient Greece* (Stuttgart) 57–85

2011. 'Alcman's first *Partheneion* and the song the Sirens sang', in Athanassaki and Bowie 2011: 33–65

2013. 'The sympotic tease', in J. Kwapisz *et al.*, eds. *The Muse at play: riddles and wordplay in Greek and Latin poetry* (Berlin) 33–43

2014. 'Stesichorus' *Geryoneis*', in L. Breglia and A. Moleti, eds. *Hespería: tradizioni, rotte, paesaggi* (Paestum) 99–105

2016. 'How did Sappho's songs get into the male sympotic repertoire?', in Bierl and Lardinois 2016: 148–64

Bowra, C. M. 1961. *Greek lyric poetry from Alcman to Simonides*, 2nd edn, Oxford

Bravi, L. 2006. *Gli epigrammi di Simonide e le vie della tradizione*, Rome

Breitenberger, B. 2007. *Aphrodite and Eros: the development of erotic mythology in early Greek poetry and cult*, New York

Brillante, C. 1998. 'L'inquietante bellezza di Eurialo: Ibico fr. 288 P.', *RCCM* 40: 13–20

Brize, P. 1980. *Die Geryoneis des Stesichoros und die frühe griechische Kunst*, Würzburg

1990. 'Herakles and Geryon (Labour x)', *LIMC* v.1: 73–85

Brown, C. 1983. 'From rags to riches: Anacreon's Artemon', *Phoenix* 37: 1–15

1989. 'Anactoria and the Χαρίτων ἀμαρύγματα: Sappho fr. 16, 18 Voigt', *QUCC* n. s. 32: 7–15

2011. 'To the ends of the earth: Sappho on Tithonus', *ZPE* 178: 21–5

Bruce, W. 2011. 'A note on Anacreon 388', *CQ* 61: 306–9

Brunnsåker, S. 1971. *The Tyrant-Slayers of Kritios and Nesiotes: a critical study of the sources and restorations*, 2nd edn, Stockholm

Brussich, G. F. 1970. 'La lingua di Timoteo', *Quaderni triestini per il lessico della lirica corale greca* 1: 51–80

1999. 'Il decreto spartano contro Timoteo e la σφραγίς dei *Persiani*', in B. Gentili *et al.*, eds. *Per Carlo Corbato: scritti di filologia greca e latina offerti da amici e allievi* (Pisa) 29–46

Bücher, K. 1899. *Arbeit und Rhythmus*, 2nd edn, Leipzig

Budelmann, F. (ed.) 2009. *The Cambridge companion to Greek lyric*, Cambridge

2013a. 'Alcman's nightscapes (frs. 89 and 90 *PMGF*)', *HSPh* 107: 35–53

2013b. 'Greek festival choruses in and out of context', in J. Billings *et al.*, eds. *Choruses, ancient and modern* (Oxford) 81–98

2018. 'Lyric minds', in Budelmann and Phillips 2018b: 235–56

Budelmann, F., and P. LeVen 2014. 'Timotheus' poetics of blending: a cognitive approach to the language of the New Music', *CPh* 109: 191–210

Budelmann, F., and T. Phillips 2018a. 'Introduction', in Budelmann and Phillips 2018b: 1–27

(eds) 2018b. *Textual events: performance and the lyric in early Greece*, Oxford

Bundrick, S. D. 2005. *Music and image in Classical Athens*, Cambridge

Bundy, E. L. 1986 [1962]. *Studia Pindarica*, Berkeley

Buongiovanni, A. M. 1990. 'Marginalia pindarica', *SIFC* 8: 121–36

Burgess, J. S. 2002. *The tradition of the Trojan war in Homer and the epic cycle*, Baltimore, MD

Burke, P. 2009. *Popular culture in early modern Europe*, 3rd edn, Farnham

Burkert, W. 1985. *Greek religion: Archaic and Classical*, trans. J. Raffan, Oxford

1987. 'The making of Homer in the sixth century BC: rhapsodes versus Stesichorus', in *Papers on the Amasis painter and his world: colloquium sponsored by the Getty Center for the History of Art and the Humanities and symposium sponsored by the J. Paul Getty Museum* (Malibu, CA) 43–62

Burnett, A. P. 1964. 'The race with the Pleiades', *CPh* 59: 30–4

1983. *Three Archaic poets: Archilochus, Alcaeus, Sappho*, London

1985. *The art of Bacchylides*, Cambridge, MA

1988. 'Jocasta in the West: the Lille Stesichorus', *ClAnt* 7: 107–54

Burris, S., *et al.* 2014. 'New fragments of book 1 of Sappho', *ZPE* 189: 1–28

Burton, D. 2011. 'Response and competition in Archaic Greek poetry', *Antichthon* 45: 58–76

Burton, J. 1998. 'Women's commensality in the ancient Greek world', *G&R* 45: 143–65

Burzacchini, G. 1976. 'Alc. 130 b Voigt = Hor. *Carm.* I 22', *QUCC* 22: 39–58

1977. "Ἔσχατον δύεται κατὰ γᾶς (= Simon. 89 P.)', *QUCC* 25: 31–41

1985. 'Some further observations on Alcaeus fr. 130B Voigt', *Papers of the Liverpool Latin Seminar* 5: 373–81

1994. 'Alc. fr. 130bV. rivisitato', *Eikasmos* 5: 29–38

1995. 'Lirica arcaica (I): elegia e giambo, melica monodica e corale (dalle origini al VI sec. a. C.)', in U. Mattioli, ed. *Senectus: la vecchiaia nel mondo classico* (Bologna) I.69–124

2005. 'Fenomenologia innodica nella poesia di Saffo', *Eikasmos* 16: 11–40

2007a. 'Saffo frr. 1, 2, 58 V. tra documentazione papiracea e tradizione indiretta', in G. Bastianini and A. Casanova, eds. *I papiri di Saffo e di Alceo* (Florence) 83–114

2007b. 'Saffo, il canto e l'oltretomba', *RFIC* 135: 37–56

Busine, A. 2002. *Les septs sages de la Grèce antique: transmission et utilisation d'un patrimoine légendaire d'Hérodote à Plutarque*, Paris

Buxton, R. G. A. 1982. *Persuasion in Greek tragedy: a study of peitho*, Cambridge

Caciagli, S. 2009a. 'Lupi o codardi nell'*Heraion* di Lesbo', *ZPE* 171: 216–20

2009b. 'Un contesto per Alcm. *PMGF* 1', *Eikasmos* 20: 19–45

2009c. 'Un serment violé chez Alcée', *REG* 122: 185–200

2010. 'Il temenos di Messon: uno stesso contesto per Saffo e Alceo', *Lexis* 28: 227–56

2011. *Poeti e società: comunicazione poetica e formazioni sociali nella Lesbo del* VII/VI *secolo a. C.*, Amsterdam

2014. 'Case di uomini, case di dèi: per un contesto di Alc. fr. 140 V.', *QUCC* n. s. 108: 57–92

2015. 'Per un nuovo testo di Sapph. fr. 2 V.', *Eikasmos* 26: 31–52

2016. 'Sappho fragment 17: wishing Charaxos a safe trip?', in Bierl and Lardinois 2016: 424–48

Cairns, D. 2011. 'Looks of love and loathing: cultural models of vision and emotion in ancient Greek culture', *Métis* 9: 37–50

Calame, C. 1970. *Etymologicum genuinum: les citations de poètes lyriques*, Rome

1977. *Les chœurs de jeunes filles en Grèce archaïque*, vol. II: *Alcman*, Rome

1983. *Alcman: introduction, texte critique, témoignages, traduction et commentaire*, Rome

1997 [1977]. *Choruses of young women in ancient Greece: their morphology, religious role, and social function*, trans. D. Collins and J. Orion, Lanham, MD

1998. 'La poésie lyrique grecque, un genre inexistant?', *Littérature* 111: 87–110

1999 [1992]. *The poetics of Eros in ancient Greece*, trans. J. Lloyd, Princeton

2005 [1987]. 'Fiction as narrative argumentation', trans. P. M. Burk, in *Masks of authority: fiction and pragmatics in ancient Greek poetics* (Ithaca, NY) 55–69

2013. 'La poésie de Sappho aux prises avec le genre: polyphonie, pragmatique et rituel (à propos du fr. 58b)', *QUCC* n. s. 104: 45–67

2015. 'Relations of sex and gender in Greek melic poetry: Helen, object and subject of desire', trans. L. Arnault and M. Masterson, in M. Masterson *et al.*, eds. *Sex in antiquity: exploring gender and sexuality in the ancient world* (London) 198–213

2016. 'The amorous gaze: a poetic and pragmatic *koinê* for erotic *melos*?', in Cazzato and Lardinois 2016: 288–306

Cameron, A. 1939. 'Sappho's prayer to Aphrodite', *HThR* 32: 1–17

Campbell, D. A. 1982. *Greek lyric poetry*, new edn, Bristol

1989. 'Going up? ἀναβῆναι in Anacreon 395 (Page)', *EMC* 8: 49–50

Canevaro, L. G. 2015. *Hesiod's Works and Days: how to teach self-sufficiency*, Oxford

Cannatà Fera, M., and S. Grandolini (eds.) 2000. *Poesia e religione in Grecia: studi in onore di G. Aurelio Privitera*, 2 vols., Naples.

Caprioli, M. 2012. 'On Alcaeus 42, Voigt', *CQ* 62: 22–38

Carey, C. 1981. *A commentary on five odes of Pindar*, Salem, NH

1989. 'The performance of the victory ode', *AJPh* 110: 545–65

1993. 'Return of the radish or Just when you thought it safe to go back into the kitchen', *LCM* 18.4: 53–55

2009. 'Genre, occasion and performance', in Budelmann 2009: 21–38

2011. 'Alcman: from Laconia to Alexandria', in Athanassaki and Bowie 2011: 437–60

2015. 'Stesichorus and the epic cycle', in Finglass and Kelly 2015: 45–62

Carmignani, L. 1981. 'Stile e tecnica narrativa in Stesicoro', in *Studi di letteratura greca* (Pisa) 25–60

Carson, A. 1986. *Eros the bittersweet*, Princeton

1990. 'Putting her in her place: woman, dirt, and desire', in Halperin *et al.* 1990: 135–69

1992a. 'How not to read a poem: unmixing Simonides from *Protagoras*', *CPh* 87: 110–30

1992b. 'Simonides painter', in R. Hexter and D. Selden, eds. *Innovations of antiquity* (New York and London) 51–64

1996 [1980]. 'The justice of Aphrodite in Sappho 1', in Greene 1996: 226–32

1999. *Economy of the unlost: reading Simonides of Keos with Paul Celan*, Princeton

Carty, A. 2015. *Polycrates, tyrant of Samos: new light on Archaic Greece*, Stuttgart

Cassio, A. C. 1999. 'Futuri dorici, dialetto di Siracusa e testo antico dei lirici', in A. C. Cassio, ed. Κατὰ διάλεκτον: atti del III colloquio internazionale di dialettologia greca (Naples) 187–214

2007. 'Alcman's text, spoken Laconian, and Greek study of Greek dialects', in I. Hajnal, ed. *Die altgriechischen Dialekte: Wesen und Werden* (Innsbruck) 29–45

(ed.) 2008. *Storia delle lingue letterarie greche*, Florence

Castellaneta, S. 2005. 'Note alla *Gerioneide* di Stesicoro', *ZPE* 153: 21–42

Catenacci, C. 2007. 'Dioniso κεμήλιος (Alceo, fr. 129, 8 V.)', *QUCC* n. s. 85: 37–9

Cavallini, E. 2000. 'Dee e profetesse nella poesia di Ibico', in Cannatà Fera and Grandolini 2000: 1.185–98

2003. 'L'ἄγνος Alceo', *AION(filol)* 25: 139–44

2006. 'Lesbo, Mileto, la Lidia (Sapph. fr. 16 e fr. 96 V.)', in M. Vetta and C. Catenacci, eds. *I luoghi e la poesia nella Grecia antica* (Alessandria) 145–58

Cavarzere, A., *et al.* (eds.) 2001. *Iambic ideas: essays on a poetic tradition from Archaic Greece to the late Roman Empire*, Lanham, MD

Cazzato, V. 2013. 'Worlds of *Erôs* in Ibycus fragment 286 (*PMGF*)', in E. Sanders *et al.*, eds. *Erôs in ancient Greece* (Oxford) 267–76

2016. 'Symposia *en plein air* in Alcaeus and others', in Cazzato et al. 2016: 184–206

Cazzato, V., and A. Lardinois (eds.) 2016. *The look of lyric: Greek song and the visual*, Leiden

Cazzato, V., *et al.* (eds.) 2016. *The cup of song: studies on poetry and the symposion*, Oxford

Ceccarelli, P. 2012. 'Naming the Aegean Sea', *MHR* 27: 25–49

Chantraine, P. 1942–53. *Grammaire homérique*, 2 vols., Paris

1968–80. *Dictionnaire étymologique de la langue grecque: histoire des mots*, 4 vols., Paris

Cingano, E. 1989. 'Tra epos e storia: la genealogia di Cianippo e dei Biantidi in Ibico (Suppl. Lyr. Gr. 151 Page), e nelle fonti mitografiche greche', *ZPE* 79: 27–38

1990. 'L'opera di Ibico e di Stesicoro nella classificazione degli antichi e dei moderni', *AION(filol)* 12: 189–224

2003. 'Entre skolion et enkomion: réflexions sur le "genre" et la performance de la lyrique chorale grecque', in J. Jouanna and J. Leclant, eds. *La poésie grecque antique* (Paris) 17–45

Cirio, A. M. 1995. 'Alceo, fr. 140 V', *RCCM* 37: 179–86

2001. 'Nuovi dati sul culto degli eroi: una interpretazione di Alceo, 140 V', in S. Ribichini *et al.*, eds. *La questione delle influenze vicino-orientali sulla religione greca* (Rome) 299–305

Citti, V. 1987. 'Il lenzuolo funebre della tirannide: a proposito di Simon. 89P.', *Prometheus* 13: 11–12

Clairmont, C. W. 1983. *Patrios nomos: public burial in Athens during the fifth and fourth centuries* BC, 2 vols., Oxford

Clarke, M. 1999. *Flesh and spirit in the songs of Homer: a study of words and myths*, Oxford

2002. 'Spartan *ate* at Thermopylae? Semantics and ideology at Herodotus, *Histories* 7.223.4', in A. Powell and S. Hodkinson, eds. *Sparta: beyond the mirage* (London) 63–84

Clay, D. 1991. 'Alcman's *Partheneion*', *QUCC* n. s. 39: 47–67

2013. 'Lesbian armour: Alcaeus fr. 140 Voigt', *Prometheus* 39: 18–24

Clay, J. S. 2001. 'The New Simonides and Homer's *hemitheoi*', in Boedeker and Sider 2001: 182–4

2016. 'How to construct a sympotic space with words', in Cazzato and Lardinois 2016: 204–16

Cohen, D. 1980. '*Horkia* and *horkos* in the *Iliad*', *RIDA* 27: 49–68

Cohen, E. E. 2015. *Athenian prostitution: the business of sex*, New York

Cole, S. G. 2004. *Landscapes, gender, and ritual space: the ancient Greek experience*, Berkeley

Colesanti, G. 1995. 'La disposizione delle armi in Alc. 140 V', *RFIC* 123: 385–408

2014. 'Two cases of submerged monodic lyric: sympotic poetry and lullabies', in G. Colesanti and M. Giordano, eds. *Submerged literature in ancient Greek culture: an introduction* (Berlin) 90–106

Coletti, M. L. 1972. 'L'autenticità di Ancr. fr. 36 Gent.', in *Studi classici in onore di Quintino Cataudella* (Catania) I.85–91

Collins, B. J. 1995. 'Greek ὀλολύζω and Hittite *palwai-*: exultation in the ritual slaughter of animals', *GRBS* 36: 319–25

Collins, D. 2004. *Master of the game: competition and performance in Greek poetry*, Washington, DC

Colvin, S. 2007. *A historical Greek reader: Mycenaean to the koiné*, Oxford

Contiades-Tsitsoni, E. 1990. *Hymenaios und Epithalamion: das Hochzeitslied in der frühgriechischen Lyrik*, Stuttgart

Coppola, G. 2005. 'La tradizione dardanide, Saffo e il fr. 44 Voigt', in A. Mele *et al.*, eds. *Eoli ed Eolide tra madrepatria e colonie* (Naples) 103–22

Csapo, E. 2004. 'The politics of the New Music', in P. Murray and P. Wilson, eds. *Music and the muses: the culture of mousike in the Classical Athenian city* (Oxford) 207–48

2008. 'Star choruses: Eleusis, Orphism, and New Musical imagery and dance', in M. Revermann and P. Wilson, eds. *Performance, iconography, reception: studies in honour of Oliver Taplin* (Oxford) 262–90

Csapo, E., and P. Wilson 2009. 'Timotheus the New Musician', in Budelmann 2009: 277–93

Cuartero, F. J. 1972. 'La poética de Alcman', *CFC(G)* 4: 367–402

Culler, J. 2015. *Theory of the lyric*, Cambridge, MA

Currie, B. 2004. 'Reperformance scenarios for Pindar's odes', in C. J. Mackie, ed. *Oral performance and its context* (Leiden) 49–69

2005. *Pindar and the cult of heroes*, Oxford

2011. 'Epinician *choregia*: funding a Pindaric chorus', in Athanassaki and Bowie 2011: 269–310

2013. 'The Pindaric first person in flux', *ClAnt* 32: 243–82

2015. '*Cypria*', in M. Fantuzzi and C. Tsagalis, eds. *The Greek epic cycle and its ancient reception: a companion* (Cambridge) 281–305

Curti, M. 1995. 'L'elmo caduto? Note a Stesicoro, Gerioneide, S15 Davies', *ZPE* 105: 1–5

Curtis, P. 2011. *Stesichoros' Geryoneis*, Leiden

D'Alessio, G. B. 1994. 'First-person problems in Pindar', *BICS* 39: 117–39

1997. 'Pindar's *prosodia* and the classification of Pindaric papyrus fragments', *ZPE* 118: 23–60

2009a. 'Defining local identities in Greek lyric poetry', in Hunter and Rutherford 2009: 137–67

2009b. 'Language and pragmatics', in Budelmann 2009: 114–29

2013. '"The name of the dithyramb": diachronic and diatopic variations', in Kowalzig and Wilson 2013: 113–32

2018. 'Fiction and pragmatics in ancient Greek lyric: the case of Sappho', in Budelmann and Phillips 2018b: 31–62

D'Angour, A. 2006. 'The New Music – so what's new?', in S. Goldhill and R. Osborne, eds. *Rethinking revolutions through ancient Greece* (Cambridge) 264–83

2011. *The Greeks and the new: novelty in ancient Greek imagination and experience*, Cambridge

2013. 'Love's battlefield: rethinking Sappho fragment 31', in E. Sanders *et al.*, eds. *Erôs in ancient Greece* (Oxford) 59–71

Dale, A. 2011a. 'Alcaeus on the career of Myrsilos: Greeks, Lydians and Luwians at the east Aegean–west Anatolian interface', *JHS* 131: 15–24

2011b. 'Topics in Alcman's *Partheneion*', *ZPE* 176: 24–38

Dale, A. M. 1969 [1951]. 'The metrical units of Greek lyric verse, III', in *Collected papers* (Cambridge) 80–102

Danielewicz, J. 2006. 'Bacchylides fr. 20a, 12 S.-M. and Sappho, P. Köln fr. I–II, 12', *ZPE* 155: 19–21

Davidson, J. F. 1987. 'Anacreon, Homer and the young woman from Lesbos', *Mnemosyne* 40: 132–37

Davidson, J. N. 1997. *Courtesans and fishcakes: the consuming passions of Classical Athens*, London

2013. 'Politics, poetics and *eros* in Archaic poetry', in E. Sanders, ed. *Eros and the polis: love in context* (London) 5–37

Davies, M. 1980. 'The eyes of love and the hunting-net in Ibycus 287 P.', *Maia* 32: 255–7

1981. 'Artemon transvestitus? A query', *Mnemosyne* 34: 288–99

1985. 'Conventional topics of invective in Alcaeus', *Prometheus* 11: 31–9

1986a. 'Alcaeus, Thetis and Helen', *Hermes* 114: 257–62

1986b. 'Symbolism and imagery in the poetry of Ibycus', *Hermes* 114: 399–405

1988a. 'Monody, choral lyric, and the tyranny of the hand-book', *CQ* 38: 52–64

1988b. 'Stesichorus' *Geryoneis* and its folk-tale origins', *CQ* 38: 277–90

2015. 'The odd couple: snake and crab in an Attic *scolion* (*carm. conv. PMG* 892)', *Eikasmos* 26: 77–82

Davies, M., and P. J. Finglass 2014. *Stesichorus: the poems*, Cambridge

Davison, J. A. 1938. 'Alcman's *Partheneion*', *Hermes* 73: 440–8

1959. 'Anacreon, Fr. 5 Diehl', *TAPhA* 90: 40–7

De Cristofaro, L. 2005. 'L'aristocratico di Mitilene, le fanciulle di Lesbo e Achille a Sciro: alcune considerazioni su Alceo 130 V.', *ARF* 7: 5–8

de Jong, I. J. F. 2001. *A narratological commentary on the Odyssey*, Cambridge

de Kreij, M. 2016. 'Οὔκ ἐστι Σαπφοῦς τοῦτο τὸ ἄισμα: variants of Sappho's songs in Athenaeus' *Deipnosophistae*', *JHS* 136: 59–72

De Libero, L. 1996. *Die archaische Tyrannis*, Stuttgart

De Martino, F. 2006. *Poetesse greche*, Bari

Debiasi, A. 2004. *L'epica perduta: Eumelo, il Ciclo, l'occidente*, Rome

Del Freo, M. 1993. 'Alc. fr. 140 Voigt: il problema delle armi', *RAL* ser. 9, vol. 4: 377–92

Delavaud-Roux, M.-H. 1995. 'L'énigme des danseurs barbus au parasol et les vases "des Lénéennes"', *RA*: 227–63

Denniston, J. D. 1954. *The Greek particles*, 2nd edn, Oxford

Depew, M. 2000. 'Enacted and represented dedications: genre and Greek hymn', in M. Depew and D. Obbink, eds. *Matrices of genre: authors, canons, and society* (Cambridge, MA) 59–79

des Bouvrie Thorsen, S. 1978. 'The interpretation of Sappho's fragment 16 L.-P.', *SO* 53: 5–23

Detienne, M. 1994 [1972]. *The gardens of Adonis: spices in Greek mythology*, trans. J. Lloyd and J.-P. Vernant, Princeton

Deubner, L. 1982a [1941]. 'Ololyge und Verwandtes', in Deubner 1982c: 607–28

  1982b [1943]. 'Zu den neuen Bruchstücken des Alkaios', in Deubner 1982c: 691–704

  1982c. *Kleine Schriften zur klassischen Altertumskunde*, Königstein

Di Benedetto, V. 1973. 'Il volo di Afrodite in Omero e in Saffo', *QUCC* 16: 121–3

  2006. 'Il tetrastico di Saffo e tre postille', *ZPE* 155: 5–18

  2010. 'Una proposta di soluzione per Saffo fr. 31.17 V', *ZPE* 175: 1–2

Dickey, E. 1996. *Greek forms of address from Herodotus to Lucian*, Oxford

Dickie, M. 1978. 'The argument and form of Simonides 542 *PMG*', *HSPh* 82: 21–33

Donlan, W. 1969. 'Simonides, fr. 4D and *P.Oxy.* 2432', *TAPhA* 100: 71–95

  1970. 'Changes and shifts in the meaning of demos in the literature of the Archaic period', *PP* 25: 381–95

Dougherty, C. 2001. *The raft of Odysseus: the ethnographic imagination of Homer's Odyssey*, Oxford

Dryer, R. R. 1965. 'Asia/*Aswia and Archilochus fr. 23', *PP* 20: 115–32

Ducat, J. 2006. *Spartan education: youth and society in the Classical period*, trans. E. Stafford *et al.*, Swansea

Dunbar, N. 1995. *Aristophanes' Birds*, Oxford

Easterling, P. E. 1974. 'Alcman 58 and Simonides 37', *PCPhS* 20: 37–43

  1995. 'Holy Thebe', in *Studia in honorem Georgii Mihailov* (Sofia) 161–7

Edmunds, L. 2006. 'The New Sappho: ἔφαντο (9)', *ZPE* 156: 23–6

2012. 'Deixis and everyday expressions in Alcaeus frs. 129 V and 130b V', in *Donum natalicium digitaliter confectum Gregorio Nagy septuagenario a discipulis collegis familiaribus oblatum*, Washington, http://chs.harvard.edu/CHS/article/display/4353

Edwards, A. T. 1985. *Achilles in the Odyssey*, Königstein

Egger, É. 1865. 'Papyrus no. 71: fragment inédit du poëte Alcman', *Notices et textes des papyrus grecs du Musée du Louvre et de la Bibliothèque Impériale* 18: 416–420A

Ehrenberg, V. 1956. 'Das Harmodioslied', *WS* 69: 57–69

Elliger, W. 1975. *Die Darstellung der Landschaft in der griechischen Dichtung*, Berlin

Ercoles, M. 2008. 'La citarodia arcaica nelle testimonianze degli autori ateniesi d'età classica', *Philomusica on-line* 7: 124–36

2010. 'Note a Tim. *PMG* 791, 221–228', *Eikasmos* 21: 111–32

2011. 'Stesichorus *PMGF* S21.1–3 (*Geryoneis*): a textual proposal', *GRBS* 51: 350–62

2013. *Stesicoro: le testimonianze antiche*, Bologna

Esposito, E. 2005. *Il fragmentum Grenfellianum (P. Dryton 50)*, Bologna

Fabbro, H. 1995. *Carmina convivalia Attica*, Rome

Falkner, T. M. 1995. *The poetics of old age in Greek epic, lyric, and tragedy*, Norman, OK

Fantalkin, A. and E. Lytle 2016. 'Alcaeus and Antimenidas: reassessing the evidence for Greek mercenaries in the Neo-Babylonian army', *Klio* 98: 90–117

Faraone, C. A. 1993. 'Molten wax, spilt wine and mutilated animals: sympathetic magic in Near Eastern and early Greek oath ceremonies', *JHS* 113: 60–80

1999. *Ancient Greek love magic*, Cambridge, MA

Faulkner, A. 2008. *The Homeric Hymn to Aphrodite: introduction, text, and commentary*, Oxford

Fearn, D. 2013. '*Kleos* versus stone? Lyric poetry and contexts for memorialization', in P. Liddel and P. Low, eds. *Inscriptions and their uses in Greek and Latin literature* (Oxford) 231–53

2018. 'Materialities of political commitment? Textual events, material culture, and metaliterarity in Alcaeus', in Budelmann and Phillips 2018b: 93–113

Fehr, B. 1984. *Die Tyrannentöter*, Frankfurt

Ferrari, F. 1986. 'Formule saffiche e formule omeriche', *ASNP* 16: 441–7

2000a. 'Due note al testo del fr. 2 di Saffo', *APapyrol* 12: 37–44

2000b. *La porta dei canti: storia e antologia della lirica greca*, Bologna

2010 [2007]. *Sappho's gift: the poet and her community*, trans. B. Acosta-Hughes and L. Prauscello, Ann Arbor

2011. 'Di Kato Simi a Mitilene: ancora sull'ode dell'ostrakon fiorentino (Sapph fr. 2 Voigt)', *PP* 381: 442–63

2016. 'La via del rifugio: Alceo, fr. 130b V.', in *E sì d'amici pieno: omaggio di studiosi italiani a Guido Bastianini per il suo settantesimo compleanno* (Florence) 473–87

Ferrari, G. 2008. *Alcman and the cosmos of Sparta*, Chicago

Ferrarini, S. 2014. 'Simonide, Leonida e la "memoria degli avi": sull'occasione e il destinatario di Simon. *PMG* 531', *Athenaeum* 102: 369–87

Fileni, M. G. 1983. 'Osservazioni sull'idea di tiranno nella cultura greca arcaica (Alc. frr. 70,6–9; 129,21–24 V., Theogn. vv. 1179–1182)', *QUCC* n. s. 14: 29–35

Finglass, P. J., and A. Kelly (eds.) 2015. *Stesichorus in context*, Cambridge

Finkelberg, M. 1998. *The birth of literary fiction in ancient Greece*, Oxford

Fisher, N. 2000. 'Symposiasts, fish-eaters and flatterers: social mobility and moral concerns in old comedy', in D. Harvey and J. Wilkins, eds. *The rivals of Aristophanes: studies in Athenian Old Comedy* (London) 355–96

Fitzhardinge, L. F. 1980. *The Spartans*, London

Foley, H. P. 1998. '"The mother of the argument": eros and the body in Sappho and Plato's *Phaedrus*', in M. Wyke, ed. *Parchments of gender: deciphering the body in antiquity* (Oxford) 39–70

Föllinger, S. 2009. 'Tears and crying in Archaic Greek poetry (especially Homer)', in T. Fögen, ed. *Tears in the Graeco-Roman world* (Berlin) 17–36

Ford, A. 2002. *The origins of criticism: literary culture and poetic theory in Classical Greece*, Princeton

2003. 'From letters to literature: reading the "song culture" of Classical Greece', in H. Yunis, ed. *Written texts and the rise of literate culture in ancient Greece* (Cambridge) 15–37

2006. 'The genre of genres: paeans and *paian* in early Greek poetry', *Poetica* 38: 277–95

Ford, B. B., and E. C. Kopff 1976. 'Sappho fr. 31.9: a defense of the hiatus', *Glotta* 54: 52–6

Fornara, C. W. 1970. 'The cult of Harmodius and Aristogeiton', *Philologus* 114: 155–80

Forsdyke, S. 2005. *Exile, ostracism, and democracy*, Princeton

Forssman, B. 1966. *Untersuchungen zur Sprache Pindars*, Wiesbaden

1975. 'Zur Lautform der lesbischen Lyrik', *MSS* 33: 15–37

Förtsch, R. 2001. *Kunstverwendung und Kunstlegitimation im archaischen und frühklassischen Sparta*, Mainz

Fowler, R. L. 1987. *The nature of early Greek lyric: three preliminary studies*, Toronto

1995. 'Alkman *PMGF* 1.45: a reprise', *ZPE* 109: 1–4

Fraenkel, E. 1910–12. *Geschichte der griechischen Nomina agentis auf -τήρ, -τωρ, -της (-τ-)*, 2 vols., Strassburg

1950. *Aeschylus: Agamemnon*, 3 vols., Oxford

Fränkel, H. 1975 [1962]. *Early Greek poetry and philosophy: a history of Greek epic, lyric, and prose to the middle of the fifth century*, trans. M. Hadas and J. Willis, Oxford

Franklin, J. C. 2010. 'Remembering music in early Greece', in S. Mirelman, ed. *The historiography of music in global perspective* (Piscataway, NJ) 1–41

2013. '"Song-benders of circular choruses": dithyramb and the "demise of music"', in Kowalzig and Wilson 2013: 213–36

Franzen, C. 2009. 'Sympathizing with the monster: making sense of colonization in Stesichorus' *Geryoneis*', *QUCC* n. s. 92: 55–72

Frede, D. 1986. 'The impossibility of perfection: Socrates' criticism of Simonides' poem in the *Protagoras*', *RMeta* 39: 729–53

Friis Johansen, H., and E. W. Whittle 1980. *Aeschylus: the Suppliants*, 3 vols., Copenhagen

Frontisi-Ducroux, F., and F. Lissarrague 1990 [1983]. 'From ambiguity to ambivalence: a Dionysiac excursion through the "Anakreontic" vases', trans. R. Lamberton, in Halperin *et al.* 1990: 211–56

Führer, R. 1968. 'Die metrische Struktur von Stesichoros' Γηρυονηΐς (P.Ox. 2617)', *Hermes* 96: 675–84

1976. 'Beiträge zur Metrik und Textkritik der griechischen Lyriker: 1. Text und Kolometrie von Simonides' Danae (fr. 543 P.)', *Nachr. Akad. Wiss. Göttingen, phil.-hist. Kl.*: 109–64

Furley, W. D. 2000. '"Fearless, bloodless . . . like the gods": Sappho 31 and the rhetoric of "godlike"', *CQ* 50: 7–15

Furley, W. D., and J. M. Bremer 2001. *Greek hymns: selected cult songs from the Archaic to the Hellenistic period*, 2 vols., Tübingen

Gagné, R. 2013. *Ancestral fault in ancient Greece*, Cambridge

Gallavotti, C. 1942. 'Nuovi carmi di Alceo da Ossirinco', *RFIC* 20: 161–81

1981. 'La primavera di Ibico', *BollClass* 2: 120–35

Gambetti, S. 2001. 'Alcuni elementi per una interpretazione storica dei *Persiani* di Timoteo', *Simblos* 3: 45–65

Gantz, T. 1993. *Early Greek myth: a guide to literary and artistic sources*, Baltimore, MD

García-Ramón, J. L. 1998–9. 'Mycenaean *e-u-de-we-ro* /Eʰu-dewelo-/ "having nice late afternoons", Homeric εὐδείελος and Cyrenaean Εὐεσπερίδες', *Minos* 33–4: 135–47

Gargiulo, T. 1996. 'Mare e vino nei *Persiani*: una congettura a Timoteo, fr. 791, 61–62 Page', *QUCC* n. s. 54: 73–81

Garner, Richard 1990. *From Homer to tragedy: the art of allusion in Greek poetry*, London

Garner, R. Scott 2011. *Traditional elegy: the interplay of meter, tradition, and context in early Greek poetry*, Oxford

Garvie, A. F. 2009. *Aeschylus: Persae*, Oxford

Garzya, A. 1954. *Alcmane: i frammenti*, Naples

Geißler, C. 2005. 'Der Tithonosmythos bei Sappho und Kallimachos: zu Sappho fr. 58 V., 11–22 und Kallimachos, Aitia fr. 1 Pf.', *GFA* 8: 105–14

2011. 'Jungfrau oder Hetäre? Das "thrakische Füllen" und seine allegorische Deutung (Anacr. *PMG* 417 ap. Heraclit. *All.* 5.10–1 und [Theoc.] *Id.* 20.11–8)', *Mnemosyne* 64: 541–55

Gellar-Goad, T. H. M. 2017. 'Failure of the textual relation: Anacreon's purple ball poem (*PMG* 358)', in A. Park, ed. *Resemblance and reality in Greek thought* (London) 46–64

Gentili, B. 1958. *Anacreon*, Rome

1960. 'Studi su Simonide', *RCCM* 2: 113–23

1964. 'Studi su Simonide: II. Simonide e Platone', *Maia* 16: 278–306

1966. 'Sul testo del fr. 287 P. di Ibico', *QUCC* 2: 124–7

1967. 'Metodi di lettura (su alcune congetture ai poeti lirici)', *QUCC* 4: 177–81

1972. 'Il "letto insaziato" di Medea e il tema dell'*adikia* a livello amoroso nei lirici (Saffo, Tegonide) e nella *Medea* di Euripide', *SCO* 21: 60–72

1973. 'La ragazza di Lesbo', *QUCC* 16: 124–8

1977. 'Eracle "omicida giustissimo": Pisandro, Stesicoro e Pindaro', in B. Gentili and G. Paioni, eds. *Il mito greco: atti del convegno internazionale (Urbino, 7–12 maggio 1973)* (Rome) 299–305

1984. 'Eros custode: Ibico, fr. 286 P. e Meleagro, *Anth. P.* 12, 157', *EClás* 87: 191–7

1988 [1984]. *Poetry and its public in ancient Greece: from Homer to the fifth century*, trans. A. T. Cole, Baltimore, MD

Gentili, B., and C. Catenacci 2007. *Polinnia: poesia greca arcaica*, 3rd edn, Messina

Gentili, B., and P. Giannini 1977. 'Preistoria e formazione dell'esametro', *QUCC* 26: 7–51

Gerber, D. E. 1982. *Pindar's Olympian One: a commentary*, Toronto

Gerkan, A. v. 1935. *Die Stadtmauern*, Berlin

Giangrande, G. 1968. 'Sympotic literature and epigram', in O. Reverdin, ed. *L'Épigramme grecque*, Entretiens Hardt vol. 14 (Geneva) 91–174

1973. 'Anacreon and the Lesbian girl', *QUCC* 16: 129–33

1995. 'Anacreon's pubic hair', *Habis* 26: 9–12

2011. 'Anacreon's sense of humour and the Greek language', *Habis* 42: 27–33

Giannini, P. 2000. 'Eros e primavera nel fr. 286 Davies di Ibico', in Cannatà Fera and Grandolini 2000: I.335–43

2004. 'Ibico a Samo', in E. Cavallini, ed. *Samo: storia, letteratura, scienza* (Pisa) 51–64

Gianotti, G. F. 1973. 'Mito ed encomio: il carme di Ibico in onore di Policrate', *RFIC* 101: 401–10

Gioia, T. 2006. *Work songs*, Durham, NC

Goff, B. 2004. *Citizen Bacchae: women's ritual practice in ancient Greece*, Berkeley

Goldhill, S. 1987. 'The dance of the veils: reading five fragments of Anacreon', *Eranos* 85: 9–18

1991. *The poet's voice: essays on poetics and Greek literature*, Cambridge

1999. 'Literary history without literature: reading practices in the ancient world', *SubStance* 88: 57–89

Goodwin, W. W. 1887. *Syntax of the moods and tenses of the Greek verb*, rewritten and enlarged edn, London

Gostoli, A. 1979. 'Osservazioni metriche sull'encomio a Policrate di Ibico', *QUCC* n. s. 2: 93–9

Gow, A. S. F. 1955. 'Two epigrams by Diotimus', *CR* 5: 238–41

Graf, F. 1985. *Nordionische Kulte*, Rome

Graziosi, B., and J. Haubold 2009. 'Greek lyric and early Greek literary history', in Budelmann 2009: 95–113

Greene, E. (ed.) 1996. *Reading Sappho: contemporary approaches*, Berkeley

2002. 'Subjects, objects, and erotic symmetry in Sappho's fragments', in N. S. Rabinowitz and L. Auanger, eds. *Among women: from the homosocial to the homoerotic in the ancient world* (Austin) 82–105

Greene, E., and M. B. Skinner (eds.) 2009. *The New Sappho on old age: textual and philosophical issues*, Washington, DC

Griffith, M. 1983. *Aeschylus: Prometheus Bound*, Cambridge

1990. 'Contest and contradiction in early Greek poetry', in M. Griffith and D. J. Mastronarde, eds. *Cabinet of the Muses: essays on classical and comparative literature in honor of Thomas G. Rosenmeyer* (Atlanta) 185–207

2006. 'Horsepower and donkeywork: equids and the ancient Greek imagination', *CPh* 101: 185–246 (part 1) and 307–58 (part 2)

Griffith, R. D. 2000. 'Tricks on ancient Rhodes', *Athenaeum* 88: 276

Griffiths, A. 1972. 'Alcman's *Partheneion*: the morning after the night before', *QUCC* 14: 7–30

Grig, L. (ed.) 2017. *Popular culture in the ancient world*, Cambridge

Gronewald, M. 1988. 'Ein Erntelied in *P. Ryl.* I 34?', *ZPE* 73: 31–2

Gronewald, M., and R. W. Daniel 2004a. 'Ein neuer Sappho-Papyrus', *ZPE* 147: 1–8

2004b. 'Nachtrag zum neuen Sappho-Papyrus', *ZPE* 149: 1–4

Gurd, S. A. 2016. *Dissonance: auditory aesthetics in ancient Greece*, New York

Hagel, S. 2010. *Ancient Greek music: a new technical history*, Cambridge

Hall, E. 1988. 'When did the Trojans turn into Phrygians? Alcaeus 42.15', *ZPE* 73: 15–18

1996. *Aeschylus: Persians*, Warminster
2006. *The theatrical cast of Athens: interactions between ancient Greek drama and society*, Oxford
Hall, J. M. 2002. *Hellenicity: between ethnicity and culture*, Chicago
2012. 'Early Greek settlement in the west: the limits of colonisation', in K. Bosher, ed. *Theater outside Athens: drama in Greek Sicily and South Italy* (Cambridge) 19–34
Halliwell, S. 2008. *Greek laughter: a study of cultural psychology from Homer to early Christianity*, Cambridge
Halperin, D. M., *et al.* (eds.) 1990. *Before sexuality: the construction of erotic experience in the ancient Greek world*, Princeton
Hamilton, R. 1989. 'Alkman and the Athenian Arkteia', *Hesperia* 58: 449–72
Hamm, E.-M. 1957. *Grammatik zu Sappho und Alkaios*, Berlin
Hammer, D. 2004. 'Ideology, the symposium, and Archaic politics', *AJPh* 125: 479–512
Hammerstaedt, J. 2009. 'The Cologne Sappho: its discovery and textual constitution', in Greene and Skinner 2009: 17–40
Hammond, N. G. L., and L. J. Roseman 1996. 'The construction of Xerxes' bridge over the Hellespont', *JHS* 116: 88–107
Hansen, M. H. 1991. *The Athenian democracy in the age of Demosthenes: structure, principles and ideology*, trans. J. A. Crook, Oxford
Hansen, O. 1984. 'On the date and place of the first performance of Timotheus' *Persae*', *Philologus* 128: 135–8
Hardie, A. 2005. 'Sappho, the Muses, and life after death', *ZPE* 154: 13–32
2013. 'Ibycus and the Muses of Helicon', *MD* 70: 9–36
Harvey, A. E. 1955. 'The classification of Greek lyric poetry', *CQ* 5: 157–75
1957. 'Homeric epithets in Greek lyric poetry', *CQ* 7: 206–23
Haslam, M. W. 1974. 'Stesichorean metre', *QUCC* 17: 7–57
1986. '*Lesbiaca* (commentary on Alcaeus?)', *Oxyrhynchus Papyri* 53: 112–25
2011. 'Text and transmission', in M. Finkelberg, ed. *The Homer encyclopedia* (Oxford) 848–55
Hatto, A. 1965. *Eos: an enquiry into the theme of lovers' meetings and partings at dawn in poetry*, London
Haubold, J. 2000. *Homer's people: epic poetry and social formation*, Cambridge
Headlam, W. 1922. *Herodas: the mimes and fragments*, Cambridge
Helly, B. 1995. *L'état thessalien: Aleuas le Roux, les tétrades et les tagoi*, Lyon
Henderson, J. 1975. *The maculate muse: obscene language in Attic comedy*, New Haven
1987. *Aristophanes: Lysistrata*, Oxford
Henrichs, A. 1978. 'Greek maenadism from Olympias to Messalina', *HSPh* 82: 121–60

1994–5. '"Why should I dance?": choral self-referentiality in Greek tragedy', *Arion* 3.1: 56–111

Herington, J. 1985. *Poetry into drama: early tragedy and the Greek poetic tradition*, Berkeley

Herzfeld, M. 1977. 'Ritual and textual structures: the advent of spring in rural Greece', in R. K. Jain, ed. *Text and context: the social anthropology of tradition* (Philadelphia) 29–50

2004. 'Rites of spring: ritual, resistance, and taxonomic regimentation in Greek cultural history', in D. Yatromanolakis and P. Roilos, eds. *Greek ritual poetics* (Washington, DC) 371–82

Herzhoff, B. 1994. 'Kriegerhaupt und Mohnblume – ein verkanntes Homergleichnis (Θ 306–308)', *Hermes* 122: 385–403

Heubeck, A., *et al.* 1988. *A commentary on Homer's Odyssey*, vol. I, Oxford

Hinge, G. 2006. *Die Sprache Alkmans: Textgeschichte und Sprachgeschichte*, Wiesbaden

2009. 'Cultic persona and the transmission of the partheneions', in J. T. Jensen *et al.*, eds. *Aspects of ancient Greek cult: context, ritual, iconography* (Aarhus) 215–36

Hobden, F. 2011. 'Enter the divine: sympotic performance and religious experience', in A. P. M. H. Lardinois *et al.*, eds. *Sacred words: orality, literacy and religion* (Leiden) 37–57

Hodot, R. 1990. *Le dialecte éolien d'Asie: la langue des inscriptions, VIIe s. a.C.– IVe s. p.C.*, Paris

Hofstetter, E. 1997. 'Seirenes', *LIMC* VIII.1: 1093–1104

Hölkeskamp, K.-J. 1999. *Schiedsrichter, Gesetzgeber und Gesetzgebung im archaischen Griechenland*, Stuttgart

Holzberg, N. 2002. *The ancient fable: an introduction*, trans. C. Jackson-Holzberg, Bloomington

Hooker, J. T. 1973. 'Sapphos βροδοδάκτυλος und Verwandtes', *GB* 1: 165–9

1977. *The language and the text of the Lesbian poets*, Innsbruck

1979. 'The unity of Alcman's Partheneion', *RhM* 122: 211–21

Hordern, J. H. 2002. *The fragments of Timotheus of Miletus*, Oxford

Hornblower, S. 1991–2008. *A commentary on Thucydides*, 3 vols., Oxford

2013. *Herodotus: Histories Book* V, Cambridge

Horrocks, G. 1981. *Space and time in Homer: prepositional and adverbial particles in the Greek epic*, New York

Hubbard, T. K. 2011. 'The dissemination of Pindar's non-epinician choral lyric', in Athanassaki and Bowie 2011: 347–64

Huber, I. 2002. 'Der Perser-Nomos des Timotheos: zwischen Unterhaltungsliteratur und politischer Propaganda', in M. Schuol *et al.*, eds. *Grenzüberschreitungen: Formen des Kontakts zwischen Orient und Okzident im Altertum* (Stuttgart) 169–95

Hullinger, D. 2016. 'Chasing a dark horse: pursuit and identity in Anacreon's "Thracian filly" fragment [417 PMG]', *Mnemosyne* 69: 729–41

Hunter, R. 2002. '"Acting down": the ideology of Hellenistic performance', in P. E. Easterling and E. Hall, eds. *Greek and Roman actors: aspects of an ancient profession* (Cambridge) 189–206

2005. '"Sweet talk": *Song of Songs* and the traditions of Greek poetry', in A. C. Hagedorn, ed. *Perspectives on the Song of Songs = Perspektiven der Hoheliedauslegung* (Berlin) 228–44

2014. *Hesiodic voices: studies in the ancient reception of Hesiod's Works and Days*, Cambridge

Hunter, R., and I. Rutherford (eds.) 2009. *Wandering poets in ancient Greek culture: travel, locality and pan-Hellenism*, Cambridge

Hunter, R., and A. S. Uhlig (eds.) 2017. *Imagining reperformance in ancient culture: studies in the traditions of drama and lyric*, Cambridge

Hunter, V. J. 1994. *Policing Athens: social control in the Attic lawsuits, 420–320 B.C.*, Princeton

Hutchinson, G. O. 2001. *Greek lyric poetry: a commentary on selected larger pieces*, Oxford

Hutzfeldt, B. 1999. *Das Bild der Perser in der griechischen Dichtung des 5. vorchristlichen Jahrhunderts*, Wiesbaden

Inglese, L. 2002. 'Simon. PMG 531,3 προγόνων δε μνᾶστις', *Eikasmos* 13: 17–22

Irigoin, J. 1952. *Histoire du texte de Pindare*, Paris

Irvine, J. A. D. 1997. 'Keres in Stesichorus' *Geryoneis*: P.Oxy 2617 fr. 1 (a)–(b) = SLG 21 reconsidered', *ZPE* 115: 37–46

Irwin, E. 1984. 'The crocus and the rose: a study of the interrelationship between the natural and the divine world in early Greek poetry', in D. E. Gerber, ed. *Greek poetry and philosophy: studies in honour of Leonard Woodbury* (Chico, CA) 147–68

Ivanov, R. 2010. 'Nietzsche redivivus: Simonides, fr. 543.11 PMG', *RhM* 153: 113–24

Ivantchik, A. I. 2002. 'Un fragment de l'épopée scythe: "le cheval de Colaxaïs" dans un partheneion d'Alcman', *Ktema* 27: 257–64

Jackson, V. 2012. 'Lyric', in R. Greene, ed. *The Princeton encyclopedia of poetry and poetics* (Princeton) 826–34

Jackson, V., and Y. Prins (eds.) 2014. *The lyric theory reader: a critical anthology*, Baltimore, MD

James, S. L., and S. Dillon (eds.) 2012. *A companion to women in the ancient world*, Chichester

Janni, P. 1965. *La cultura di Sparta arcaica: ricerche*, vol. 1, Rome

Janssen, T. H. 1984. *Timotheus Persae: a commentary*, Utrecht

Jarva, E. 1995. *Archaiologia on Archaic Greek body armour*, Rovaniemi

Jedrkiewicz, S. 1989. *Sapere e paradosso nell'Antichità: Esopo e la favola*, Rome

Jenkyns, R. 1982. *Three classical poets: Sappho, Catullus and Juvenal*, London
Johnson, M. 2009. 'A reading of Sappho poem 58, fragment 31 and Mimnermus', in Greene and Skinner 2009: 162–75
Johnson, W. R. 1982. *The idea of lyric: lyric modes in ancient and modern poetry*, Berkeley
Johnston, R. W., and D. Mulroy 2004. 'Simonides' use of the term τετράγωνος', *Arethusa* 37: 1–10
Jones, G. S. 2014. 'Voice of the people: popular symposia and the non-elite origins of the Attic *skolia*', *TAPhA* 144: 229–62
  2016. 'Observing genre in Archaic Greek *skolia* and vase-painting', in Cazzato and Lardinois 2016: 146–84
Jouanna, J. 1999. 'Le trône, les fleurs, le char et la puissance d'Aphrodite (Sappho I, v. 1, 11, 19 et 22): remarques sur le texte, sur les composés en -θρονος et sur les homérismes de Sappho', *REG* 112: 99–126
Jourdain-Annequin, C. 1989. *Héraclès aux portes du soir: mythe et histoire*, Paris
Kakridis, J. T. 1966. 'Zu Sappho 44 LP', *WS* 79: 21–6
Kantzios, I. 2005. 'Tyranny and the symposion of Anacreon', *CJ* 100: 227–45
  2010. 'Marginal voice and erotic discourse in Anacreon', *Mnemosyne* 63: 577–89
Käppel, L. 1992. *Paian: Studien zur Geschichte einer Gattung*, Berlin
Karanika, A. 2007. 'Folk songs as ritual acts: the case of work-songs', in M. Parca and A. Tzanetou, eds. *Finding Persephone: women's rituals in the ancient Mediterranean* (Bloomington) 137–53
  2009. 'The *ololygê* in the *Homeric Hymn to Apollo*: from poetics to politics', in L. Athanassaki *et al.*, eds. *Apolline politics and poetics* (Athens) 67–77
  2014. *Voices at work: women, performance, and labor in ancient Greece*, Baltimore, MD
Kauffmann-Samaras, A. 1996. 'Paroles et musiques de mariage en Grèce antique: sources écrites et images peintes', in O. Cavalier, ed. *Silence et fureur: la femme et le mariage en Grèce* (Avignon) 435–48
Kehrhahn, T. 1914. 'Anacreontea', *Hermes* 49: 481–507
Kelly, A. 2015. 'Stesichorus' Homer', in Finglass and Kelly 2015: 21–44
Kennell, N. M. 2010. *Spartans: a new history*, Oxford
Kidd, D. 1997. *Aratus: Phenomena*, Cambridge
Kierdorf, W. 1966. *Erlebnis und Darstellung der Perserkriege: Studien zu Simonides, Pindar, Aischylos und den attischen Rednern*, Göttingen
Kivilo, M. 2010. *Early Greek poets' lives: the shaping of the tradition*, Leiden
Kleingünther, A. 1933. Πρῶτος εὑρετής: *Untersuchungen zur Geschichte einer Fragestellung*, Leipzig
Klinck, A. L. 2002. 'Sappho and her daughters: some parallels between ancient and medieval women's song', in A. L. Klinck

and A. M. Rasmussen, eds. *Medieval woman's song* (Philadelphia) 15–28

Kokkorou-Alewras, G. 1990. 'Herakles and the Lernaean Hydra (labour 11)', *LIMC* V.1: 34–43

Koniaris, G. L. 1967. 'On Sappho, fr. 16 (L.P.)', *Hermes* 95: 257–68

Korzeniewski, D. 1974. 'De Binnenresponsion in den *Persern* des Timotheos', *Philologus* 118: 22–39

Kossatz-Deissmann, A. 1997. 'Troilos', *LIMC* VIII.1: 91–4

Kowalzig, B. 2007. *Singing for the gods: performances of myth and ritual in Archaic and Classical Greece*, Oxford

Kowalzig, B., and P. Wilson (eds.) 2013. *Dithyramb in context*, Oxford

Kowerski, L. M. 2005. *Simonides on the Persian Wars: a study of the elegiac verses of the 'New Simonides'*, New York

Kranz, W. 1961. 'Sphragis: Ichform und Namensiegel als Eingangs- und Schlußmotiv antiker Dichtung', *RhM* 104: 3–46 and 97–124

Kretschmer, P. 1917. 'Literaturbericht für das Jahr 1914: Griechisch', *Glotta* 8: 249–70

Krischer, T. 1968. 'Sapphos Ode an Aphrodite (typologische Bemerkungen)', *Hermes* 96: 1–14

Krummen, E. 2013. '*Kolombôsai, klinai* und eine lydische Mitra: Alkman als Dichter der orientalischen Epoche Spartas', in P. Mauritsch and C. Ulf, eds. *Kultur(en): Formen des Alltäglichen in der Antike* (Graz) 19–44

2014 [1990]. *Cult, myth, and occasion in Pindar's victory odes: a study of Isthmian 4, Pythian 5, Olympian 1, and Olympian 3*, trans. J. G. Howie, Prenton

Kullmann, W., and M. Reichel (eds.) 1990. *Der Übergang von der Mündlichkeit zur Literatur bei den Griechen*, Tübingen

Kurke, L. 1991. *The traffic in praise: Pindar and the poetics of social economy*, Ithaca, NY

1992. 'The politics of ἁβροσύνη in Archaic Greece', *ClAnt* 11: 91–120

1994. 'Crisis and decorum in sixth-century Lesbos: reading Alkaios otherwise', *QUCC* n. s. 47: 67–92

1997. 'Inventing the *hetaira*: sex, politics, and discursive conflict in Archaic Greece', *ClAnt* 16: 106–50

1999. *Coins, bodies, games, and gold: the politics of meaning in Archaic Greece*, Princeton

2007. 'Archaic Greek poetry', in H. A. Shapiro, ed. *The Cambridge companion to Archaic Greece* (Cambridge) 141–68

2011. *Aesopic conversations: popular tradition, cultural dialogue, and the invention of Greek prose*, Princeton

Lambin, G. 1992. *La chanson grecque dans l'antiquité*, Paris

1998. 'Les "délices" d'Harmodios (Aristophane, *Acharniens*, v. 1093)', *RPh* 72: 59–64

2002. *Anacréon: fragments et imitations*, Rennes

2013. *Timothée de Milet: le poète et le musicien*, Rennes

Lanata, G. 1960. 'L'ostracon fiorentino con versi di Saffo: note paleografiche ed esegetiche', *SIFC* 32: 64–90

1996 [1966]. 'Sappho's amatory language', trans. W. Robins, in Greene 1996: 11–25

Langdon, M. K. 2015. 'Herders' graffiti', in A. P. Matthaiou and N. Papazarkadas, eds. *Axon: studies in honor of Ronald S. Stroud* (Athens) 49–58

Lardinois, A. 1996. 'Who sang Sappho's songs?', in Greene 1996: 150–72

2009. 'The new Sappho poem (*P.Köln* 21351 and 21376): key to the old fragments', in Greene and Skinner 2009: 41–57

Lasserre, F. 1989. *Sappho: une autre lecture*, Padua

Latacz, J. 1985. 'Realität und Imagination: eine neue Lyrik-Theorie und Sapphos φαίνεταί μοι κῆνος-Lied', *MH* 42: 67–94

1990. 'Die Funktion des Symposions für die entstehende griechische Literatur', in Kullmann and Reichel 1990: 227–64

Lazzeri, M. 2008. *Studi sulla Gerioneide di Stesicoro*, Naples

Ledbetter, G. M. 2003. *Poetics before Plato: interpretation and authority in early Greek theories of poetics*, Princeton

Lefkowitz, M. R. 2012. *The lives of the Greek poets*, 2nd edn, London

Lelli, E. 2006. *Volpe e leone: il proverbio nella poesia greca (Alceo, Cratino, Callimaco)*, Rome

Lenz, L. 1994. 'Zwei Flaneure: Anakreon 54 D. (= 388 PMG) und Horaz' 4. Epode', *Gymnasium* 101: 483–501

Leo, G. M. 2015. *Anacreonte: i frammenti erotici: testo, commento e traduzione*, Rome

Lerza, P. 1978. 'Su un frammento della *Gerioneide* di Stesicoro', *Atene e Roma* n. s. 23: 83–7

1979. 'Nota a Stesicoro', *Atene e Roma* n.s. 24: 41–3

Leumann, M. 1950. *Homerische Wörter*, Basel

LeVen, P. A. 2011. 'Timotheus' eleven strings: a new approach (*PMG* 791. 229–36)', *CPh* 106: 245–54

2014. *The many-headed Muse: tradition and innovation in late Classical Greek lyric poetry*, Cambridge

2018. 'Echo and the invention of the lyric listener', in Budelmann and Phillips 2018b: 213–33

Lewis, D. M. 1988. 'The tyranny of the Pisistratidae', in J. Boardman *et al.*, eds. *The Cambridge ancient history*, vol. IV² (Cambridge) 287–302

Liberman, G. 1992. 'Lire Sappho dans Démétrios, *Sur le style*', *QUCC* n. s. 40: 45–8

1999. *Alcée: fragments*, 2 vols., Paris

2007. 'L'édition alexandrine de Sappho', in G. Bastianini and A. Casanova, eds. *I papiri di Saffo e di Alceo* (Florence) 41–65

2016. 'Some thoughts on the symposiastic catena, *aisakos*, and *skolia*', in Cazzato *et al.* 2016: 42–62

Lidov, J. 2009. 'The meter and metrical style of the new poem', in Greene and Skinner 2009: 103–17

2010. 'Meter, colon, and rhythm: Simonides (*PMG* 542) and Pindar between Archaic and Classical', *CPh* 105: 25–53

2016. 'Songs for sailors and lovers', in Bierl and Lardinois 2016: 55–109

Liebermann, W.-L. 1980. 'Überlegungen zu Sapphos "Höchstwert"', *A&A* 26: 51–74

Lissarrague, F. 1995. 'Women, boxes, containers: some signs and metaphors', trans. E. Brulotte, in Reeder 1995: 91–101

1996. 'Regards sur le mariage grec', in O. Cavalier, ed. *Silence et fureur: la femme et le mariage en Grèce* (Avignon) 415–33

1999. 'Publicity and performance: *kalos* inscriptions in Attic vase painting', trans. R. Osborne, in S. Goldhill and R. Osborne, eds. *Performance culture and Athenian democracy* (Cambidge) 359–73

Littlewood, A. R. 1968. 'The symbolism of the apple in Greek and Roman literature', *HSPh* 72: 147–81

Livrea, E. 2007. 'La vecchiaia su papiro: Saffo, Simonide, Callimaco, Cercida', in G. Bastianini and A. Casanova, eds. *I papiri di Saffo e di Alceo* (Florence) 67–81

2016. 'Novità su Saffo nella poesia alessandrina: la chiusa del fr. 31 V. e due letture ellenistiche dell'ode', *Eikasmos* 27: 57–71

Lloyd-Jones, H. 1974. 'Simonides, *P.M.G.* 531', *CR* 24: 1

Long, A. A. 1968. *Language and thought in Sophocles: a study of abstract nouns and poetic techniques*, London

Lonsdale, S. H. 1993. *Dance and ritual play in Greek religion*, Baltimore, MD

Luginbill, R. D. 1995. 'Ibycus 286: the beleagured heart', *Maia* 47: 343–7

Lundon, J. 2007. 'Die fehlende Silbe im neuen Kölner Sappho-Papyrus', *ZPE* 160: 1–3

Luppe, W. 2004. 'Überlegungen zur Gedicht-Anordnung im neuen Sappho-Papyrus', *ZPE* 149: 7–9

Maas, M., and J. M. Snyder 1989. *Stringed instruments of ancient Greece*, New Haven

Mace, S. 1993. 'Amour, encore! The development of δηὖτε in Archaic lyric', *GRBS* 34: 335–64

Maehler, H. 1963. *Die Auffassung des Dichterberufs im frühen Griechentum bis zur Zeit Pindars*, Göttingen

2000. 'Beobachtungen zum Gebrauch des Satz-Asyndetons bei Bakchylides und Pindar', in Cannatà Fera and Grandolini 2000: II. 421–33

Magnani, M. 2013a. '*Carmina popularia*: origine e sviluppo della raccolta', *Paideia* 68: 543–73

2013b. 'Note marginali ai *Carmina popularia*', *Eikasmos* 24: 45–66

Magnelli, E. 2015. 'Omero (*Il.* II 311–316) ma soprattutto Alcmane (*PMGF* 89) in *4 Mac.* 14,16s.', *Eikasmos* 26: 27–30

Maingon, A. D. 1980. 'Epic convention in Stesichorus' *Geryoneis: SLG* S15', *Phoenix* 34: 99–107

Malkin, I. 1994. *Myth and territory in the Spartan Mediterranean*, Cambridge

Malnati, A. 1993. 'Revisione dell'ostrakon fiorentino di Saffo', *APapyrol* 5: 21–2

Manuwald, B. 2010. 'Ist Simonides' Gedicht an Skopas (PMG 542) vollständig überliefert?', *RhM* 153: 1–24

March, J. R. 1987. *The creative poet: studies on the treatment of myths in Greek poetry*, London

Marcovich, M. 1983. 'Anacreon, 358 *PMG* (ap. Athen. XIII.599 c)', *AJPh* 104: 372–83

Mariotti, I. 1987. 'Ibico, Omero e la vicenda delle stagioni', in *Filologia e forme letterarie: studi offerti a Francesco Della Corte* (Urbino) 1.67–77

Markwald, G. 1986. *Die Homerischen Epigramme: sprachliche und inhaltliche Untersuchungen*, Königstein

Maronitis, D. N. 2004 [1984]. 'The heroic myth and its lyrical reconstruction', trans. D. Connolly, in *Homeric megathemes: war, homilia, homecoming* (Lanham, MD) 77–88

Martin, H. 1972. *Alcaeus*, New York

Martin, R. P. 1993. 'The seven sages as performers of wisdom', in C. Dougherty and L. Kurke, eds. *Cultural poetics in Archaic Greece: cult, performance, politics* (Cambridge) 108–28

2007. 'Outer limits, choral space', in C. Kraus *et al.*, eds. *Visualizing the tragic: drama, myth, and ritual in Greek art and literature* (Oxford) 35–62

2017. 'Crooked competition: the performance and poetics of *skolia*', in E. J. Bakker, ed. *Authorship and Greek song: authority, authenticity, and performance* (Leiden) 61–79

Martín Vásquez, L. 1999. 'The song of the swallow', *CFC(G)* 9: 23–39

Marzillo, P. 2010. *Der Kommentar des Proklos zu Hesiods Werken und Tagen*, Tübingen

Marzullo, B. 2009. *Il 'miraggio' di Alceo*, Berlin

Maslov, B. 2015. *Pindar and the emergence of literature*, Cambridge

Massimi, A. 1959. 'Schedae Sapphicae', *GIF* 12: 26–35

Masson, O. 1951. 'Encore les "Épodes de Strasbourg"', *REG* 64: 427–42

Mastronarde, D. J. 1994. *Euripides: Phoenissae*, Cambridge

Maurach, G. 1968. 'Schilderungen in der archaischen Lyrik: zu Alkaios Fr. Z 34', *Hermes* 96: 15–20

McEvilley, T. 1972. 'Sappho, fragment two', *Phoenix* 26: 323–33

McKeown, J. C. 1979. 'Augustan elegy and mime', *PCPhS* 25: 71–84

Mehl, V. 2008. 'Parfum de fêtes: usage de parfums et sacrifices sanglants', in V. Mehl and P. Brulé, eds. *Le sacrifice antique: vestiges, procédures et stratégies* (Rennes) 167–86

Meyerhoff, D. 1984. *Traditioneller Stoff und individuelle Gestaltung: Untersuchungen zu Alkaios und Sappho,* Hildesheim

Miller, D. G. 2013. *Ancient Greek dialects and early authors: introduction to the dialect mixture in Homer, with notes on lyric and Herodotus,* Boston

Miller, M. C. 1992. 'The parasol: an oriental status-symbol in Late Archaic and Classical Athens', *JHS* 112: 91–105

1997. *Athens and Persia in the fifth century* BC: *a study in cultural receptivity,* Cambridge

Mollard-Besques, S. 1954. *Musée national du Louvre: catalogue raisonné des figurines et reliefs en terre-cuite grecs, étrusques et romains,* 5 vols., Paris

Molyneux, J. H. 1992. *Simonides: a historical study,* Wauconda, IL

Monoson, S. S. 2000. *Plato's democratic entanglements: Athenian politics and the practice of philosophy,* Princeton

Morani, M. 1990. 'Rileggendo il notturno di Alcmane: considerazioni filologiche e linguistiche', *Orpheus* n. s. 11: 221–44

Morantin, P. 2009. 'L'hymne à Artemis d'Anacréon (*PMG* 348 = Gent. 1)', *QUCC* n. s. 91: 81–94

Morelli, G. 1963. 'Un antico carme popolare rodiese', *SIFC* 35: 121–60

Morgan, K. A. (ed.) 2003. *Popular tyranny: sovereignty and its discontents in ancient Greece,* Austin

2008. 'Generic ethics and the problem of badness in Pindar', in I. Sluiter and R. M. Rosen, eds. *Kakos: badness and anti-value in classical antiquity* (Leiden) 29–57

2015. *Pindar and the construction of Syracusan monarchy in the fifth century* BC, New York

Moritz, L. A. 1958. *Grain-mills and flour in classical antiquity,* Oxford

Morris, I. 1986. 'The use and abuse of Homer', *ClAnt* 5: 81–138

1996. 'The strong principle of equality and the Archaic origins of Greek democracy', in J. Ober and C. Hedrick, eds. *Dēmokratia: a conversation on democracies, ancient and modern* (Princeton) 19–48

Morrison, A. D. 2007. *The narrator in Archaic Greek and Hellenistic poetry,* Cambridge

Most, G. W. 1981. 'Sappho fr. 16.6–7 L-P', *CQ* 31: 11–17

1994. 'Simonides' ode to Scopas in contexts', in I. J. F. de Jong and J. P. Sullivan, eds. *Modern critical theory and classical literature* (Leiden) 127–52

1995. 'Reflecting Sappho', *BICS* 40: 15–38

Mueller-Goldingen, C. 2001. 'Dichter und Herrscher: Bemerkungen zur Polykratesode des Ibykos', *AC* 70: 17–26

Murnaghan, S. 1992. 'Maternity and mortality in Homeric poetry', *ClAnt* 11: 242–64

Murray, O. 1988. 'Death and the symposion', *AION(archeol)* 10: 239–57

1990. *Sympotica: a symposium on the symposion*, Oxford

Muth, S. 2008. *Gewalt im Bild: das Phänomen der medialen Gewalt im Athen des 6. und 5. Jahrhunderts v. Chr.*, Berlin

Nagy, G. 1974. *Comparative studies in Greek and Indic meter*, Cambridge, MA.

1979. *The best of the Achaeans: concepts of the hero in Archaic Greek poetry*, revised edn, Baltimore

1990. *Pindar's Homer: the lyric possession of an epic past*, Baltimore, MD

1993. 'Alcaeus in sacred space', in Pretagostini 1993b: 1.221–5

2007. 'Did Sappho and Alcaeus ever meet? Symmetries of myth and ritual in performing the songs of ancient Lesbos', in A. Bierl *et al.*, eds. *Literatur und Religion*, vol. 1: *Wege zu einer mythisch–rituellen Poetik bei den Griechen* (Berlin) 211–69

Napolitano, M. 2000. 'Simonide, fr. 531.3 Page: πρὸ γόων, προγόνων, o altro?', *SemRom* 3: 205–15

Natale, A. 2009. 'Spigolature sull'*Encomio a Policrate* di Ibico (fr. S 151 Davies)', *BollClass* 30: 55–83

Neer, R. 2002. *Style and politics in Athenian vase-painting: the craft of democracy, ca. 530–460 BCE*, Cambridge

Neri, C. 2003. 'Sotto la politica: una lettura dei *carmina popularia* melici', *Lexis* 21: 193–260

Neri, C., and F. Citti 2005. 'Sudore freddo e tremore (Sapph. fr. 31,13 V ~ Sen. *Tro.* 487s. ~ Apul. *Met.* I 13, II 30, X 10)', *Eikasmos*: 51–62

Neuberger-Donath, R. 1977. 'Sappho 31.2s.', *AClass* 20: 199–200

Nicholson, N. 2000. 'Pederastic poets and adult patrons in late Archaic lyric', *CW* 93: 235–59

Nicosia, S. 1977. *Tradizione testuale diretta e indiretta dei poeti di Lesbo*, Rome

Nieddu, G. F. 1993. 'Parola e metro nella *sphragis* dei *Persiani* di Timoteo (*PMG* fr. 791, 202–236)', in Pretagostini 1993b: II.521–9

Nøjgaard, M. 1964–7. *La fable antique*, 2 vols., Copenhagen

Norsa, M. 1937. 'Versi di Saffo in un ostrakon del sec. II a.c.', *ASNP* ser. II, vol. 6: 8–15

Nöthiger, M. 1971. *Die Sprache des Stesichorus und des Ibycus*, Zurich

Noussia Fantuzzi, M. 2013. 'A scenario for Stesichorus' portrayal of the monster Geryon in the *Geryoneis*', *Trends in Classics* 5: 234–59

Oakley, J. H., and R. H. Sinos 1993. *The wedding in ancient Athens*, Madison, WI

Obbink, D. 2001. 'The genre of *Plataea*: generic unity in the New Simonides', in Boedeker and Sider 2001: 65–85

2009. 'Sappho fragments 58–59: text, apparatus criticus, translation', in Greene and Skinner 2009: 7–16

2014. 'Two new poems by Sappho', *ZPE* 189: 32–49

2016a. 'The newest Sappho: text, apparatus criticus, and translation', in Bierl and Lardinois 2016: 13–33

2016b. 'Ten poems of Sappho: provenance, authenticity, and text of the new Sappho papyri', in Bierl and Lardinois 2016: 34–54

Ober, J. 2003. 'Tyrant killing as therapeutic *stasis*: a political debate in images and texts', in Morgan 2003: 215–50

Ogden, D. 2008. *Perseus*, London

Olson, S. D. 2002. *Aristophanes: Acharnians*, Oxford

Onians, R. B. 1951. *The origins of European thought about the body, the mind, the soul, the world, time, and fate*, Cambridge

Ormand, K. 2014. *The Hesiodic Catalogue of Women and Archaic Greece*, Cambridge

Ornaghi, M. 2008. 'I Policrati ibicei: Ibico, Anacreonte, Policrate e la cronografia dei poeti della "corte" di Samo', *AOFL* 1: 14–72

Osborne, R. 2009. *Greece in the making, 1200–479 BC*, 2nd edn, London

Ostwald, M. 1969. *Nomos and the beginnings of the Athenian democracy*, Oxford

Pace, C. 1996. 'Anacreonte e la palla di Nausicaa (Anacr. fr. 13 G = 358 *PMG*, 1–4)', *Eikasmos* 7: 81–6

Page, D. L. 1938. *Euripides: Medea*, Oxford

1951a. *Alcman: the Partheneion*, Oxford

1951b. 'Ibycus' poem in honour of Polycrates', *Aegyptus* 31: 158–72

1951c. 'Simonidea', *JHS* 71: 133–42

1955. *Sappho and Alcaeus: an introduction to the study of ancient Lesbian poetry*, Oxford

1960. 'Anacreon fr. 1', in *Studi in onore di Luigi Castiglioni* (Florence) II. 659–67

1971. 'Poetry and prose: Simonides, *P.M.G.* 531, Ibycus 298', *CR* 21: 317–18

1973. 'The Geryoneïs', *JHS* 93: 138–54

Pallantza, E. 2005. *Der Troische Krieg in der nachhomerischen Literatur bis zum 5. Jahrhundert v. Chr.*, Stuttgart

Palmisciano, R. 1996. 'Simonide 531 P: testo, dedicatario e genere letterario', *QUCC* n. s. 54: 39–53

Palumbo Stracca, B. M. 1981. 'Ibico, *PMG* 286: osservazioni metriche', *BollClass* 2: 143–9

2014. 'I canti di questua nella Grecia antica (1): il *Canto della rondine* (*PMG* 848)', *RCCM* 56: 57–78

Papadimitropoulos, L. 2016. 'Ibycus *PMGF* 287: love and disgrace', *Prometheus* 42: 25–9

Parker, H. N. 1993. 'Sappho schoolmistress', *TAPhA* 123: 309–51

Parker, R. 1983. *Miasma: pollution and purification in early Greek religion*, Oxford

1989. 'Spartan religion', in A. Powell, ed. *Classical Sparta: techniques behind her success* (London) 142–72

2005. *Polytheism and society at Athens*, Oxford

2011. *On Greek religion*, Ithaca, NY

Parry, H. 1965. 'An interpretation of Simonides 4 (Diehl)', *TAPhA* 96: 297–320

Pavese, C. O. 1967. 'Alcmane, il *Partenio* del Louvre', *QUCC* 4: 113–33

1992a. *Il grande Partenio di Alcmane*, Amsterdam 1992

1992b. 'Su Ibyc., fr. 5, 12P.: παιδόθεν', *Eikasmos* 3: 43–5

1995. 'Arch. 2 T. = 2 W. ἐν δορί', in L. Belloni *et al.*, eds. *Studia classica Iohanni Tarditi oblata* (Milan) 1.335–40

Payne, M. 2006. 'On being vatic: Pindar, pragmatism, and historicism', *AJPh* 127: 159–84

Pearson, A. C. 1917. *The fragments of Sophocles*, 3 vols., Cambridge

Pelliccia, H. 1991. 'Anacreon 13 (358 *PMG*)', *CPh* 86: 30–6

1992. 'Sappho 16, Gorgias' *Helen*, and the preface to Herodotus' *Histories*', *YClS* 29: 63–84

1995a. 'Ambiguity against ambiguity: Anacreon 13 again', *ICS* 20: 23–34

1995b. *Mind, body, and speech in Homer and Pindar*, Göttingen

2009. 'Simonides, Pindar and Bacchylides', in Budelmann 2009: 240–62

Pelling, C. 1991. 'Thucydides' Archidamus and Herodotus' Artabanus', in M. A. Flower and M. Toher, eds. *Georgica: Greek studies in honour of George Cawkwell* (London) 120–42

1997. 'Aeschylus' *Persae* and history', in C. Pelling, ed. *Greek tragedy and the historian* (Oxford) 1–19

Peponi, A.-E. 2004. 'Initiating the viewer: deixis and visual perception in Alcman's lyric drama', *Arethusa* 37: 295–316

2007. 'Sparta's prima ballerina: *choreia* in Alcman's second *Partheneion* (3 *PMGF*)', *CQ* 57: 351–62

2012. *Frontiers of pleasure: models of aesthetic response in Archaic and Classical Greek thought*, Oxford

2016. 'Lyric vision: an introduction', in Cazzato and Lardinois 2016: 1–15

Pereira, M. H. d. R. 1961. *Sobre a autenticidade do fragmento 44 Diehl de Anacreonte*, Coimbra

Perelli, A. 1993. 'Variazioni sul cavallo vecchio (Tibullo e altri)', *RCCM* 35: 119–36

Pernigotti, C. 2001. 'Tempi del canto e pluralità di prospettive in Saffo, fr. 44 V.', *ZPE* 135: 11–20

Péron, J. 1982. 'Le poème à Polycrate: une "palinodie" d'Ibycus?', *RPh* 56: 33–56

1987. 'Demi-chœurs chez Alcman: Parth. 1, v. 39–59', *GB* 14: 35–53

Perotti, P. A. 1988. 'Alcmane fr. 89 P. (= 58 D., 49 G., 159 C.)', *Vichiana* 17: 261–9

Petropoulos, J. C. B. 1993. 'Sappho the sorceress – another look at fr. 1 (LP)', *ZPE* 97: 43–56

1994. *Heat and lust: Hesiod's midsummer festival scene revisited,* Lanham, MD

2003. *Eroticism in ancient and medieval Greek poetry,* London

Petrovic, A. 2007. *Kommentar zu den simonideischen Versinschriften,* Leiden

Pfeiffer, R. 1959. 'Vom Schlaf der Erde und der Tiere (Alkman, fr. 58 D.)', *Hermes* 87: 1–6

Pfeijffer, I. L. 2000a. 'Playing ball with Homer: an interpretation of Anacreon 358 *PMG*', *Mnemosyne* 53: 164–84

2000b. 'Shifting Helen: an interpretation of Sappho, fragment 16 (Voigt)', *CQ* 50: 1–6

Pfisterer-Haas, S. 2003. 'Mädchen und Frauen im Obstgarten und beim Ballspiel', *MDAI(A)* 118: 139–95

Picard, C. 1962. 'Où fut à Lesbos, au VIIe siècle, l'asyle temporaire du poète Alcée?', *RA* 2: 43–69

Pintaudi, R. 2000. 'Ermeneutica *per epistulas*: l'ostrakon fiorentino di Saffo (*PSI* XIII 1300)', *APapyrol* 12: 45–62

Pipili, M. 2000. 'Wearing an other hat: workmen in town and country', in B. Cohen, ed. *Not the classical ideal: Athens and the construction of the other in Greek art* (Leiden) 153–79

Pirenne-Delforge, V. 2001. 'La genèse de l'Aphrodite grecque: le "dossier crétois"', in S. Ribichini et al., eds. *La questione delle influenze vicino-orientali sulla religione greca* (Rome) 169–87

Pirenne-Delforge, V., and G. Pironti 2014. 'Héra et Zeus à Lesbos: entre poésie lyrique et décret civique', *ZPE* 191: 27–31

Pitotto, E. 2011. 'Note testuali e interpretative a Ibico, S 151, vv. 23–26: limiti umani ed encomio poetico', in A. Balbo et al., eds. *Tanti affetti in tal momento': studi in onore di Giovanna Garbarino* (Alessandria) 711–22

Podlecki, A. J. 1966. 'The political significance of the Athenian "tyranni-cide"-cult', *Historia* 15: 129–41

1968. 'Simonides: 480', *Historia* 17: 257–75

Pöhlmann, E. 1990. 'Zur Überlieferung griechischer Literatur vom 8.–4. Jh.', in Kullmann and Reichel 1990: 11–30

Pöhlmann, E., and M. L. West 2012. 'The oldest Greek papyrus and writing tablets: fifth-century documents from the "tomb of the musician" in Attica', *ZPE* 180: 1–16

Poltera, O. 1997. *Le langage de Simonide: étude sur la tradition poétique et son renouvellement*, Bern

2008. *Simonides lyricus: Testimonia und Fragmente*, Basel

Pomeroy, S. B. 2002. *Spartan women*, New York

Ponzio, A. 2001. 'Tradizione di un frammento alcaico (frg. 347 V.)', in M. Cannatà Fera and G. B. D'Alessio, eds. *I lirici greci: forme della comunicazione e storia del testo* (Messina) 63–7

Porro, A. 1989. 'Un commentario papiraceo ad Alceo e il fr. 130B Voigt', *Aevum(ant)* 2: 215–22

1994. *Vetera Alcaica: l'esegesi di Alceo dagli Alessandrini all'età imperiale*, Milan

Porter, J. I. 2010. *The origins of aesthetic thought in ancient Greece: matter, sensation, and experience*, Cambridge

Porter, J. R. 1994. *Studies in Euripides' Orestes*, Leiden

Pötscher, W. 1998. 'Γλαύκη, Γλαῦκος und die Bedeutung von γλαυκός', *RhM* 141: 97–111

Power, T. 2010. *The culture of kitharôidia*, Washington, DC

2011. 'Cyberchorus: Pindar's Κηληδόνες and the aura of the artificial', in Athanassaki and Bowie 2011: 67–113

Prauscello, L. 2006. *Singing Alexandria: music between practice and textual transmission*, Leiden

2007. 'Le "orecchie" di Saffo: qualche osservazione in margine a Sapph. 31, 11–12 V. e alla sua ricezione antica', in G. Bastianini and A. Casanova, eds. *I papiri di Saffo e di Alceo* (Florence) 191–212

2009. 'Wandering poetry, "travelling" music: Timotheus' muse and some case-studies of shifting cultural identities', in Hunter and Rutherford 2009: 168–94

2016. 'Sappho's book 4 and its metrical composition: the case of *P.Oxy.* 1787 reconsidered', *MD* 76: 53–71

Preisshofen, F. 1977. *Untersuchungen zur Darstellung des Greisenalters in der frühgriechischen Dichtung*, Wiesbaden

Prest, N. 1989. 'Note alla *Gerioneide* di Stesicoro', *Sileno* 15: 69–75

Pretagostini, R. 1993a. 'Vicende di una allegoria equestre: da Anacreonte (e Teognide) ad Asclepiade', in Pretagostini 1993b: III.959–69

(ed.) 1993b. *Tradizione e innovazione nella cultura greca da Omero all'età ellenistica*, 3 vols., Rome

Price, T. H. 1978. *Kourotrophos: cults and representations of the Greek nursing deities*, Leiden

Priestley, J. M. 2007. 'The φαρος of Alcman's *Partheneion* 1', *Mnemosyne* 60: 175–95

Prins, Y. 1999. *Victorian Sappho*, Princeton

Privitera, G. A. 1967. 'La rete di Afrodite: ricerche sulla prima ode di Saffo', *QUCC* 4: 7–58

1969. 'Ambiguità antitesi analogia nel fr. 31 L.P. di Saffo', *QUCC* 8: 37–80

2013. 'Il "sudore" giambico di Sapph. 31.13 Voigt ed Erodiano', *RAL* 24: 5–12

Probert, P. 2015. *Early Greek relative clauses*, Oxford

Puelma, M. 1995 [1977]. 'Die Selbstbeschreibung des Chores in Alkmans grossem Partheneion-Fragment (fr. 1 P. = 23 B., 1 D. v. 36–105)', in *Labor et lima: Kleine Schriften und Nachträge* (Basel) 51–110; originally published in *MH* 34 (1977) 1–55

Puelma, M., and F. Angiò 2005. 'Sappho und Poseidippos: Nachtrag zum Sonnenuhr-Epigramm 52 A.-B. des Mailänder Papyrus', *ZPE* 152: 13–15

Pugliese Carratelli, G. 1990. *Tra Cadmo e Orfeo: contributi alla storia civile e religiosa dei Greci d'Occidente*, Bologna

Pulleyn, S. 1997. *Prayer in Greek religion*, Oxford

Purves, A. 2014. 'Who, Sappho?', in D. Cairns and R. Scodel, eds. *Defining Greek narrative* (Edinburgh) 175–96

Quinn, J. D. 1961. 'Cape Phokas, Lesbos – site of an Archaic sanctuary for Zeus, Hera and Dionysus?', *AJA* 65: 391–3

Raaflaub, K. A. 2003. 'Stick and glue: the function of tyranny in fifth-century Athenian democracy', in Morgan 2003: 59–93

2004. *The discovery of freedom in ancient Greece*, Chicago

Race, W. H. 1982. *The classical priamel from Homer to Boethius*, Leiden

1983. '"That man" in Sappho fr. 31 L-P', *ClAnt* 2: 92–101

1989. 'Sappho, *fr.* 16 L-P. and Alkaios, *fr.* 42 L-P.: romantic and classical strains in Lesbian lyric', *CJ* 85: 16–33

Radke, G. 2005. *Sappho Fragment 31 (LP): Ansätze zu einer neuen Lyriktheorie*, Stuttgart

Rawles, R. 2006. 'Notes on the interpretation of the "New Sappho"', *ZPE* 157: 1–7

2012. 'Early epinician: Ibycus and Simonides', in P. Agócs *et al.*, eds. *Reading the victory ode* (Cambridge) 3–27

2013. 'Aristophanes' Simonides: lyric models for praise and blame', in E. Bakola *et al.*, eds. *Greek comedy and the discourse of genres* (Cambridge) 175–201

Redfield, J. M. 2003. *The Locrian maidens: love and death in Greek Italy*, Princeton

Reeder, E. D. 1995. *Pandora: women in classical Greece*, Princeton

Renehan, R. 1984. 'Anacreon fragment 13 Page', *CPh* 79: 28–32

Richer, N. 2012. *La religion des Spartiates: croyances et cultes dans l'Antiquité*, Paris

Rickert, G. 1989. Ἑκών *and* ἄκων *in early Greek thought*, Atlanta

Rijksbaron, A. 2002. *The syntax and semantics of the verb in Classical Greek: an introduction*, 3rd edn, Amsterdam

Risch, E. 1962. 'Der göttliche Schlaf bei Sappho: Bemerkungen zum Ostrakon der Medea Norsa', *MH* 19: 197–201

1974. *Wortbildung der homerischen Sprache*, 2nd edn, Berlin

Rissman, L. 1983. *Love as war: Homeric allusion in the poetry of Sappho*, Königstein

Robbins, E. 1980. '"Every time I look at you...": Sappho thirty-one', *TAPhA* 110: 255–61

1991. 'Alcman's *Partheneion*: legend and choral ceremony', *CQ* 44: 7–16

1993. 'The education of Achilles', *QUCC* n. s. 45: 7–20

Robert, L. 1960. 'Recherches épigraphiques: v. Inscriptions de Lesbos', *REA* 62: 285–315

Rocconi, E. 2003. *Le parole delle muse: la formazione del lessico tecnico musicale nella Grecia antica*, Rome

Rodríguez Somolinos, H. 1994. 'De nuevo sobre Alceo 130b,10 V. (ἐοίκησ' ἀλυκαιχμίαις)', *Eikasmos* 5: 23–8

Rosenbloom, D. 2006. *Aeschylus: Persians*, London

Rosenmeyer, P. A. 1991. 'Simonides' Danae fragment reconsidered', *Arethusa* 24: 5–29

1992. *The poetics of imitation: Anacreon and the Anacreontic tradition*, Cambridge

1997. 'Her master's voice: Sappho's dialogue with Homer', *MD* 39: 123–49

2004. 'Girls at play in early Greek poetry', *AJPh* 125: 163–78

Rosenmeyer, T. G. 1966. 'Alcman's *Partheneion* 1 reconsidered', *GRBS* 7: 321–59

Rösler, W. 1975. 'Ein Gedicht und sein Publikum: Überlegungen zu Sappho Fr. 44 Lobel-Page', *Hermes* 103: 275–85

1980. *Dichter und Gruppe: eine Untersuchung zu den Bedingungen und zur historischen Funktion früher griechischer Lyrik am Beispiel Alkaios*, Munich

1990. 'Realitätsbezug und Imagination in Sapphos Gedicht φαίνεταί μοι κῆνος', in Kullmann and Reichel 1990: 271–87

Rossi, L. E. 1971. 'I generi letterari e le loro leggi scritte e non scritte nelle letterature classiche', *BICS* 18: 69–94

Rozokoki, A. 2006. *Ανακρέων: εισαγωγή, κείμενο, μετάφραση, σχόλια*, Athens

2008. 'Stesichorus, Geryoneis S 11 SLG: the dilemma of Geryon', *WS* 121: 67–9

2009. 'Some new thoughts on Stesichorus' *Geryoneis*', *ZPE* 168: 3–18

Rubinstein, L. 2004. 'Ionia', in M. H. Hansen and T. H. Nielsen, eds. *An inventory of Archaic and Classical poleis* (Oxford) 1053–1107

Ruijgh, C. J. 1971. *Autour de 'te épique': études sur la syntaxe grecque*, Amsterdam

Rutherford, I. 1997. 'Odes and ends: closure in Greek lyric', in D. H. Roberts *et al.*, eds. *Classical closure: reading the end in Greek and Latin literature* (Princeton) 43–61

2001a. 'The New Simonides: toward a commentary', in Boedeker and Sider 2001: 33–54

2001b. *Pindar's paeans: a reading of the fragments with a survey of the genre*, Oxford

2007. 'Two notes on Simonides' Plataea-poem', in B. Palme, ed. *Akten des 23. Internationalen Papyrologen-Kongresses* (Vienna) 633–6

Saake, H. 1971. *Zur Kunst Sapphos: motiv-analytische und kompositionstechnische Interpretation*, Munich

Salvador Castillo, J. A. 1994. 'El símil homérico de la μήκων (*Il.* 8.302–308)', *CFC(G)* 4: 227–45

Sampson, C. M. 2016. 'A new reconstruction of Sappho 44 (*P.Oxy.* x 1232 + *P.Oxy.* xvii 2076)', in T. Derda *et al.*, eds. *Proceedings of the 27th International Congress of Papyrology* (Warsaw) 53–62

Sbardella, L. 2012. *Cucitori di canti: studi sulla tradizione epico-rapsodica greca e i suoi itinerari nel vi secolo a.c.*, Rome

2014. 'The Trojan War myth: rhapsodic canon and lyric alternatives', in G. Colesanti and M. Giordano, eds. *Submerged literature in ancient Greek culture: an introduction* (Berlin) 61–75

Schefold, K. 1992. *Gods and heroes in late Archaic Greek art*, Cambridge

1997. *Die Bildnisse der antiken Dichter, Redner und Denker*, 2nd edn, Basel

Schironi, F. 2016. 'Alcman's semi-choruses – in the text . . . and beyond it', *MD* 76: 33–52

Schlesier, R. 2011a. 'Aphrodite reflétée: à propos du fragment 1 (LP / V) de Sappho', in F. Prescendi and Y. Volokhine, eds. *Dans le laboratoire de l'historien des religions: mélanges offerts à Philippe Borgeaud* (Geneva) 416–29

2011b. 'Presocratic Sappho: her use of Aphrodite for arguments about love and immortality', *Scientia Poetica* 15: 1–28

2013. 'Atthis, Gyrinno, and other *hetairai*: female personal names in Sappho's poetry', *Philologus* 157: 199–222

Schmitz, T. A. 2013. 'Erzählung und Imagination in Sapphos Aphroditelied (frg. 1 V)', in B. Dunsch *et al.*, eds. *Epos, Lyrik, Drama: Genese und Ausformung der literarischen Gattungen* (Heidelberg) 89–103

Schnapp, A. 1997. *Le chasseur et la cité: chasse et érotique en Grèce ancienne*, Paris

Schönberger, O. 1980. *Griechische Heischelieder*, Meisenheim

Schrenk, L. 1994. 'Sappho frag. 44 and the "Iliad"', *Hermes* 122: 144–50

Schütrumpf, E. 1987. 'Simonides an Skopas (542 PMG)', *WJA* 13: 11–23

Schwartz, A. 2009. *Reinstating the hoplite: arms, armour and phalanx fighting in Archaic and Classical Greece*, Stuttgart

Scodel, R. 1986. 'Literary interpretation in Plato's *Protagoras*', *AncPhil* 6: 25–37

1996. 'Self-correction, spontaneity, and orality in Archaic poetry', in I. Worthington, ed. *Voice into text: orality and literacy in ancient Greece* (Leiden) 59–79

Scott, J. A. 1905. 'Additional notes on the vocative', *AJPh* 26: 32–43

Scully, S. 1990. *Homer and the sacred city*, Ithaca, NY

Seaford, R. 1990. 'The imprisonment of women in Greek tragedy', *JHS* 110: 76–90

Segal, C. 1983. 'Sirius and the Pleiades in Alcman's Louvre *Partheneion*', *Mnemosyne* 36: 260–75

1985. 'Stesichorus', in P. E. Easterling and B. M. W. Knox, eds. *The Cambridge history of classical literature* (Cambridge) 186–201

1998. 'Beauty, desire, and absence: Helen in Sappho, Alcaeus, and Ibycus', in *Aglaia: the poetry of Alcman, Sappho, Pindar, Bacchylides, and Corinna* (Lanham, MD) 63–83

Sevieri, R. 2011. *Timoteo: I Persiani*, Milan

Shapiro, H. A. 1989. *Art and cult under the tyrants in Athens*, Mainz

1992. '*Mousikoi agones*: music and poetry at the Panathenaia', in J. Neils, ed. *Goddess and polis: the Panathenaic festival in ancient Athens* (Princeton) 53–75

1994. *Myth into art: poet and painter in classical Greece*, London

2012. *Re-fashioning Anakreon in Classical Athens*, Munich

Shipley, G. 1987. *A history of Samos, 800–188 BC*, Oxford

Silk, M. 1974. *Interaction in poetic imagery with special reference to early Greek poetry*, Cambridge

2010. 'The language of Greek lyric poetry', in E. J. Bakker, ed. *A companion to the ancient Greek language* (Oxford) 424–40

Simon, E. 1997. 'Héra en Béotie et en Thessalie', in J. de La Genière, ed. *Héra: images, espaces, cultes* (Naples) 83–6

Simonini, L. 1979. 'Il fr. 282 P. di Ibico', *Acme* 32: 285–98

Sisti, F. 1967. 'L'ode a Policrate: un caso di recusatio in Ibico', *QUCC* 4: 59–79

Slater, W. J. 1978. 'Artemon and Anacreon: no text without context', *Phoenix* 32: 185–94

Slings, S. R. 1990. 'The I in personal Archaic lyric: an introduction', in S. R. Slings, ed. *The poet's I in Archaic Greek lyric: proceedings of a symposium held at the Vrije Universiteit Amsterdam* (Amsterdam) 1–30

1991. 'Sappho fr. 1.8 V.: golden house or golden chariot?', *Mnemosyne* 44: 404–10

Smith, A. C. 2011. *Polis and personification in Classical Athenian art*, Leiden

Snell, B. 1931. 'Sapphos Gedicht φαίνεταί μοι κῆνος', *Hermes* 66: 71–90

Snodgrass, A. M. 1964. *Early Greek armour and weapons: from the end of the Bronze Age to 600 BC*, Edinburgh

1974. 'An historical Homeric society?', *JHS* 94: 114–25

Snyder, J. M. 1991. 'Public occasion and private passion in the lyrics of Sappho of Lesbos', in S. B. Pomeroy, ed. *Women's history and ancient history* (Chapel Hill) 1–19

Sommerstein, A. H., and I. C. Torrance (eds.) 2014. *Oaths and swearing in ancient Greece*, Berlin

Sordi, M. 1958. *La lega tessala fino ad Alessandro Magno*, Rome

1998. Review of B. Helly, *L'état thessalien*, *Gnomon* 70: 418–21

Sourvinou-Inwood, C. 1983. 'A trauma in flux: death in the 8th century and after', in R. Hägg, ed. *The Greek renaissance of the eighth century BC: tradition and innovation* (Stockholm) 33–48

1995. *'Reading' Greek death to the end of the Classical period*, Oxford

Spelman, H. 2014. 'Placing Aphrodite: Alcaeus fr. 296B and Horace *C.* 4.1', *ZPE* 189: 53–63

2015. 'Alcaeus 140', *CPh* 110: 353–60

2017. 'Sappho 44: Trojan myth and literary history', *Mnemosyne* 70: 740–57

2018. *Pindar and the Poetics of Permanence*, Oxford

Stamatopoulou, M. 2007. 'Thessalian aristocracy and society in the age of epinikian: from Archaic Greece to the Roman Empire', in S. Hornblower and C. Morgan, eds. *Pindar's poetry, patrons, and festivals* (Oxford) 309–41

Stanford, W. B. 1939. *Ambiguity in Greek literature: studies in theory and practice*, Oxford

Stark, R. 1956. 'Bemerkungen zu zwei Alkaios-Fragmenten', *RhM* 99: 172–8

Stehle, E. 1996 [1990]. 'Sappho's gaze: fantasies of a goddess and young man', in Greene 1996: 193–225

1997. *Performance and gender in ancient Greece: nondramatic poetry in its setting*, Princeton

2009. 'Greek lyric and gender', in Budelmann 2009: 58–71

Stein-Hölkeskamp, E. 1989. *Adelskultur und Polisgesellschaft: Studien zum griechischen Adel in archaischer und klassischer Zeit*, Stuttgart

Steiner, D. 1999. 'To praise, not to bury: Simonides fr. 531 P', *CQ* 49: 383–95

2001. *Images in mind: statues in Archaic and Classical Greek literature and thought*, Princeton

2005. 'Nautical matters: Hesiod's *Nautilia* and Ibycus fragment 282 *PMG*', *CPh* 100: 347–55

Steinrück, M. 1995. 'Lautechos bei Anakreon', in F. De Martino and A. H. Sommerstein, eds. *Lo spettacolo delle voci* (Bari) 173–92

308WORKS CITED

Stevens, P. T. 1976. *Colloquial expressions in Euripides*, Wiesbaden

Stüber, K. 1996. *Zur dialektalen Einheit des Ostionischen*, Innsbruck

Stulz, H. 1990. *Die Farbe Purpur im frühen Griechentum: Beobachtet in der Literatur und in der bildenden Kunst*, Stuttgart

Svenbro, J. 1975. 'Sappho and Diomedes', *Museum Philologum Londiniense* 1: 37–49

1976. *La parole et le marbre: aux origines de la poétique grecque*, Lund

1993 [1988]. *Phrasikleia: an anthropology of reading in ancient Greece*, trans. J. Lloyd, Ithaca, NY

Swift, L. 2010. *The hidden chorus: echoes of genre in tragic lyric*, Oxford

2016. 'Visual imagery in parthenaic song', in Cazzato and Lardinois 2016: 255–87

Taplin, O. 1980. 'The shield of Achilles within the *Iliad*', *G&R* 27: 1–21

Taylor, M. W. 1991. *The tyrant slayers: the heroic image in fifth-century* BC *Athenian art and politics*, 2nd edn, Salem, NH

Tedeschi, G. 2015. 'Scrittura e μουσική nell'antica Grecia', *AOFL* 10.1: 3–26

Thomas, R. 1989. *Oral tradition and written record in Classical Athens*, Cambridge

Too, Y. L. 1997. 'Alcman's *Partheneion*: the maidens dance the city', *QUCC* n. s. 56: 7–29

Tortorelli, W. 2004. 'A proposed colometry of Ibycus 286', *CPh* 99: 370–6

Trenkner, S. 1958. *The Greek novella in the Classical period*, Cambridge

Treu, M. 1954. *Sappho*, Munich

Tribulato, O. 2010. 'Literary dialects', in E. J. Bakker, ed. *A companion to the ancient Greek language* (Oxford) 388–400

Trumpf, J. 1960. 'Kydonische Äpfel (Ibykos fr. 6D.)', *Hermes* 88: 14–22

Tsantsanoglou, K. 2008. 'The banquet of the gods and the picnic of the girls: observations on Sappho fr. 2 V. (with an appendix on Ibycus *PMGF* 286)', *Eikasmos* 19: 45–69

2012. *Of golden manes and silvery faces: the Partheneion 1 of Alcman*, Berlin

Tsitsibakou-Vasalos, E. 1990. 'Stesichorus' *Geryoneis*, *SLG* 15 I–II', Ἑλληνικά 41: 7–31

1991–2. 'Stesichorus, *Geryoneis* S11.5–26: the dilemma of Geryon', Ἑλληνικά 42: 245–56

1993. 'Alcman's partheneion *PMG* 1, 13–15: Αἶσα, Πόρος and ἀπέδιλος ἀλκά: their past and present', *MD* 30: 129–51

Tsomis, G. 2001. *Zusammenschau der frühgriechischen monodischen Melik (Alkaios, Sappho, Anakreon)*, Stuttgart

2003. 'Eros bei Ibykos', *RhM* 146: 225–43

Turner, E. G. 1987. *Greek manuscripts of the ancient world*, second edn, revised and enlarged by P. J. Parsons, London

Tzamali, E. 1996. *Syntax und Stil bei Sappho*, Dettelbach

Ucciardello, G. 2005. 'Sulla tradizione del testo di Ibico', in S. Grandolini, ed. *Lirica e teatro in Grecia: il testo e la sua ricezione* (Naples) 21–88 forthcoming. 'Textual notes on Alcman, fr. 1 PMGF'

Ulf, C. 2014. 'Formen von Konsumption, Lebensstilen und Öffentlichkeiten von Homer bis Theognis', *Klio* 96: 416–36

van Dijk, G.-J. 1997. *Ainoi, logoi, mythoi: fables in Archaic, Classical, and Hellenistic Greek literature*, Leiden

van Minnen, P. 1997. 'The performance and readership of the *Persai* of Timotheus', *APF* 43: 246–60

van Wees, H. 1994. 'The Homeric way of war: the *Iliad* and the hoplite phalanx', *G&R* 41: 1–18 and 131–55

1998a. 'A brief history of tears: gender differentiation in Archaic Greece', in L. Foxhall and J. Salmon, eds. *When men were men: masculinity, power and identity in classical antiquity* (London) 10–53

1998b. 'Greeks bearing arms: the state, the leisure class, and the display of weapons in Archaic Greece', in N. Fisher and H. van Wees, eds. *Archaic Greece: new approaches and new evidence* (London) 333–78

Vermeule, E. 1979. *Aspects of death in early Greek art and poetry*, Berkeley

Vernant, J.-P. 1980 [1973]. 'Marriage', trans. J. Lloyd, in *Myth and society in ancient Greece* (New York) 45–70

1991 [1979]. '*Panta kala*: from Homer to Simonides', trans. F. I. Zeitlin, in *Mortals and immortals: collected essays*, ed. F. I. Zeitlin (Princeton) 84–91

Vetta, M. 1982. 'Studi recenti sul primo *Partenio* di Alcmane', *QUCC* n. s. 10: 127–36

1983. 'Un capitolo di storia di poesia simposiale (per l'esegesi di Aristofane, *Vespe* 1222–1248)', in M. Vetta, ed. *Poesia e simposio nella Grecia antica: guida storica e critica* (Rome) 117–31

2000. 'Anacreonte a Samo e l'Artemide dei Magneti', in Cannatà Fera and Grandolini 2000: II.671–82

Visconti, A. 2004. 'Riflessioni sull'azione politica di Pittaco a Mitilene', *Incidenza dell'antico* 2: 149–69

Voigt, E.-M. 1961. 'Zu Sappho 55a, 6 Diehl', *Hermes* 89: 251–3

Wærn, I. 1951. Γῆς ὀστέα: the kenning in pre-Christian Greek poetry, Uppsala

Walker, J. 2000. *Rhetoric and poetics in antiquity*, New York

Wallace, R. W. 2009. 'Plato, *polikilia*, and New Music at Athens', in E. Berardi *et al.*, eds. *Poikilia: variazioni sul tema* (Rome) 201–13

Wallinga, H. T. 1993. *Ships and sea-power before the great Persian War: the ancestry of the ancient trireme*, Leiden

Watkins, C. 2007. 'The golden bowl: thoughts on the New Sappho and its Asianic background', *ClAnt* 26: 305–25

West, M. L. 1965. 'Alcmanica', *CQ* 15: 188–202

1966a. 'Conjectures on 46 Greek poets', *Philologus* 110: 147–68

1966b. *Hesiod: Theogony*, Oxford

1967a. 'Alcman and Pythagoras', *CQ* 17: 1–15; repr. in West 2011–13: III.37–58

1967b. 'Prose in Simonides', *CR* 17: 133

1970a. 'Burning Sappho', *Maia* 22: 307–30; repr. in West 2011–13: II.28–52

1970b. 'Melica', *CQ* 20: 205–15

1971. 'Stesichorus', *CQ* 21: 302–14; repr. in West 2011–13: II.78–97

1975. 'Some lyric fragments reconsidered', *CQ* 25: 307–9

1978. *Hesiod: Works and Days*, Oxford

1980. 'Iambics in Simonides, Bacchylides and Pindar', *ZPE* 37: 137–55

1981. 'Simonides' Danae fragment: a metrical analysis', *BICS* 28: 30–8

1982a. *Greek metre*, Oxford

1982b. 'Metrical analyses: Timotheos and others', *ZPE* 45: 1–13

1992a. 'Alcman and Spartan royalty', *ZPE* 91: 1–7; repr. in West 2011–13: II.17–24

1992b. *Ancient Greek music*, Oxford

1993. *Greek lyric poetry: the poems and fragments of the Greek iambic, elegiac, and melic poets (excluding Pindar and Bacchylides) down to 450 BC*, Oxford

1999. 'The invention of Homer', *CQ* 49: 364–82; repr. in West 2011–13: I.408–36

2002. 'The view from Lesbos', in M. Reichel and A. Rengakos, eds. *EPEA PTEROENTA: Beiträge zur Homerforschung* (Stuttgart) 207–19; repr. in West 2011–13: I.392–407

2005. 'The New Sappho', *ZPE* 151: 1–9; repr. in West 2011–13: II.53–66

2011–13. *Hellenica: selected papers on Greek literature and thought*, 3 vols., Oxford

2013. *The epic cycle: a commentary on the lost Troy epics*, Oxford

2014. 'Nine poems of Sappho', *ZPE* 191: 1–12

West, W. C. 1969. 'The trophies of the Persian Wars', *CPh* 64: 7–19

Wiater, N. 2005. 'Eine poetologische Deutung des σηκός in Simon. fr. 531 PMG', *Hermes* 133: 44–55

2010. 'Der utopische Körper: die Interpretation frühgriechischer Lyrik am Beispiel von Sappho frg. 31 LP', in S. Elit *et al.*, eds. *Antike – Lyrik – Heute: griechisch-römisches Altertum in Gedichten von der Moderne bis zur Gegenwart* (Remscheid) 23–49

Wide, S. 1893. *Lakonische Kulte*, Leipzig

Wiesmann, P. 1972. 'Was heisst κῶμα? Zur Interpretation von Sapphos "Gedicht auf der Scherbe"', *MH* 29: 1–11

Wilamowitz-Moellendorff, U. v. 1886. *Isyllos von Epidauros*, Berlin

1889–90. *Commentariolum grammaticum*, vol. IV, Göttingen

1890. 'Zu Plutarchs Gastmahl der Sieben Weisen', *Hermes* 25: 196–227

1900. *Die Textgeschichte der griechischen Lyriker*, Berlin

1903. *Timotheos: Die Perser*, Leipzig

1913. *Sappho und Simonides: Untersuchungen über griechische Lyriker*, Berlin

1921. *Griechische Verskunst*, Berlin

Wilkinson, C. L. 2013. *The lyric of Ibycus: introduction, text and commentary*, Berlin

Willi, A. 2008. *Sikelismos: Sprache, Literatur und Gesellschaft im griechischen Sizilien (8.–5. Jh. v. Chr.)*, Basel

2011. 'Language, Homeric', in M. Finkelberg, ed. *The Homer encyclopedia* (Oxford) 458–64

2012. '"We speak Peloponnesian": tradition and linguistic identity in post-Classical Sicilian literature', in O. Tribulato, ed. *Language and linguistic contact in ancient Sicily* (Cambridge) 265–88

2017. 'Towards a grammar of narrative voice: from Homeric pragmatics to Hellenistic stylistics', in N. W. Slater, ed. *Voice and voices in antiquity* (Leiden) 233–59

Williams, R. 1983. *Keywords: a vocabulary of culture and society*, revised edn, London

Williamson, M. 1995. *Sappho's immortal daughters*, Cambridge, MA

1998. 'Eros the blacksmith: performing masculinity in Anakreon's love lyrics', in L. Foxhall and J. Salmon, eds. *Thinking men: masculinity and its self-representation in the classical tradition* (London) 71–82

Wilson, P. 2003. 'The sound of cultural conflict: Kritias and the culture of *mousikē* in Athens', in C. Dougherty and L. Kurke, eds. *The cultures within ancient Greek culture: contact, conflict, collaboration* (Cambridge) 181–206

2004. 'Athenian strings', in P. Murray and P. Wilson, eds. *Music and the Muses: the culture of mousikē in the Classical Athenian city* (Oxford) 269–306

Winkler, J. J. 1990 [1981]. 'Double consciousness in Sappho's lyric', in *The constraints of desire: the anthropology of sex and gender in ancient Greece* (New York) 162–87

1996 [1981]. 'Gardens of nymphs: public and private in Sappho', in Greene 1996: 89–109

Wohl, V. 1999. 'The eros of Alcibiades', *ClAnt* 18: 349–85

Woodbury, L. E. 1953. 'Simonides on ἀρετή', *TAPhA* 84: 135–63

1979. 'Gold hair and grey, or the game of love: Anacreon fr. 13: 358 *PMG*, 13 Gentili', *TAPhA* 109: 277–87

1985. 'Ibycus and Polycrates', *Phoenix* 39: 193–220

Xanthou, M. G. 2015. 'Maternal figures in the Stesichorean blueprint: Althaea, Calllirhoe and the Lille queen', *QUCC* n. s. 111: 29–57

Yatromanolakis, D. 1999. 'Alexandrian Sappho revisited', *HSPh* 99: 179–95

2004. 'Ritual poetics in Archaic Lesbos: contextualising genre in Sappho', in D. Yatromanolakis and P. Roilos, eds. *Greek ritual poetics* (Washington, DC) 56–70

2007. *Sappho in the making: the early reception*, Cambridge, MA

2008. 'P. Colon. inv. 21351+21376 and P. Oxy. 1787 fr. 1: music, cultural politics, and Hellenistic anthologies', *Ελληνικά* 58: 237–55

2009. 'Ancient Greek popular song', in Budelmann 2009: 263–76

2012. 'Sappho', *Oxford Bibliographies Online*, www.oxfordbibliographies.com

2016. 'Greek symposion', *Oxford Bibliographies Online*, www.oxfordbibliographies.com

Zaikov, A. V. 2004. 'Alcman and the image of the Scythian steed', in C. J. Tuplin, ed. *Pontus and the outside world: studies in Black Sea history, historiography, and archaeology* (Leiden) 69–84

Zarker, J. W. 1965. 'King Eëtion and Thebe as symbols in the *Iliad*', *CJ* 61: 110–14

Zellner, H. 2006. 'Sappho's supra-superlatives', *CQ* 56: 292–7

2007. 'Sappho's alleged proof of aesthetic relativity', *GRBS* 47: 257–70

INDEX